Diné

Diné
A HISTORY OF THE NAVAJOS

Peter Iverson
Featuring photographs by Monty Roessel

University of New Mexico Press
Albuquerque

To Kaaren

To Karina, Jaclyn, Bryan, Robert, and Robyn

And to the future of the Navajo Nation

Library of Congress Cataloging-in-Publication Data

Iverson, Peter.
Diné : a history of the Navajos / text by Peter Iverson ;
photographs by Monty Roessel.—1st ed.
    p. cm.
Includes bibliographical references and index.
ISBN 0-8263-2714-1 (cloth : alk. paper) — ISBN 0-8263-2715-X
(pbk. :alk. paper)
  1. Navajo Indians—History. I. Roessel, Monty. II. Title.

  E99.N3 I88 2002
  979.1004'972—dc21

                              2002006407

Contents

List of Illustrations & Maps

Acknowledgments

In the spring of 1969, I applied for a teaching position at Navajo Community College, a new institution established by the Navajo Nation. The college hired someone else, who then backed out of the assignment right before classes began that fall. Navajo Community College needed to find a person young and foolish enough to take on this assignment at the last possible minute. I hardly hesitated before I agreed to come to Many Farms.

The years I spent at the college changed the course of my life. They fundamentally influenced my perspective on Native history in general and Navajo history in particular. Living and working in Diné Bikéyah helped me understand the importance of the land, the ways in which the Navajos incorporate new elements, and the significance of historic events. This time furnished a foundation. Through the decades, many Diné teachers have taught me. It has been an honor and a pleasure to work with Monty Roessel to produce *Diné: A History of the Navajos* and *"For Our Navajo People": Diné Letters, Speeches, and Petitions, 1900–1960*.

My interest in Navajo history did not begin in 1969. Rather, it started during my childhood, when I began to see photographs and hear the stories from my grandparents' time in Navajo country. During the 1930s and early 1940s, my grandfather served as a principal in Indian Service schools at Fort Wingate, Keams Canyon, and Toadlena. One of my mother's sisters was married at St. Michaels; another sister employed her camera to capture lasting images of a transitional time. My mother made a number of trips to visit her parents in Diné Bikéyah. In an age when people still wrote letters, they wrote all the time—and they saved their correspondence.

Perhaps because my grandparents never drank anything stronger than coffee, went to mass all the time, ate the vegetables they grew in their own garden, and voted Democratic, they lived into their nineties. During my first autumn in Navajo country, I drove over to southern California to see them. They informed me that my colleagues, silversmith Kenneth Begay and linguist William Morgan, had been students at Fort Wingate during the time my grandfather served as its principal. I returned to Many Farms armed with the Wingate yearbook and more stories.

Even now I still meet people who remember my grandparents. I think of my relatives each time I return to the Navajo Nation. I am glad to have the opportunity to thank them once again for sparking my interest in this remarkable community. I also would like to thank my father, who died in 1994, and my mother, who continues to instruct me, for helping me to appreciate the importance of history, memory, stories, and place. As always, I want to express my gratitude to Kaaren, whose love, patience, strength, and grace make better each of my days. To Erika, Jens, Anna, Scott, Lissa, Tim, and Laurie, my appreciation for your interest in and support of this book and for all that you have taught and given me. To David, Paul, Yoko, Alice, Vi, Joe, Diane, Dick, Becky, David, Terry, and Mark, my thanks for your love, understanding, and encouragement.

Diné: A History of the Navajos and *"For Our Navajo People": Diné Letters, Speeches, and Petitions, 1900–1960* have been informed and inspired by many Diné teachers. I cannot name them all, but I want to begin by thanking Monty Roessel for this collaboration and for his friendship. Thanks, too, to Francis Becenti, Clifford Beck, Kenneth Begay, AnCita Benally, Bahe Billy, Jennifer Nez Denetdale, Anthony Chee Emerson, Larry Emerson, Ned Hatathli, Dean Jackson, Jack Jackson, Rex Lee Jim, Jennie Joe, Priscilla Kanaswood, Carol Lujan, B. Kay Manuelito, Richard Mike, William Morgan, Mabel Myers, Betty Reid, Ruth Roessel, Luci Tapahonso, Francis Teller, Carl Todacheene, Glojean Todacheene, Laura Tohe, Harry Walters, and Peterson Zah, for all that you have shared with me.

David Aberle, John Adair, William Adams, Carol Behl, Hank Blair, David Brugge, Bruce Burnham, Kathleen Chamberlain, Lee Correll, Wade Davies, Bill Donovan, Charlotte Frisbie, Steve and Gail Getzwiller, Bruce Gjeltema, Ann Hedlund, Klara Kelley, Larry Kelly, Bill Malone, Laura Moore, William Moore, Bob McPherson, Don Parman, Steve Pavlik, Bill Quinn, Marian Rodee, Bob Roessel, Scott Russell, Orit Tamir, Mark Trahant, Scott Travis, Tara Travis, Bob Trennert, Mark Winter, Marsha Weisiger, David Wilkins, Robert Young, Paul Zolbrod, and others too numerous to mention have aided my understanding of Navajo history and culture.

I want to express my appreciation to AnCita Benally, David Brugge, Margaret Connell-Szasz, Jennifer Nez Denetdale, Charlotte Frisbie, Adelaide Iverson, David Iverson, Erika Iverson, Jens Iverson, Kaaren Iverson, Scott Travis, and Tara Travis for their careful and perceptive reading. Thanks to AnCita Benally for providing the appropriate diacritical markings for Navajo words. I thank editor Beth Hadas, director Luther Wilson, and associate director David Holtby of the University of New Mexico Press, who embraced this endeavor right from the start and helped shepherd these books to prompt publication. Thanks, too, to production manager Dawn Hall, supervisory editor Amy Elder, designer

Melissa Tandysh, and copyeditor Barbara Kohl for their support and assistance. My thanks as well to Pat Etter and Chris Marin of Arizona State University, Evelyn Cooper of the Arizona Historical Foundation, Rose Diaz and Mary Alice Tsosie of the University of New Mexico, Lisa Gezelter and Paul Wormser of the National Archives in Laguna Niguel, Joel Barker of the National Archives in Denver, John Ferrell of the National Archives in Seattle, Laine Sutherland of Northern Arizona University, Jim Dildane of Arizona Historical Society in Flagstaff, and George Miles of Yale University for their assistance. I would like to express my gratitude to Arizona State University, Northern Arizona University, the University of Arizona, the Museum of Northern Arizona, Yale University, Hubbell Trading Post and the National Park Service, and the National Archives in Laguna Niguel, Denver, Seattle, and Washington, D.C., for materials reprinted in *"For Our Navajo People."*

Fellowships from the John Simon Guggenheim Memorial Foundation and the National Endowment for the Humanities helped support research and expedited the completion of these volumes. Arizona State University supported this project in many ways, including a sabbatical leave. My department chair, Noel Stowe, offered consistent encouragement and assistance. Colleagues Roger Adelson, Angela Cavender Wilson, Rachel Fuchs, Susan Gray, Kyle Longley, Beth Luey, Carol Lujan, Steve MacKinnon, Susan Miller, James Riding In, Jim Rush, Kay Sands, Laura Tohe, Bob Trennert, Phil VanderMeer, Myla Vicenti Carpio, and Matt Whitaker expressed interest in and offered support for this project. Research assistants Laurie Arnold and Jane Lawrence furnished invaluable help. Undergraduate students in my introduction to Navajo history classes proved enthusiastic in their consideration of primary source materials.

I would like to close with a special note of thanks for my doctoral students in American Indian history, past and present, at Arizona State University. They have contributed to this endeavor in many ways. To Steve Amerman, Laurie Arnold, Rebecca Bales, Carol Behl, AnCita Benally, Gerald Betty, Marc Campbell, Al Carroll, Brian Collier, Wade Davies, Julie Davis, Daniel d'Oney, Andrew Fisher, Gretchen Harvey, John Heaton, Paivi Hoikkala, Becky James, Richard Kitchen, Jane Lawrence, Michael Lawson, Tracy Leavelle, Jaakko Puisto, Scott Riney, Mara Rutten, Jeff Shepherd, Victoria Smith, Tara Travis, Myla Vicenti Carpio, and Scott White, my continuing appreciation for the privilege of working with you.

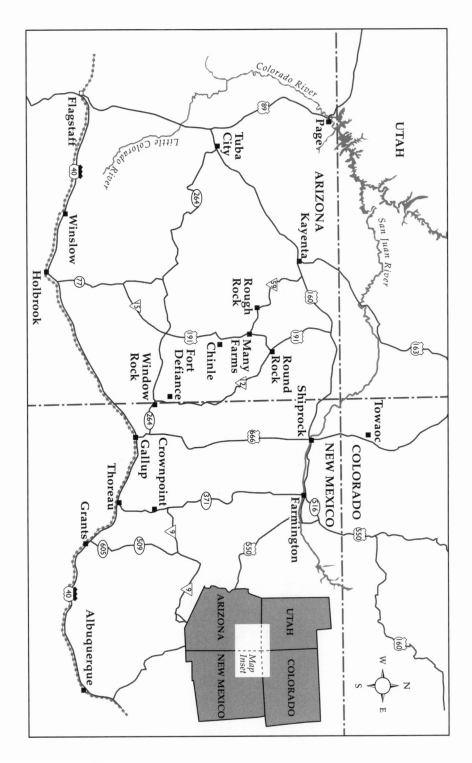

Map 1. Four Corners area

Map 2. The Navajo Nation today

Introduction

They are the children of Changing Woman.

They are called the Navajos. They call themselves Diné.

They are the largest American Indian nation in North America with a population in 2002 of more than 290,000 people. The Navajo Nation officially encompasses 25,000 square miles in northeastern Arizona, northwestern New Mexico, and southeastern Utah. However, Diné Bikéyah, the Navajos' country, extends well beyond these boundaries. It lies within the four mountains that the Diné consider sacred. It is here, the Navajos believe, that they belong. It is here, they know, that they will stay.

Because their history is so long and so complicated, because their community is so sizable, because their land base is so extensive, because their culture is so rich, countless writers have attempted to tell a portion of their story. However, most of these volumes focus on one local community, consider a specific dimension of Navajo life, or concentrate on a narrow span of time. Anthropologists have dominated the field of Navajo studies and their concerns have generally been more immediate in time and more localized than those of individuals trained in history. Only one Navajo scholar, Jennifer Denetdale, has completed doctoral work in history; a second, AnCita Benally, is about to receive her degree. Few non-Navajo historians have ventured into Navajo country, and with the notable exception of scholars such as Wade Davies and Robert McPherson, most have emphasized the evolution of federal Indian policy rather than the Diné themselves. Although non-Navajo anthropologists such as David Brugge, Charlotte Frisbie, and Klara Kelley have routinely worked with Diné collaborators, almost no non-Navajo historians have done so.

This book and *"For Our Navajo People": Diné Letters, Speeches, and Petitions, 1900–1960* reflect our deep-rooted connections to the Navajo Nation. Peter Iverson's grandfather served as a principal in Navajo schools in the 1930s and early 1940s. Iverson came to Many Farms in 1969 to teach at Navajo Community College (now Diné College) during its first years. Since 1986, he has taught American Indian history at

1

Arizona State University, three hours from the Nation's border. Monty Roessel is a member of the Navajo Nation. A former editor of the *Navajo Times* and *The Navajo Nation Today*, he has spent all but four years of his life in Diné Bikéyah.

Peter Iverson has had primary responsibility for the text and Monty Roessel has had primary responsibility for the visual images in *Diné* and *"For Our Navajo People,"* yet the books also mirror Iverson's interest in photography and Roessel's interest in history. This volume has been shaped by our shared questions and concerns.

Diné: A History of the Navajos provides the first account we have of the Navajos from their origins until the first years of the twenty-first century. Its emphasis is on the past century and a half. This book takes appropriate advantage of past scholarship, but it is based on extensive new archival research, Navajo oral and written history, interviews, and firsthand observation. This story is told from the inside out rather than the outside in. This book portrays Navajos as agents of their own destiny, rather than as victims. Although the Diné have faced racism, oppression, and hostility, through the centuries they have found ways to adapt, adjust, and continue.

Two photo essays by Monty Roessel furnish an initial declaration and a closing synthesis. The first photo essay introduces the central importance of the people's association with the land. The second photo essay portrays contemporary Diné life, including the five major Navajo sports, which Roessel insists are either rodeo, rodeo, rodeo, rodeo and basketball, or basketball, basketball, basketball, basketball, and rodeo.

Four central themes provide the foundation for *Diné*. The first is defense and survival. Throughout the course of Navajo history, there is an understanding that the people, the animals, and the land must be defended in order for the Diné to survive. In the early days, the Navajos dealt with Spanish efforts to establish administrative authority over them, to limit their expansion, and to press their women and children into servitude. They also had to contend with other Native peoples, such as the Comanches and Utes, who raided, attempted to appropriate livestock and crops, and to kidnap members of the Diné community. During the "Fearing Time" of the 1860s, the Navajos tried to avoid surrender and exile. Some of them succeeded. Others did not, but even if ultimately captured or killed, they knew the importance of defending the mountains, the people and their livestock, and the land itself. A third critical time in Navajo history came with the livestock reduction era of the 1930s and 1940s. Here again the Diné attempted to defend their animals and their lands, believing their very survival was at stake. A final example would be the military service of Navajos during not only World War II, but other wars as well. Diné members of the armed forces consistently spoke about fighting not only for America but also for their own country within the United States. The Code Talkers linked themselves to the Hero Twins, recognizing the parallels between their quest and the heroic deeds of these cultural heroes.

A second theme is adaptation and incorporation. The Navajos have always brought in new people, new ideas, and new elements and, over time, made them Navajo. The livestock brought by the Spaniards furnishes an early case in point. The Navajos took the animals, wrapped them in the strands of their own stories, and made them theirs. Over the course of centuries other peoples joined up with the Diné. The clan system clearly delineates a number of groups who chose to live with the Navajos and whose children certainly were brought into the larger Diné community. At different points in their history, the Diné have expanded their weaving repertoire by using design elements that have been brought in from the outside, such as the "Oriental" patterns of the early twentieth century. The Native American Church stands as a third instance of incorporation. A final case in point would be rodeo and basketball, for many years now "traditional" pastimes.

A third theme is expansion and prosperity. The Navajos believed that for their society and culture to prosper they had to expand in a number of different ways. In part, this meant territorial expansion, as we can see in Spanish and Mexican colonial times and during the American period. The Diné needed more land for their sheep and they associated expansion with new possibilities. They pushed in the colonial era and in the U.S. national era to claim and control new terrain. Thus, the original Navajo reservation established through the 1868 treaty grew to four times its original size through various executive order additions. In the 1950s, the internal network of roads and schools expanded because of federal investment and increased tribal revenues. The expansion of legal services and systems has also been important in our own time.

A final theme is identity and continuation. To be Navajo meant to respect the old ways and to find the means to continue in a new day. The people looked to Changing Woman for inspiration and reaffirmation. They signed a treaty in 1868 that allowed them to preserve a separate sense of self. While many other Indian communities viewed the whole treaty-making process with disappointment and despair because of so much being lost, the Navajos celebrated their continuation in the heart of their old country. The declaration of nationhood by the Navajos in the late 1960s offers another example. A recent case in point would be the Treaty Day celebration held in 1999.

Chapter 1 stretches from Diné origins until the mid-nineteenth century, when the United States claimed Navajo country following the conclusion of the war with Mexico. It brings forth the Navajos' stories of their beginnings and the contours of early Diné culture, including their acquisition and possession of livestock. The chapter examines relations between the Navajos and other Native peoples as well as their contact with the Spanish and Mexican priests, administrators, soldiers, miners, farmers, and ranchers. The chapter discusses the results of that contact, and conflict as well, and considers Diné migration out of the Dinétah (the initial Navajo country) and the infusion of new people.

Chapter 2 examines the tumultuous generation from 1846 to 1868, including the immediate tension and conflict between the United States and the Navajos, the campaign to force Diné acquiescence to American authority, the Long Walk to exile at Fort Sumner, New Mexico, incarceration, and the negotiation of the Treaty of 1868, which permitted those Navajos who had been imprisoned to join their friends and relatives who had evaded capture.

Chapter 3 begins with the return home and then analyzes an era of remarkable revitalization and expansion from 1868 until 1901, while chapter 4 considers the period from 1901 to 1923, which culminated in the establishment of the Navajo Tribal Council. Within these two chapters we review the expansion of the Navajo economy, the growth of the reservation, and the significant roles played by traders, agents, missionaries, and school personnel. These chapters bring forth the conflicts that permeated this era over schooling, boundaries, and status. In addition, they delineate the growing concern on the part of federal employees and other observers over the condition of the Navajo lands and the discovery of oil and subsequent pressure for development of this resource. This enormously important period, largely neglected by historians who have emphasized the eras of the Long Walk and livestock reduction, proved central to the evolution of the Navajo Nation.

Chapter 5 offers an analysis of key Diné leaders during the 1920s and 1930s, such as Chee Dodge and Thomas Dodge, and the Dodges' rival, Jacob C. Morgan. It documents the start, development, and impact of livestock reduction as well as attempted federal innovations in health care and education and changing patterns of religious observance. The evolution of the Tribal Council is discussed in considerable detail. Dimensions of Diné resistance to livestock reduction and elements of that program are presented here for the first time, revealing an even more complicated and fascinating era, whose legacy continues to our own day. The colonial nature of the "Indian New Deal" receives significant attention, as does the changing nature of trader-Navajo relations.

Chapter 6 starts with the years of World War II and the importance of Diné involvement in that struggle, including the participation of the Code Talkers. It ponders how the World War II experience helped encourage the Diné to push for more equal status, including the right to vote, and to campaign for more improved educational opportunities. The Navajo Nation's acquisition of its first legal counsel, Norman Littell, also influenced these years and affected the start of the long battle with the Hopis over land. New tribal ambitions were made possible by oil discoveries and development and the passage of the Navajo-Hopi Rehabilitation Act of 1950, which funneled millions of dollars for improved roads, schools, and other institutions.

Chapter 7 begins with the election of Raymond Nakai in 1962. It discusses the establishment of important new educational institutions and the formation of other significant entities such as the legal services program. Here we introduce Peter MacDonald, who, together with Peterson Zah, dominated Diné political life for the remainder of the twentieth century. This chapter reviews efforts for self-determination in education, health care, economy, and government. Chapter 8 focuses on vital recent developments, including urbanization, the rivalry between MacDonald and Zah; MacDonald's conviction, imprisonment, and eventual return home; the conflict between the Hopis and the Navajos; the status of women; education; health care; basketball and rodeo; and individual artists.

Diné: A History of the Navajos brings forth a concise analysis of Navajo origins and early development. It argues that unfortunate policies and actions on the part of outsiders (from the days of New Spain to our own time) as well as their very presence have harmed the Diné, but also forced or encouraged them to develop a culture in which new elements would continue to be incorporated and in which innovation would be prized. Third, it offers more nuanced analyses of Navajo leaders in the twentieth century, including Chee Dodge, Thomas Dodge, Jacob Morgan, Sam Ahkeah, Paul Jones, Annie Wauneka, Raymond Nakai, Peter MacDonald, and Peterson Zah. It also reconsiders the period between the Long Walk and livestock reduction eras—from 1868 to 1933—which fundamentally shaped modern Navajo life. Although hardly ignoring the importance of political developments, the book gives new attention to dimensions of life outside of the Navajo capital of Window Rock (Tségháhodzání or "Perforated Rock"). Finally, it provides a more complete portrait of the Diné through visual materials and through the consistent employment of Navajo voices.

Given the size of the Navajo Nation, the richness of its history, and the voluminous nature of its literature, it has often been difficult to decide what to include and what to omit. This is not a short book, but it could have been considerably longer. *Diné* tries to furnish representative rather than exhaustive examples and to furnish evocative illustration rather than endless documentation. The footnotes and a supplementary list of readings will lead readers to additional sources.

This book underscores how Navajo identity is rooted in this particular place. Navajo history does not begin with some long, wonderfully vague and imprecise journey by an isolated community of people who remained magically intact for centuries before shouldering their way into what became the American Southwest. Navajo history does not start in Alaska or northwestern Canada or along the Rocky Mountains or in the Great Basin. It does not transpire in isolation or in separation. It begins with Changing Woman, with the Hero Twins, with monsters, and with blue horses. It begins with the sacred mountains.

"We believe in old values and new ideas," declares the poet Luci

Tapahonso. The Navajos' vibrant culture has never stood still. Through time it has demonstrated that it is through contact with others that a community truly enjoys vitality. All along the way, the Diné have incorporated new elements, new peoples, and new ways of doing things. The artist R. C. Gorman smiles and proclaims that his people have borrowed or stolen everything they call theirs—and improved upon them. In time, whether it be a so-called squash blossom necklace or a modern sport called basketball, it will not matter where it came from. It becomes Navajo. The historian AnCita Benally insists that the essential question is not when her people supposedly arrived or how the language they now speak is or is not related to others spoken thousands of miles away. The real question, she emphasizes, is why so many individuals and peoples through the centuries have chosen to become Navajo. Through the centuries Navajos have brought in all sorts of other folks—Puebloans, Apacheans, and others—and, in time, made them, or their children, or their children's children, into Diné.

Most archaeologists claim a relatively recent arrival by Navajos in the U.S. Southwest; most linguists cite similarities between the language the Diné speak to other languages spoken by Native peoples in northwestern Canada and Alaska. These debates are important, but also, in the end, irrelevant. If the Navajos today are, in part, descended from peoples who migrated to the south and to the east, if they speak a language that bears a resemblance to languages spoken elsewhere, they are, nevertheless, a community that started within this particular environment. All that may have occurred prior to what happened here is prelude. Prior to this place, there were no Navajos. Without this place, there could be no Diné.

The traditional stories thus say: This is where we began and this is where we were meant to be. The stories the Navajos tell about their more recent history say: This is where we fought and struggled to stay and this is where we will remain. Each day there are reminders of those accounts for the Diné who live within the boundaries of the sacred mountains. Each day there can be reinforcement of an understanding, constructed through the centuries, that the past and the present and the future are one, and that merging of time is based upon what has happened, is happening, and will happen here. Each generation knows uncertainty and experiences challenge, yet each realizes it must do its part to make sure that the Diné continue—that past promises are remembered, past events are commemorated, past sacrifices are recalled, past hopes are realized, and new imagination and inspiration are encouraged.

1

"Black Clouds Will Rise": To 1846

After we get back to our country it will brighten up again and the Navajos will be as happy as the land, black clouds will rise and there will be plenty of rain.

—Barboncito, 1868

BEGINNINGS

It begins with the land. It begins with the first light of morning. It begins with the white shell mountain. It begins with spring.

Luci Tapahonso writes:

Hayoolkaalgo Sisnajini nihi neel'iih leh.
Blanca Peak is adorned with white shell.
Blanca Peak is adorned with morning light. . . .
She is the brightness of spring.
She is Changing Woman returned. . . .
Because of her we think and create
Because of her we make songs.
Because of her, the designs appear as we weave.
Because of her, we tell stories and laugh.[1]

Before this land, this light, this mountain, this season, there could be no Diné. So rooted in this particular place, this extraordinary environment, are the Navajos that one cannot imagine them elsewhere. The mountains are placed there for the Diné; they are to live within these mountains.

But one can imagine a certain scene, a vital moment in their history. It is the summer of 1868. Most of the Diné are in exile—incarcerated on a decidedly different earth hundreds of miles from their homeland. Their leaders are negotiating with federal representatives about their future residence. Barboncito declares: "Our grandfathers had no idea of living in any country except our own. . . . When the Navajos were first created four mountains and four rivers were pointed out to us, inside of which we should live, that was to be our country and was given to us by the first woman of the Navajo tribe."

General William Tecumseh Sherman raises the possibility of sending the people to Indian Territory. Barboncito responds: "I hope to God you will not ask me to go to any other country except my own." When the Navajos eventually persuade the government negotiators to allow them to go home, they are overjoyed. Barboncito says: "After we get back to our country it will brighten up again and the Navajos will be as happy as the land, black clouds will rise and there will be plenty of rain."[2] As the people made their way back toward their home country, the old men and the old women began to weep with gladness when they first saw Tsoodził (Mount Taylor), the sacred mountain that marks the southern Navajo boundary. They had returned to Diné Bikéyah—the Navajo country—where the Holy People wished them to live. The agreement forged at Fort Sumner—the Treaty of 1868—clearly marked a major turning point in Navajo history. Had the Navajos been coerced into permanent exile in Oklahoma, their history would have been decidedly different.

That is, in fact, what their traditional oral histories proclaim. Through consideration of these stories one can begin to gain an essential appreciation for the nature of Diné identity and understand why the Navajos have been so tenacious in the defense of their land. This chapter thus begins with a brief summary of some central elements of these stories and then traces the history of the Diné in the American Southwest to 1846. In this overview one may see fundamental qualities of the people: adaptation, incorporation, and continuation.

THE EMERGENCE

The stories say that the Navajos emerged into this world after a long and difficult journey that took them from the First World (the Black World) to the Second World (the Blue World) to the Third World (the Yellow World) to the Fourth World (the Glittering World). First Man (Áłtsé Hastiin) and First Woman (Áłtsé Asdzáá) are formed in the Black World, which also contained various Insect Beings.

Quarreling in the Black World among the Insect Beings forces them to climb to the Blue World, where Blue Birds (Dólii), Blue Hawks (Ginitsoh Dootł'izhí), Blue Jays (Jigí), and Blue Herons (Táłtl'ááh Ha'alééh) resided, together with other Insect Beings. First Man and First Woman soon discovered different animals, including Wolves (Ma'iitsoh), Wildcats (Nashdoiłbáhí), Badgers (Nahashch'id), Kit Foxes (Ma'iiłtsooí), and Mountain Lions (Nashdoitsoh).[3]

Once again, quarreling forced another migration, this time to the Yellow World. Here the mischievous Coyote causes problems for one and all that eventually lead to a flood that carries everyone to the Glittering World, the site of the six mountains: in the east (Blanca Peak or

Sacred Mountain of the East: Sis Naajiní, Blanca
Peak, Colorado. Photograph by Monty Roessel.

Sacred Mountain of the South: Tsoodził, Mount
Taylor, New Mexico. Photograph by Monty Roessel.

Sacred Mountain of the West: Dook'o'oosłííd, San Francisco
Peaks, Arizona. Photograph by Monty Roessel.

Sacred Mountain of the North: Dibé Nitsaa, Hesperus
Peak, Colorado. Photograph by Monty Roessel.

Sis Naajiní), the south (Mount Taylor or Tsoodził), the west (San Francisco Peaks or Dook'o'oosłííd), the north (Mount Hesperus or Dibe Nitsaa), the center (Huerfano Mountain or Dził Na'oodiłii), and the east of center (Gobernador Knob or Ch'ool'í'í). The first four mountains also were associated with a particular color and a particular season. They were the four sacred mountains that mark the traditional boundaries of Diné Bikéyah.

Now the world as the Navajos would know it continued to be shaped. The stories tell of the first hogan being constructed, the first sweat bath being taken, the four seasons being established, day and night being created, the stars being placed in the sky, and the sun and the moon coming into existence. The Glittering World encompasses both beauty and difficulty. In one episode after another, listeners hear the consequences of improper behavior, and learn about the difficulties that may ensue through carelessness or thoughtlessness. The people had to learn as well about planning and resourcefulness in order for them to survive.[4]

During this time Changing Woman (Asdzáá Nádleehí) is born. Discovered on top of Gobernador Knob, she grew in twelve days to womanhood. The first puberty ceremony (Kinaaldá) was conducted for her, with many of the Holy People (Diyin Dine'é) participating. Talking God (Haashch'éíłti'í) conducted the final night ceremony, when he presented the twelve Hogan songs (Hooghan Biyiin) still employed today. According to Navajo elder Mike Mitchell, this ceremony represents the original Blessingway.[5]

Changing Woman becomes pregnant and gives birth to twin boys, who become known as Born for Water (Tóbájíshchíní) and Monster (or Enemy) Slayer (Nayee' Neizghání). The twins embark upon a long and dangerous journey, filled with challenges that call upon them to employ all the good qualities emphasized in Navajo life. They visit their father, the Sun Bearer, who gives them weapons to employ against the monsters then plaguing the people. The twins return to kill One Walking Giant (Ye'iitsoh Łá'í Naagháíí), whose dried blood may be seen in the form of the lava flow near Tsoodził. They also slay Tsé Nináhálééh, the Monster Bird who lived on top of Shiprock (Tsé bit ' aí, or "Winged Rock").[6]

Although these exploits relieved the Diné of much suffering, the people needed additional help to improve their lives. Some Navajo accounts credit Changing Woman with the creation of livestock, while other stories have the twin boys returning to see the Sun Bearer, who gave them livestock as well as special prayers and medicine songs to be used for proper care of these animals. Regardless of how they were obtained, the horses are of four colors, each linked with one of the seasons and one of the sacred mountains: white, blue (or turquoise), yellow (or red), and black. Changing Woman is also important for her role in creating the first Navajo clans. She rubbed the skin from her breast, her back, and from under her arms to create Kiiyaa'áanii (Towering House), Honágháhnii (One Walks Around You), Tódích'íi'nii (Bitter Water), and Hashtł'ishnii

(Mud) clans. Eventually there would be sixty clans, with perhaps a third of them tied to peoples of Puebloan descent. The clan system is matrilineal, with the individual inheriting his or her clan from his or her mother.[7]

Changing Woman, Born for Water, and Monster Slayer are central figures in Navajo history and culture. Diné traditional scholar Harry Walters concludes: "Their exploits and heroic deeds set order, balance and harmony in the world. Changing Woman's gift of mother's instinct and affection are the basis for the matrilineal clan system. The exploits of Monster Slayer and Born for Water are the basis for Navajo healing and protection ceremonials. The accomplishments of all three, mothers and sons, defined new terms and set standards of behavior on how the people should live and what to expect of life."[8]

A proper life embodies hózhǫ́, defined by anthropologist Charlotte Frisbie as "continual good health, harmony, peace, beauty, good fortune, balance, and positive events in the lives of self and relatives."[9] If chaos had prevailed prior to the fourth world, the Blessingway ceremony opens the way to an era Walters terms the Hózhǫ́ójí period. The onset of this era is tied to increased contact between and among peoples of Athabaskan and Pueblo heritage. This is the foundation for the way of life that will become known as the Navajo. Blessingway is the fundamental informing and organizational force in Navajo ceremonialism. The standard anthropological analysis posits its formulation well after European contact, with significant evolution in the 1700s, when in the wake of the Spanish return in 1692 Puebloan peoples fled their home country and often joined Navajo communities. Walters disagrees, contending that the absence of extended references to livestock in the core ceremonial tales and the emphasis on corn and corn pollen speak to an aboriginal origin.

Thus, the Blessingway ceremonial's adaptation and development are tied to a time of extended contact with Puebloan peoples, whereas the roots of the Enemy Way ceremonial may be linked to contact with people who have ties to the southern Plains, especially the Plains Apaches and the Comanches. Walters sees Plains elements in the Enemy Way, citing "the use of scalps, give-aways, name-calling songs, and the round dance." Not all Diné share this perspective, but this observation is indicative of the new questions being raised about the evolution of Navajo culture.[10]

The Navajo traditional accounts do not contradict all of the archaeological or linguistic research that has been carried out over the past century. Navajos do not necessarily deny a connection with other Native peoples who speak a version of a language that has been classified as belonging to the Athabaskan (or Athapaskan) language category. The journey delineated in the traditional stories is not unlike the journey that non-Navajo archaeologists and linguists insist the Diné took from northwestern Canada and Alaska. There are, however, significant differences in some elements of Navajo traditional stories and the stories told by academic archaeologists and anthropologists.

The site of the first Kinaaldá: Dził Na'oodiłii, Huerfano Mountain, New Mexico. Photograph by Monty Roessel.

Historian AnCita Benally's work helps to clarify commonalities and differences. Benally is completing her Ph.D. in history at Arizona State University. Highly regarded for her skill in the Navajo language, she is well versed in traditional Diné knowledge. She acknowledges Navajo and Apache linguistic ties, not only with Native communities in Alaska and Canada, but also with people such as the Hupas, who reside today in northern California. However, she contends that Diné traditional knowledge adds a component essential in understanding the full picture. Archaeologists and anthropologists, for example, still cannot reach a consensus on the route or routes that Athabaskans took in their migration or how these affiliated peoples became separated.[11]

A traditional story tells of a terrible fire that lasted for a long time and permanently divided people into the two groups who are today labeled Northern Athabaskan and Southern Athabaskan. Another story relates how people traveled from south to north to find their relatives from whom they had been separated during a time of confusion and disagreement. These stories, Benally notes, assume "a time when all people considered Diné and who are called Athapaskan today were united as one people." The splintering that took place was followed by a time when different clan groups found one another and made an effort to reunify. As they also met with other groups, there often occurred exchanges of "gifts, ideas, and friendship. A number of them became a part of the traveling Diné and eventually became fully integrated into Diné society." On occasion, some of "the original Diné adopted small groups of other peoples and proclaimed them their relatives, either to share the same clan name or to become, as a group, related clans of a different name." "Diné clans adopting new people," she adds, "pledged to maintain kinship and social alliances with them."[12]

"Today," Benally observes, "almost every single group that the Diné came in contact with through trading, marriage, war or social events is represented by a clan group." Thus, people from Jemez Pueblo, San Felipe Pueblo, the Utes, the Chiricahua Apaches, the Zunis, other Puebloans, Paiutes, and even Spanish/Mexican groups were integrated in time into the Diné. In time they all became one people. They were all Diné.[13]

Recent archaeological research is calling into question routes of migration, length of residence, and other fundamental dimensions of aboriginal occupation of North America. Perhaps a major volcanic fire that took place roughly 1,600 years ago did have the effect reported by the traditional stories. Perhaps climate change occurred in a pattern allowing for south to north as well as north to south migration. Perhaps future archaeologists will find evidence to support the connection with the Pacific Coast that the Hupa presence connotes and of which traditional Diné stories speak but for which there is not presently "scientific" evidence.[14] As Klara Kelley and Harris Francis remark in an important essay, absence of evidence is not necessarily evidence of absence.[15]

In any event, there is sufficient uncertainty, and archaeological research is at such a comparatively early stage of development, that we have every right to be skeptical about orthodox archaeological accounts in which Navajos arrive essentially intact as a linguistic community, but curiously empty-handed otherwise. In these renditions, the Diné too often lurch onto the Southwestern stage as nomadic vagabonds. In such renditions other communities must teach them how to survive. Such scenarios doom the Navajos to second-class citizenship, demote them to newcomers in a new land, and relegate them to the category of upstarts whose eventual ambition becomes arrogance, in stark contrast to sedentary and supposedly always peaceful Puebloan groups.

Conventional archaeological and anthropological accounts too often deny the power and the essential truth of the traditional Navajo account of their origins. They disregard the obvious parallels between the Diné story of their emergence and the archaeological-linguistic evidence about a people's long journey and eventual emergence into the region. They tend to be so caught up in arcane detail that they don't ask the right questions and miss the larger picture.[16]

Perhaps one should not be surprised that the archaeologists who are the most completely grounded in Navajo history and culture—who are either Navajo themselves, or like David Brugge and Klara Kelley, have

Cliff Palace, an Anasazi site in Mesa Verde, Colorado.
Photograph by Ansel Adams. Still Pictures Division,
National Archives, College Park, Md.

worked closely with Navajo colleagues for decades—are precisely the ones who are the most skeptical about this perspective. Kelley and her Navajo collaborator, Harris Francis, conclude that "many scholars have assumed that a speech community, an endogamous community, and the users of distinctive material culture are all the same people in one neat self-contained package that is also stable for a long time."[17]

When one begins to find such a convenient combination suspect, as Kelley and Harris observe, things start to fall apart. And then a new, dramatic picture of the Southwest begins to come into focus. Brugge observes, "[T]he sacred traditions would indicate that the Navajos' ancestors were living in close association with the Anasazi, that their homes and camps were intermingled with the settlements of the village dwellers, and that their wanderings took them throughout the country among the various Anasazi centers." He then notes "the most curious aspect of the distribution of places named in the sacred texts is that they seem to concentrate at the old Anasazi centers, Mesa Verde and Mancos Canyon, Canyon de Chelly, the Hopi Mesas, Aztec Ruins and Chaco Canyon in particular."[18]

Much of the most recent archaeological research is pushing back the supposed "time of arrival" for the Apacheans—the Navajos and the Apaches—into the Southwest. Rather than the late 1400s or the early 1500s, more evidence now points to some time in the twelfth or thirteenth century. Archaeologist Alan Downer, for example, has revised his estimate to the 1100s.[19] The 1400s, as we have seen, may more properly be classified as the time when a distinctive Navajo culture began to emerge.

THE NAVAJOS AND THE ANASAZI

Such reconsideration is essential, indeed pathbreaking, but it ultimately avoids a central question: From whom are the Navajos of today descended? There is little debate about the ability of the Diné through time to incorporate other peoples into their ranks, to make them or their children into Navajos, with equal status and standing. There is also little debate about the ability of the Diné through time to incorporate useful elements of other cultures or to take advantage of their contact with others to add to their base of ceremonial ritual and cultural understanding.[20]

Kelley and Francis, along with such Navajo scholars as Walters, AnCita Benally, and Clyde Benally, see the Diné biological and cultural heritage as complex. They acknowledge the likelihood of multiple sources for that heritage. Kelley and Francis state: "Probably all post-contact Southwestern Indian communities, including Apachean groups, incorporate genealogical descendants of both Precolumbian residents of the central Colorado Plateau and other Postcolumbian emigrants onto the Plateau. No one modern ethnic group can reasonably claim to be exclusive descendants of the Precolumbians." They add, "Those Navajo who acknowledge connections with Anasazi limit the connections to certain specific Navajo clans,

White House Ruins, an Anasazi site in Canyon de
Chelly, Arizona. Photograph by Ansel Adams. Still
Pictures Division, National Archives, College Park, Md.

specific aspects of Navajo ceremonialism, or specific Precolumbian archaeological sites."[21]

Part of the conventional wisdom about the aboriginal Southwest has been to place the Navajos in opposition to the Anasazi. "Ana" does mean enemy in the Navajo language and Navajos are said to avoid the Anasazi sites because of their antagonism toward these communities as well as their reluctance to be in contact with places where people have died. At the same time, Puebloan communities within the region have assumed a proprietary air about the Anasazi. They have determined that when the great Anasazi population centers at Chaco Canyon, Mesa Verde, and elsewhere were abandoned during the thirteenth century, those who departed eventually joined or established new Puebloan entities. The similarity between Anasazi and Pueblo housing in and of itself has given that association a kind of obvious inevitability.[22]

Particularly within the past generation, Navajos have begun to reconsider their association with the Anasazi. Some of the Diné now claim a connection between their history and Anasazi history. Given the pattern through the centuries of incorporation of other peoples or fusion of others' cultural elements with those of the Navajos, they contend, is it not possible that some of the Anasazi chose to join with other people to form the group that we now call Navajo? If one accepts Walters's notion that some of the Diné ancestors lived near Anasazi for generations, then the claim for a Navajo link to the Anasazi becomes not only possible, but probable. Downer, now head of the Navajo Nation's Historic Preservation Office, has come to believe in an earlier arrival period for the Athabaskan speakers. Otherwise, he believes one must accept the notion that the Navajos had a curious proclivity for using old wood in their buildings. To the critics who say that the Diné simply employed old wood from other buildings, Downer replies, "I can't understand what would motivate these people to consistently use wood that's 200 years old."[23]

As one might well anticipate, such contentions are greeted derisively and dismissed by members of contemporary Pueblo communities, especially at Hopi, as well as by many anthropologists and archaeologists. Nevertheless, the Navajos have been sufficiently persuasive in regard to their claim for an association with the Anasazi that Chaco Canyon National Historic Park and Mesa Verde National Park have both agreed to grant the Navajos the status of affiliation with the Anasazi, and therefore consult the Diné as well as Pueblo communities in regard to dealing with Anasazi human remains and artifacts.[24]

Kelley and Francis have made some especially significant observations in regard to cultural continuity and change. They deride the notion that "societies are normally (or even ever) self-contained, self-sufficient, endogamous communities in which ethnicity, language, and culture coincide and remain stable for a long time." They add, "In the real world, ethnic identities, marriage and political networks, and speech communities overlap and therefore perpetually destabilize each other." Kelley and Francis remind us of the Navajo stories that feature such elements as turquoise, obsidian, and shell, which are not to be found within the immediate surroundings. Could these Apacheans, they ask, have been traders who helped link different regions? Could those trading activities have encouraged not only contact but also eventual commingling of these evolving, emerging groups within the Southwest?[25]

Trade surely represented a centrally important dimension of Native life in the period prior to the arrival of Europeans. In all parts of Native North America, extensive trade networks existed, allowing people a thousand miles away from the ocean to possess, for example, abalone shell. It permitted the Navajos, for instance, to possess enough abalone for their stories to present one of their holy mountains, the San Francisco Peaks, as being cloaked in abalone. On the local level, trade enabled less sedentary groups, such as the people who were becoming the Navajos, to exchange products from the hunt or from pastoralism for other products from more sedentary communities, such as Hopi. Relatively recent antagonism between the Navajos and Hopis over competing claims to land should not obscure the undeniable fact that these two groups through the centuries have often enjoyed very amicable relations, including trade, and, for that matter, marriage.

Brugge summarizes: "Navajo cultural changes must have involved immigration, instruction, diffusion, and even local inspiration, sometimes under the pressure of necessity, at other times perhaps more in response to opportunity." In the end, he concludes, Navajo adaptations within the Southwest and to "Old World peoples have left remarkably little that can be traced to their Northern Athapaskan ancestors aside from language and basic cultural themes such as individualism, fear of the dead, high status for women, pragmatic and optimistic outlook, and, as a corollary to the last, flexibility in adapting to new situations." Many of the ways in which Navajos express themselves, Brugge argues, may eventually have come to be seen as "traditional," but were clearly influenced by other peoples and cultures. Those who joined or became part of the Navajos brought ideas, knowledge, and material items with them. The expansion of the Diné cultural repertoire therefore came about through infusion of new people rather than by borrowing or duplication.[26]

Navajo archaeology is relatively young, and a great deal remains to be sorted out. Those interested in the first centuries of the Diné can anticipate important new findings in the next few decades that will deepen significantly our understanding of these years. Even now, although much remains in the shadows, scholars are gaining a sharper picture of the ways in which the people we now call Navajo emerged.

Before the Spaniards came, the people who were becoming the Navajos were centered in an area to the east of the present reservation. The Dinétah ("among the Diné") in northwestern New Mexico formed an important part of the early Navajo country for more than two centuries, from the 1500s or earlier through the late 1700s, when pressures from the Spaniards as well as conflicts with the Comanches and the Utes encouraged the Diné to move out of the area.[27]

The cradle of Navajo civilization, the place of Changing Woman's birth, the Dinétah is a rugged stretch of land to the east of present-day Farmington, New Mexico. Today the Bureau of Land Management manages most of this area. Here, in a challenging environment, the basic form of Navajo culture took shape. Although few Diné live in the area today, Dinétah remains a mecca to Navajos interested in their history and heritage.

Dominated by the distinctive peak of Gobernador Knob, Dinétah is home to a rich legacy of painted and carved ceremonial art. James M. Copeland, for example, concludes that over thirty-five Dinétah sites contain material relating to Monster Slayer and Born for Water. Pueblitos— little rock houses—also dot the landscape. The pueblitos looked familiar to early twentieth-century archaeologists. To most scholars, the presence of the pueblitos indicated not merely the presence of Puebloan refugees in the area but their influence in everyday Diné life.

Additional archaeological research raised fundamental questions about who had constructed the pueblitos. The sites contained the kind of broken pottery one could observe at Pueblo sites, but they also yielded some shards that differed from the remnants of Puebloan pottery. One contemporary source offers a vivid description: "The stone rooms, too, were both familiar and strange. Their walls rose in loosely stacked columns of rock, not the carefully bonded masonry of the Pueblo world, and their roof beams bore the marks of light metal axes, not the heavy stone choppers of the Ancient builders. Doorways were narrow; low and cramped. Often the only way in or out was through the roof. And outside, on the mesa tops, were the wheel-spoke patterns of fallen forked-stick hogans and sweatlodges—the architecture of ancestral hunters and gatherers becoming farmers."[28]

If the pueblito differed from a pueblo, then the forked-pole hogan represented an amalgamation of Athabaskan and Puebloan influences. Brugge has outlined the probable sources of architectural features in the following manner:

1. Forked-pole construction—probably a local innovation about 1700 to meet the need for more substantial homes
2. Solid walls—probably due to influence of Pueblo peoples used to more permanent homes
3. Wood as a basic material—Athabaskan tradition
4. Covering of vegetal material—probably a continuation of a tradition of thatch-like covering among Athabaskans
5. Earth covering—probably of Puebloan origin
6. Conical shape—Athabaskan

7. Orientation—local innovation in the Puebloan tradition of orientation of buildings
8. Hearth location—Athabaskan and Puebloan
9. Ash heap—Puebloan, but see number 10
10. Scattered trash—Athabaskan
11. Vestibule—Athabaskan
12. Door slabs—probably a Puebloan tradition adapted to local conditions

The functional sources of the forked-pole hogan also represented a mix:

13. Primary dwelling—Athabaskan
14. Working area—Athabaskan and Puebloan
15. Ceremonial structure—Athabaskan and Puebloan
16. Limited storage—Athabaskan and Puebloan
17. Meeting place—Athabaskan and Puebloan
18. Seasonal occupation—Athabaskan

This pattern, Brugge emphasizes, does not furnish an example of the much-publicized Navajo ability to incorporate new elements. Rather, it is a "fusion of two cultural traditions."[29]

THE NAVAJOS AND THE SPANIARDS

In the fields, in the hunt, and in battle, Navajos fully appreciated that their success hinged on more than hard work. They needed to pray, to hold the appropriate ceremonies, and to reconsider the promise of the Diné Bikéyah. They recognized that life was fragile, that harmony within oneself and within one's family could prove elusive, and that contact with others might provide new benefits or pose unanticipated dilemmas. Nevertheless, the promise of finding something better usually outweighed the danger of discovering something worse. Already it was becoming a society noteworthy for its members' willingness to look around the corner and over the next hill, for their curiosity about what might be gained by exploration and inquiry, and for their determination to do something well. Is it any wonder that others might consider joining such a people—less enamored of routine and more tolerant of innovation?

Such a society inherently embraced expansion. Once the people acquired a few horses, they wanted or needed more horses—and more land for them. Once they obtained a few sheep, they understood the benefits of having more—and the necessity of finding a place for them. Such an approach guaranteed that the Navajos would gain a reputation. They challenged other Indians' claims to particular territory. The Navajos did not think much of the notion of prior appropriation, or first in time, first in right. They opted for a pragmatic doctrine that emphasized beneficial use. This perspective guaranteed a continuing chance for prosperity, but it also ensured continuing opportunities for trouble.

Well before the Americans came, the Navajos began to develop a reputation. The Pueblo communities often welcomed them as trading partners, but resented the unwillingness of the Navajos to grant them primacy, that is, to acknowledge dutifully the Pueblo claim to prior appropriation. Pueblo villages offered bases for forays well beyond the mesas or valleys where they made their homes. Through their journeys for salt or eagle feathers or other items, their people believed that they had made such territory their own. The Navajos could not accept and did not accept this presumption. How could you call land your own when you did not live on it or near it, and if you made significant use of it only on rare occasions?

The Comanches and Utes, daring raiders in their own right, did not welcome the Navajo emergence as a force to be reckoned with in the region. These peoples delighted in their own courage, celebrated their ability to steal horses, or for that matter, people. The Navajo oral tradition brims over with accounts of Comanche and Ute attempts, sometimes successful, to steal their horses, their children, or their sisters or mothers.

The arrival of the Spaniards did not create instantaneous conflict for the Navajos, because the initial Spanish presence in the Rio Grande Valley lay well to the east of Navajo country. But the Spanish were committed to expansion, too, and even the Navajo appreciation for Spanish generosity for bringing such wonderful beings as horses, sheep, cattle, and goats could not forestall eventual conflict. The Diné would wrap such animals in the strands of their own stories, give credit to their own deities, and never even nod in the direction of New Spain for improving their lives. After all, the Spaniards did not possess turquoise horses. They did not have a chant that proclaimed:

> I am the Sun's son.
> I sat on the turquoise horse.
> He went to the opening in the sky.
> He went with me to the opening.
> The turquoise horse prances with me.
> From where we start the turquoise horse is seen.
> The lightning flashes from the turquoise horse.
> The turquoise horse is terrifying.
> He stands on the upper circle of the rainbow.
> The sunbeam is in his mouth for his bridle.
> He circles around all the people of the earth
> With their goods.
> Today he is on my side
> And I shall win with him.[30]

New Spain changed the lives, altered the cultures, and influenced the destinies of all Native peoples in the region. However, as the pioneering student of the Southwest Edward Spicer observed several decades ago, it would be the people on the margins of New Spain who would be most profoundly impacted by the Spanish incursion. The Spaniards employed forced imposition, persuasion, and demonstration in their efforts to produce cultural change. The more sedentary the Native population and the closer its location to Spanish outposts, the more likely it would be to experience the full brunt of the first element of that trinity.[31] This is not to suggest that the Navajos were beyond the reach of Spanish colonialism. They were not. But given their character and their lack of proximity, most Diné clearly did not confront the daily imposition of Spanish will in the same manner as Puebloan communities, especially those situated in the Rio Grande Valley. The Navajos were far more able to pick and choose, to take advantage of non-directed cultural change, even amidst the complications, and, at times, the horrors brought by the Spanish presence.

Cultural change came in different ways. Navajos did not always just borrow new methods and concepts. Often immigrant peoples, both Puebloan and Apachean, brought new ideas to the Navajos. For example, during this period the Comanches decimated the Plains Apache and drove them far to the south, where many survived in remnant groups or merged with other Native groups. Other Apacheans may have joined the Navajos after being displaced by the Utes. Native newcomers to Navajo society could introduce new approaches to farming or to ceremonial practice or bring additional livestock into Navajo country. Thus, Pueblo women may well have been the ones who primarily introduced Navajos to sheep and influenced their raising of sheep.[32]

Sheep, goats, horses, and cattle were all central to the evolution of Diné society and economy, but from the beginning, the sheep mattered most. As anthropologist Gary Witherspoon has observed, "[T]he central symbol of Navajo social organization is motherhood . . . [T]he meaning of this symbol is found in the reproduction and maintenance of life. It is not surprising, therefore, that the Navajo find a conceptual relationship between sheep and motherhood."[33] When Percy Deal spoke at a "Sheep Is Life" conference at Diné College in Tsaile, Arizona, in the summer of 1999, he said, "My mother taught us that the sheep is our mother. They will care for you." Another Diné a generation before had expressed the same sentiment: "Dibé wolyéii nimá át'é; dibé iiná niliínii át'é" ("Those called sheep are your mother; sheep are life").[34]

Sheep furnished security, became an integral part of one's identity, and influenced how Diné social groups were organized. Like other Native peoples who lived in fragile and uncertain environments, the Navajos worried about the possibility of hunger and possible starvation. Their skill as farmers and their ability to care for their sheep provided the base for social cooperation and mutual interdependence. They began to have greater confidence not only in today, but in tomorrow as well. The acquisition of sheep, horses, cattle, and goats transformed their future. Without the addition of livestock, the Navajos might have been just another Native community in the region. They certainly would have carved out an interesting niche. They would have experienced their fair share of compelling incidents and claimed their fair share of impressive leaders. But they would not have become the largest and most powerful Native community in the Southwest, let alone North America.[35]

The sheep, the *churra*, became known eventually as the *churro* in the United States. The churro accompanied early Spanish conquistadors and ranchers and quickly established itself as a key resource, both for meat and wool. The Navajos quickly recognized its attributes, and during the late sixteenth and seventeenth centuries the Diné employed time-honored techniques—trading and raiding—to begin to develop flocks of their own.[36]

Students of Navajo weaving have noted the importance of two other elements introduced by residents of New Spain: indigo dye (from Mexico) and bayeta, "that rare red fabric dyed with cochineal (a cactus louse)." Stefani Salkeld writes, "Navajo women deftly unraveled, re-carded, and re-spun this prized fabric to use in their own weaving."[37] Diné women observed the work of Spanish and Pueblo weavers; those Puebloans who came to live with the Navajos played a role in this evolution. Weaving authority Joe Ben Wheat says that the Navajos "adopted, without change, the wide vertical loom, together with the various techniques of spinning, dying, and weaving." They quickly proved their talents and their industry by producing a surplus for trade by the early 1700s, suggesting, Wheat contends, that they had become proficient weavers before the revolt of 1680.[38]

New Spain empowered the Navajos, but its overall relationship with the Diné varied enormously across time and space. Spanish policies and the caliber of administrative leadership in Santa Fe did not remain constant. An era of colonial reform, as implemented in Spain in 1720, could not entirely eradicate misunderstanding and violence, but made major, extended conflicts less likely. Conversely, a governor determined to profit personally from his administrative position could single-handedly cause a rapid deterioration in relations.

The culture of New Spain reflected the specific objectives of those Spaniards who chose to make the long journey to the region. They were men on the make: representatives of the Crown seeking to further their careers, and often to use their positions for personal financial gain; individuals who sought their fortunes in the area's minerals or in land where they could raise livestock; and priests who attempted to convert the Indians to a new faith and way of life. Spaniards were united in their dismissal of Native cultures—they would have considered such terminology an oxymoron—but they competed with each other for Native labor and other indigenous resources. The Spanish felt no need to consult with people they considered to be barbarians; the king gave to his colonists not only Indian land but the right to the labor of those Indians unfortunate enough to occupy specific parcels of real estate.[39]

The Spaniards brought considerable cultural baggage to the Americas, including the collective experience of dealing with North Africans, commonly called "the Moors," over seven centuries. Only with the final defeat of the remaining Islamic center in Granada in 1492 could "Spain" become a reality. The reconquest, or the crusade to eradicate Islamic authority may have ended, but the experience remained fresh in the minds of the Spaniards. It made Spanish migrants something other than ambassadors for cultural pluralism. Seven centuries had stiffened their resolve to conquer people different from themselves and to use any means necessary to achieve that goal.

Many students of Southwestern history have stressed the brutality that so often characterized New Spain's policies and actions. Acoma Pueblo will always remember that fateful occasion, now four centuries ago, when the Spaniards under Juan de Oñate fought and defeated the people, killing perhaps eight hundred of them and carrying out the most vindictive of all possible punishments against another five hundred, including about eighty men over the age of twenty-five who each had one foot cut off. Two Hopi boys who had the great misfortune of visiting Acoma at the time of the confrontation had their right hands sliced away.[40] David Warren, the historian from Santa Clara Pueblo, declares, "That something happened is far more important for us than when it happened."[41] He must not have been surprised when some of the good citizens of New Mexico saw fit to erect a new statue of Oñate near Santa Fe in 1999, that some other good citizens quickly carried out their own punishment. They cut off one of the statue's feet.

Historians of the Southwest have been so preoccupied with the Pueblo revolt of 1680 that they have largely ignored Spanish-Navajo relations both before and after that fateful event. In fact, the Navajos fought their share of battles with New Spain, even if they did not play a central role in the revolt or experience anything as climactic as the terrible event at Acoma. Many of their military engagements and confrontations took place prior to 1700, thus mirroring the general pattern of Spanish-Indian relations in the region, although the Diné surely had their share of problems with New Spain in the late 1700s, for example, as well.

Spanish-Navajo contact during the 1500s is difficult to track, in part because of the dispersed nature of the Navajo population; the Diné are far from being a unified nation but rather constitute a series of autonomous groups with highly localized leadership patterns. It was not always clear to the Spaniards just which Native group they were dealing with from one moment to the next, especially in the earlier years. Over time they began to realize that the Navajos shared, with some variation, a common language, common rituals, and common values, and upon special occasions attempted to transcend local allegiance in the interests of a more unified response to some contemporary challenge, but local authority almost always prevailed. Moreover, there are uncertainties surrounding the terms the Spaniards chose to employ. Francisco Coronado in 1540 may have encountered a group of Navajos; Antonio de Espejo met people the Spaniards called Querechos south of Mount Taylor, who seem rather likely to have been Diné. Raids by Navajos forced the Spaniards in 1609 to abandon hopes for San Gabriel del Yunque, between the Chama River and the Rio Grande.[42]

The first specific Spanish references to the Navajos as Navajos came in 1626 and 1630. In 1626, Fray Geronimo de Zarate Salmeron wrote of "the Apache Indians of Navaju"; the Tewa word "navahu" means "large area of cultivated lands." Four years later, Fray Alonso de Benavides calls the Navajos "very great farmers, for that /is what/ 'Navajo' signifies—'great planted fields.'"[43]

In the period leading up to the Pueblo revolt of 1680, the Spaniards often suspected the Diné of conspiring with Pueblo communities against them. The Navajos, no doubt, would have used the term "alliance" rather than "conspiracy," and they had a very specific reason for their animosity and for carrying out raids of reprisal. Although they certainly raided Spanish communities from time to time for livestock and other material items, Navajo raids often were sparked by the capture of Diné individuals for the Spanish slave trade. Frank McNitt and David Brugge have documented the degree to which Navajo people were seized for this inhumane institution. The Navajos suffered more from Spanish slavery than any other Native group.[44] The Spaniards rationalized involuntary servitude in language familiar to any person who has studied the history of the American South. They also spoke about teaching the Diné a lesson, but on that score the Spaniards hardly ever succeeded. The Navajos have been accused of many things through the centuries, but never of pacifism. Whenever Spain decided to teach them a lesson, the Diné had ways of offering New Spain some instruction of their own.

The eventual revolt of 1680 was preceded by a series of events that, at least in retrospect, made the rebellion not altogether surprising. For example, in 1650, Jemez, Isleta, Alameda, Sandia, and San Felipe joined with some Apaches and Navajos in an effort to overthrow Spanish rule. The attempt failed and nine Pueblo leaders were hanged and others sold into slavery. As Brugge observes, such failures remain significant; they may have fueled the fires that eventually swept over New Mexico in 1680, and they demonstrated the ability of different Native communities to unify around a common goal.[45] At the same time, one must recall that Puebloan communities had a fierce sense of independence and that factionalism frequently prevailed within individual villages. Various combinations of motives could foster factionalism or promote alliances. Navajos, along with other Apacheans, offered things of value to Puebloan groups. The Navajos' abilities as equestrians promised to be useful in times of conflict.

AnCita Benally adds, "Game meat, salt, dressed skins, and wild plant foods were among the products available from Apacheans. Village farmers on the other hand produced agricultural goods and woven cloth as well as ceramics and domesticated animal products like turkey meat. In addition to these resources each group provided refuge for each other, whether that refuge was from enemies, the weather, famine, or a place to stay while traveling, trading or to wait out a bad winter."[46]

In 1659, Bernardo Lopez de Mendizabal became governor of New Mexico. McNitt observes: "While his predecessors had made handsome profits in the acquisition or sale of Indian slaves, Governor Lopez apparently was determined to use his three-year term of office to make a fortune." In the course of his administration, many Navajos were killed or dragged away into bondage. A slave owner himself, Lopez made a personal profit through the now flourishing slave trade, ordering raids against Navajo communities and then having the captives taken to Sonora, where they were sold.[47]

As indigenous resentment and anger toward New Spain increased in the generation before 1680, the Spanish grew increasingly frustrated over raiding and over the unwillingness of many Natives to fully acknowledge the legitimacy of the Spanish Crown or the Spanish church. The Diné proved an elusive foe. In 1675 and twice in 1678, Spanish governors authorized military campaigns against the Navajos. During both efforts, hundreds of Pueblo men joined the Spanish ranks, either because they had been coerced to do so or because they had some grievance of their own. These initiatives resulted in the massive destruction of Navajo fields of corn, the capture of men, women, and children, and the killing of other Diné.[48]

Although some individual Navajos surely participated in the revolt of 1680, most Diné did not directly join the highly successful rebellion that killed several hundred Spaniards and drove the others into exile. The Spaniards returned in 1692 under Diego de Vargas. Many Pueblo people feared reprisals and fled into hiding. The Hano community of Tewa speakers was established at Hopi during this time. The Pueblo of Laguna, to the west of the Rio Grande, either began or expanded at this time. Other Puebloans in the years that followed chose to join Navajo groups. As already has been noted, those who became part of Diné settlements may have been attracted by what they saw there as well as unhappy with the tenuous situations in their home locales.

The historical literature customarily emphasizes that the Spaniards returned in 1692 a somewhat chastened lot, determined to act less harshly toward Native peoples. However, the first two decades of the eighteenth century witnessed constant campaigns against the Navajos, inaugurated in 1705 by a major effort that Jemez and other Pueblo refugees with the Diné also had to endure. Once again, the Navajos paid a price: The Spaniards destroyed many of their fields, killed an undetermined number of Diné, and took still others captive. Governor Francisco Cuervo y

Valdez observed that he had waged war against the Navajos "because of their great crimes, their audacity, and their reckless depredations upon the frontiers and pueblos of this kingdom."[49] This campaign did not occur in isolation; Rick Hendricks and John P. Wilson—the editors of the campaign journal of Roque Madrid, a contemporary Spanish soldier—note that "for more than a decade thereafter, full-scale Spanish military expeditions were carried out against the Navajos almost without surcease."[50] Seven campaigns were launched in 1709 alone, but by the 1720s, policymakers in Madrid implemented a reform program that curtailed both Spanish aggression and thus the Navajo retaliatory strikes against Spanish communities and Puebloan groups who had chosen or been coerced into fighting the Diné. Directives from Madrid had little effect on the Utes and Comanches, however, and Navajo difficulties with these groups, who sometimes allied with each other, continued unabated.[51]

The absence of extended, continuing confrontations with New Spain and crop failures and diseases, especially smallpox, experienced by many Puebloan communities helped open the door even wider to Diné territorial expansion. The Canyon de Chelly area thus became by the end of the eighteenth century more fully the heart of Diné Bikéyah. The stream of new people into the ranks of the Navajos, coupled with the needs and hopes of an expanding Diné population pushed more and more people westward. This movement clearly had important consequences for the generations to come. The movement helped inspire the vast livestock holdings of the Navajos and enabled them to claim a major land base in the Southwest. It strongly affected their perspective and their options when the American intrusion came in the mid-nineteenth century. It also allowed large numbers of the Diné to be out of harm's way—that is to say more fully removed from the eventual renewed push for control by Spanish and Mexican authorities in the late eighteenth and early nineteenth centuries.[52]

Canyon de Chelly became a significant population center in the 1700s. Navajos used its streams to grow corn and peach trees. Its walls allowed for protection; its vantage points permitted the Diné to spy on strangers from a long distance. As time went on, the Diné became progressively more confident of their capacity to repel unwanted intruders. Brugge notes that "friends and relatives from more than a hundred miles away would retreat to this citadel when enemies threatened." He adds, "Few were the raiding parties that had the temerity even to enter the canyons and fewer still those that dared stay long enough to do any real damage."[53]

However, in 1805 the Spanish attempted to extend the reach of their authority well into Diné Bikéyah. In a series of military operations, the Spaniards determinedly pushed all the way to Canyon de Chelly. A Sonoran named Antonio Narbona took hundreds of men from Sonora plus a hundred New Mexican men into the canyon, where they proceeded to attack a Diné bastion. This confrontation produced the legendary tragedy of Massacre Cave. Navajo oral tradition records that a great many women, children, and elders were hiding in a cave in the adjoining Canyon del Muerto. They were hundreds of feet above the canyon floor and almost entirely hidden from the view of the troops below. It is said that an old woman who had been a Spanish captive overestimated the security of her perch and began to yell insults, in Spanish, at the distant Hispanic soldiers. She had been treated very badly, and when this opportunity appeared, she could not contain her wrath. In the process she divulged their hiding place. The Spanish soldiers fired round after round in the general direction of the cave, killing over a hundred of the Diné, with another thirty-three taken captive. Antonio Narbona failed to mention the massacre in his final report.[54]

Not all Diné, of course, could move far to the west and not all wished to do so. One band, known through most of its history as Cañoncito illustrates the diversity of the Diné. The Navajos from this community became known as the "Enemy Navajos" (Diné Anaa'í) because, under duress, they allied themselves with the Spaniards and the Mexicans against other groups of Diné. In 1787, the people of Cañoncito agreed to participate in Spanish campaigns against the Apaches and to accept Spanish control in exchange for protection. After the Americans claimed the region, they would again side against other Diné. New Spain hoped to impose comparable terms on other branches of the Diné, but could not do so.[55]

Even with all these concessions and capitulations, Cañoncito did not know peace. Continuing Hispanic intrusions prompted a series of attacks and counterattacks at the turn of the nineteenth century. Treaties signed in 1805 and 1819 did not achieve all the Cañoncito people hoped. Moreover, the later treaty formally ceded to the Spanish much of the Navajo land in the Dinétah, over which Cañoncito actually had no authority. The 1819 agreement permitted the Spaniards to appoint a man known as Joaquin, from Cañoncito, as the area's "captain general." These arrangements infuriated the Dinétah Navajos, who bestowed the term of "Enemy Navajo" on the people of Cañoncito, thereby ensuring their continuing and future separation from the rest of the Diné.[56]

Spanish correspondence and administrative records reveal the challenges, frustrations, and illusions of attempted colonial rule. As the eighteenth century progressed, the Navajos were mentioned more specifically and more frequently, with the collective administrative voice reaching new decibel levels. The penmanship is often exquisite, but the hand cannot hide annoyance at these "Navajos" or "Nabajoes," who were clearly not behaving like docile subjects. They were allying with another group and were definitely up to no good.[57] They stole some horses and then vanished, leaving a Spanish pursuer to confess: "I have been in search of the stolen herd of horses taken by the Navajos, and have been unable to find any clue of their tracks." He blamed the disappearance not, heaven forbid, on his own ineptitude, or on Navajo knowledge of the land. Rather, "they have been favored by the heavy rains which have been excessive." For

Canyon de Chelly, Arizona. Photograph by Ansel Adams.
Still Pictures Division, National Archives, College Park, Md.

good measure, he also blamed the Jicarillas "in company with the
Navajos," who did know the country. On another occasion, the reporter
conceded, "It has been impossible to bring about the general meeting of all
of the Chiefs of the Navajo tribe on account of the heavy snow."[58]

The castigation of climate helps rationalize the inability of the Spanish
to coerce the Navajos into obedience. Even if they showed up, even if they
chose to sign some piece of paper, the Diné did not seem exactly persuaded that their behavior must change. The Spanish scribes commented
on this recalcitrance time and again. They were certainly agitated by the
Navajos' actions. Nemesio Salcedo, for example, warned that the Navajos
"may relapse into committing hostilities."[59]

POMEGRANATES BECOME SQUASH BLOSSOMS

During the final four decades of Spanish-Mexican administration of the
Southwest, in the first half of the nineteenth century, various bands of
Navajos alternately fought, agreed to peace, and fought again against these
outsiders and against neighboring Indian communities. Two specific inci-

dents illustrate some of the tensions and complications of this era: the Mexican expedition to Navajo country in 1835 and the Diné attack upon the Hopi village of Oraibi in 1837. In both instances, Navajo oral history offers us a more comprehensive sense of these battles.

The 1835 expedition symbolized the recurring effort on the part of Santa Fe to punish the Navajos for their raids and to demand acceptance of Spanish authority. On this occasion, perhaps a thousand men, mostly Hispanic along with some allies from Jemez Pueblo, ventured into Diné Bikéyah, intent upon administering a lesson the Diné would long remember. As they approached the Chuska Mountains (Ch'óóshgai, white spruce), they entered a pass between the Chuskas and the Tunicha Mountains (Tónítsaa, much water) that the Navajos called Béésh Łichii'í Bigiizh, after the chert or flint found there.[60]

As far as we know, the Spaniards did not bring along buglers to announce their arrival, but they might as well have done so. The pass is located at 8,800 feet and from near the summit, not far from present-day Crystal, New Mexico, one can see far to the east, as the wrinkled, brown land flattens toward the horizon. The Navajos knew the Spaniards were coming, and they had ample time to prepare a less than hospitable welcome. The leader of the assembled two hundred Diné who ambushed the intruders was one of the first of the people to emerge from the anonymity of group history. He is known to us by a Spanish name, Narbona.

An elder by this time, perhaps in his late sixties, Narbona had grown up in the Chuskas and knew the area as only a native of the region could. He prepared his men to wait until the invaders were strung out in a long line in order to make their way up to and through the pass. Tradition has it that Narbona compared that line to a long branch and that he proclaimed the branch could quickly be cut into firewood. At just the right moment, the Diné descended upon the Spaniards and the people from Jemez, promptly decimating the column of weary and unwary soldiers.[61]

Also in the 1830s, the Navajos attacked the Hopi village of Oraibi. According to Diné leader Scott Preston's presentation of a traditional narrative, a Navajo man named Darts at the Enemy had been killed by a young Hopi and the Diné sought revenge. When they reached the Hopi village, a few Navajos baited the Hopis to chase them, and then when they did so, Preston recounts, "the main Navajo force, which had remained hidden, came together to cut off their retreat. They chased the Hopis out into the flat." Then, he says, "the other force, which was attacking from the north (and which had approached from the west) did likewise. Then the arrow . . . feathered with buzzard feathers was shot over the village. It went smoothly over, without a wobble." This omen indicated the Navajos would succeed. They won a decisive victory, killing many Hopis. The Diné remembered the event by a name they bestowed upon Oraibi: "Sharp Point of the Mountain Runs into Water."[62]

The experiences of the final years of Spanish-Mexican administration could not prepare the Navajos for the kind of demands the Americans would make upon them beginning in the 1840s. Because the Diné were a long way from Santa Fe, and because of the nature of colonial administration, the Spanish and Mexican presence remained inconsistent and, at least from time to time, avoidable. Although the Spaniards and the Mexicans wanted to deal with the Navajos as one people, they had neither the resources nor, in the end, the commitment necessary to force lasting subjugation. As the Diné would soon discover, the Americans represented a different kind of presence and a different determination.

The Spanish-Mexican period was enormously important in Navajo life. The contact with the Spaniards, the Mexicans, and the many different Native communities transformed the Navajos from a minor to a major player on the Southwestern stage. The Diné had demonstrated that cultures are more likely to thrive not in isolation but through continuing contact, even conflict, with other groups. By the time the Americans came, the foundation of Navajo culture had been established. In addition to the introduction of sheep and other livestock, this period saw the evolution of weaving. In both weaving and, later, in silversmithing, the Navajos would continue to demonstrate their capacity for learning initially from others and ultimately developing forms of cultural expression that, regardless of their derivation, would emerge as fundamentally, centrally Navajo.

Silversmithing did not really emerge as a Diné art form until after the incarceration at Fort Sumner, but two prominent "traditional" design elements within silversmithing trace their origins to the Spanish-Mexican period. Before Navajos became silversmiths, they themselves wore silver and they saw other people, particularly the Spaniards and Mexicans, wear silver. Arthur Woodward, an important student of the evolution of Diné silversmithing, writes, "During the latter part of the eighteenth and the first few decades of the nineteenth century, the trousers and jackets of the Mexican men were profusely decorated with silver buttons and clasps. The bridle trappings of Mexican horses were covered with glittering silver. Suspended from the head stall of Spanish horses was a crescent-shaped bit of silver, the ends of the crescent often terminating in two tiny hands." The round silver buttons from Spanish or Mexican clothing became the beads in Diné necklaces. From the city of Granada, which means pomegranate in Spanish, came the inspiration for silver pomegranates that "dangled from trouser legs and jackets of New Mexican dandies." Anglo Americans eventually labeled these ornaments "squash blossoms." The Navajos first wore them as earrings before they strung them together to create necklaces, centering in the crescent with two tiny hands, which is called a *naja*.[63] Like the squash blossom, the naja is connected to Islamic Spain, surely a version of the Islamic crescent.

Islamic influence would also manifest itself in weaving, but primarily after 1868 when Anglo-American traders introduced designs from Turkey and other areas to Diné weavers, who, characteristically, soon made their own versions of them. That development is discussed in some detail in a subsequent chapter. Other more immediate points in the evolution of Navajo weaving merit brief explication here. Although the United States had yet to claim the Southwest, American influence had already started to permeate the region during the final years of Mexican administration. Kate Peck Kent, an authority on the history of Navajo weaving, points to the importance of the Santa Fe Trail, which, beginning in the early 1820s "linked New Mexico to the central United States and furnished an additional outlet for weavings, as well as bringing new yarn to the weavers. Navajo blankets of the period," Kent notes, "were considered superior to those produced on treadle looms by Hispanic weavers in the Rio Grande villages and were coveted by Mexicans, Anglos, and Indians alike."[64]

Josiah Gregg understood that the Diné had become a people who mattered. Writing in *The Commerce of the Prairie,* an 1840s publication that still is regarded as one of the classic books of the American frontier, Gregg did not necessarily portray the Navajos in the most positive of terms. But, in reading his reflections, one can see that the Diné had most assuredly and deservedly garnered his attention.

Gregg estimated the Navajo population at "about 10,000 souls." He labeled them "certainly the most important, at least in a historical point of view, of all the northern tribe(s) of Mexico. . . ." Gregg added, "They now manufacture a singular species of blanket, known as the Serape Navajo, which is of so close and so dense a texture that it will frequently hold water almost equal to gum-elastic cloth. It is therefore highly prized for protection against the rains."[65]

Gregg mentioned "the present predatory and somewhat unsettled habits of the Navajoes," but acknowledged "they cultivate all the different grains and vegetables to be found in New Mexico." He also made note of their "extensive herds of horses, mules, cattle, sheep, and goats of their own raising which are generally celebrated as being much superior to those of the Mexicans; owing, no doubt, to greater attention to the improvement of their stocks."

He reported that the missionaries had not had much success converting the Diné: "They now remain in a state of primitive paganism—and not only independent of the Mexicans, but their most formidable enemies." And thanks to the Mexican government's "repeated acts of cruelty and ill-faith well calculated to provoke hostilities" one could understand why the Navajos and other tribes seemed so constantly at war.[66]

Only a matter of months after Gregg penned his observations, General Stephen Watts Kearny's Army of the West marched triumphantly into Santa Fe. Governor Manuel Armijo had departed for Chihuahua, bequeathing New Mexico to the United States, a nation he called "that faithless and perfidious power." Acting Governor Juan Bautista Vigil y Alarid told the citizens of New Mexico: "[I]t is for us to obey and respect the established authorities, no matter what may be our private opinion. . . . No one in this world can successfully resist the power of him who is stronger." On August 18, 1846, Kearny pledged to the New Mexicans: "We mean not to murder you or rob you of your property. Your families shall be free from molestation; your women secure from violence. . . . In our government all men are equal. We esteem the most peaceable man, the best man. . . ."[67] Four days later, Kearny issued a proclamation in which he repeated his promises. This time, however, he clarified the status of the Navajos in this new order. Kearny said the United States would "protect the persons and property of all quiet and peaceable inhabitants within its boundaries against their enemies: the Eutaws, the Navajoes, and others. . . ."[68]

For the Navajos, such a declaration could mean only one thing. It meant war.

A Portfolio of Photographs
by Monty Roessel

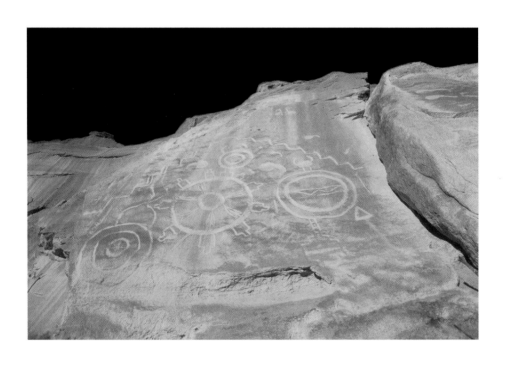

Diné: A History of the Navajos

Diné: A History of the Navajos

Diné: A History of the Navajos

Diné: A History of the Navajos

Diné: A History of the Navajos

Diné: A History of the Navajos

Diné: A History of the Navajos

Diné: A History of the Navajos

Diné: A History of the Navajos

Diné: A History of the Navajos

Diné: A History of the Navajos

Diné: A History of the Navajos

Diné: A History of the Navajos

Diné: A History of the Navajos

Diné: A History of the Navajos

2

"We Must Never Forget": 1846–1868

We must never forget their screams and the last we saw of them—
hands, a leg, strands of hair floating.

—*Luci Tapahonso, 1993*

THE TREATY AS TRIUMPH

"You are here," Luci Tapahonso's aunt would always say, "because of what happened to your great-grandmother long ago."

"I think that is what kept us alive. We believed in ourselves and the old stories the holy people had given us." But all along the way, not all the people could survive. "Some of the old people fell behind and they wouldn't let us go back and help them."

Others drowned attempting to cross the Rio Grande: "Some babies, children, and some of the older men and women were swept away by the river current. We must never forget their screams and the last we saw of them—hands, a leg, strands of hair floating."[1]

Luci Tapahonso would not forget. She would tell the story to the next generation, who would tell it to the next. It is a story of trauma and loss. But it is also a story of survival and continuation. It is a story that encompasses the coming of the Americans, the Long Walk, the time at Hwéeldi, and the signing of the treaty. It is a story that turned out differently than one would have assumed.

The historian Bernard DeVoto called 1846 "the year of decision."[2] In that fateful year, a sizable portion of the North American West started to become part of the western United States. The Navajos were among many Native peoples whose lands the United States claimed. By this time in our country's history, a clear pattern had emerged in regard to those peoples and those lands. The westward movement of the Americans sooner or later engulfed Indian communities. Americans justified the process of dispossession by declaring that Indians weren't using their lands to full advantage.

"You are in the way." That is, in the end, what the Americans said. It did not matter how many of one's people spoke English, went to Christian church services, or lived in houses. Indians represented an obstacle to "progress," a deferral of dreams. "You will lose your lands," the Americans said. "If you resist, you will lose your lives."

When Stephen Watts Kearny marched into Santa Fe in 1846, it seemed as though another inevitable chapter had begun. To most Anglo-American residents of New Mexico Territory (which also encompassed Arizona until the 1860s), the Diné represented an obstacle to the kind of rapid economic development they hoped to witness in the region. The years from 1846 to 1868 did witness an onslaught upon the Navajos and their way of life. However, when the Navajos signed the treaty of 1868, they achieved a great triumph. For the Navajos the treaty signified not defeat, but victory, and not disappearance, but continuation. The agreement allowed the Diné to return to a portion of their home country.

The treaty that carved out the initial acreage for the Navajo reservation remains a source for celebration. Unlike so many other Indian communities in the nineteenth century, the Diné through the treaty regained a central part of their traditional lands. By contrast, the Chiricahua Apaches, the western Lakotas, and most other Native groups lost valuable economic, social, and cultural resources. The most devastating outcome of all involved forced removal from one's own country. Removal meant that you had forsaken your ancestors; removal meant that you were separated from the place of your beginnings.

Alexis de Tocqueville, the French observer of America, understood the process. Just a few years prior to 1846, he wrote in *Democracy in America* about the dispossession of the Cherokees. De Tocqueville rehearsed how they had been uprooted from the Southeast and had been pushed along what later became known as the "Trail of Tears" to Indian Territory. Despite all the federal government's endless prattle about isolation and separation for the Native peoples in the Indian Territory, de Tocqueville could hear the clock ticking. "In a few years the same white population that now flocks around them will doubtless track them anew to the solitudes of the Arkansas," he predicted. "They will then be exposed to the same evils, without the same remedies; and as the limits of the earth will at last fail them, their only refuge is the grave."[3]

If asked about the future of the Diné, de Tocqueville no doubt would have held forth in equally articulate and depressing terms. Those Indian communities could not win. They would lose their lands, their lives, and their futures. They would be cast aside, flotsam in the wave of American "progress" washing across the continent. As the observations of New Mexico's acting governor made evident, such generalizations did not have to be limited to Indians. Who, after all, had the power to stand up to the United States?

In the history of any people there are certain defining moments that say something about the character and determination of the group. As important as they were, those men who negotiated and signed the treaty of 1868 were not the only significant actors in this story. Inspiration came from the elders who insisted that the people would continue. Sustenance came from those who conducted the religious ceremonies that were essential to Diné well-being. Resolve came from young women who sought a future for their children free from terror, mercifully removed from the point of a bayonet. In the actions of the thousands who found a way not to go into exile and the thousands more who endured the time away from Diné Bikéyah, an ability to endure hardship and to believe in the future could be discerned.

For many, if not most American Indian communities who signed treaties with the United States, that moment was experienced and is remembered not with gladness but with despair. Historian Robert F. Berkhofer, Jr., once wrote that Americans believed in expansion with honor—that treaty making involved a kind of demonstration that they were law-abiding, honorable people.[4] But for Indians, the treaties were never voluntary. They never involved gain, but always seemed to involve acquiescence and giving away land. Often treaty making was dishonorable. It frequently made "chiefs" out of individuals not empowered to represent all the people; it sanctioned the theft and lasting appropriation of hills, lakes, and mountains that possessed sacred significance.

Yet the signing of the Navajo treaty on June 1, 1868, defined the heart of a homeland rather than ripping the heart out of a people. June 1, 1868, became known as Treaty Day, as important in its own way as July 4, 1776, became to Americans. In a ceremony held 131 years later, the people remembered. They gathered on the Northern Arizona University campus in Flagstaff on June 1, 1999, to commemorate Treaty Day. During the previous year an original copy of the treaty (Naałtsoos Sání) had been on display at Cline Library. Thousands had made a pilgrimage to Flagstaff to see it. The document was about to be returned to Washington, D.C., but the Diné had come to demonstrate their respect prior to its departure. Speaker of the Navajo Nation Edward T. Begay concluded, "What our leaders were able to accomplish at Hwéeldi was to give us a land, a home within the four sacred mountains, and a purpose as a people to live with our new partner, the United States, as a nation and a semi-independent entity within these borders."[5]

THE AMERICANS

In 1846, such an outcome appeared unlikely at best. Kearny's public pronouncement that identified the Navajos as enemies quickly set the tone for an assertive American diplomatic position. Even before the war with Mexico had ended with the signing of the Treaty of Guadalupe Hidalgo in 1848, the United States had moved abruptly to assert its authority over the Diné and their lands.

Before Kearny departed for California and a continuing war against Mexico, he invited Navajos to Santa Fe to discuss the new order. Few responded to his summons other than a handful of Diné who no doubt lived near Santa Fe and were curious to learn more about these newcomers. Those who did not come figured the next move was up to Kearny. They did not have long to wait. On October 2, 1846, Kearny dispatched Colonel Alexander W. Doniphan of the 1st Regiment Missouri Mounted Volunteers into Navajo country, carrying instructions to force the Diné to release any and all prisoners and property "which may have been stolen from the inhabitants of the territory of New Mexico," and to "require of them such security for their future good conduct, as he may think ample and sufficient, by taking hostages or otherwise." Diné near the Rio Grande were sufficiently unimpressed by Kearny's presence in their neighborhood that on the following day, October 3, they raided the community of Polvadera, only twelve miles from where Kearny's command was camped, and took off with an ample supply of cattle and horses. Some of Kearny's men, called in to chase the Navajos, got close enough to recover the cattle, but not the horses.

An exasperated Kearny issued another proclamation in which he made note of "the frequent and almost daily outrages committed by the Navajos upon the persons and property of the inhabitants of the Rio Abajo, by which several lives have been lost, and many horses, mules and cattle stolen from them." Responding to the local inhabitants' pleas to go after the Diné, Kearny gave them his blessing "to form war parties, to march into the country of their enemies, the Navajoes, to recover their property, to make reprisals and obtain redress for the many insults received from them." He added an "expansion with honor" postscript: "The old, the women and the children of the Navajoes must not be injured."[6]

While Kearny was declaring open season on the Diné, not all the residents of New Mexico had uniformly negative comments to make about the Navajos. Governor Charles Bent's letter to Secretary of State James Buchanan on October 15, 1846, and a subsequent letter to Commissioner of Indian Affairs William Medill on November 10, 1846, suggested mixed emotions and reflected the kind of ambivalence that the Navajos already seemed to inspire in Anglo Americans. Although not happy with Diné behavior, the governor had to admire some of their achievements. He described the Navajos to Buchanan:

> They are a warlike and wealthy tribe, there being many individuals among them whose wealth is estimated as far exceeding that of any other person in this Territory. Their principal wealth consists of immense herds of horses, mules, sheep, and cattle. . . . These Indians have permanent villages, and cultivate all the grains and fruits known to the Spaniards in this climate. They manufacture blankets of rare beauty and excellence.

Bent noted the Navajos "do not destroy the Mexicans, because they actually prefer that they should continue to raise stock for them to drive off. Until these Indians are effectually subdued," Bent emphasized, "they will continue to blight the prosperity of that portion of this Territory which is exposed to their depredations." In his letter to Medill, Bent cheerfully contradicted his earlier depiction. In the space of a few weeks, the Diné had been transformed into a people with "no permanent villages or places of residence" who "roam over the country between the river San Juan on the north and the waters of the Gila on the south." According to the governor, the Navajos possessed 30,000 cattle, 500,000 sheep, and 10,000 horses, mules and asses, "it not being a rare instance for one individual to possess 5000 to 10,000 sheep and 400 to 500 head of other stock, and their horses are said to be greatly superior to those raised by the Mexicans."[7]

Doniphan departed Santa Fe in late October. By late November the Americans had succeeded in convincing some of the Navajos to sign a peace treaty, the first of seven negotiated between the Diné and the United States between 1846 and 1868. Narbona was among those to travel to a place the Navajos called Shush Bitoh or Bear Springs (Ojo del Oso, the Mexicans labeled it), the future site of the new Fort Wingate, near present-day Gallup. The elderly Narbona, now nearing eighty years of age, signed the treaty. Narbona had traveled to the edge of Santa Fe to gain a firsthand impression of the Americans. He decided they were a force to be reckoned with and cautioned other Diné to be wary of their military strength.[8]

Zarcillos Largos took advantage of the occasion to express his annoyance with "the new men," as Narbona had labeled the Americans:

> Americans! You have a strange cause of war against the Navajos. We have waged war against the New Mexicans for several years. . . . We had just cause for all this. You have lately commenced a war against the same people. You are powerful. You have great guns and many brave soldiers. You have therefore conquered them, the very thing we have been attempting to do for so many years. You now turn on us for attempting to do what you have done yourselves. . . . This is our war. We have more right to complain of you for interfering in our war, than you have to quarrel with us for continuing a war we had begun long before you got here.[9]

Zarcillos Largos expressed the hope that the Americans would allow the Navajos "to settle our own differences" with the Mexicans, but such a scenario could hardly be sanctioned by the new power in Santa Fe. The Americans promoted expansion with honor; the more quickly peace could be forged, the more rapidly expansion could take place. The unratified treaty of Bear Springs is significant for its formal declaration of the Navajos' status. Not only were the Spaniards and Mexicans of New Mexico included in the term "American people," but the treaty also found room for the Pueblo Indians to be brought under that umbrella. Such a definition emphasized the separate status people like the Navajos and the Apaches had been given in the American Southwest.[10]

The treaty is also an important illustration of American alacrity. Within the span of a few months, the United States had already insisted upon such negotiations. By autumn of the following year, Major Robert Walker marched his battalion into Canyon de Chelly. The Diné apparently scattered at the sight of these first American intruders, leaving the hungry soldiers to fend for themselves. Walker's contingent managed to survive for some time on mule, dog, and wild parsley.[11] In addition to demonstrating that Americans were not picky eaters, the U.S. presence symbolized American determination to see and to be seen. The Navajos had been put on notice that the "new men" would never be far away.

Colonel John Macrae Washington became one of these new men in the autumn of 1848, when he showed up in Santa Fe as the new military commander and provisional governor of New Mexico. In February 1849 he informed the adjutant general in Washington of the need for the "wild tribes" to "change from their present roving habits to the pursuit of agriculture, from the savage state to that of civilization."[12] In his employment of such language, Washington very much expressed the sentiments of the day. In the mid-nineteenth century savagery and civilization were seen as different stages of human development. The very word "savage" had evolved from the Latin "silvaticus," or "man of the woods." In 1859, Charles Darwin would publish his theory of evolution in *On the Origin of Species* and observers of human societies were declaring that cultures evolved as well. Whether depicting Indians in a romantic way, as did Henry Wadsworth Longfellow in "Hiawatha" in 1851, or in an unromantic way, as did the average Anglo American on the frontier, Americans believed that most, if not all, Indians must be compelled upward out of "savagery" and "barbarism" into the higher stage of "civilization." If this "improvement" required coercion, then so be it.[13]

Colonel Washington soon embarked upon his own fateful effort to hasten the process along. The Navajos' "repeated depredations," he told the adjutant general, really left him no alternative but to march into Diné Bikéyah. In August 1849, reinforced by "a detachment of Pueblo Indians and Mexican militia," the troops passed through Torreon, Pueblo Pintado, Chaco Canyon, and the Tunicha mountains to Canyon de Chelly. But before the conclusion of treaty discussions and the signing of this second treaty on September 9, 1849, the Americans instigated a confrontation in the vicinity of that pass where Narbona had won his great victory. This tragic event could easily have been avoided.

A Navajo rode by on a horse that the Americans claimed had been stolen. They called upon the Diné man to give up his horse. When he declined to do so, Colonel Washington refused to back down. He ordered his men to fire on the offender. Chaos erupted in the camp, with seven

Navajos, among them Narbona, losing their lives in the senseless fracas. Colonel Washington did not mourn Narbona's loss. Several weeks later, he summarized what had happened: "Among the dead of the enemy left on the field was Narbona, the head chief of the nation, who had been a scourge to the inhabitants of New Mexico for the last thirty years."[14]

This murder, however, was far more consequential than the colonel could appreciate. That the Americans would kill a frail old man of great standing in his community told the Diné something about the character of the newcomers. Those who had witnessed these senseless deaths were embittered by what they had seen. Narbona's son-in-law, Manuelito, seemed particularly angry.

This time the Senate ratified the treaty on September 9, 1850. The head signatories to what became known as the treaty of 1850 were Washington and Agent James Calhoun for the United States and Mariano Martinez and Chapitone for the Diné. The Navajos, not surprisingly, did not accord this agreement any of the respect they later felt for the treaty of 1868. They understood it for what it was: an arrangement negotiated in haste and signed under duress. The main, practical significance of the treaty came in one clause: "the Government of the United States will establish such military posts and agencies, and authorize such trading-houses, at such time and in such places as said Government may designate."[15]

FORT DEFIANCE (TSÉHOOTSOOÍ: "MEADOW BETWEEN THE ROCKS")

The door was now opened to the construction of a fort in Navajo country. Given the prevailing American attitudes toward the Navajos, the fort would have an unoriginal but still symbolically significant name: Fort Defiance. Americans had given the same name to a fort constructed decades before in Shawnee country. Defiance was more imposing, at least, than Fauntleroy, the name temporarily affixed to another military installation not far away. Agent Calhoun, for one, thought the forceful federal stance to be the correct one. His letter of October 1, 1849, to the commissioner of Indian affairs offered a concise summation of his opinion about the Diné. "The Navajos," he argued, "commit their wrongs from a pure love of rapine and plunder."[16] By 1851, Fort Defiance had been constructed in the southern portion of Navajo country, where the Diné community of the same name is situated today. Major snow storms that November made for an abbreviated harvest of alfalfa. The soldiers stationed there under the command of Major Electus Backus nicknamed it "Hell's Gate."[17]

John Macrae Washington left his post in the autumn of 1849, to be replaced by Colonel John Munroe, who, in turn, was succeeded by William Carr Lane. Backus also departed after a relatively brief stay. He had formed a quite positive view of the Navajos. In a letter to ethnologist Henry Schoolcraft on February 10, 1853, Backus declared: "As a nation of Indians, the Navajoes do not deserve the character given them by the people of New Mexico. From the period of their earliest history, Mexicans have injured and oppressed them to the extent of their power; and because these Indians have redressed their old wrongs, the degenerate Mexicans have represented them as a nation of thieves and assassins." Not a man to mince words, Backus concluded his epistle leaving little doubt about his judgment. He noted that the Navajos' "name has become a terror to their pusillanimous and effeminate enemies. . . ." Backus believed "their country is, generally, too poor to excite the cupidity of the whites; yet it is well suited to their own wants," and he expressed the hope that the government would protect the Diné "from the incursions of that reckless portion of our citizens, which is but too frequently found hovering upon our remote frontiers."[18]

As noted in the first chapter, the continuation of the trade through which Navajo children and adults became enmeshed in captivity and slavery severely hindered attempts made to reduce Navajo raiding and to promote Diné cooperation with American authorities. A January 27, 1852, council at Jemez sought to discover the primary reasons behind the Navajos' intransigence. When he summarized this session for Governor James S. Calhoun, Agent John Greiner quoted the words of Armijo, one of the Diné leaders who blamed the slave trade for most of the difficulties: "Is it American justice that we must give up everything and receive nothing? More than 200 of our children have been carried off and we know not where they are. The Mexicans have lost but few children in comparison with what they have stolen from us. . . . My people are yet crying for the children they have lost." Greiner wrote that he was "so well convinced with the truth of the remarks of Armijo that I confess that I had little to say."[19]

Nevertheless, the mood in New Mexico could hardly be called conciliatory. Governor Calhoun issued a proclamation in 1851 urging citizens to form volunteer units that would be under his direction. They would be "authorized to attack any hostile tribe of Indians which may have entered the settlements for the purpose of plunder and depredation." Just to remove all doubt about who might be included under the label of "hostile tribe," Calhoun also relayed messages to the different Pueblo communities demanding that they "abstain from all friendly intercourse with the Navajo Indians." Should the Diné "dare to come into your neighborhood," Calhoun informed them, "you are authorized to make war upon them, and to take their animals and such other property as they may have with them."[20]

New Mexico governors often issued proclamations and calls for citizen action during the era. They did not burden an already empty treasury. And like all politicians, the governors wanted to show that they cared. At the same time, the pragmatic Diné knew empty rhetoric when they heard it. They also realized the limitations of New Mexico's ability to restrain or respond to them. Agent Greiner noted that the territory did not even have a thousand troops. Moreover, he had calculated their value: "Our troops are of no earthly value. They cannot catch a single Indian. A dragoon mounted will weigh 225 pounds. Their horses are all as poor as carrion. The Indians have nothing but their bows and arrows and their ponies are as fleet as deer. Cipher it up. . . . Heavy dragoons on poor horses who know nothing of the country, sent after Indians who are at home anywhere and who always have some hours' start, how long will it take to catch them? So far, although several expeditions have started after them, not a single Indian has been caught."[21]

Nor were the Diné necessarily committed to endless raiding and chasing. Agents such as Backus, who came in without preconceived conclusions about their charges, reported better results. The actions of the Navajos clearly evidenced a willingness to work toward peace under the right set of circumstances, which included people they could trust or at least with whom they could communicate.

Backus related one example in the autumn of 1851. Forty Hopis came into Fort Defiance on behalf of some of the Diné, who wanted to reach an agreement that would allow for peace. Backus assured the Hopis of his serious desire to gain such an accord. The Hopis left to so inform the Navajos. Six days later "a formidable body of Navajos, well mounted, and armed with guns, lances, bows, and arrows, presented themselves in front of the garrison, and solicited an interview." The Navajos promptly reached agreement on a document comprising two articles, in which they promised to remain at peace and enter into negotiations with American authorities for a lasting peace. Backus reported no further problems during the remainder of his time at Fort Defiance.[22]

A conscientious agent could make a difference in the attitude of any indigenous group, but he faced a nearly impossible assignment. He was often caught among competing interests for Native lands and frequently had to deal with factions within the tribe itself. The rapid turnover of personnel, the isolation, and the weather often posed problems. Incompetent and insensitive men outnumbered those who could be considered dedicated and understanding. It is not surprising that Indian communities often gave these individuals nicknames that reflected their appearance or their attitude. Thus, the anxious young man at Pine Ridge in South Dakota in 1890 quickly earned a Lakota name meaning "Young Man Afraid of Indians." The Navajos would have more positive names for Henry Dodge. They generally called him Bi'éé'łichi'í (Red Shirt).

The successor to John Greiner, Dodge arrived in June 1853. He had the distinct advantage of having worked in Navajo country. He knew what he was getting into and held no illusions about the nature of his job. A year after his arrival, Dodge came to Santa Fe, accompanied by forty-two Navajos and five hundred sheep that the Diné had "borrowed" not long before. A writer for the Santa Fe *Gazette* was impressed that the incidents of Navajo raiding had diminished drastically and was astonished that the Diné actually were returning the sheep. He gave full credit to Dodge for the turnaround. Manuelito observed that the sheep had been stolen by thieves who had since run away; the Diné had "bad people" in their midst, he acknowledged, but so did all other groups of human beings.[23]

Dodge reported that the Navajos had ten thousand people and 250,000 head of livestock and impressive yields of wheat, corn, pumpkins, melons, and peaches. Given their holdings and their dreams for the future, the Diné had a very definite stake in proper decision making about their lands. They also believed quite strongly in the ideal of reciprocity and sought to impress the non-Indians of New Mexico with the degree to which they had bought into this ideal. The Navajos had the opportunity to show their commitment to the goal of reciprocity in response to an incident that took place in November 1854. A Diné man killed a soldier at Fort Defiance. The Diné not only acknowledged responsibility but also brought in the person responsible. They agreed that he should be hanged. As Dodge reported, the army did not hesitate to carry out the sentence and the guilty party soon was *"dead dead dead."*[24]

Had Dodge lived he might well have made a difference at this juncture of Diné history. He surely would have tried to improve cross-cultural communication and he would have appreciated the different perspectives people had, depending on their age, life experience, and gender. Unfortunately, Apaches killed him while he was out hunting south of Zuni. He was only forty-five years old. Without him, an already tense situation became all the more combustible.[25]

Just prior to this tragic development, pressures had escalated within New Mexico for a more binding treaty. Governor David Meriwether took the lead in calling the latest treaty council, and a gathering convened north of Fort Defiance in July 1855. After hearing Meriwether's proposal, the Diné pondered its merits. Zarcillos Largos did not attend the second day's session, sending word that he was returning the staff and medal given to him by the federal government in recognition for his central role in representing the Navajos. With Zarcillos Largos's resignation, a successor had to be found, and the Diné selected Manuelito.[26]

Manuelito and his colleagues did not like what the governor had proposed. They felt that he did not recognize the appropriate and true limits of Diné Bikéyah and in general they believed the restrictions and limitations imposed by the treaty to be excessive. Eventually the governor wore down their opposition. Reluctantly each of the Diné representatives, including Manuelito, Segundo, Aguila Negra, Hijo del Juanico, Mariano Martinez, and Zarcillos Largos, affixed their marks to the "Articles of Agreement and Convention." The Navajos had to give up 20 million acres and were promised a pittance—$102,000 a year for twenty-one years—for all that land. Fate smiled on the Diné, however, as once again the U.S. Senate did not ratify the treaty.[27]

The governor's secretary provided another useful description of the Navajos, in which he apparently forgot to include censure along with his

Manuelito, Navajo resistance leader. National
Anthropological Archives, Washington, D.C.

praise. W. W. H. Davis underlined the economic productivity of the Diné, including their two hundred thousand head of sheep, their more than ten thousand horses, and their agricultural bounty of corn, wheat, beans, pumpkins, melons, and peaches. He praised their weaving skills and labeled the people "industrious and laborious." "In many respects," Davis argued, "the Navajos are the most interesting tribe of Indians in our country, and their history, manners, and customs are not unworthy of an investigation."[28]

General William Thomas Harbaugh Brooks could have benefited from such an investigation, if he had bothered to read it. Unfortunately, Brooks appeared not to be inclined toward thoughtful review or careful inquiry. The wrong man at the wrong place at the wrong time, Brooks became the commander of Fort Defiance in 1857. He came in with an already formed conclusion about the proper way for him to fulfill his responsibilities and nothing he witnessed during his first months in Diné Bikéyah caused him to change his mind. Independence, Brooks reported to the assistant adjutant general in April 1858, encouraged the Navajos to be "self confident, arrogant," and "presumptuous." "They can only be prosperous," he alleged, "when a strong arm, and one that they dread, is over them and ready to strike at any offense given."[29]

The Navajos promptly obliged and furnished an offense. A southerner, Brooks had brought an African-American male slave (known simply as Jim) and a female slave with him to Fort Defiance. An unidentified Navajo shot Jim in the back with an arrow. According to Navajo traditional accounts, the African-American woman provoked the attack. She had mistreated a Diné woman at the fort. This kind of action demanded a response, and the attack on Jim represented another version of reciprocity. Seriously wounded, Jim clung to life for several days, but finally passed away four days later. Brooks had already concluded that war with the Navajos was inevitable, and this incident merely added fuel to a considerable flame. So, in essence, concluded the Santa Fe *Gazette*. The Diné did not like Brooks and they did not want to give up anyone within their ranks to the officer. Finally, in an effort to placate Brooks, they killed a Mexican captive, brought him into the fort and announced that they had apprehended the guilty party and were bringing him in the interests of justice. This was obviously not the person Brooks had sought and he remained unimpressed with the workings of the Diné traditional justice system.[30]

And so war began—not war on the scale the Navajos would experience a few years hence, but war, nevertheless. Brooks admitted that until the Diné were willing to give up the actual murderer of his slave, he did not want the conflict to end. The campaign appeared to cost the Navajos far more than the American forces. In the seven or eight battles that took place over the course of the four-month conflict, at least two hundred Navajos were killed, far more fatalities than the U.S. troops experienced. The peace treaty negotiated at Fort Defiance at Christmas between Colonels B. L. E. Bonneville and James L. Collins for the United States and fifteen Diné leaders "included the establishment of an east boundary for the Navajos, payment of indemnification by the tribe for depredations committed since August 15, the release of all captives by both parties involved, [and] waiver of the demand for the surrender of the murderer who touched off the war." In addition, the United States "reserved the right to send expeditions through Navajo country and to establish military posts." Huerto was appointed as head chief of the Diné. Perhaps the most difficult pill for the Navajos to swallow came with the insistence by the Americans that Sandoval and the other Diné from the Cañoncito area—the "enemy Navajos" who had continued to ally themselves with the Americans and who had been a real thorn in the side of the Diné—had to be considered a part of the Navajo Nation. The details that had been presented, discussed, and debated, however, once again became irrelevant, since, mercifully for the Navajos, the U.S. Senate did not ratify the treaty.[31]

The Senate often refused to ratify treaties. Many senators disliked paying any money to Indian nations or reserving land for them. With or without ratification of this treaty, the likelihood of a major war between the two sides had been increased by the latest confrontation. Each party had reason to escalate the conflict. The Navajos clearly could not have been pleased with the terms of the treaty, while many Americans appeared to back Brooks. The Diné had tolerated the intrusion of institutions such as Fort Defiance. Now they wanted to expel the U.S. Army from their midst.

The next significant stage of the struggle involved the Navajo attempt to capture Fort Defiance. The Diné nearly succeeded in realizing this objective in the spring of 1860. At about four o'clock in the morning on April 30, 1860, led by Manuelito and Barboncito, approximately a thousand of them launched a painstakingly designed plan of attack. Only superior firepower on the part of the beleaguered three companies of the Third Infantry prevented the Diné from achieving an extraordinary triumph. One observer in Santa Fe, James Donaldson, called it "the most daring attack by the Indians that has taken place since I was in the Army, and indicates a spirit that will become dangerous if not checked."[32]

Had the Navajos succeeded they might have delayed the drive to remove them from their own country, but perhaps this result simply would have accelerated the process. The initial proponent of removal was actually not James Carleton, governor and commander of New Mexico Territory, but rather his commanding officer, General Edward R. S. Canby. Canby had become convinced that by placing the Navajos on a reservation or reservations removed from their home country, the federal government would at least have a chance to impose its will on them. An ample supply of skeptics, including Donaldson, denied the Navajos would change. "You might as well make a hyena adopt the habits of a poodle dog," he huffed.[33]

Canby took his turn at a campaign in Navajo country with a foray begun in the autumn of 1860. The usual pattern prevailed. Canby expressed pleasure at the damage done to the Navajos and optimism about the difference the campaign would make. He proceeded to negotiate a treaty in February 1861 with forty-nine Navajo leaders, including Barboncito, Manuelito, Armijo, and Ganado Mucho. The Diné promised once again to submit to American authority, control the actions of their people, "establish themselves in pueblos," and adhere to an eastern boundary. The U.S. Senate once again refused to ratify the accord.[34]

CARLETON, CARSON, AND NAVAJO REMOVAL

The ongoing struggle of the American Civil War eventually forced Canby to move on from New Mexico. He handed control over New Mexico Territory to Carleton in 1862. Carleton's ascension marked another crucial turning point in the crisis. Determined to bring an end to Native resistance in the territory, he targeted both the Mescalero Apaches and the Navajos for removal, isolation, and incarceration, and decided to place them together in one location to enforce a different future for both communities. Although from today's perspective Carleton's attitudes seem culturally insensitive and strikingly inappropriate, his basic approach represented the ideas of a great many Americans who perceived the establishment of reservations as a solution to what was deemed "the Indian problem."

In the 1840s, the U.S. federal government had adopted a new approach in Indian affairs. It moved responsibility for Native concerns from the War Department to the Interior Department and anticipated the placement of Indians on federal trust land—reservations—as a means of assimilating them into American life. The reservation system was designed to offer an alternative to extinction for Native peoples. Policymakers hoped that isolating and controlling Indians on reservations would encourage non-Indian "settlement" and development of the interior West. Given the problems of proximity in the past, the government sought to move Indians beyond harm's way to some of America's least attractive, most remote terrain.

In concert with isolating Native peoples, federal officials thought that it was high time to remake them in the American image. The flood of immigrants to America and the subsequent assimilation of many of these newcomers encouraged the belief that required schooling of the young, conversion to Christianity for all, and the eventual division of reservation land into privately held individual parcels of real estate could, in the unconsciously ironic words of one commissioner of Indian affairs, "make the Indians feel at home in America." Carleton's plan, therefore, should not be seen as some wild, idiosyncratic scheme. It definitely emerged from the priorities and perspectives of the era. Ultimately the reservation envisioned by Carleton symbolized the two overarching impulses of "white"

Americans toward different peoples "of color": segregation and assimilation. Those two goals conflicted with each other, with some ironic results. Reservations could become cultural enclaves. The reservation boundary could become a working ethnic boundary that permitted its occupants to maintain languages and to develop viable modern identities as members of a reservation community. This, obviously, is not what the policymakers or most other Americans had in mind.[35]

In the second half of the nineteenth century, federal policymakers, state officials, and especially non-Indian residents of Arizona Territory and New Mexico Territory perceived reservations to be temporary institutions. Blithely disregarding the standard language of the treaties, which stipulated a continuing commitment on the part of the federal government as a trustee for an Indian nation, these individuals considered reservations to be transitional in nature. They constituted an expedient means to deal with the demands of the present but they hardly were intended as a permanent fixture on the American map. The entire American experience had reinforced this lesson. At some point in the not-too-distant future, non-Indians would once again be able to push and shove their way onto Indian land. Federal administration of the reservation continued to be influenced by non-Indian demands for access to Native resources. But as reservations did exist, many Americans wanted to use them to try to push Indians up the ladder to the next stage of social evolution—that elusive state the whites called "civilization."

Carleton envisioned the reservation as a place where the Navajos would be transformed. Their children would learn how to read and write. The Diné would be taught "the art of peace" and "the truths of Christianity" and soon would "acquire new habits, new values, new modes of life." In time, he predicted, "the old Indians will die off and carry with them the latent longings for murder and robbing: the young ones will take their places without these longings: and thus, little by little, they will become a happy and contented people . . ."[36]

Carleton's vision meshed with that of Commissioner of Indian Affairs William P. Dole, whose annual report submitted in November 1861 also furnished a blueprint for military action and forcible separation of the Navajos from other New Mexicans. The current situation, he contended, "demands the earliest possible interposition of the military force of the government, not only to preserve the lives and possessions of our resident citizens, but also to punish the Navajos and other "hostile tribes . . . for barbarous atrocities they are continually committing." The concentration of the Indians on "suitable reservations" would remove them from "a wild and predatory life, gaining a scant subsistence by the chase and an irregular and imperfect cultivation of the soil."[37]

In 1857, the position of superintendent of Indian affairs had been separated from that of governor; the person appointed to the superintendent's post, James S. Collins, also vigorously campaigned for reservations. Again and again, Collins offered vitriolic assessment of the Navajos, whom he continually termed "savages." By the autumn of 1862, Collins had reached the boiling point. The government had to act immediately. "Procrastination," he emphasized, "serves only to accumulate the evils to be remedied and increases the difficulties to be overcome."[38]

The crusade for reservations was also often inspired by a particular interest in the natural resources or the agricultural potential of Native land. By confining Indian communities to specific plots of land, the reservation system "opened" considerable acreage for "development" by non-Indians. The non-Indians customarily argued that they would use the land more productively—they were, after all, "civilized"—and that it would be not in their best interests but in the best interests of America for Indians to be shoved out of the way. Hence Carleton's justification to the Army in Washington for removing the Navajos: "By the subjugation and colonization of the Navajo tribe we gain for civilization their whole country, which is much larger in extent than the state of Ohio, and, besides being the best pastoral region between the two oceans, is said to abound in the precious as well as the useful metals." Carleton admitted to Adjutant General Lorenzo Thomas that "the exodus of this whole people from the land of their fathers is not only an interesting but a touching sight. They have fought us gallantly for years on years. . . . They have defended their mountains and their stupendous canyons with a heroism which any people would be proud to emulate." The Navajos, he contended, knew it was "their destiny . . . to give way to the insatiable progress of our race."[39]

In a prior generation, the campaign for removal of the Five Tribes of the southeast—the Cherokees, Chickasaws, Choctaws, Creeks, and Seminoles—had succeeded, in part, because the federal government had a specific site (what would be deemed Indian Territory) set aside for them. It gave the process of removal a kind of concrete reality by suggesting a direction and a focus. For Carleton's campaign to succeed, he also needed a specific place for the Navajos. In 1854, Carleton had visited the area along the Pecos River commonly called the Bosque Redondo. He had registered his enthusiasm about the site's suitability for a military post, with "abundant" fuel available from local timber and thousands of acres of "arable land, which for richness, and depth of soil will compare favorably with that of the Missouri Bottoms." Here Carleton created Fort Sumner, named after his former commanding officer, Edward Vose Sumner.[40]

It turned out to be a disastrous choice. A board of officers that he appointed to select a specific site anticipated its liabilities. The board visited Carleton's recommended location and discovered all sorts of shortcomings: "It is remote from the depot of supplies and from the neighborhoods that supply forage. Building material will have to be brought in from a great distance. The water of the Pecos contains much unhealthy mineral matter. A large part of the valley is subject to inundation by the spring floods." Carleton read the report and proceeded to ignore all its caveats.[41]

Although consensus had been reached on the need for action if not on the location itself, it remained a verdict violently objected to by the people who were supposed to benefit from it. How could the Navajos be convinced, compelled, or coerced onto a reservation? They would not want to leave their home country, to be sure, so they would have to be forced from the sacred mountains. Carleton saw this as a straightforward assignment. "The Navajo Indians have got to be whipped," he wrote.[42] He turned to Christopher "Kit" Carson to head the campaign that would force most of the Diné to depart from Diné Bikéyah.

Even during his lifetime Kit Carson had achieved legendary status. Born in Kentucky in 1809, Carson had come west and become famous. He had served in the army and had been an Indian agent, and possessed the kind of decisiveness and determination that Carleton sought. Carson knew that he had to go after the heart of Navajo country—Canyon de Chelly—and achieve results if his overall campaign were to have any chance at all for success.[43]

Carson carried out the kind of campaign that people do not forget. There are still stories being told about Bi'éé Łichíí'ii (the soldiers of Red Clothes) and the heavy-handed initiative that dislodged the people from their homes and lands—stories that illustrate in a poignant manner the importance of these events and these individuals in Navajo history.

Although Carson has garnered most of the attention devoted to the effort to force the Diné into exile, he did not act by himself. Carson knew, for example, that the Utes could furnish some of the necessary knowledge of the land, and with the recent animosity between the Utes and the Navajos, he figured correctly that the Utes would be valuable additions to his forces. Other Indian communities, including the Hopis and the Zunis, contributed men and knowledge of the terrain. Carson carefully chose his company commanders, picking experienced soldiers. He generally selected people he knew, those whom he believed he could count on in the heat of battle.[44]

Carson's campaign was brief, blunt, and, when combined with a particularly difficult winter, very effective. The maelstrom of destruction and death brought by Carson and his men and their Native allies had the desired effect. Thousands of Navajos were starving or freezing to death; countless others had died. They went to Fort Wingate and then went on the Long Walk, but this did not mean they had surrendered forever. It meant that they wanted to survive and they wanted their children to realize some kind of future.

THE LONG WALK
The Long Walk was not a walk. It was a forced march driven by harshness and cruelty far more than it reflected any kind of kindness or respect. The Navajos who made the journey several hundred miles south

and east to Fort Sumner did not know where they were going, how long it would take for them to get there, what they would find when they got there, or how long they would be there. They had to assume they would always be incarcerated; they had to believe they had been torn away from their mountains and their sheep, never to return.

The Long Walk was not a single event. Neal Ackerley has documented fifty-three different episodes of the Long Walk, dating from August 1863 through the end of 1866. In some instances just a handful of people made the journey; in other cases, hundreds of Diné were herded along to Fort Sumner. The trip took several different routes, beginning in the Fort Wingate area, heading toward Albuquerque, and then branching south to the Bosque. The time of the year, the inclinations of the army personnel in charge, and the general well-being of those making the trek all affected the experience.[45]

It would have been difficult even if the distance had not been extensive. It would have been trying even if the weather had been good. It would have been hard for a young man or woman in good health. It would have been frightening even if the people had been properly fed and clothed. It would have been far worse for the elderly, the young, the ill, and the physically challenged. It would have been terrible for a woman about to give birth or one who gave birth along the way. It would have been awful for those who had been separated from other family members and who did not know where they were and whether they were alive or dead. It would have been excruciating for all who were inadequately clothed and fed. It would have been miserable in the ice and snow of winter or in the unrelenting heat of the summer. And it would be remembered.

If they survived the march the Navajos all wound up in the same location, a destination that surpassed their fears. Hwéeldi was a nightmare that would not go away when the dawn finally came. Flat, barren, and nearly treeless, it was an empty landscape. There were no mountains to be seen. Imagine those who became ill and who died far from home. Consider all the men who could no longer hunt or ride or demonstrate their courage or their generosity. Picture the people trying to eat rancid bacon and to drink the miserable, alkaline water from the river.

Despite the miserable circumstances in which they found themselves, religious leaders could still provide some of the ceremonies that even in this place might bring hózhǫ́. Even in this place the Diné looked at the clothing worn by the Anglo women at the fort and thought about how it might be adapted for use back home, if they ever saw that home again. As time went on they began to recognize a degree of commonality, regardless of clan and of where they had lived before. They had to endure the continuing attacks by Comanches and others who delighted in the Diné having nowhere to hide and no way to retaliate. This place, like all prisons, made the people vow that if they ever escaped or were somehow freed, they would never take the land and the sky of Diné Bikéyah for granted, and they would celebrate each day of freedom. And it would be remembered.

When the day finally arrived that the Americans came and talked to their leaders about the Diné leaving this place, it must have seemed too good to be true. For the young, the memories of home had become increasingly vague and disturbingly uncertain. For the elderly and the ill, the possibility of seeing the homeland again one final time was a reed to clutch and hold onto and not let go. For the weavers who longed to recreate old patterns and to create new ones, it was surely a prospect so exciting that they could barely stand it. Then they heard that the small man with a beard, the one they called General Sherman, wanted to send them instead even farther away from the mountains. Then their hopes, which had suddenly flickered with life, were extinguished with equal, shocking rapidity. But then they heard that Barboncito and the others had stood tall, spoken well, and been persuasive. They heard they would be going home to the land of Changing Woman. They would begin a very different kind of journey from the one that had brought them to this place. And it would be remembered.

The Carson campaign, the Long Walk to Fort Sumner, and the years spent at Hwéeldi, like other major episodes in Navajo history, should be viewed through the dual lenses of Diné traditional history and standard archival history. The stories and the written records both contribute to our understanding of these vitally important events. A careful reading of both, as with the different accounts of Navajo origins, reveals that each perspective largely corroborates the other, even when one factors in the self-serving, no-fault soliloquies that upon occasion both Navajo and non-Navajo participants at the time and through the years might add to the overall historical record.

From time to time, students of Navajo history present revisionist accounts, designed to change our essential view of a participant or an event. A new biography of Carson, for example, or a new treatise on the conditions of the Long Walk will surface. The authors make strenuous efforts to improve our general judgment of Carson's character and actions or to soften our condemnation of the army's treatment of the Diné as the Navajos were "escorted" to the Bosque Redondo.[46] But an analysis of the available materials tends to bring us back to generally well-established conclusions: (1) the non-Indians in the Southwest did have reason for grievances against the Navajos for their continual pattern of raiding, even if not all the Diné participated in such ventures; (2) the Carson campaign and the Long Walk to Fort Sumner inflicted enormous suffering and trauma on the Diné; (3) the years spent by some of the Diné at Hwéeldi and the years spent by other Diné apart from Hwéeldi had a powerful effect on Navajo identity and the Navajo future; and (4) the ability of the Navajo leadership to succeed in their negotiations with the American commissioners so that the Diné were able to return to a portion of their homeland marked a major turning point in Navajo history.

The non-Indian and even some of the non-Navajo Indian residents of the Southwest used the Diné as scapegoats for anything that went wrong and identified as Diné any stranger or group of strangers who committed any violent act. Nevertheless, it is true that the Navajos did attempt to gain more livestock and other valued items. Even though the Anglo and Mexican accounts include overly dramatic hand-wringing, racist stereotyping, and self-serving, holier-than-thou declarations, Anglos and Mexicans did not invent or misrepresent every last incident. Even if these individuals often behaved badly or worse on a great many occasions, even if one can argue that the Southwest would have been well served if many of these folks had just kept going to California or had remained south of the Gila or considerably south of the Sandias, one can understand why they complained so frequently.

That Anglos and Mexicans and Indians who were not Navajo would document at great length the nature and extent of a variety of Diné transgressions is not startling. What may be surprising is the degree to which many Navajo traditional accounts accept at least partial responsibility for the overall situation. Some of the storytellers admittedly do not acknowledge any culpability. Frank Goldtooth will say, "It has been said that the reason why the people were marched to Hwéeldi was because, as we were told over and over, they had been stealing. We were no stealers. . . . We were branded as being a bunch of thieves because they couldn't find any other excuse to make us march to Hwéeldi." However, another Diné storyteller will grant that at least some of the responsibility for conflict and for war lies with the Navajos themselves. Sometimes this acknowledgment is more indirect. Howard Gorman will say "most of us were not harming anybody," rather than "none of us were harming anybody," and that the Long Walk "began because of the behavior of a few Diné." Charley Sandoval will say, "It was the Diné's own fault to be rounded up" for they "had been having war with other tribes." Helen Begay will say in telling her grandmother's story that while "[s]ome Navajos did not steal," others did steal from "the enemies," including the Mexicans, the Utes, the Comanches, and the Jicarilla Apaches. Theft led to fighting, and fighting led to war. Ultimately she concluded, "the Navajos brought the war on themselves."[47]

If there is sometimes that concession, the Diné stories do not condone how the Carson campaign was conducted. Howard Gorman's vivid description is representative of many accounts of how Carson went about his business: "Unexpectedly, Bi'éé Łichíí'í [Red Clothes' Soldiers] arrived, destroying water wells—contaminating them, breaking the rocks edging the water holes or filling up the holes with dirt so they became useless. They also burned cornfields and the orchards of peaches."[48] Curly Tso adds: "It was horrible the way they treated our people. Some old handicapped people, and children who couldn't make the journey, were shot on the spot, and their bodies were left behind for crows and coyotes to eat."[49]

The stories tell of people freezing or starving to death, even though most of them had done nothing wrong, or being shot without reason by the soldiers. There were men, women, and children who chose death rather than capture. Gus Bighorse remembered people hiding who jumped off cliffs: "[S]ome families just jump down because they don't want to be shot by the enemy. They commit suicide." Bighorse cried, even though he was not supposed to do so. It was bad enough to see the people get shot. This was worse.[50]

The reports from the soldiers offer additional details. Albert H. Pfeiffer led an expedition through Canyon de Chelly in January 1864, taking as prisoners Diné who "were half-starved and naked." He killed "one Squaw who obstinately persisted in throwing rocks and pieces of wood at the soldiers."[51] Navajo oral historical accounts and government reports speak of the problems posed by Mexican citizens who hated the Navajos and tried to harm them as they were being marched to Fort Sumner. Gus Bighorse condemns what took place on the Long Walk: "The trip is on foot. People are shot on the spot if they say they are tired or sick or if they stop to help someone. If a woman is in labor with a baby, she is killed. Many get sick and get diarrhea because of the food. They are heartbroken because their families die on the way."[52] Luci Tapahonso recounts: "Two women were near the time of the births of their babies and they had a hard time keeping up with the rest. . . . Some army men pulled them behind a huge rock, and we screamed out loud when we heard the gunshots. The women didn't make a sound but we cried out loud for them and their babies."[53]

Lieutenant George Pettis wrote to his wife on February 26, 1864, describing the last section of the Long Walk, from Los Pinos to Fort Sumner. It took, he noted, "15 long weary days, most of the time in the mountains, three ranges of which I crossed over—the total distance in that time was 242 miles." It had been a harrowing ordeal. "While in the mountains we experienced very cold weather and some of the time having no water, but what we obtained by melting snow, and part of the time, we had no wood either to keep us warm, or melt our snow. . . . Everything must have an end, so we finally arrived here safely. . . . I had fed the last of the Indian provisions the day before, and my company were quite out of provisions. Four of the Indians died and were buried on the road, so I got here with 239 of the Red Skins, they causing me very little trouble other than feeding such a large number every day."[54]

Men like Captain John Thompson demonstrated their determination to destroy the Diné environment. He marched through the canyon in late July, cutting down every peach tree he could find. In a branch of the canyon he discovered about 200 peach trees and had them cut down. It turned out that he was just developing momentum. During the first two days of August he "cut down 1800 fruit trees (peach) all of which were bearing fruit and a large number of small fruit trees which are not included in the above number." On August 3, Thompson "cut down 500 of the best peach trees I had ever seen in the country[,] every one of them bearing fruit." Thompson noted that "[a]fter this work of destruction had been perfected," he destroyed five acres of corn. The next day he decimated a six-acre field of corn and beans and cut down 600 peach trees. The following two days witnessed the axing of another 600 peach trees. On August 7, Thompson came across another orchard and leveled an additional 450 trees.[55] By this time, Diné resistance in the area had already been crushed. Perhaps the army simply wanted to remove evidence that contradicted the image of Navajos as full-time nomadic wanderers.

Many Navajos resisted incarceration but eventually concluded they had no choice other than to surrender. The most prominent of these was Manuelito, who in the spring of 1864 informed the Americans that he and his group did not want to go to the Bosque but wanted to remain in their home area and plant crops. The proud Diné leader held out as long as he could. No doubt embarrassed by Manuelito's unwillingness to participate in his grand experiment on the Pecos, Carleton eventually ordered his arrest in March 1865. Manuelito still refused. Finally in September 1866, worn down by all that he and his people had endured, he came to Fort Wingate and from there went on to Hwéeldi.[56]

The Hopi village of Walpi. Photograph by Ansel Adams.
Still Pictures Division, National Archives, College Park, Md.

Several thousand Diné never went to Fort Sumner. The Navajos who avoided the Long Walk generally lived in the western and northwestern reaches of Diné Bikéyah. Black Mesa, the canyon country north of present-day Kayenta, and the rugged terrain around Navajo Mountain afforded opportunities to hide. Herbert Zahne summarizes what happened: "Some Navajos never went to Fort Sumner. A lot of them hid in the deep canyons or on the mountains, such as at Navajo Mountain and other rugged areas where they couldn't be found. They managed to avoid the enemies and survive."[57] Ernest Nelson adds: "My own ancestors didn't go on the Long Walk. . . . When enemies came for them they flew down into the canyon gorge behind Navajo Mountain."[58] Frank Goldtooth concludes: "[A] lot of people managed to avoid the long march to Hwéeldi. They hid in rugged areas, cliff dwellings, and other places where enemies were not likely to find them."[59] Gus Bighorse lists the names of thirty warriors who stayed with him in this area: Deenasts'aa', Bilatsoohii, Bizhi Dizah, Ayóó'aníldílii, Hadah Adeetiin, Bilíí Łání, Tadídíín, Ha't'iłch'ałí Sání, Bilíí' Łizhiní, Bilíí' Łigaii, Bidzaanézí, Łók'aa' Ch'ígainii, Tł'áschhí'í, Nitł'ai, Tł'ízítání, Ts'aa' Bíheestł'óonii, Tódích'íí'nii Sání, Tł'ahnii Bidághaa' Łichí'í, Yistł'inii, Bitł'ízí Łigaii, Tł'aa'í Nééz, Béégashii Łaní, Nidaaz/Ndaaz, Bilódii, Nééz, Béésh Łigaii, Béésh Łigaii Yitsidii, Bigodii, Chíshí Nééz, and Bidághaa' Łitsooí. Even if individuals remained free, they agonized over the fates of those who had been captured. Bighorse relates that each day and each night they would pray for them and "and for the white people who are holding all these people captive, pray to soften the white soldiers' hearts to let those people go free."[60]

The Diné who avoided capture merit more attention than they have received. Their success is important for several reasons. Their presence in the west and north continued to strengthen Diné claims to these areas and to encourage the process through which the reservation land base would be extended in the years after 1868. They also played an important role in the revitalization of the Navajo economy following the treaty of 1868, because although their lives had been disrupted, they had not been completely fragmented. For example, when Navajos returned to the area of Canyon de Chelly, they found other Diné already present, tilling the fields. Their use of and claims to portions of this region became part of the struggle for lands at the heart of the conflict between the Diné and the Hopi. Even during this time Hopis pressured, attacked, and killed some of the Navajos who had made their way into the region.[61]

HWÉELDI

In many ways Fort Sumner resembled a typical military outpost of its day. The compact fort included housing for the soldiers, stables and corrals, a parade ground, a hospital, a prison, shops for the carpenter and the blacksmith, a guardhouse, a dining room, and rooms to store food supplies.

Given its function, Fort Sumner also contained an office for the Indian agent and a separate hospital that contained classrooms and a kitchen in addition to a room for surgery and rooms for the housing of patients. An extensive amount of land was assigned for farming purposes, both to feed the prisoners and as part of the effort to teach them "the arts of peace." Little attention or consideration was given to housing for the incarcerated Diné. The people did the best they could to carve out or erect shelter for themselves on the almost treeless plain, but they had little to work with and as a result they suffered from both winter's cold and summer's heat. They struggled to maintain a belief that somehow, someday they would be free, that they could see the mountains again.

Just as those Diné who went to Hwéeldi did not all go there at the same time, not all Navajos remained at the Bosque Redondo until the summer of 1868. Some Navajos escaped the confines of Fort Sumner. Those who tried to escape recognized that there were serious penalties for those who were caught and great dangers for those who fled toward freedom. Concern for other captured loved ones could prompt plans for escape and could also discourage such efforts. The constant raids by Comanches and other tribes infuriated the Diné, who felt powerless to defend themselves. When the Comanches succeeded in kidnapping children or stealing horses, the compulsion to "desert," as the army phrased it, became all the stronger.

Critics questioned the viability of Fort Sumner before the Navajos arrived, throughout their sojourn, and even after the treaty had been

The Diné at Hwéeldi, Fort Sumner, New Mexico.
National Archives, Washington, D.C.

signed. Michael Steck, the New Mexico Territory superintendent of Indian affairs, took an intense dislike to Carleton and lost no opportunity to ridicule what some called "Fair Carletonia." He and other opponents of Carleton had a lot of ammunition. William Howard Moore, for example, contracted with the federal government to provide flour for Hwéeldi. The Mescalero Apaches who were imprisoned at Fort Sumner before the Navajos arrived began to become violently ill. The flour brought in by Moore contained "bits of slate, broken bread, and something that resembled plaster of paris. It was an old ploy of western contractors," Gerald Thompson informs us, "to load up their flour sacks with such foreign junk in order to make an even greater profit." Remarkably, Moore later gained a contract to bring beef to the fort, and true to character, overcharged the government.[62]

The Navajos and Apaches suffered other indignities during their sojourn in addition to bad flour and attack by other Indian groups. The people were always hungry, even after they learned how to prepare coffee and bacon. Yasdesbah Silversmith says that "a great number of Diné died of dysentery." Rations proved to be woefully insufficient and farming efforts generally failed. The Navajos were proud of their abilities as farmers and some Diné made a genuine effort in the fields. However, insects, the vagaries of the New Mexico climate, and the alkaline soil all conspired against productivity and good health. Rita Wheeler sums up the deplorable circumstances: "Many people died at Hwéeldi—of various diseases, starvation, exposure and attacks by enemies." The Diné had to be concerned about not only human enemies, but also wolves and other wild animals that sometimes ventured into the fort, killing both people and livestock.[63]

Letters from soldiers at the fort support Diné complaints. George Pettis described the environment in less than enthusiastic terms, calling the fort "a terrible place." He described the river as "a little stream winding through an immense plain, and the water is terrible, and it is all that can be had within 50 miles; it is full of alkali and operates on a person like castor oil—take the water, heat it a little, and the more you wash yourself with common soap, the dirtier you will get."[64]

The desperate circumstances at the fort forced some Diné women into prostitution and syphilis became a significant problem among the people. Navajo individuals who suffered from a variety of illnesses proved reluctant to enter the fort's hospital. When the terminally ill died in that institution, it only reinforced cultural taboos against occupying a place where death had occurred. Historian Robert Trennert concludes that the Diné "suffered from severe medical problems, many of which plagued them for years afterward. They were underfed, confined to crowded and unsanitary camps, mentally distressed, and treated by doctors using alien procedures."[65]

As they did under other circumstances, the Diné turned to ceremonial leaders for assistance during the time at the Bosque. Many Navajo oral histories give credit to the ceremonies and those who conducted them for promoting harmony and balance among the people and making it more likely that they would get through this ordeal. In the final days before the American commissioners reached a decision about the fate of the Diné, Mose Denejolie recounts how the people surrounded a coyote and Barboncito did "what is called [the] Ma'ii Bizéé'nast'áán (Put Bead in Coyote's Mouth) ceremony." The coyote faced east; Barboncito "caught the animal and put a piece of white shell, tapered at both ends, with a hole in the center, into its mouth. As he let the coyote go free," Denetjolie relates, "she turned clockwise and walked off timidly, with her tail between her legs—toward the west." At Barboncito's command, the people opened up their circle and let the coyote go free. Barboncito then concluded, "There it is, we'll be set free." Four days later, they learned they would be able to go home.[66]

The road to the treaty signing at Fort Sumner began, appropriately enough, in the mountains. It began a long way from Navajo country in a place called the Big Horns in northern Wyoming. By the 1860s these mountains had become part of the home country of the western Lakotas. In the 1860s a man named John Bozeman helped blaze a trail through these mountains for white men who sought wealth in the gold fields of southern Montana. The Lakotas protested the presence of these trespassers; the American government hastily constructed forts along the trail and rushed in soldiers to protect these citizens.

In 1866, Captain William Fetterman entered the Big Horns. A young, impetuous army officer, he boasted of his own ability and derided the military might of the Lakotas and their allies. Fetterman is supposed to have said: "Give me eighty men and I will ride right through the entire Sioux nation." As the old Lakota joke goes, he was half right. He got halfway through. On a December morning, Fetterman rode out from Fort Phil Kearny with eighty men under his command. The Lakotas suckered him into directing his men into a box canyon, a dead-end valley from which there could be no retreat. They swooped down the hillsides of this beautiful valley and killed Fetterman and all his men. The white men first called it the Fetterman fight and soon thereafter the Fetterman massacre.

In the town of Laramie, Wyoming, where they named dusty streets after men such as Canby, Custer, Gibbon, Hancock, Harney, Kearney, Ord, Sheridan, and Steele, they gave a short, dead-end road the appropriate appellation of Fetterman. Observers noticed Fetterman in more important places as well. The shock waves generated by the disaster in the Big Horns pushed the federal government to take action about the situation in the West. In 1867, Congress created the Peace Commission and gave it major responsibilities. Its members—a mix of civilian and military representatives, a blend of humanitarian concerns and pragmatic priorities—were supposed to negotiate with Indian tribes, establish new reservations, and,

Barboncito, leading negotiator of the 1868 Treaty.
National Anthropological Archives, Washington, D.C.

in sum, work for expansion with honor.[67] This process did not necessarily work out well for the Native peoples concerned. Another one of the 1868 treaties, signed at Fort Laramie, is a case in point. The Lakotas signed the treaty after they had secured the rights to their sacred Black Hills. Then gold was discovered in Paha Sapa and the federal government acted dishonorably, obtaining a fraudulent "agreement" in 1876 that threw open the doors to the Lakota cathedral to people who could not and would not respect this sacred ground. The 1868 Fort Laramie Treaty did not represent a triumph but rather a painful reminder of what should have been.

General William T. Sherman and Lewis Tappan came to the Bosque Redondo to negotiate a treaty that in many ways resembled the Fort Laramie Treaty in some of the boilerplate language it employed and some of the priorities it endorsed, such as education and the ability to build new transportation networks across Native land. Nevertheless, from June 1, 1868, to our own day, the Diné would see the treaty in the proper way, as a document that attested to their determination to continue as a people.

By the summer of 1867, it had become painfully evident that "Fair Carletonia" would soon be no more. Carleton himself was no more in terms of New Mexico. He had been relieved of his command the year before, a casualty of incessant local criticism, mismanagement, and, ultimately, a bad idea at the wrong time. However, Carleton's departure did not solve Fort Sumner's problems.

An incident in the summer of 1867 exemplified the deteriorating situation. Two Navajos had provided information that other Navajos were lurking in the area and stealing horses from the fort. The acting commander chose Second Lieutenant William Henry Bragg to take twenty-one cavalrymen out the next night and bring back the horses. The soldiers went out, found the Navajos, rounded up a first installment of one hundred horses and demanded that the Diné return with them to the fort while Bragg and three others got the rest of the herd.

However, the horses did belong to the Navajos, who did not want the cavalry to steal them. En route to the Bosque, they stampeded the horses and then drove them off. The soldiers shook their heads and went back to the fort. Bragg, in the meantime, had acquired fifty more horses; they too were stampeded and dispersed. Bragg sent the trio of Americans back to reacquire the fifty horses, but the Navajos fired on them and the men hurried back to Bragg, who wheeled them around and charged back toward the Diné, who by now had become a cadre of two hundred and who forced Bragg and company back to the fort. There they ran into a very drunk Major Elisha W. Tarlton and his drinking buddy Lieutenant Charles Porter. Tarlton sent Porter and the men back to get the horses.

In the momentary standoff that followed, a soldier fired a shot, and then the Diné charged the twenty army men. Six of the cavalry were killed and three others seriously wounded. The Navajos chased the survivors back toward the fort. They could have killed them all, but they pulled up and stopped at the top of the hill south of Fort Sumner, much to the astonishment of soldiers and Navajos watching from the fort.

Manuelito, the symbol of Navajo resistance, then rushed out from the fort and accompanied another lieutenant, with whom he had become friends, back to the Navajos. Despite the interference of a still-drunk Tarlton, the Navajos kept their horses and the surviving army men kept their lives.

Things continued to deteriorate after that point. Scurvy swept through the fort, pigs ran wild on the fort grounds, and Comanches attacked at their leisure, seemingly on a daily basis. When the federal government decided to take Barboncito, Manuelito, and a handful of other Diné back to Washington, D.C., in the spring of 1868 to impress upon them the size and power of the American nation, the Navajos gave the officials an earful. Barboncito told one and all that if they did not negotiate a treaty to allow the Diné to return home, there would be a total rebellion among the remaining Navajos at the fort.[68]

NEGOTIATING THE TREATY

By the time Sherman and Tappan came to the Bosque, then, the question had become not whether Fort Sumner would continue to hold the Navajos, but rather where the people would go. Sherman initially had preferred that the Diné be moved to Indian Territory; Tappan had advocated a return to their home country.[69] The general had been especially annoyed at the Tarlton affair. He did not need to be convinced about the need to close down the fort and had been moved by a plea to be able to return home that Navajo women had presented him. Sherman told the assembled Diné representatives on May 28, 1868, that he knew the people had worked hard, but their situation had not improved: "[Y]ou have no farms, no herds, and are now as poor as you were when the government brought you here." Barboncito responded that many Diné and many animals had died. They were in the wrong place: "Our grandfathers had no idea of living in any other country except our own. . . . When the Navajos were first created, four mountains and four rivers were pointed out to us, inside of which we should live, that was to be our country, and was given to us by the first woman of the Navajo tribe."[70]

Barboncito proceeded to speak in an eloquent way about the Diné's condition and their need to return home. When he finished, Sherman raised the possibility of having the Navajos go to Indian Territory. The general sang the praises of its potential, but added: "If you don't want that we will discuss the other proposition of going back to your own country and if we agree we will make a boundary line outside of which you must not go except for the purpose of trading. . . . You must live at peace and you must not fight other Indians." After Sherman concluded his remarks, Barboncito said, "I hope to God you will not ask me to go to any other country than my own. It might turn out another Bosque Redondo. They told us this was a good place when we came, but it is not."[71]

Sherman asked that the Diné delegate ten of their men to represent them the following day. The Navajos chose Delgadito, Barboncito, Manuelito, Largo, Herrero, Chiqueto, Muerto de Hambre, Hombro, Narbono, and Armijo, with Barboncito selected as chief or primary spokesman for the group. Barboncito soon sensed that Sherman and Tappan were going to go along with the Diné desire to return home. He said: "After we get back to our country, it will brighten up again and Navajos will be as happy as the land. Black clouds will rise and there will be plenty of rain. Corn will grow in abundance and everything will look happy."

Barboncito then demonstrated how important the matter of Navajos being held as slaves or captives remained to the Diné by pressing the commissioners on this issue. Although Sherman said that the latter had to be resolved through the courts, he then added: "We will do all we can to have your children returned to you. Our government is determined that the enslavement of the Navajoes shall cease and those who are guilty of holding them as peons shall be punished."

The council adjourned to the following day. The treaty had been prepared and Sherman read it to those assembled. The Diné heard the translation and then offered their approval. Sherman described the reservation boundaries and Barboncito responded, "We are very pleased with what you have said, and well satisfied with that reservation; it is the very heart of our country and it is more than we ever expected to get." After the Diné gained approval for the addition of Narbono Segundo and Ganado Mucho to their delegation, the council soon adjourned until June 1, when the treaty was signed. Each Navajo representative, with one exception, made a thumbprint next to his name on the document. Delgado, however, had learned to write his name, and proudly inscribed it on the treaty.[72]

As the Navajos prepared to leave the Bosque Redondo, Barboncito and others no doubt reflected on all that had happened to the Diné and all that they had made happen over the past five years. They would never forget the tragic dimensions of this experience. They would always carry with them the trauma of the Carson campaign and the Long Walk, the painful exile from Diné Bikéyah, and the many indignities and insults that they had had to endure. At the same time, they would recall that they had made their way through this crisis. They had learned as they went through so much with each other, that they had much in common. The U.S. government had insisted on dealing with them as one people, and this era had increased their own sense of themselves in this way.[73] They had continued to expand their material cultural repertoire during this period, becoming acquainted with the art of silversmithing, beginning to learn about how the yarns of Germantown, Pennsylvania, might add new elements to their weaving, and finding in the attire of the women at the fort an appearance they thought they could work with to create something of their own. They had begun to use flour, and that would lead to fry bread. In time the blouse and the dresses and the fry bread would be considered traditional, but their beginnings can be traced to this place and this time.[74]

And so they began the necessary preparations for a different kind of long walk—one that would take them back to their home country. They had defended their mountains. They had begun to see themselves as a great people, destined to do great things.

That, too, would be remembered.

3

"Our Beloved Country": 1868–1901

When they reached Fort Wingate many were in a hurry and started tak-
ing off, saying, "We're lonely for our beloved country."
—Francis Toledo, 1973

COMING HOME

At last, the day came—that day they had hoped for, but could not fully imagine. Mothers spoke softly as they attempted to calm their excited and anxious children. The elders sighed. They could not quite believe the promise of deliverance from Hwéeldi. The young adults stirred at the prospect of a new life, one without soldiers. Even with all the escapes, even with all the deaths, more than seven thousand Diné remained at the fort. The people noticed the haste of the preparations. It seemed as though the Bilagáana (Anglos, white people) were also eager to be out of this terrible place. In less than three weeks, the necessary arrangements had been completed. On June 18, 1868, the soldiers shouted for the people to get ready to leave. They were ready.

It is said that some of the people had taken their belongings and had moved as far to the west as they could within the fort. They wanted to be just that much closer to home. Now, finally, the Diné formed a line, and that line extended for a full ten miles. It stretched across the alkaline horizon of the Bosque Redondo. Had they been in the Chinle Valley that chain of humanity would have reached from Chinle past the site of Valley Store.

The Diné experienced wildly conflicting emotions as they finally departed. Elation mixed with memory; prospect collided with deeply etched recollection. They remembered the terror of the Long Walk; they recalled those who had died. Now they had to retrace the steps of that horrible experience. What about crossing the Rio Grande? What about the kind of treatment they would receive from the soldiers? Such questions leavened the excitement they felt as they began their journey. Most of the people had to walk, with fifty-six army wagons carrying the aged and ill. A pitiful remnant of their once great herds also trailed along: 940 sheep,

1,025 goats, and 1,550 horses. "Never mind," the people muttered, "we are going home."[1]

This moment resonates today in the collective memory of the Diné. In her poem, "It is Said," Marilyn Help concludes, "It is said / When the Diné people were released, / It was a great day. / The Diné saw and recognized the peak / Mount Taylor and they wept. / I can hear the words of the ancient ones: / Be strong. It is said / Remember the Diné way." In *We'll Be In Your Mountains, We'll Be In Your Songs*, Help and Ellen McCullough-Brabson report there is an old Navajo song, "Shí Naashá" ("I am going"), that may date to the return home from the Bosque Redondo. It speaks to the emotions of that moment:

> Ahala ahalago naashá ghą.
> Shí naashá ghą, shí naashá ghą,
> Shí naasha lágo hózhǫ́ la.
> Shí naashá ghą, shí naashá ghą,
> Shí naasha, ladee hózhǫ́ǫ́ lá.
> (I am going in freedom.
> I am going in beauty all around me.
> I am going, I am going, in beauty
> It is around me.)[2]

The Diné inched their way through San Carlos and Tijeras Canyons. They managed to ford the Rio Grande without disaster. Eventually the sacred mountain of the South came into view, the one the white people called Mount Taylor. The old people wept at the vision of that beautiful land formation, rising in grandeur, welcoming them home. Weary but determined, the Diné attempted to pick up the pace.[3] In the 1970s, Francis Toledo said, "When they reached Fort Wingate many were in a hurry and started taking off, saying, 'We're lonely for our beloved country.' But they were told not to take off until they got to Fort Defiance where rations could be issued to them."[4] Akinabh Burbank observed that additional sheep "had been promised as part of the treaty" and "at Fort Defiance they received their sheep." She added, "Then, the White Men told the people, 'Now you are on your own, go your way; now that you have some sheep, take care of them.'"[5]

The Diné proceeded to do just that. In the first decades following the treaty of 1868, they expanded their herds and added to their land base. During an era when most other Native communities in the West were losing their lands and confronting diminished opportunities, the Diné, for the most part, experienced a different fate. Yet even during this period of revitalization, complications arose. Arizona, New Mexico, and Utah expanded, too, and the once isolated lands being incorporated into the Navajo reservation started to become contested ground. The federal commitment to inflicting formal education on Diné children also raised concerns. The demands of the regional and national economy and a changing federal perspective about the development of Indian lands also affected the people. At the beginning of a new century the Diné perceived that the fight over lands and lives had just begun.

The Navajos made their homes both within and outside the main reservation. Some of the Diné who returned from Fort Sumner, in fact, chose not to go all the way to Fort Defiance. As the group proceeded west from Albuquerque, about four hundred Navajos, including one of the treaty signers, Delgadito, departed to return to their home country to the north. They joined with some of the "enemy Navajos" to form what became known as the Cañoncito Navajo community and today is called Tóhajiileehí (Where the Water Is Drawn Up Out). Another detached enclave formed at Alamo (or T'iistsoh, "Big Cottonwood Tree"), west of Socorro. Individuals leaving the fort made this locale a destination, too, joining relatives or friends. In time, land would be withdrawn from the public domain and would be allotted for these communities, thus providing a base for future generations. In 1874, a third such niche became established at Ramah (or Tł'ohchiní, "Wild Onions") south and east of Gallup, near Zuni. All three would remain as Navajo, separate from the "big reservation."[6]

In the meantime, the precise size and location of the "big reservation" remained somewhat elusive. In the words of historian John Kessell, General Sherman had crafted "a basic and expedient misunderstanding." The treaty delineated a precise area "bounded on the north by the 37th degree of north latitude, south by an east and west line passing through the site of old Fort Defiance, in Cañon Bonito, east by the parallel of longitude which, if prolonged south, would pass through old Fort Lyon, or the Ojo-de-oso, Bear Spring, and west by a parallel of longitude about 109 degrees 30 minutes west of Greenwich, provided it embraces the outlet of the Canon-de-Chelly, which cañon is to be all included in this reservation. . . ." However, Sherman realized that the Diné or any other American population did not think of their home country in terms of degrees and minutes west of Greenwich and he also recognized the challenges of translation from English to Diné. So he added his own description: "We have marked off a reservation for you, including the Cañon de Chelly, and part of the valley of the San Juan, . . . about (100) one hundred miles square. It runs as far south as the Cañon Bonito, and includes the Chusca mountain, but not the Mesa Calabesa you spoke of; that is the reservation, we suggest to you, it also includes the Carresa / Carrizo / mountain, and the bend of the San Juan River, not the upper waters."[7]

The actual area covered by the treaty turned out to be roughly half of "one hundred miles square"—3,328,302 acres rather than about 6,400,000 acres, and did not begin to provide a sufficient base for the Diné. It did not even include all of Canyon de Chelly. It omitted a good deal of the Dinétah, failing to deliver much of the terrain that would have been incorporated in Sherman's description. Moreover, although Article 9 of the treaty opened the door for a railroad to be built through Navajo country, neither Sherman nor Tappan broached this rather delicate subject.[8]

It did not take long for some of the complications of this "misunderstanding" to be revealed. But even before the major dilemmas became fully evident, the Navajos proceeded to interpret the treaty's meaning. They simply moved on to land that they considered theirs. Most Diné did not seek new horizons, but rather they returned to the general areas they had occupied and used prior to their incarceration. The United States had not erected a fence nor had it put up signs noting formal boundaries within which the people had to reside and within which their livestock had to be maintained. In addition, General Sherman had instructed them at the time of the treaty negotiations that any Navajos willing to live outside the reservation should be able to do so. The Navajos assumed, understandably enough, that in the absence of constraints they had every right to use the land that had been theirs before. This assumption immediately stretched the Diné population well beyond the rectangle of reservation that would have appeared on some federal map never to be viewed by the Navajos themselves.

At first this demographic expansion appeared to pose relatively little difficulty. The railroad had yet to be built and the non-Indian population in most of Diné Bikéyah remained sparse. Conflicts continued with the Hopis and the Utes, but given a record of past antagonism, friction may have appeared to be an inevitable element in regional life. In the absence of major demographic pressure from non-Indians, the federal government proceeded to make two crucially important decisions. It chose to add to the initial Diné land base established by the treaty and it contributed to the rapid growth of the numbers of livestock possessed by the Navajos. These choices fundamentally altered the course of the Navajo future. They furnished a foundation that could not be eroded and established a pattern for Diné life in the twentieth century.

The Diné did not for a moment ever doubt the appropriateness of their movements. They had come home or come out of hiding and begun the process of reclaiming a homeland. They would never forget the events of this time of troubles, but at the same time, they could now begin to look to tomorrow. They went about the demanding but ultimately fulfilling process of expanding their holdings of livestock and claiming the land and water resources necessary for their animals. In a larger sense, as the people built new hogans, began new families, and acquired new livestock, they started to believe in a future that only recently had seemed impossible to realize. When they received communications from the white men who served as federal agents or who ventured into Navajo country to open trading posts, there now seemed to be a clear, consistent message, an unblinking green light that said "go."

Federal actions in the first few critical years that followed were influenced by the essential ideals and goals of the so-called peace policy, inaugurated during the administration of Ulysses S Grant. Policymakers and reformers embraced assimilation and ventured a cautious but heartfelt optimism about the Native capacity for progress. They believed reservations would not always be needed; they concluded Indians could become equal citizens in the Republic, given appropriate and sufficient assistance.[9] In the meantime, they called upon the government to invest in Native progress. During the final years of the century, federal officials reassessed this perspective, with devastating consequences for the Diné in the early 1900s. Even so, the period from 1868 to 1901 allowed the Navajos to consolidate their gains and established a substantial cultural and economic foundation that subsequent policy reversals could not obliterate.

The transition, nevertheless, included some traumatic moments. Not all the Diné prospered in this new age, and resentment and jealousy led in some cases to social and cultural confrontations. Before the reservation land base was expanded and prior to the takeoff of the Navajo economy, there was significant tension within Diné society, exacerbated by the federal decision to cut off rations a decade after the treaty had been signed. More than a few people went hungry. At this time, a number of Navajos were accused of practicing witchcraft, or the deliberate attempt to cause evil. In the traditional belief system of the people, certain individuals (usually male) are capable of inflicting illness or death through malevolent

Navajo delegation to Washington, D.C., Manuelito and his wife, Juanita, are in first row, center. Smithsonian Institution.

powers they have acquired. Diné took matters into their own hands and killed individuals whom they concluded had been guilty of practicing witchcraft. Soon the Navajo society regained its customary balance. The Diné economy proceeded to experience more than a decade of increasing prosperity and the terror caused by the witchcraft dissipated as suddenly as it had erupted.[10]

ADDITIONS TO THE RESERVATION

Sherman contributed to the expansion of the reservation. He informed President Rutherford B. Hayes in 1878 that the western boundary had not been set sufficiently to the west; it should "be pushed twenty miles west." Although Congress had passed a law in 1871 that ended formal treaty making, the president could still create reservations as well as add land to or delete land from an existing reservation, without the need for congressional approval. Hayes concurred with Sherman and issued an executive order on October 28, 1878, extending the reservation accordingly.[11]

In 1878, the territories of Arizona, New Mexico, and Utah had not yet gained admission as states. If federal policymakers were not always persuaded about the potential for Navajo development, many of them also expressed significant doubts about the economic promise of the Southwest. Senator Albert Beveridge of Indiana, for example, who at the turn of the century chaired the committee that reviewed territorial progress, delayed Arizona and New Mexico's bid for equal status. He worried about the economic base of the territories and decried the presence of Mexican Americans and American Indians. Passage of the Reclamation Act of 1902, however, began to open the door to statehood. The Salt River Project in Arizona became one of the first initiatives funded through the new law. By February 14, 1912, both Arizona and New Mexico had gained statehood. Despite the virulent anti-Mormon prejudice of the era, Utah gained statehood in 1890. That emotion had not subsided entirely by this date, but the Church's formal disavowal of polygamy expedited Utah's inclusion in the Union.[12]

Once statehood had been achieved for all three of the states in which the Navajo reservation was situated, further additions to the Diné land base became increasingly problematic. The president did not require congressional approval in order to issue an executive order, yet the reality of political life dictated caution in the face of significant congressional opposition from the affected state or states. If Washington preached with increasing fervor the gospel of Western development, then it inevitably gave greater weight to non-Indian pressure for access to and use of the land than to the needs and desires of Indian communities.

Thus, the additions made during this period became all the more important. The map illustrates how the various directives furnished valuable supplements to the Diné estate. Executive orders of January 6, 1880,

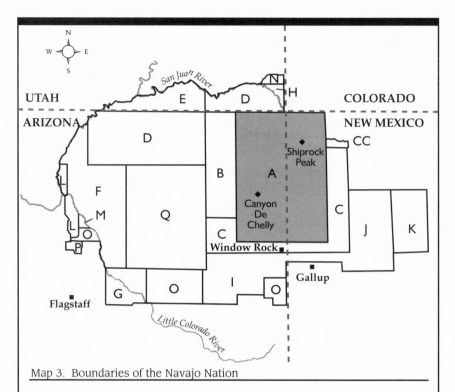

Map 3. Boundaries of the Navajo Nation

A   Original treaty reservation.
    June 1, 1868.

B   Executive-order addition.
    October 29, 1878.

C   Executive-order addition.
    January 6, 1880.

CC Originally a part of C; withdrawn
    from the reservation by executive
    order, May 17, 1884; restored by
    executvie order, April 24, 1886.

D   Executive-order addition.
    May 17, 1884.

E   The Paiute Strip. Originally a
    part of D; in 1892 restored to
    the public domain; in 1908
    withdrawn for the use of various
    Indians; restored to public
    domain in 1922; in 1929 again
    withdrawn from entry; 1933
    transferred permanently to the
    Navajo reservation.

F   Executive-order addition.
    January 8, 1900.

G   Executive-order addition.
    November 14, 1901.

H   Executive-order addition.
    March 10, 1905.

D   Executive-order addition.
    November 9, 1907.

J   Executive-order addition.
    November 9, 1907; restored to
    public domain by executive
    order of January 16, 1911.

K   Executive-order addition.
    November 9, 1907; restored to
    public domain by executive order
    of December 30, 1908.

L   Tusayan Forest addition.
    Act of May 23, 1930.

M   Executive-order addition.
    May 7, 1917.

N   Act of March 1, 1933.

O   Arizona Boundary.
    Act of June 14, 1934.

P   Tusayan Forest addition.
    Act of February 21, 1933.

Q   Executive-order reservation cre-
    ated on December 16, 1882, for
    the Hopis and other "Indians."

Source: Peter Iverson, *The Navajo Nation* (Albuquerque: University of New Mexico Press, 1983), 14.

May 17, 1884, and April 24, 1886, nearly encircled the original rectangle of Navajo land; executive orders of May 17, 1884, and November 19, 1892, extended the reservation to the west in Arizona and to the north in Utah. President William McKinley added more land east of the Colorado River, including Tuba City, on January 8, 1900; Theodore Roosevelt authorized the "Leupp extension" (so named after Commissioner of Indian Affairs Francis Leupp) on November 14, 1901.[13]

Yet another executive order created a reservation for the use of the Hopis (or Moquis, as they were often called at this time), and, ambiguously, "for the use and occupancy of the Moqui, and such other Indians as the Secretary of the Interior may see fit to settle thereon." By the time of this decree, Native populations had been consolidated on some reservations. The northern Arapahoes, for example, came to the eastern Shoshone reservation of Wind River in Wyoming. The Gros Ventres of northern Montana had to accommodate themselves to the addition of the Assiniboines to the Fort Belknap reservation. The Navajos already occupied portions of the acreage included in President Chester Allan Arthur's order. Even in his own time, Arthur seemed destined for obscurity, but this one action guaranteed for him a kind of perverse immortality. The December 16, 1882, order practically ensured conflict between the two peoples since it failed to clarify which land should be occupied by the Hopis or the "other Indians." Designed more to protect the Hopis from intrusions by whites than to settle specifically competing land claims by the Hopis and the Navajos, the order did little to still the complaints about trespass and theft continually lodged by one tribe against the other. For the people who made this land their home, it meant eventual disaster.[14]

The map of the Navajo Nation could have been made far more precise and Navajo landholdings could and should have been made more extensive. Those with the authority to do so could have created a clear line of demarcation, separating the Hopis and the Navajos. They could have avoided some, if not all, of the crazy-quilt complications of what became known as the checkerboard area, by more clearly and assertively defining appropriate Navajo land occupation in New Mexico, to the south and east of the present reservation. On the other hand, one must consider what did happen and contrast the Navajo situation with that of so many other Native nations. The Diné added land at a time when most Indian groups lost acreage and they remained in the cultural center of their world. That result was hardly inevitable, as the example of another Athabaskan people, the Chiricahua Apaches, demonstrates. The Chiricahuas lost their land base in Arizona and New Mexico and never regained it.

Disputes continued over where the Navajos should live, where they should graze their livestock, and where they should hunt. Diné utilization of land became increasingly contested. Non-Indians frequently accused the Navajos of theft or trespass and took the law into their own hands in their efforts to find "justice." Innocent Diné and Diné raiders alike faced the wrath of some Anglo newcomers. As historian Robert McPherson has documented, the northern Navajo frontier witnessed a number of violent incidents in the final years of the nineteenth century. The contrary and cantankerous individual sometimes caused a maelstrom. Some of the white men who had come to the area were not exactly people of the highest character, and they appeared to derive their greatest pleasure in life from making everyone around them miserable. A man like Henry L. Mitchell thus could create all by himself "a cauldron of conflict" along the San Juan River. The non-Mormon rancher labeled the Navajos as "terrors, cutthroats, thieves, and murderers"; at the same time he could not stand the "damn Mormon outfit" in the area. In time local authorities learned to disregard nearly anything he said. Eventually Mitchell left the region, but not before several lives had been lost because of the poisonous environment he had helped to create. In at least one instance Mitchell accused Navajos of an act of violence for which the Utes were responsible.[15] This example of mistaken identity was hardly unique. Given their general reputation in the region, the Navajos frequently found themselves being blamed for the acts of others.

Some years proved worse than others. A period of relative calm could be followed by one bout of violence or confrontation after another. Agent Edward Plummer certainly had to deal with more than his share of incidents during his tenure in Fort Defiance from 1893 to 1896. Consider the year of 1893 as a case in point. Thomas Keam informed Plummer that two Navajos had stolen goods from his store, ranging from twelve cans of baking powder and two corduroy coats to four "fancy robes" and, inevitably, sugar and coffee.[16] Ralph P. Collins, the superintendent at Keams Canyon, backed up Keam's claim, adding, for good measure: "The Navajoes around here have been stealing horses and breaking into homes ever since I have been here."[17] His successor, C. W. Goodman, reported "several articles were stolen from the store room of the school by a band of Navajos." He also relayed the complaint of Tom Polacca, a prominent Hopi rancher who alleged that Navajos had "settled" by his springs with stock. "I might add also," Goodman noted, "that a great many Navajos seem to be making themselves very much at home on the Moqui reservation."[18] The sheriff of Apache County, W. R. Campbell, asked the agent to help him serve warrants on various Navajos.[19] W. A. Daugherty alleged that Black Horse and his followers were stealing horses and cattle from non-Indians along the San Juan River. The Zuni governor charged that the Diné were grazing their animals on Zuni land and finding a way for their livestock to "constantly" invade his grain fields.[20]

Others added their accusations or objections in 1893. Walter Hinnes of Cortez, Colorado, said that Navajos had stolen five horses and then had taken them over "on the Navajo side."[21] S. V. Berlin, A. C. Honaker, William Hyde, and James W. Hanna declared they were "compelled to complain of trespass of the Navajo Indians and their stock upon the range that is already almost depleted on account of the prolonged drouth [sic] and former trespass. . . ."[22] From the Coolidge, New Mexico, area, W. R. Jones lodged his own distinctive protest. Jones clearly liked apostrophes better than he liked periods, or for that matter, the Diné: "I would like to know what you can do about the Indian's having our horse's I want you to have them brought in if you can I know the have them they have been killing my cattle I can not turn out a hourse or cow but what they have got them wright away. See about it as soon as possible. Your's Resp."[23] The agent at Fort Apache, H. Cousins Jennings, informed Plummer that, "Your Navajos are expert horse thieves occasionally. They frequently bring horses here for sale and on their return steal a few from the Indians here and sell on their return trip . . ."[24]

Plummer heard as well in 1893 from C. H. Fancher, general agent of the Atlantic and Pacific Railroad. Fancher asked that "the Indians" be "confined to their reservation, so as to relieve this company from the great wrong it suffers of being unable to induce settlers to come on the territory occupied by the Indians, outside of their reservation." He took a deep breath and then vented his emotions in a seventy-eight-word sentence: "As the matter stands now with the Indians scattered all over our railroad grant, nothing will induce settlers to occupy territory already occupied by Indians, know[ing] as they do that their efforts in producing crops and raising stock will, in case of success, only result in raising products for the Indians, without receiving any benefits therefrom, as it is well known that these Indians, in a quiet way, help themselves to whatever they desire without regard to ownership." He expressed a widely shared Anglo perspective. "The Indians," Fancher contended, "have a reservation amply large to graze their stock."[25] This period constituted simply the first phase of a progressively more complicated and vexing pattern of conflict over the lands surrounding the railroad.

Once in a while an Anglo spoke up against the thefts and violence that the Diné themselves had had to endure. Charles Babbitt, secretary of the Coconino Cattlemen's Association, noted in 1893 "the stealing of some Navajo Ponies, by some persons that are in this vicinity." But this expression of concern is clearly an exception to the general pattern. Even Plummer was forced upon occasion to acknowledge that Navajos did take horses from others and from each other. In his best Victorian manner, he wrote to Jennings on one occasion: "I have the honor to inform you that a horse was stolen from a Navajo by another Navajo recently and was sold to an Apache Indian near Holbrook, Indian Territory, five days ago."[26] By the early 1890s, then, non-Navajo farmers and ranchers in Arizona, New Mexico, and Utah had become more strident in their pleas against Diné expansion. They urged law enforcement personnel to crack down on people such as Black Horse.[27]

With the limited number of sheriffs and police officers, law enforcement personnel were more likely to investigate a crime or an armed confrontation than actually prevent bloodshed. For example, on November

18, 1899, the *Coconino Sun* reported that a group of Navajos had taken on William Montgomery, whom they accused of stealing four of their horses. They "held him up at the point of their guns," the *Sun* noted, "and otherwise abused him." Montgomery then went to Flagstaff, obtained the warrants for the arrest of the people who had confronted him, and, accompanied by a deputy sheriff and two other men, journeyed to the Navajo camp outside of town. The attempt to serve the warrants touched off what the *Sun* called "one of the most desperate conflicts ever to be fought in the Southwest." In the chaos that ensued, Montgomery and at least two of the Navajos were killed. A missionary from the Tuba City (Tó Naneesdizí, or "Place of Water Rivulets") area, William R. Johnston, who was traveling to Flagstaff, encountered some of the surviving Diné in the Leupp area. Already acquainted with one of these Diné, Johnston helped mediate a surrender and trial at which the Navajo defendants were acquitted of murder charges.[28]

LIVESTOCK, WEAVING, AND TRADING POSTS

In the final decades of the nineteenth century, the Navajos added substantially to their livestock holdings. They did so through a three-part program of federal bequest, trade with surrounding Indian and non-Indian populations, and, upon occasion, the time-honored option of a long-term loan without permission. It is quite unclear how much they relied on each of these options to bolster their herds of sheep, cattle, goats, and horses, for the various reports by the different agents assigned to Navajo country turn out to be less instructive than one might initially anticipate in regard to the actual amount of livestock. Historian Marsha Weisiger concludes that not until 1930 when the Bureau of Indian Affairs (BIA) began "to try to make accurate accounts at sheep dipping vats, do we get a really good sense of the number of small stock grazing the entire Navajo range." By that time, "the range supported at least some 575,000 sheep and more than 186,000 goats, not to mention other domestic animals."[29] Few animals had accompanied the Diné home from the Bosque, so growth of Navajo livestock holdings bordered on the astonishing. As long as the reservation land base kept expanding and the climate kept cooperating, the rapid increase in livestock could generally be managed successfully. Once new land became harder to come by or once the climate became less beneficent, the Diné would be in trouble.

Even during this period there could be heard the beginning peals of warning echoing from reports filed from agents stationed in Fort Defiance. The federal agents and the traders both promoted this acceleration because the expansion was very much in their interest. The agent could say to Washington that the Diné were demonstrating their potential as productive pastoralists, while the traders' own livelihood depended on the volume of trade created by the Navajos. More wool, more mutton, and more blankets meant more money for these frontier entrepreneurs. They advocated rapid expansion rather than slow growth. They hoped for and pressured the Diné to realize maximum immediate yield rather than sustained yield over a more extended period of time.

The network of traders expanded quickly in this interval. Many of the traders were members of the Church of Jesus Christ of Latter-day Saints (LDS), who migrated into Navajo country from the surrounding areas. The operations of traders possessed names like Burnham, Foutz, McGee, and Tanner. They became multigenerational, ongoing family concerns with their own stake in not only an expanding marketplace but also in establishing new posts for family members. Just as the Mormons utilized considerable expertise in finding promising sites for new LDS communities in the larger region, so, too, did they generally employ good judgment in choosing locations for new posts.[30]

The full impact of the Mormon involvement in the trading post business would be felt in subsequent years. In this first generation, some key participants were non-Mormons who influenced in a crucial way the development of the Navajo society and economy. Thomas Keam, Juan Lorenzo Hubbell, the Wetherills, and the Babbitt brothers rank among the most prominent individuals in this congregation.[31] Keam's enterprise bequeathed the family name to Keams Canyon. The name of Hubbell will always be associated with the community of Ganado (Lók'aahnteel, or "Wide Reeds"), the base of the Hubbell empire, and the name of Babbitt is tied to Flagstaff, even if their CO Bar ranch and brand paid ongoing tribute to their former hometown of Cincinnati, Ohio.

The agents and traders were kind enough on many occasions to record their observations of this transitional period. Their observations are self-serving, but a close reading of their surviving reports and epistles augments our sense of the era and the challenges the Diné confronted in forging a permanent place on the Colorado Plateau. Consider, for example, these candid observations in 1869 proffered by Agent Frank T. Bennett. They once again reflect the mixed image being created of the Navajos as well as that cautious optimism of the age. Bennett listed the population at 8,500 and compared the Diné with the Irish. "They are more like the Irish than any people I can compare them with. Brave, hardy, industrious, restless, quick-witted, ready for either mischief, play, or hard work, they are people that can be guided into becoming the most useful of citizens, or, if neglected, the most troublesome of outlaws. . . . They were equally given to the vices of stealing, gambling, and licentiousness when not employed, and to the virtues of the most indefatigable perseverance in farming, stock-raising, trading with their neighbors, the Moqui Pueblos, and weaving garments, when at work."[32]

Bennett remained at Fort Defiance and dutifully submitted an even more extensive report the following year to his superior, one William Clinton, the superintendent of Indian affairs for New Mexico Territory.

Although the federal government much preferred the Indians to become farmers rather than ranchers, Bennett argues that these Indians were better off being cowboys: "On the 30th of May, just as their crops were coming up nicely and everything looked well for a large crop, we were visited by a severe storm of sleet and snow, accompanied by severe frost, it froze hard for three nights, making ice on our acequias, and everything they had planted (except wheat and peas) was cut to the ground. I think that at this time, they were the most sorrowful, down-hearted, discouraged set of people that could be well imagined."[33] In the following year, the commissioner of Indian affairs recorded: "The Navajoes have raised less corn and other crops during the present summer than usual, owing to the shortness of the season, and it will be necessary to provide them with supplies until their crops can mature next year."[34] In 1879, Agent Galen Eastman observed that "very little rain has fallen here this year," and with the "unusually severe" drought, "the Navajo Indians will not raise one-fourth of their usual crop of corn, wheat, and vegetables. . . ."[35] Nor did the next year bring an improvement: "A succession of two years' drought placed these Indians in a very bad condition, and more especially during the past year many of them were in a starving condition . . ."[36]

Although the Navajos were accomplished farmers, farming at this altitude seemed best undertaken on a small scale; the livestock appeared to be far better suited to the land on which the Diné found themselves. Moreover, the women quickly developed a strong vested interest in the livestock industry that, once established, could not be quickly or readily uprooted. Weisiger summarizes: "Diné women held power in their communities, where mothers, daughters, and sisters formed strong bonds of interdependence and men often stood on the periphery." She adds, "But women's power did not rest merely on female solidarity. Women were important to economic production, and significantly they also controlled the means of their own production: livestock and land. . . . It was the intertwining of these strands—stock ownership, matrilocal residence, and matrilineal land-use patterns—that gave women power over their lives. Like the individual fibers of a braided cord, each reinforced the other."[37]

The social and cultural world in which Diné women and men lived encouraged them to own more livestock. A large, thriving herd testified to one's ability to work hard and to take good care of the animals. That care involved not only daily diligence but also ritual knowledge, for without the proper prayers and observances, the animals entrusted to the Diné by the Holy People would not do well. If one had more sheep, one could also be more generous in providing for older or less prosperous relatives, more easily pay a ceremonial leader, and exert more influence in one's community.[38] There were, in sum, real, tangible, valuable rewards for having more rather than fewer livestock.

More sheep encouraged, too, the evolution of the weaving industry. In the short term, the results seemed decidedly mixed. The government brought in merinos rather than churros and Diné women struggled with the "short, kinky, and greasy" merino fleece. This transition encouraged another: the employment of commercial rather than hand-spun yarn. Alice Kaufman and Christopher Selser pinpoint the change: "In 1855 the best weavers used bayeta, Saxony, and hand-spun yarns. By 1880 many of the best weavers were using, almost exclusively, commercial American synthetic-dyed three- and four-ply Germantown yarn." As the new century began, Diné weavers were beginning to meet a series of interrelated challenges, including those "of new yarns and new dyes to master, of new designs to embrace and transform, of new uses and functions for weaving, and, finally, of a new world of customers."[39] From this beginning, the next generation developed the truly outstanding regional styles, such as Two Grey Hills, Crystal, Teec Nos Pos, and Ganado.

The trading post emerged as a focal point in the workings of Navajo life. As early as 1883, traders bought more than 1.3 million pounds of Navajo wool, perhaps three hundred thousand sheep pelts, and one hundred thousand goat hides. Successful traders demonstrated some of the same traits valued among the Diné, particularly hospitality and generosity. The economic collapse of 1893 delayed rather than eliminated the possibilities of this emerging economy. Somewhat larger-than-life individuals, such as Juan Lorenzo Hubbell, positioned themselves to cast a still longer shadow in the new century, when the maturation of the marriage between the Santa Fe Railway and the Fred Harvey Company opened up almost unimaginable markets.[40]

The advent of the trading post brought with it the potential for economic advance for individual Navajos, but it also carried with it some undesirable complications. The traders assumed a certain authority within the workings of the Diné world. Their decisions about the value of one's weaving or one's wool made a difference in Diné financial well-being. At this time nearly all the traders were non-Navajos, and since in this first generation almost none of them chose to marry a Diné woman, the Navajos had minimal leverage over how these outsiders did business. In these days before paved roads and pickup trucks, Navajo communities were isolated and individuals usually could not deal with a trader other than the one who happened to be situated in their vicinity. This kind of monopoly promoted paternalism and inevitably, some abuse of power. The people could joke about a trader's idiosyncrasies, make up a not-always-flattering nickname for him, and tell stories about him, but they could not really boycott him. And he knew it. At the same time, any sensible trader stood to benefit if the people with whom he dealt enjoyed some degree of prosperity. Self-interest had to be combined with some concern for his clients' situation. J. L. Hubbell emphasized that no "intelligent Indian trader desires to live among a community of Indian paupers." He stressed that "The first duty of an Indian trader is to look after the material welfare of his neighbors." Hubbell hastened to add, "This

Navajo silversmith and a young girl. Photograph by Milton Snow.
Archives and Manuscripts, Arizona State University.

does not mean that the trader should forget that he is here to see that he makes a fair profit for himself, for whatever would injure him would naturally injure those with whom he comes into contact."[41]

Thomas Keam concurred. An Englishman, Keam carved out a career in Arizona as a trader and a federal agent. He had the most elegant, Victorian handwriting of any trader who ever ventured into Diné Bikéyah. Others might not agree with the sentiments that Keam may have expressed in one of his frequent epistles, but they certainly could not claim that those letters were illegible. Keam would have labeled himself strong willed; his critics called him stubborn. He would have called himself independent; his critics said he was out of control. He certainly had his opinions about the Navajos and Hopis and did not hesitate to express them to a variety of correspondents. Writing to Commissioner of Indian Affairs J. D. C. Atkins from Keam's Canon (as he spelled it) on January 2, 1886, he concluded that the Navajos were more "intelligent and thrifty, ready and willing to work," whereas the Hopis, although "not so intelligent, are industrious, and being community dwellers are more dependent on each other."[42]

SCHOOLS BUT FEW STUDENTS

The first teachers in Diné Bikéyah faced challenges that bordered on the overwhelming. Few children enrolled and even fewer remained. Parents resisted the notion of placing their children in boarding schools. They missed the labor that the children provided in helping to look after the livestock, but most of all, they missed the children themselves. Even those Diné parents inclined to enroll their children in order to equip them to deal with a changing world tended to grow discouraged about the kind of education their sons and daughters received. Their condemnation of the schooling available resounded in Navajo country and throughout Native North America.[43]

The treaty of 1868 had called on the federal government to provide a teacher and classroom for every thirty children who could be "induced or compelled" to enroll. The "peace policy" shifted considerable responsibility for Indian education to the churches.[44] Thus, the first classroom for Navajo children inaugurated following the treaty came under the auspices of the Presbyterian Church. A church missionary, James Roberts, attempted to teach a small number of Diné children, but soon abandoned his efforts. A federal agent explained that Roberts had found the Navajos to be "uncommonly bright and promising," but that some of them had not behaved well. "[T]he vagabonds of the tribe," he said, "stole his chickens, milked his cow, threatened his kitchen by burglariously breaking in at night, and kept Mrs. Roberts on the rack of anxiety daily."[45]

Charity A. Gaston had the distinction of being the first full-time teacher. Arriving in October 1869, Gaston appeared to get off to a good start, but student absences limited what she could accomplish. Agent Bennett closed down the school in April before the scheduled conclusion of the term. Gaston labeled her students as "easily controlled," but she believed it would "take time to teach them to persevere in efforts to gain knowledge." Annoyed by the frequent absences, she declared her students to be "quick to learn" and possessing "retentive memories," but also observed they were "unused to constant application of the mind."[46]

John. V. Lauderdale recognized that parental anxiety about the schools curtailed enrollment. However, he also emphasized another recurring dilemma: Who would teach at such schools? Indian reservation schools in the late nineteenth century occasionally attracted the best and the brightest, but they were more likely to draw the worst and the worn-out. Inadequate pay, poor housing, isolation, and lack of support discouraged most potential teachers. Lauderdale argued that Navajo schools needed "*live* men, not those who are nearly gone with consumption, and too feeble to work more than a couple of hours per day."[47]

Bennett's successor, W. F. Hall, delineated continuing problems with attendance. He suggested in 1872 that the best way to overcome "irregularity in attendance" would be to establish "an industrial school." "There is little in their present surroundings to attach them to their studies or advancement in this respect," he observed. Hall believed that the next generation of the Diné would "prove an important and valuable portion of the American people in this Territory. . . . They are industrious, skillful, willing and eager to work when they get reasonable compensation for their labor . . ."[48]

The next agent, William F. M. Arny, clarified how few Navajos had enrolled in school at any time. "There are two thousand nine hundred and two children on the reservation," Arny noted, "scarcely twenty of whom know the alphabet." He called on the government to invest in an industrial school at the agency that two hundred children could attend.[49] The commissioner of Indian affairs agreed with the need to educate more Navajo children, calling in 1874 the "establishment of boarding schools among them an imperative necessity."

However, Congress continued to be reluctant to provide sufficient funding for such schools. Even when some funds were finally obtained for a new school building, inclement weather and problems in obtaining appropriate construction materials delayed progress. And when the new building finally was completed in Fort Defiance, Navajos did not exactly rush in and fill it to capacity. John Bowman commented in 1885 that the agency now had an adequate building and good teachers. He had pulled out all the stops to get children to come; he had, he admitted, "argued, coaxed, begged, bribed, and threatened," but with imperfect success. "All that is needed," Bowman concluded, "is the necessary number of children."[50]

Boarding schools faced the same problems throughout Indian country.

Students missed their parents and home. They did not like being punished for using the Navajo language. And so much at these odd new institutions seemed so different that the young people never adjusted to them. Frank Mitchell remembered: "One of the problems we faced . . . was that we did not know how to eat at a table. We had to be told how to use the knife, fork, and spoons. And when we started eating, we were so used to eating with our fingers that we wanted to do it that way at school, and we had to be taught. Although we had things there to eat with, like a fork, we had never used them at home, so we did not know what they were or how to use them; so we always wanted to stick our fingers in our food."[51]

A handful of Navajo parents decided to send their children to school. The prominent Navajo leader Manuelito numbered among this small contingent. Manuelito is supposed to have told Chee Dodge: "[T]he whites have many things which we Navajos need. But we cannot get them. It is as though the whites were in a grassy canyon and there they have wagons, plows, and plenty of food. We Navajos are up on a dry mesa. We can hear them talking but we cannot get to them. My grandchildren, education is the ladder. Tell our people to take it."[52]

From that point until our own day, BIA teachers have exploited those last two sentences. Manuelito's words continued to be affixed to classroom bulletin boards throughout Navajo country. Although one might question whether he used these precise words, Manuelito truly embraced the importance of education and backed up that endorsement in the most meaningful way. When the opportunity came to send his two sons and a nephew off to the leading Indian school of its day, Richard Henry Pratt's Carlisle Indian Industrial School in Pennsylvania, Manuelito did not equivocate. He sent all three boys back east. This act of faith met with tragic consequences. All three boys died, one son and the nephew from tuberculosis during a visit home, and the other at Carlisle.[53]

Fewer than four dozen Navajo students ever attended Carlisle during its years of operation from 1879 to 1917. No Diné ever graduated from the school. However, one of the students, Tom Torlino, personified for many critics the kind of cultural onslaught all students confronted in the boarding schools of this time. Pratt hired photographers to take "before and after" images of the students in order to dramatize the kind of "civilizing" effect the institution had upon its students. Torlino thus was photographed upon enrollment in 1880 and again after he had been enrolled at the school for three years. The contrast between the two images is dramatic, but in the hail of criticism that surrounds this subject, one never hears about what happened to Torlino. In fact, like a great many other students at boarding schools, he weathered the experience as best he could, and went home. He farmed his land and lived out his days, no doubt glad to be a long way from Pennsylvania, but not traumatized to the point of complete inactivity.[54]

Some other Diné students attended off-reservation boarding schools but

Tom Torlino upon arrival at Carlisle Indian Industrial School. Photograph by J. N. Choate. Museum of New Mexico.

Tom Torlino after three years at Carlisle.
Photograph by J. N. Choate. Museum of New Mexico.

far closer to home. During the 1880s and 1890s, twenty-three other such institutions opened their doors. With the exception of a few schools, such as Mt. Pleasant in Michigan and Morris in Minnesota, they were almost all in the West. Off-reservation schools competed vigorously with each other for students as they tried to reach their maximum enrollments.[55] School principals and superintendents thus recruited new pupils through a variety of means, including appeals to Indian agents. One such letter from the newly opened boarding school in Grand Junction, Colorado, helped encourage the agent at Fort Defiance to send some Navajo students in that direction. He took thirty-one. Twenty-three remained after one year, with the other eight running away, somehow making their way "over the mountains and through deep snow" to their homes.[56] One of these pupils who stayed, Jacob C. Morgan, whom the school's superintendent praised in 1893 as one who "is learning the carpenter's trade and promises to become a fine workman," eventually became chairman of the Navajo Tribal Council.[57]

Morgan typified many Native students who attended the early boarding schools. His mother had died and during his time in Grand Junction, his father also passed away. For students whose parents had died or who came from either poverty-stricken or dysfunctional families, the schools offered shelter, clothing, food, and supervision. The schools thus became a kind of last resort, a final option for children who could not be cared for in some other way.[58]

Other elements figured in decisions about school enrollment. Family ties were often influential. A younger sister or brother could choose to attend a school in which an older sibling was already enrolled. The success or failure or the positive or negative experiences of a family member at a particular school might well determine whether another relative decided to go there. In multitribal, off-reservation schools, the presence or absence of other members of one's own community could influence the decision. Not surprisingly, students from the same Indian nation tended to support each other, including speaking their own languages, so frowned upon at these schools. Certain schools also gained reputations, deserved or otherwise, as being stronger institutions than the ones that might be available nearby. Finally, the larger off-reservation schools encompassed more grades of instruction; students who wished access to higher levels usually had to attend one of these schools.[59]

However, such considerations lay in the future for most prospective pupils, for they remained prospective pupils. Parents resisted the imposition of schooling because schooling threatened their authority, contradicted the priorities they were trying to inculcate in their children, and removed their sons and daughters from the daily life of the community, including participation in and attendance at religious rituals. As they heard more about the boarding schools, they came to fear the institutions as a kind of death trap from which their children would not return. They had good reason for this dread.

Chee Dodge as a young man. Photograph by
Ben Wittick. Museum of New Mexico.

Diseases spread rapidly in the confines of boarding schools and the physicians on hand, like the teachers, varied enormously in their competence. After considerable soul searching, some parents relented and allowed one or more of their children to go away to school, only to have them not return. Agent C. E. Vandever reported that of the approximately seventy children attending school at Fort Defiance in 1890, five did not survive the year. Two boys and three girls perished from pneumonia. They were hardly the only fatalities to be recorded in this era and not all fatalities stemmed from this cause. There were also frequent runaways and any runaway, especially during the winter, ran a dangerous gauntlet that could be life threatening.[60]

By the 1890s, one man among the Diné had demonstrated through his own success that a working knowledge of the English language and a better understanding of the workings of American culture could translate into significant wealth and influence. He became known as Henry Chee Dodge and eventually as Chee Dodge; the Diné called him Hastiin Adiits'a'ti—or "Man who Interprets" or "Man who Understands (Languages)." His mother belonged to the Ma'iideshgizhnii or Coyote Pass Clan. There remains doubt about the identity of his father, who was killed during his son's infancy, but in all likelihood, he was of Spanish or Mexican descent.[61]

Chee Dodge was probably born in the late 1850s. According to Brugge, Navajo tradition declares that his mother was killed by the Hopis just before the Long Walk. The boy went on the Long Walk and returned to Diné Bikéyah after the treaty was signed. Agent William Arny had concluded that Dodge was the son of Henry Dodge, whose name he had taken in tribute to the late agent. Based on this probably mistaken assumption, Arny took a strong interest in the boy's future and made sure that he enrolled in the school at Fort Defiance. Dodge did not remain in school long, but he learned enough to furnish a foundation. Knowledge of English opened the door to a unique future. By 1882, he had become the official interpreter for the agency in Fort Defiance. During the 1880s, on several occasions he demonstrated the tact and determination that later would be hallmarks of a remarkable political career. Chee Dodge also knew how to make money and save money. He and Stephen H. Aldrich formed a partnership to gain control of the Round Rock Trading Post; together with the brother of Juan Lorenzo Hubbell, Charles Hubbell, Dodge ran the post. He returned to employment with the Fort Defiance agency by 1892, just in time to get fully involved in the Black Horse affair at Round Rock (Tsé Nikání, or "Round Flat-Topped Rock").[62]

When Dodge assumed this position again, Dana L. Shipley had just taken over as agent at Fort Defiance. Zealous to a fault, Shipley was determined to boost the meager totals of Navajos enrolled in school. He took Diné policemen with him on his recruitment outings, showing that he meant business. In 1892, accompanied by the police, Shipley went looking for some Diné students. At one point, they divided into three

Bilii Liziinii (Black Horse), a leading resistance figure, with Taijoni.
Photograph by Simeon Schwenberger. Smithsonian Institution.

groups; one probed the Carrizo Mountains, one left for Chinle, and a third, headed by Shipley, traveled to Round Rock.[63]

Black Horse was already a fierce opponent of the American presence. Schools symbolized for Black Horse the power now held by the Americans. He fully realized that the schools sought to move the children away from Diné traditions. Informed about Shipley's intentions, Black Horse traveled to Round Rock, determined to prevent the agent from achieving his objective of acquiring thirty Diné children for schooling. A standoff ensued, testing Chee Dodge's considerable diplomatic and linguistic skills and revealing Shipley's lack of either attribute.

The agent promptly began to lambaste Black Horse, although in a subsequent letter to the commissioner of Indian affairs he preferred to say that he "reminded" him. Shipley reprimanded Black Horse, lecturing him about "how he and his people by their conduct were abusing the confidence that had been placed in them by the Government in its greatness in granting them full pardon for all past offenses when from starvation they were compelled to surrender as prisoners of war in 1862 and 1863." In addition, the agent argued that such schooling was necessary for the "advancement" of the Diné and "assured them as to what their opposition would surely lead and the punishment that would surely follow if they disregarded my instructions, and the wish of the Department."[64]

Shipley's clumsy, heavy-handed approach put Black Horse in a kind of box. He could not now back off from his demands, for to do so would have risked public humiliation. Shipley, predictably, perceived the Diné man as "obstinate," as one who "refused to compromise in any way." The agent described, from his vantage point, what happened next:

> He worked on his followers to such an extent that they rushed on me, and very violently overpowered me and removed me from the building in which the council was held. Here they continued their violence on my person, until a very powerful friendly Navajo, assisted by my police, the trader Chee and his clerk, Mr. Hubbell, succeeded in tearing me away from them and getting me in the middle of the trader's store again.[65]

The enraged Diné held Shipley hostage for the next day and a half before the arrival of American soldiers put an end to the standoff. Shipley could not leave bad enough alone. He called for a detachment of ten to fifteen men to be summoned from Fort Wingate and stationed over the winter at Round Rock, with "at least one company" also stationed at the agency "for protection." Ten days later Shipley wrote to the commanding officer at Fort Wingate, renewing his demand for soldiers, who were needed, as he put it, "to maintain my authority." He added, "In view of the fact that Black Horse and his band have refused to recognize or yield to my authority as Agent, I hereby renew my request for the use of troops in sufficient number to make the arrest of Black Horse, and those responsible for the trouble."[66]

But no soldiers came. The commanding officer at Fort Wingate decided to reject Shipley's request. "The trouble with Black Horse and his band should be settled if possible," he determined, "without the assistance of the military." The situation should be resolved "through the good influences of the leading men of the tribe" rather than dispatching troops "to make arrests or force children into the school at Fort Defiance."[67]

At a November 25, 1892, meeting, the Diné explained why they had resisted the agent. Gordy eloquently stated their case. "When we put our children in school," he emphasized, "it is like giving our hearts up, and when the Superintendent takes our children it hurts us very much." Gordy continued: "The name we have given this superintendent is Billy Goat. A billy goat is always butting all the rest of the sheep and imposing on them, and we think this is a good name for him. . . . We make this complaint to you white people who want to see children well-treated. And now we want a new superintendent who will take interest in our children and treat them as we do."[68]

Angry parents began to document the abuses at the school. One parent said, "When I brought my boy to school he had two eyes. . . . The next time I saw him he had only one. I don't know how it happened." Another Diné reported that the superintendent had been "catching some of the boys by the throat," and that he had put his hands over their mouths and had smothered them. A Diné mother charged that her son "was confined as a prisoner in the belfry of the school building for the period of two days without food." After that period, he "was allowed to go out in the school yard with handcuffs on his ankles." Her son had then escaped the school and attempted to reach his home, not quite a mile away. He crawled on his hands and knees for most of that distance and then collapsed. His mother found him and carried him inside.[69]

The agency carpenter wrote to Shipley on November 24, 1892, and provided corroborating testimony: "Mr. Wadleigh is guilty of vile and inhuman treatment of the Navajo boys in school, by placing them in handcuffs on their hands in the dark and poorly ventilated cellar of the old school building. This cellar, as you know, is at the present time and was when I came here used as a storage room for salt pork, barrels of vinegar and syrup, kerosene oil, rotten potatoes and spoiled fresh meats . . ."[70]

Wadleigh and Shipley both soon resigned but what happened at Round Rock and what had happened at the agency school would be remembered. Such incidents caused many of the Diné to resist sending their children to school, even as some of them began to recognize certain potential benefits of schooling. Many parents could not bring themselves to entrust the lives of their precious children to people who had not earned their trust.

The government opened another school at Keams Canyon in 1887. Navajo pupils joined Hopi pupils at this institution. Here the government

Faculty, staff, and students at the Fort Defiance boarding school.
Photograph by Cosmos Mindeleff. Smithsonian Institution.

had an opportunity to demonstrate that it could furnish a more humane environment in which to educate children. However, the initial reports from Keams Canyon differed little from those resounding from Fort Defiance. Shipley's successor, Edward Plummer, visited the Keams school. His letter to the commissioner of Indian affairs, dated December 26, 1893, presented a devastating indictment. He charged that eighty to one hundred pupils were crowded into a dormitory space designed for far fewer people. Scarlatina and mumps took their toll on many children.[71]

Moreover, the superintendent of the Keams Canyon school had written months before, lamenting the government's unwillingness to employ force to compel attendance. Superintendent C. W. Goodman reported that the school had opened in September "with somewhat less than thirty pupils. I have been out among the Indians, and find that it will be very difficult to fill the school by mere persuasion." He suggested that, "If a show of force is made, or if they know definitely that force will be resorted to in case of necessity, they will doubtless send in their children cheerfully and with good grace."[72] Such an attitude, of course, went a long way toward explaining why that cheer and grace were so often absent.

In an effort to boost school enrollment and impress some of the Diné with the realities of modern American life, in 1893 Agent Plummer persuaded some Diné to attend the Columbian exposition in Chicago. Most of those who made the journey were startled by the size of the city and the overall pace and demands of contemporary industrial life. They were not taken by all they witnessed; a visit to a local meatpacking plant proved once again that one should not know too much about how sausages were created. Nevertheless, what they had seen had a profound impact. One Diné compared white people to ants. They were, he explained, "industrious, working all the time; they are thick, coming and going all the time." He had doubted Plummer when the agent had attempted to explain the number of white people in the entire country. When he returned home to Diné Bikéyah he had gained a new sense of America. He was struck by how Americans tended to discard the old and embrace the new. It was, he said, like going from an old Mexican cart "to a Studebaker wagon."[73]

In the short term, the visit to Chicago heightened the interest of some Diné in the utility of education. Plummer reported: "The educational value of the visit of the chiefs to Chicago can scarcely be appreciated by anyone except those who have seen the results." Enrollment briefly surged at the Fort Defiance school, but continuing health care problems and negative images of school personnel curtailed the long-term effect of the Chicago experience. The commissioner of Indian affairs could deny that a school principal tended toward "immoderate use of morphine," but once such rumors started, they could be difficult to dispel. Despite the protests of federal officials that the Diné could soon expect their schools to be less threatening to the health of their children, in fact epidemics continued to sweep through the dormitories. Inadequate sewer systems and crowded living conditions left children vulnerable to a variety of illnesses.[74] At century's end, few observers could be optimistic that this appalling situation would be remedied in the near future.

USING THE LAND

In 1893, the national economy spiraled into depression. The effects of the Panic of 1893 reverberated in Navajo country. Even though the Diné economy had undergone a period of rapid expansion that allowed the benefits of prosperity to be widely shared within Navajo society, the Diné could not avoid the widespread economic downturn, exacerbated by a drought of major proportions. In 1893, Plummer declared the situation in Diné Bikéyah "worse than it has been for a number of years." He laid the blame on "a succession of very dry seasons, which have caused a great scarcity of foliage, very poor crops, loss of many sheep and ponies from starvation during the winters, and a very poor yield of wool." Many Navajos, he concluded, would have to "steal or starve."[75]

Even the proud Black Horse was compelled to request provisions.

Chee Dodge wrote to Plummer on May 31, 1893, from his trading post at Round Rock that Black Horse wanted him to send provisions. "Black Horse says that he is pretty hard up and hungry," Dodge said. Not that long ago Black Horse had held an Indian agent hostage. Now hunger held him hostage and would not let him go. Although he would never have asked for help from Shipley, it could not have been easy to ask for help from anyone affiliated with Fort Defiance.[76]

Nor did the outlook improve much during the remainder of the decade. The range remained in trouble and thus the people did, too. Widespread suffering, however, did not prevent the Diné from confronting escalating pressure for their land to be employed to maximum economic advantage. Non-Navajos were beginning to suspect that they had made a rather substantial error in allowing so many acres to be reserved for exclusive use by the Diné. Geological surveys started to reveal that the Navajo land would prove to be more valuable than had initially been assumed. In particular, preliminary investigation had indicated that the reservation might well yield major financial returns from tapping its mineral resources.

The economy of the western states at this time may best be described as colonial. Corporations headquartered almost entirely outside of the West dominated the workings of this regional economy. These interests attempted to exploit the natural resources of the West and Western politicians and business leaders were all too willing to assist in the process, seeing in it both the opportunity for public expansion and private gain. Federal enclaves thus came under tremendous regional and national pressure as a variety of folks with a stake in development lobbied for resources to be "unlocked." Completion of the transcontinental railroad expedited the shipment of goods and materials and thus accelerated the demand that western forests be chopped down, western rivers be dammed, and western oil and coal be extracted.[77]

The reassessment of land policy within the Indian Office, as the BIA was then labeled, began in earnest in the 1890s. Passage of the General Allotment Act in 1887 started to "open" reservation land for development. After the acreage on allotted reservations was doled out to individual Indians, the remaining "surplus" lands could be sold to outsiders. Moreover, the act permitted individual landholdings to be sold after an initial twenty-five-year trust period. Subsequent legislation allowed that period to be reduced. In addition, inheritance problems began to mount. The initial allotment had been for 160 acres for the head of a family. That amount had been based on the old Homestead Act of 1863. A total of 160 acres might be adequate for a farm on the edge of the western frontier, but it did not provide an adequate land base for self-sufficiency in the more arid West. Moreover, Indians tended not to subscribe to the European notion of primogeniture—that the eldest member of the next generation would inherit the land. Native peoples usually figured that those other family members who had not been smart enough to be born first also merited land. So, in most communities an already too-small plot would be divided up several ways. This approach may have offered equity but it also nearly guaranteed a parcel of land too small to be of much use. The resulting situation encouraged, if not forced, individuals to sell or lease their holdings. Soon a crazy-quilt land pattern divided up many reservations. Economic development had never been easy in these locales, but the ravages of allotment began to make it almost impossible.[78]

Those reservations fortunate enough to avoid allotment did not escape the workings of American capitalism. If their lands somehow contained significant natural resources, members of a particular nation could expect corporate representatives coming to knock on their door. The Navajos were no exception. An 1891 federal law specifically permitted Indian communities to lease land for mineral exploration and development. After an initial discovery of oil seeps in 1879 near Mexican Hat, Utah, it would only be a matter of time before corporations came knocking.[79]

When the Navajos had to respond to corporate inquiries and demands, they confronted several significant problems. One involved language. Lease agreements featured the kind of impenetrable prose that only attorneys can create. They presented a festoon of interminable clauses that novices in the law struggled to comprehend. A few Diné, such as Chee Dodge or Jacob Morgan, knew English well enough to be able to decipher the meaning of these strange documents, but for the average member of the Navajo Nation, the proposed agreements might just as well have been written in Hungarian.

Of course, the language of the agreements made it sound as though somehow the lease would be a great blessing for the people, as though somehow the agreement really had come about because the people had sought it, or had insisted upon it. The language of the agreements made it sound as though unproductive land, not wanted for any reason by the Diné, would be put to productive employment. However, the rapid expansion of the Navajo livestock industry meant that most of Diné Bikéyah would be claimed for grazing. Thus, a second concern became the matter of individual, family, and community rights and opportunities versus a development that promised some financial return benefiting the tribe as a whole. A third issue centered on approval of leases. Who could or should sign or refuse to sign such agreements? Should such a group represent all of the Navajo Nation or primarily or exclusively the immediate region of the proposed activity? At the beginning of the 1900s, the Navajos had no tribal council or business committee authorized to act on behalf of all Diné.

George F. Huff of Greensburg, Pennsylvania, knocked on the Diné door in 1901. He seemed to seek approval for a relatively small amount of land, 640 acres, somewhere in the Carrizos, for exploration and exploitation. A group of Navajos assembled at Fort Defiance to consider the request. None hailed from the immediate vicinity of the proposed lease site. They waded through the swamp of legal provisions. It is not surprising that those assembled balked. They asked for more time and reconvened in November. This time, a congressman from Pennsylvania, John Dalzell, was on hand to lend support to his constituent's application. Agent G. W. Hayzlett encouraged the Diné to sign. And they did, perhaps influenced in part by the economic depression that still pervaded the reservation. "Henry Dodge" signed his name; the other nine men placed an "X" next to their names on the paper. The first name under Dodge's on the lease was none other than that of Black Horse.[80]

The Navajos quickly learned a lesson that other Indian groups had learned about treaties and agreements. This kind of document could be altered after they had signed it. In this instance, Huff had substituted the entire reservation for 640 acres in the language of the agreement. The secretary of the interior, in a relatively rare fit of responsibility, actually refused to sign the amended lease. Operating ostensibly under the 640-acre restriction, Huff's employees proceeded to act as though the amended document actually had been approved. They scoured the entire reservation looking for oil. Ultimately Huff failed to comply with some of the lease's provisions and the lease was cancelled.[81] The overall experience had provided a striking lesson about the need for vigilance. It, too, would be remembered.

During the past generation, the Navajos had come home, expanded their livestock holdings, recorded impressive achievements with their weaving, and added precious acres to their land base. However, conflicts with their neighbors, growing pressure from the federal government to send more of their children to school, and the attempt by outsiders to exploit their beloved country's resources all signified that what limited isolation they had enjoyed had surely come to an end. The Diné had to be prepared to honor their ancestors' sacrifices. They had to be all the more committed to remaining on and protecting the land. And they had to be ready for that next knock on the door. They knew, somehow, they would not have long to wait.

4

"A Short Rope": 1901–1923

The President has given you a long rope . . . so that you can graze as far as you wish; it is just like a man that has a good horse; when he pickets him out he gives him a long rope in good grass and lets him graze as far as he can, and when he has a mean horse, he gives him a short rope with his head tied up close to a post and he gives only a little feed.

—Chee Dodge, 1905

PRELUDE TO STOCK REDUCTION

Yanapah and Sam listened as patiently as they could to the visitor. As white people tended to do, he spoke far too long. They concluded he was not especially well educated, for he could only speak one language. But their teacher at the San Juan School had told them that he was an important man and they should listen carefully to what he had to say. Eventually the white man stopped talking, and the next day they were required to write about his message. Yanapah remembered: "Mr. Abbott said the resone they want us to go to school is to learn to take care of our self and to live like a white people. Also he said the white people are keep coming close to this country he said pettey soon they will be lots of white people among us in this country. . . ." Sam recalled: "Yesterday Mr. Abbott talked to the Navajos in the chapel. He said he was glad to see them come and make their own living so the white people don't get their lands away from them . . ."[1]

F. H. Abbott may never have seen what Yanapah Tsosie and Sam Ahkeah wrote that spring day in 1910 and he could not know that Sam Ahkeah one day would become chairman of the Navajo Tribal Council. Abbott eventually served as assistant commissioner and as acting commissioner of Indian affairs. A self-righteous and arrogant man, he knew nothing about the Diné. However, he knew his own people and he knew what the Navajos should anticipate. As more non-Navajos came into the area, they would place new demands on the Diné and their land.

The 1901–1923 period marked a significant transition in the lives of the Diné. More outsiders criticized their livestock raising and grew concerned about the pattern of soil erosion. Heightened federal and Christian efforts to compel their children to attend school characterized this era. The twin scourges of trachoma and tuberculosis also racked the reservation. Despite such troubles, the Navajos achieved a great deal. Aided by advocates such as Father Anselm Weber of St. Michaels, they added to their land base. Their weavers and silversmiths created remarkable new work. And in 1923, their Tribal Council met for the first time. In spite of such accomplishments, this time proved difficult for most of the Diné. It may be seen as a prelude to the 1930s, when livestock reduction would be imposed. The danger signals were surely evident, at least in retrospect. Chee Dodge, for one, saw trouble coming at a very early point. "The President," he told an assembled group of the Diné in 1905, "has given you a long rope . . . so that you can graze as far as you wish; it is just like a man that has a good horse; when he pickets him out he gives him a long rope in good grass and lets him graze as far as he can, and when he has a mean horse, he gives him a short rope with his head tied up close to a post and he gives only a little feed."[2] By the early 1920s, the Navajo situation increasingly resembled that of the mean horse.

The federal government began to subdivide the administrative structure of the Navajo area. In 1901, Tuba City became the headquarters for the western Diné, with the superintendent (the more glorified title that now designated the administrator once called the agent) in charge of the portions of the reservation brought in by the executive orders of 1884 and 1900. The next year witnessed the establishment of a separate agency at Keams Canyon for the lands occupied by the Hopis and the surrounding territory occupied by the Navajos (subsequently the "joint-use" area) created through the executive order of 1882. In 1903, the government established the San Juan or northern agency to administer the northern half of the area provided by the 1868 treaty; the southern half, called Navajo, continued to be administered from Fort Defiance. Four years later Crownpoint became the agency headquarters for Pueblo Bonito (later known as Eastern Navajo). This action was taken in conjunction with an ill-fated addition to the reservation as well as to administer part of the 1880 executive order lands. Finally, in 1908, the small Leupp agency was formed, centered in the community of that name, to supervise the 1901 executive order supplement.[3]

With this new structure in place, the federal government attempted to impose its priorities on the Diné. As Frederick Hoxie has argued, in the first decade of the twentieth century assimilationist rhetoric persisted but a transition had begun to occur in American popular thought about American Indians. "Optimism and a desire for rapid incorporation," Hoxie concludes, "were pushed aside by racism, nostalgia, and disinterest."[4] The Navajos bore the brunt of that racism and endured the manufactured nostalgia of photographers, such as Edward Curtis, who portrayed them as "a vanishing race." "The Vanishing Race," the Curtis photograph of a group of Navajos riding into the distance, each individual image progressively more indistinct, was copyrighted in 1904. "The thought this picture was meant to convey," Curtis observed, "was the Indians as a race, already shorn of their tribal strength and stripped of their primitive dress, are passing into the darkness of an unknown future."[5]

This assumption of imminent disappearance would plague the Diné, in one way or another, throughout the twentieth century. Even as their population increased and their position as a power within the Southwest became more evident, the Navajos kept confronting a version of the "vanishing race." The federal government failed to deal with the crisis confronting Diné who lived off the reservation, in part because officials assumed that the Navajos would not continue as an identifiable community. From one decade to the next tourists would be informed solemnly by traders and others with a vested interest in the matter that Navajo weaving was about to disappear and they had better purchase rugs right away. From one decade to the next, Navajo culture was considered unchanging but brittle, frozen but fragile, at once somehow present from time immemorial and yet about to disintegrate.

There has always been a curious dichotomy in how non-Indians perceive American Indian peoples. One prevailing image has tended to be positive, indeed romantic; the other has tended to be negative, indeed racist. During this era both images began to crystallize in regard to the Diné. For Americans who lived some distance from the Southwest, Navajos assumed a romantic image. All Navajos appeared to live in or near Monument Valley or Canyon de Chelly. Postcard images promulgated by the Santa Fe Railway, the Fred Harvey Company, and other such enterprises fixed the Diné in the popular imagination as people who all wore a lot of silver all the time, drove their sheep incessantly through towering sand dunes, and rode horses, but never rode in a truck or a car, let alone owned such a vehicle. For Chee Dodge, who owned a Buick touring car, and for many other Diné, this stereotype became an increasing concern.[6] But they also expressed their anxiety about a different kind of stereotype promulgated within the Southwest. This image portrayed the Diné as lazy, unproductive, and incompetent. Non-Indian ranchers promoted this stereotype with a vengeance. They deliberately contrasted their own virtues with what they deemed Navajo vices. They stressed their own self-reliance and self-sufficiency as well as their responsibility and competence. They charged that the Navajos lacked all these attributes. On one occasion, a New Mexico stockgrowers' association described the Navajos as "Indians that now roam promiscuously over the open range, taking with them a lot of under fed dogs that are forced to live off the calves and sheep of the stockmen. These Indians never develop water, but simply use the water, and grass around the water, that the stockman has, in many instances, gone to great expense to develop." It pictured the Navajos as "pilfering over the country" and as showing "no appreciation" for "advanced ideas of progress."[7]

If most Americans demonstrated little concern for moving beyond such stereotypes, Southwesterners became more and more interested in the resources of the Navajo reservation and the area adjoining it. Non-Indian ranchers and farmers from Arizona, New Mexico, and Utah tried to end or restrict Diné land expansion. Mining companies sought access to Navajo land. At the same time, conservationists called for efficient, productive, and proper use of America's natural resources. With the American frontier supposedly ended, so that further expansion was impossible, Americans had to employ these resources to feed, clothe, and house an ever-growing population. Commissioners of Indian Affairs William A. Jones (1897–1905), Francis E. Leupp (1905–1909), Robert G. Valentine (1909–1913), Cato Sells (1913–1921), and Charles H. Burke (1921–1929) successively attempted to surpass their predecessors in pushing for full production on this acreage. Each pushed Indians to lease or sell their lands to outsiders. When Native communities stubbornly insisted on using the land themselves, that employment was subjected to unprecedented scrutiny.

The Navajos' situation proved especially complicated for several reasons. The reservation was situated in three territories (later three states). A series of executive orders attempted to add land to the original base established by the treaty of 1868. Navajos and non-Navajos made evolving, competing claims on the reservation land and the land adjacent to it. The checkerboard legacy of the railroad land grant south and east of the reservation essentially guaranteed conflict and confusion.

Historian Lawrence Kelly has furnished a useful summary of the making of the checkerboard. Congress chartered the Atlantic and Pacific Railroad Company to build a railroad from Springfield, Missouri, to the California state line. To support this initiative, Congress provided a generous grant of land: forty sections per mile. "In 1876," Kelly explains, "all of the original grant except that portion from Albuquerque, New Mexico, to the California state line was forfeited (24 Stat., 123) and the remainder passed into the control of the St. Louis and San Francisco Railroad Company." The Atchison, Topeka, and Santa Fe Railway purchased a one-half interest in 1880 in the St. Louis and San Francisco charter. "In 1894," Kelly continues, "the Atlantic and Pacific Railroad Company was formally liquidated; what remained of the land grant was divided between the two owners. . . . An affiliate, the Santa Fe Pacific Railroad Company, took control of the Santa Fe landholdings and the St. Louis and San Francisco entrusted its lands to a subsidiary known as the New Mexico and Arizona Land Company." Just for good measure, in 1884 the Aztec Land and Cattle Company purchased a million acres, primarily located in Arizona, from the St. Louis and San Francisco. Kelly concludes: "Much of the land given to the Navajos by executive-order action lay within the northern limits of the original Atlantic and Pacific land grant. Thus, where this occurred, alternate sections of the executive-order reservation belonged not to the Navajos but to one or more of the three land companies."[8]

Aggressive cattle and sheep interests in Arizona and New Mexico lobbied for access to lands occupied by Diné, both on and off reservation. They sought to "return" to the reservation the approximately four thousand Navajos who, through no fault of their own, resided off of it and who, in fact, had never resided on it. All of these Diné lived in the Diné Bikéyah and all had prior claims to the land but since the acreage they occupied was situated in the greater checkerboard area, they lived in highly contested terrain.

The Navajos who lived on the reservation were damned if they did and damned if they didn't. Had they reduced their livestock holdings substantially they would have been criticized for not being sufficiently productive. On the other hand, by obtaining maximum yield from their land, they were charged with overgrazing their livestock. Long before John Collier became commissioner in 1933—indeed before Collier even knew the Navajos existed—the Diné were being scolded for having too many sheep, too many horses, too many goats, and too many cattle. As early as the 1880s, Agent Dennis Riordan called for the number of Navajo goats and sheep to be reduced by one-half to two-thirds.[9]

Agents and special inspectors reserved particular scorn for the horses, or as they generally preferred to label them, the "worthless ponies." In a weak moment some Diné might have granted that they had more horses, individually and collectively, than they probably required. The more traditional among them took comfort in the obligation they had to look after these beings provided by the Holy People; the more pragmatic might have merely shrugged their shoulders, and reminded some nosy inspector that no market existed for them. In any event, they would have added, they did not mind having them around.

The Diné did not take a passive stance toward anything and they definitely did not do so in regard to their livestock. Garrick Bailey and Roberta Bailey emphasize that the Navajos differed from Anglo ranchers by factoring both market and subsistence value into their economics. Horses had more subsistence value than bureaucrats and non-Indians realized; they were used for transportation, in farming and ranching, and for food. Sheep were used to feed people at ceremonies, to pay healers for conducting those ceremonies, and for food as well as for wool. Goats and cattle also were used for milk and for food. Most outsiders did not understand or did not value such reasoning. Moreover, they did not realize or did not want to acknowledge the degree to which the Diné were beginning to adjust the composition of their livestock. The number of horses declined while the number of sheep increased. Nevertheless, by the 1920s, the old subsistence lifestyle became harder to maintain. The pragmatic Diné started to use wage work in order to participate more fully in the cash economy. More than a few Navajos found employment with the railroad.[10]

Inspector H. S. Traylor's 1916 report on Navajo land use, however, gave no indication that any progress had been achieved. "The horses," he sneered, "are mere Indian ponies. Outside of the government horses, I doubt if there are 100 good salable horses on the Reservation." He added, "It does not matter how much money, cattle or sheep a Navajo may have, or how well he lives, his wealth is gauged by his neighbors solely on the number of horses he owns." Traylor denied that a Navajo "would sell at a market price, even if his horses could meet the requirements of the buyers. As it is," he concluded, "the 30,000 horses destroy hundreds of thousands of acres with no good result other than from those few who carry their owners or draw their wagons."[11]

For superintendents like Samuel Stacher of Crownpoint and for commissioners like Cato Sells, horses represented hoofed disaster. When Stacher moaned about the lack of a market for surplus horses, even Sells had to acknowledge "you will probably experience some difficulty in procuring a satisfactory price for them." Then the commissioner had an inspiration. He came up with a solution that would reduce federal expenditures while improving the lot of "the Indians," as he insisted on calling the Navajos. "In a number of the large cities and other places in the country," Sells noted, "horse meat is being used for food and it has occurred to me that the Indian ponies might be slaughtered for that purpose and issued to the Indians in lieu of beef." The cost-conscious Texan continued: "The constantly increasing price of beef has necessitated a material reduction in the amount of beef issued to the Indians and if you feel that this plan can be adopted to advantage and without serious objection on the part of the Indians it would be possible to increase the amount of meat issued to them."[12] Stacher's response discreetly dismissed Sells's scheme. He informed the commissioner that "quite a number of the Indians have been butchering ponies for food, thereby saving sheep and cattle for market. Unfortunately, there is no demand or no sales for lamb this year."[13] Sells proved persistent on this point. He later advised Stacher that "a number of superintendents" had been able to dispose of horses and burros "to advantage on account of the demand for their hides." Sells encouraged Stacher to contact Inspector J. J. Terrell at San Carlos, "who has lately disposed of several carloads of such animals." Stacher might have informed Sells that several carloads would not exactly have much impact on the Navajo. Instead, he apparently chose not to reply.[14]

Sells and his ilk ranted about horses, but the primary problem lay elsewhere. Severe drought from 1898 through 1904, followed by wetter than usual years, followed by more drought, combined with the extraordinary increase in the number of Navajo livestock to take a devastating toll. The Navajos grazed sheep, goats, horses, and cattle. Each chewed and ate differently; each had its own impact on the range. The combination of animals had a greater effect than if the Diné had only grazed one type of livestock. Too many animals killed individual plants and restructured "the vegetative community." In addition, the increasing numbers of livestock run by Anglo-American ranchers to the south and to the east of the existing reservation and the discovery of oil in northwestern New Mexico limited both the Navajo range and the possibilities of acquiring badly needed additional land. The end result was an untenable situation that seemed to deteriorate with each passing year. Well before the New Deal it had appeared to reach a crisis stage.[15]

If the Navajos raised too much livestock for the land they had available, they were simply following an old western tradition. Just as there were divisions within the Diné ranks, with some operators, such as Chee Dodge and his wife, owning a great many animals and others but a few, there were some large-scale Anglo operators and some small outfits. The more sizable Anglo enterprises had all the more reason to find new land and they did so frequently at the expense of the Diné. In 1909, for example, Joseph E. Maxwell, the superintendent of the Leupp Training School, wrote to the commissioner of Indian affairs to lobby for a fee to be levied on non-Navajo cattle grazing on Diné land "for the reason that it is justice and for the further reason that it will tend to limit the number of cattle coming on the reservation during the five months for which the privilege is granted." The Anglo ranchers were grazing livestock on Navajo winter range. "During the past two years," Maxwell commented, "a great many cattle belonging to the white men have come into the country and have devoured the winter range belonging to the Indians and used the water on the range, which has worked a hardship on the Indians."[16]

Had the ranchers been only slightly more persuasive, they might well have succeeded in opening the entire Navajo reservation for lease and for eventual private purchase. Most students of the Diné past have not treated this very definite possibility with sufficient seriousness. In *Lone Wolf v. Hitchcock* (1903), the U.S. Supreme Court had thrown open the Kiowa, Apache, and Comanche lands in Indian Territory. It concluded that regardless of the language employed in various treaties or agreements, ultimately the Congress had the power to do as it pleased in regard to Native landholdings. In other words, even if a particular Indian community objected to the process, it did not matter. Congress could abrogate a treaty, as long as it deemed it in the best national interest. Non-Indians seized upon the decision to lobby successfully for the opening of other reservations. Special Agent James McLaughlin specifically utilized *Lone Wolf* to pry open hundreds of thousands of acres for non-Indian occupation at Crow and Flathead in Montana, Rosebud in South Dakota, Uintah in Utah, and Wind River in Wyoming. He argued that Indians had more land than they needed and white people could use the land to greater advantage.[17] Anyone at all familiar with the Navajo economy would have protested that the Diné did not have too much land, but too little. However, the size of the Navajo reservation made it an easy target. Most non-Indians had not actually been on the reservation, but they somehow knew that the Diné had more land than they needed.

Chee Dodge's response to an inquiry from Secretary of the Interior Franklin K. Lane in 1914 demonstrated that the federal government did consider seriously more general allotment or the opening of the Navajo reservation. "I am among the very few members of the tribe who could get along if they had their property and were entirely independent of the Indian Bureau," Dodge observed, "but this condition would not be a good thing for the tribe." He added, "If placed under state government, the Navajos would never be educated and civilized; what good people have been trying to do for us would be undone and the tribe would be ruined and pauperized within a very short time." Dodge concluded, "The character of our reservation is such that its division or allotment is not feasible and would prove our ruin . . . [O]ur reservation ought to be kept intact and land within the reservation belonging to the railroad company and to the state ought to be secured for us; we need it and are willing to pay for it by pledging and selling our ripe timber."[18] Although the Navajos would prevail in regard to the prevention of allotment on the main reservation, consolidation and extension of their land base proved difficult.

ANSELM WEBER'S TIRELESS CRUSADE

Father Anselm Weber of St. Michaels Mission emerged as a key figure in this struggle. Weber worked indefatigably for Diné land interests from soon after he arrived in Diné Bikéyah in 1898 until his death in 1921. He helped obtain the vitally important addition to the southern portion of the Navajo reservation in 1907. This supplement added the area just south of Ganado, including the country around Wide Ruins, down to Chambers. Weber also took on railroad and livestock interests as he battled for individual Diné on the checkerboard lands. He wrote thousands of letters to the Office of Indian Affairs, individual superintendents such as Stacher, the Land Office, the Board of Indian Commissioners, members of the U.S. House of Representatives and the U.S. Senate, the Santa Fe Railway, and the Bureau of Catholic Indian Missions. His insistent voice made a difference.[19]

Weber's letter to Senator Charles Curtis of Kansas on November 24, 1909, underlined his anxiety about the prospect of allotment on the reservation, especially in regard to the new lands added to the Arizona side. After noting "the avowed policy of the Indian Office to allot lands to Indians and to throw open their Reservations," Weber argued that allotment would not work at Navajo because of the land. Allotment may work "where the Reservations are agricultural in character," he concluded, but most of the Navajo reservation "is good for grazing purposes only; and large tracts are not even good for grazing purposes for lack of water." Dry farming has not been successful elsewhere, he told Curtis. "Shall we," he asked, "expect an Indian to make a living on a ten acre or even on an 80 acre tract where an American fails on his homestead of 160 or even 320 acres?" Weber wrote, "On many a quarter section, even a half dozen goats would starve."[20]

Weber had no doubt about what would happen if allotment were to be inflicted on the Navajo reservation. He labeled such an action "impracticable and fatal to the progress, if not, ultimately, to the very existence of the Navajos." Weber had ample evidence to support his claim. In 1907, two extensions of the reservation had been made in New Mexico, but then they were returned to the public domain. Navajos who had taken allotments quickly began to be induced, through one means or another, to abandon them. Without land, they had no future. Weber disparaged the idea that this population could somehow be absorbed into the reservation economy, for "there is about as much stock on the Reservation as the range will bear; But if similar conditions should prevail on the present Reservation (and they will prevail if the Reservation is allotted and thrown open); where will they go?" If the federal government wanted to allot the reservation in the name of "survival of the fittest," Weber did not like the odds. The "nobility of character" of the Navajos would be overwhelmed by "the sand and grit and persistence and impudence of cowboys and sheepmen."[21]

The issue would not go away. In 1917, Weber published a summary statement entitled, "The Navajo Indians: A Statement of Facts." This twenty-six-page fusillade against the prospect of allotment demonstrated that the notion of dividing the Navajo estate and opening it for non-Navajo settlement remained a very strong possibility. Weber remarked that in Navajo and Apache counties in Arizona and San Juan and McKinley counties in New Mexico, "a given area supports through agriculture and stock raising two Indians to one white man." He asked, "Then why should these reservations be opened up? Because the proportion, two to one, is too small? Must three or four Indians make a living where but one white man could subsist? That an Indian can and does make a living, where a white man would starve does not prove that an area which supports one white person can support an indefinite number of Indians."[22]

Weber spoke straightforwardly about current conditions. "It is universally admitted that the range in Arizona and New Mexico is overstocked," he acknowledged, "and run down and in danger of being ruined, hence the Kent Leasing Bill, H.R. 10,539." Weber added, "But, the Navajo Reservation is stocked heavier and its range is more overgrazed and run down than the range in other parts of these United States." He quoted E. O. Wooton of the New Mexico Agricultural Experiment Station in regard to the status of Navajo reservation lands and lands occupied by the Navajos in New Mexico. Wooton had stated that the "part of the Territory lying northwest of Grants between the Santa Fe Railroad and the Colorado and Arizona borders is a region of rather poor carrying capacity, and now has been badly overstocked by sheep for years." Weber concluded, "The clamor of these two vast, underdeveloped states for opening the overstocked and overgrazed Navajo Reservation seems rather ludicrous." However, Weber knew the proponents of the notion meant business, despite "thousands of acres" on the reservation lacking "vegetation enough to founder a humming bird." In the end his opposition proved critical to defeating the proposal to allot the Arizona reservation extension. Once that victory had been achieved, the prospects for allotment of the entire reservation began to wither. Yet the opening of the reservation for unrestricted non-Indian use remained an attractive idea to many individuals living in the vicinity of the Navajo Nation. Farmington, New Mexico, interests, including the town's newspaper, favored abolishing the reservation altogether. Sometimes they cloaked their desire for Diné land in a charade of concern. They said they wanted to liberate the Navajos from federal control. What they really wanted was the land.[23]

Allotment thus represented a kind of double-edged sword. Weber employed allotment to assist individual Diné land claims in this area. Several thousand Navajos took allotments in order to try to hang on to fragments of the land. However, allotment also threatened to break up the entire Navajo reservation. Many proponents of allotment saw it as a means to an end. They were less interested in having Navajos take over particular plots of land and much more interested in splintering the reservation. If that objective had been obtained, Navajo life would have been altered forever.

The ongoing problems of occupancy and ownership within the checkerboard region revealed the kind of chaos and disaster that would have attended allotment and sale of "surplus" land on the main reservation. In the end, Weber and his allies could only record partial victories. In 1921, Congress passed a law that attempted to consolidate the checkerboard area. Kelly reports, "No exchanges were effected under the law, however, until 1931, because the regulations issued by the Bureau were so complicated as to make compliance nearly impossible." Some Navajos who occupied the public domain gained allotments while others did not. Those who acquired their own land sometimes lost it while others managed to hold on to their precious parcels. The railroad and the non-Indian livestock interests constituted formidable foes and inheritance introduced additional complications. Navajos living in the checkerboard area generally had to use poorer land than their counterparts on the reservation, and, as a result, they tended to be less prosperous and more vulnerable ultimately to tuberculosis and other illnesses. Partial victories against them surpassed what could be expected under such circumstances. A law proposed by Arizona representative Marcus Aurelius Smith that "no Reservation shall be created, nor shall any addition be made to one heretofore created, within the limits of the States of New Mexico or Arizona, except by act of Congress" gained unanimous approval and soon the principle was applied to all the states.

New executive-order reservations had been blocked. The Navajos would have to be on guard to protect their interests in the immediate future.[24]

Superintendent Stacher appealed unsuccessfully time and again to Commissioner Sells. "Too bad that all these greedy white stockmen from around the state wish to freeze out two or three thousand Navajos for the benefit of less than a dozen white stockgrowers," Stacher observed on one occasion in 1918. Since Sells had been unmoved by prior entreaties, a desperate Stacher resorted to patriotism: "The Huns have over-run Belgium and devastated their country with the result that thousands are starving," he wrote during World War I. "Is this great republic going to permit a few whites to over-run the Indian country, and they be driven to poverty and starvation??? Here is an opportunity for us to carry out a big drive for Liberty and Justice here at home." However, neither flag waving nor dramatic punctuation proved effective in changing the commissioner's mind on this subject.[25]

Stacher searched in vain for one elected representative who would stand up for the Navajos. He could not locate anything resembling a profile in courage: "The plan to extend the reservation has been blocked. No one in politics seems to care a rap about what becomes of the Navajo and is willing to see him crowded out from his little range in the desert where he has been content to plug along. . . . Where is the law maker that raises his voice in his behalf?"[26]

Newly minted senators, such as Albert Fall of New Mexico and Henry Ashurst of Arizona, had other priorities. They both worked overtime to limit Diné landholdings off the reservation and to halt expansion of the reservation. They believed in equity for the Navajos as long as that meant giving each member of the tribe who resided off the reservation the same chance to fail. They believed in progress for the Navajos as long as that meant bringing the Diné "into regular contact with an 'advanced' society." They believed in development for the Navajos as long as that meant opening their reservation to mining interests. They believed in integration for the Navajos as long as that meant integrating their natural resources into the American economy. If this all ultimately encouraged exploitation and suffering, then Fall and Ashurst believed it taught the Diné, to borrow Hoxie's phrase, "the virtues of self-reliance and the evils of backsliding."[27]

Anselm Weber battled cancer for the last few years of his life and finally succumbed on March 8, 1921. Chee Dodge's niece, Agnes Chester, joined other Diné in mourning his passing. She feared for the future: "[N]ow the white people can do what they want with us. Now, too, the white people can do everything they please with our lands."[28]

Superintendent Peter Paquette feared for the future, too. The veteran employee had witnessed the steady deterioration of the Navajo range. By the autumn of 1922, he despaired. "I find that conditions are deplorable," he informed the commissioner. Paquette predicted that the Diné would "suffer a great loss of stock if the winter is at all severe." Could Washington help?[29] Assistant Commissioner E. B. Meritt expressed sympathy but pleaded penury. "The Office is sorry to learn this and is unable to offer any suggestions for meeting this situation at this time," he said, given "the lack of available funds and the high price of feed."[30] At a time when the Department of the Interior was pouring millions of dollars into massive new irrigation projects that greatly benefited self-reliant, self-sufficient non-Indian farmers and ranchers in the Southwest, somehow no money could be found for their counterparts on the Navajo reservation.

AUTHORITY, RESISTANCE, AND REBELLION

The agency superintendents did not have the easiest job in the world. They sometimes received directives from the commissioner of Indian affairs that they agreed with, but they also faced other suggestions or demands that they did their best to ignore. And in certain instances, they acted quite independently in efforts to establish their own authority, for example, or to enforce policies, such as school attendance. Depending on the attitude of the superintendent, the stakes of the confrontation, and the political, economic, and social climate of the moment, Navajos could go along with a request or a demand or they could oppose it strenuously. More noteworthy for their determination than their tact, they sometimes transformed a difficult assignment into an impossible one. Agency superintendents who demanded automatic and total acceptance of their authority did not always receive the respect and obedience they craved. Men like Reuben Perry and William Shelton became main characters in three stories that continue to be told by the Diné. In the Diné renditions of the Tol Zhin confrontation, the Bai-a-lil-le incident, and the Beautiful Mountain (Dził k'i Hózhoni, or "Mountain Beautiful on Top") "uprising," the superintendents were not portrayed as heroes. Those roles went to Anselm Weber and Chee Dodge, individuals who intervened to deescalate these confrontations.

The Tol Zhin affair erupted in the autumn of 1905. A young Navajo woman had accused Tol Zhin of sexual assault. He had reached agreement on restitution with the girl's family and had made the necessary payment to them of one white horse. But Perry neither approved of traditional systems of judgment nor of the punishment itself. He drove his buckboard to Chinle (Hínítí, or "Water Outlet") fully intent on arresting Tol Zhin. Word of Perry's intentions reached a group of Tol Zhin's friends, who proceeded to intercept Perry's buckboard, surround him, and threaten to kill him. Perry was carrying a gun, but the Navajos pinned back his arms and prevented him from using the weapon. Only by pardoning Tol Zhin did Perry manage to free himself from his captors.[31]

Perry soon thereafter journeyed to St. Michaels to tell Anselm Weber and Chee Dodge about this incident. They advised him that a dangerous precedent had been established. They believed that he needed to apprehend those who had forced him to turn over Tol Zhin or else resign as superintendent. Perry, not surprisingly, elected the first option. He summoned a combined force of some Navajo men who served as tribal policemen and soldiers from Fort Wingate to go out and apprehend those who had ambushed him. This party did arrest Tol Zhin and Winslow, but Dlad, Ts'osini Biye, Diné Ligaii, and Ush-tilly avoided capture.[32] For a good number of Diné, this resistance seemed ill-advised and likely to cause problems out of all proportion to the incident itself. The well-known silversmith and leader, Peshlakai, was among this group. He, Atsitty Yazza Begay, and Bish Klah even signed a statement on November 29, 1905, in which they pledged to "support and uphold the authority of the government" and to assist in capturing the four men "who are known to have committed crimes in direct violation of the treaty with the United States."[33] Eventually, Diné Ligaii was arrested. The other three men hid out in the Crystal area, together with another man who had been involved in the incident, Doo Yalti'i. Finally other Diné agreed to go out and bring them in.

Perry had felt humiliated by what had happened to him and sought revenge through his recommendation of a stiff sentence for the seven Diné. He urged that Tol Zhin, Denet Lakai, and Glahdy, whom he labeled "ringleaders," be sentenced to two years in prison, with the other men each sentenced to one year. Commissioner Francis Leupp reported to the secretary of the interior that Perry believed that "these prisoners belong to the vicious, criminal, and worthless clan" among the Navajos. The commissioner listed examples of other "troublesome Indians" who had been sentenced to prison away from their home communities, including nineteen Hopis who had resisted allotment and in 1894 had been sentenced to prison on Alcatraz, where they remained from January 3, 1895, to August 1896. He seconded Perry's recommended prison sentences, adding that this time should be spent in hard labor at Alcatraz. Leupp labeled the seven "among the most ignorant and lawless people with whom the Office has to deal," individuals who "have always maintained an attitude of contempt toward the Government except when faced with the practical demonstration of the power of the Government to exercise force when it becomes necessary to substitute force for gentle methods." He predicted much good could come from this action, because the prisoners upon return "will have very interesting stories to tell their friends of the railroads and steamboats and populous cities they have seen, and of other wonders calculated to convey to the absolutely untutored Indian mind its only conception of the numbers and power of the whites; and these will go a long way toward quenching any further desire to defy the authority of the Government."[34]

The secretary of the interior approved the sentences and the men served them, although their time on Alcatraz wound up being reduced. An Indian Rights Association investigation about "the seven troublesome Navajo Indians," as Acting Commissioner C. F. Larrabee termed them, and other concerns expressed about their health encouraged the secretary of war to authorize their removal "to a more favorable climate."[35] In August 1906, the seven moved to balmy Fort Huachuca in southern Arizona Territory. No doubt they did have stories to tell, but they may not have been exactly the moral lessons Leupp had in mind. In any event their experiences did not deter all forms of Diné resistance to colonial authority, as is clear in the confrontation surrounding Ba'áliilii.

Superintendent William Shelton was also known as Naat'aanii Nééz (or "Tall Boss"). The head of the San Juan Agency had a forceful personality and strong opinions. His idea of consensus was to have everyone agree immediately with him. Shelton believed almost all of the Diné to be "friendly and loyal," but there were a few from whom he "always expected trouble."[36] When a Navajo individual such as Ba'áliilii publicly disagreed with him and called on others to resist his authority, that definitely fit Shelton's notion of trouble.

On October 29, 1907, troops from Fort Wingate rode into Ba'áliilii's camp to take him into custody. Ba'áliilii and his followers resisted the intruders. The soldiers killed two of them. Shelton demanded that Ba'áliilii and another person, Polly, receive ten years in prison at hard labor, with seven others serving two-year terms. Leupp agreed with this recommendation and soon Fort Huachuca had more involuntary residents. However, a few weeks later Leupp began to have second thoughts about how the matter had been handled, and he asked Father Weber to review what had transpired. Weber scrutinized the events and found fault with Shelton. He condemned the superintendent's "arbitrary and autocratic" actions and recommended that Shelton be replaced. The Arizona Supreme Court eventually decided that the Diné had been unlawfully imprisoned and set them free in August 1908. The federal government chose not to appeal this decision. In the meantime, Shelton remained on the job.[37]

The Beautiful Mountain episode of 1913 also involved Superintendent Shelton. He dispatched members of the local Navajo police force to arrest Histałí Yázhí on the grounds of polygamy. He was reported to have married three sisters, but family history records the wives as being a mother and two daughters. After his first wife had died, he had asked one of the two daughters to marry him. She replied that she would only do so if he would take responsibility as well for her mother and her sister. To make sure he would fulfill that responsibility, she suggested that he follow traditional Navajo custom in such situations. Although she alone would be his partner, the three of them would live with him. Although such an arrangement made sense to Histałí Yázhí, it outraged Superintendent Shelton. Shelton dispatched the police to arrest Histałí Yázhí, but when the police reached Histałí Yázhí's place they learned he had gone hunting. Rather than wait for his return, the police took his three women into custody and brought them back to Shiprock. The three women were incarcerated in the local jail, known to the Diné as Shelton's hotel because of his tendency to imprison Navajos in it. Histałí Yázhí, accompanied by his father, Bizhoozhí, and ten other men, stormed into Shiprock to confront Shelton. When they learned that Shelton was attending a country fair in Durango, they decided to take immediate action. They overpowered the guard at the jail, retrieved the women, and returned to Beautiful Mountain. Shelton returned from Durango to discover unexpected vacancies at his hotel. He had warrants sworn to arrest the twelve "rebellious Navajos," charging them with, among other things, riot, horse theft, and deadly assault.[38]

Superintendent Paquette intervened. He conferred with Weber and Chee Dodge at St. Michaels; then Weber, Dodge, Peshlakai, Charley Mitchell, and Black Horse searched for Histałí Yázhí. They located him at an Enemy Way ceremony in the Lukachukai area. Histałí Yázhí and others proclaimed their innocence and their contempt for Shelton. Eventually, Weber and Paquette journeyed to Histałí Yázhí's home community, situated above Sanostee, New Mexico. There, accompanied by Diné interpreter Frank Walker and three other Navajo men, they spoke with Bizhoozhí and Histałí Yázhí and most of the others wanted by the law. Bizhoozhí told Paquette and Weber: "I do not think we have done anything wrong. They came and stole the women and we stole them back. . . . Mr. Shelton is mean to us. He stands out ready to jump on us. We are like small birds hiding in the rocks. . . ." The men said Shelton had

Part of the Shiprock Agency near Shelton's hotel. Photograph by Leo Crane. Leo Crane Collection, Special Collections, Cline Library, Northern Arizona University. Neg. no. NAU.PH.658.633

threatened to castrate them so they could not have any more sons. They would not surrender; they had plenty of food and supplies and were in the process of building barricades.[39]

Shelton had had enough. He requested troops, and much to Weber's and others' astonishment and dismay, the federal government actually acceded to Shelton's demand. A total of 240 soldiers, 5 cooks, 16 mule drivers, 256 horses, 40 mules, 300 rounds of ammunition per man, and 8 commissary wagons traveled by train from Fort Robinson, Nebraska, to Gallup. At least the four troops of the 12th Cavalry had been placed under the command of General Hugh Scott, someone quite familiar with the Diné. Paquette, Dodge, Weber, and Doctor Norbert Gottbrath scurried to Gallup to cut off the troops before they proceeded north. Scott assured the quartet that he only wanted to present a show of force in the hopes of prompting surrender. Mid-November snow and rain greeted Paquette and company as they left Gallup, and Paquette's car kept getting stuck on the gumbo road. It took them all night and until four o'clock the next afternoon to make the thirty-mile trip back to Fort Defiance. Paquette then decided to remain at the agency, while the other three men traveled to Crystal, took three of Dodge's horses, and rode through the Chuskas to Sanostee. Scott and his troops had already arrived, with some of the soldiers having volunteered to push the general's automobile all the way from Gallup to Tohatchi, a distance of more than forty miles. Scott finally abandoned his vehicle and rode in to Sanostee on horseback.[40]

Members of the national press naturally expressed delight at this evolving melodrama. They began filing stories from New Mexico that inflated the standoff into something likely to produce Beautiful Mountain's answer to the Alamo. Although the Navajos had no great desire to fight, it had not been that long in the Diné memory since Kit Carson, and the embattled group at Beautiful Mountain did not trust Scott, let alone Shelton. More time passed. When Thanksgiving Day arrived, Scott was determined to observe the occasion, regardless of the circumstances. The soldiers and some of the Navajos proceeded to wolf down a fine holiday dinner. The repast did, admittedly, include a few minor modifications, including the substitution of mutton for turkey.[41]

Over the next two days, Scott did his best to explain to the people from Beautiful Mountain why these individuals had to surrender. Chee Dodge spoke separately with several of the Diné, trying to assure them that things would turn out all right. The accused Diné finally decided to go to Santa Fe for their trial, as long as Dodge and Weber would go with them. At the trial, Judge William H. Pope dismissed all charges but unlawful assembly and handed out sentences from ten to thirty days, to be served in the Gallup jail. This outcome clearly had to be perceived as a triumph for Beautiful Mountain and a slap at Shelton.[42] The superintendent did his best to downplay his irritation at the light sentences. "I am glad to say that our Indian troubles seem to be about settled," he wrote to Stacher. "It has never been anything like the papers reported."[43]

These three examples of resistance to colonial administration mirror the widespread rejection in Navajo country of arbitrary, imposed rule. The Diné demonstrated that they distinguished between and among outsiders who came to work on the reservation. A person like Anselm Weber earned admiration from many Diné, even if they did not necessarily support Catholic missionary work. A person like William Shelton inspired other emotions. The Navajos, as always, were not opposed to change, but they wanted to ensure that innovations in their culture would be incorporated on their own terms. They wanted administrators and ministers to demonstrate qualities that they valued among themselves. They knew full well the kind of power that the federal government had at its disposal and they knew they could pay a price for resistance. Yet if it mattered sufficiently, if the imposition really could be harmful, then they knew they had an obligation to reject it, regardless of the cost.

During these years, the Navajos kept dealing with outsiders who believed it their duty to change Diné behavior or belief. The missionaries for various Christian churches tried to convert them to Christianity. If the missionaries stayed long enough, if they gained some minimal knowledge of the language or became proficient in it, then they often became more pluralistic in their outlook. The superintendents were, in their own way, also missionaries. They could be just as zealous and often considerably more heavy-handed. If the trading post became a kind of meeting ground, the agency headquarters remained more of a colonial outpost, more of a circle of covered wagons that isolated the people inside and separated them from the very people they were supposed to serve. Within this compound, individuals could indulge in pastimes rather removed from the everyday concerns of the Diné. Tennis captured the interest of a number of federal employees and modest courts were constructed. No golf courses were created, even though the potential for sand traps no doubt occurred to more than one federal employee.

The commissioners of Indian affairs also were given to lengthy sermons and extended harangues. They thundered against nine-day ceremonies. They complained about the Diné being nomadic. They furnished one sermon after another to the beleaguered superintendents. They kept saying, "Do this, do that," all the while complaining of their lack of funds.

The superintendents varied, of course, in how they approached their jobs, which did not remain exactly the same from one generation to the next. But most superintendents felt isolated. They were foreigners in a land that never could become their home. Their frequent insistence on their authority suggests in the end a kind of insecurity masked by false bravado. In a thousand and one ways the Navajos kept reminding these administrators that they were Diné, rather than "the Indians," and they would continue to be Diné. They would remind them that this country would continue to be Diné Bikéyah, that the land truly belonged to them. One day, they all knew, a man like Shelton would be gone. They knew, contrary to Curtis's beliefs, that they were not vanishing. They would remain.

In this regard, Chee Dodge's personal and financial relationships with the superintendents and missionaries become all the more intriguing. Dodge was in a position to help people who became his friends, and some of the superintendents and the priests at St. Michaels certainly could be included in that category. For example, he loaned Reuben Perry and Peter Paquette $800 on one occasion and $3,000 to Perry at another time. Anselm Weber received a loan of $1,460 from Dodge, and the Franciscan Fathers at St. Michaels and Chinle also benefited from Dodge's generosity. These were not small sums, particularly when one factors in inflation. It must have given Dodge both pleasure and satisfaction to provide this assistance, especially given the negative stereotypes of the day about Navajos.[44] It is also fair to assume that Dodge's generosity did not hurt his relationship with these people in positions of authority.[45]

Most of the challenges to "authority" are not revealed in the written records, although there are wonderful exceptions, such as a letter from Nelson Etcitty, who wrote in April 1922 about his dismissal by Superintendent Stacher. Stacher had fired him from his custodial position at Crownpoint for such transgressions as turning out the school's lights at the appropriate time; Etcitty did not know that Stacher wanted to stay up and play cards. "I have been sent to school by the Indian Office and I am going to show it has not been fruitless," he wrote.[46] Stacher did not appreciate this "smart Aleck letter," and chided Etcitty for his disloyalty.[47] But Etcitty, like thousands of other Navajos, did not believe in blind obedience. They tried to maintain their integrity and independence, even if it came at a price.

More than a few Diné men and women endured incarceration. They rarely had attorneys and they often were confused about why they were "in trouble." They were not always convicted, of course, and their punishment not always severe. Some even made light of a short sentence, as they did with their alternative name for the Shiprock jail. However, the prospect of Alcatraz and Fort Huachuca or the state penitentiaries in Florence, Arizona, or Santa Fe, New Mexico, were quite another matter. Any prisoner in one of these locations faced the prospect of extended separation from family, community, and friends. Few prisoners spoke English fluently and thus there could be genuine confusion about their own situation and real trauma at lack of communication with relatives. "I think I get out of this place sometime in the summer or in this fall," wrote Willie George from the state penitentiary in Santa Fe, but in fact he was not quite sure. He had written four times to his parents and he had not received a response. He wondered why.[48] John Yazza, also imprisoned in Santa Fe, said, "I do not know how much longer I have to stay here." He asked Stacher "to find out why my folks do not write or answer my letters."[49]

Willie George asked Stacher to tell his grandfather he was all right. And there was one more thing. "Ask him about my horse," he said.[50]

TUBERCULOSIS, TRACHOMA, AND THE FLU

In common with many other Native communities, the Navajos endured terrible problems with the twin scourges of tuberculosis and trachoma. A highly contagious disease, tuberculosis reached epidemic proportions among the Navajos. A 1912 survey suggested that more than 8 percent of the Diné had contracted tuberculosis. Trachoma was also spread by a virus and could cause impaired vision or blindness. Both diseases spread rapidly in the crowded conditions in the boarding schools.[51]

The great flu epidemic of 1918 did not spare the Diné. It hit the reservation in October and devastated all of the agencies. The epidemic did not last long, but its death toll was overwhelming. Over two thousand Navajos lost their lives. Robert Trennert noted several causes for this total: The "government facilities could not cope with the demand and were completely overwhelmed." Both Navajo and non-Navajo healers or medical personnel also got sick and could not continue with their work. Trennert believes that the Navajo "fear of the dead" caused the Diné to flee "from outbreak sites, carrying the disease with them as they moved into the back country." He concludes, "[I]n some cases so many family members were sick that no one could care for the sick. Many thus perished from pneumonia or starvation."[52]

Rose Mitchell became ill with the flu. "I got so weak," she later recalled, "I couldn't get up, and people started carrying me outside in a blanket when I needed to go out. After I got too weak to stand up on my own, I don't remember much; my mind seemed to be some place else and everything started getting confused." Mitchell's father decided that their relatives should "all move closer together, so we could help each other get through it." Then he "started gathering different plants and making medicines for the People to use." Mitchell reported that her father said "none of our ceremonies would help cure us from that. He said this kind of sickness, this epidemic, had nothing to do with any of our ceremonies, not even the small ones. Instead the best thing we could do was to use our Blessingway prayers, to ask that the sickness stay away from us and all our relatives, and all other Navajos, or to ask that it only touch down lightly, if we were already sick."[53]

As it did with conditions on the range, inadequate federal investment severely limited progress. Superintendent Evan W. Estep, Shelton's successor at Shiprock, became increasingly traumatized by what he observed. "We have plenty of patients but no money," he wrote to Commissioner Sells. Estep asked that a medical inspector be sent to Shiprock.[54]

Schoolchildren were at severe risk owing to conditions in boarding schools. "For some time past," Estep noted, "our children have been running down. We have cut our school room duties materially by direction of the physician and devoted the time thus taken from academic work to physical training in the open air." He added, "There may have been results that justified the procedure, but the fact remains that many of children continue to lose weight or at least do not increase in weight like healthy, growing children should do. We have lost a number of them during the year as the monthly reports show—too many when there was no epidemic of any kind. There are two in the hospital now who will most likely die and so far as I can get at it there is no very clear diagnosis of the causes—'intermittent fever' being about as close as we can get to it. A very promising girl went to the hospital last week. I do not expect her to come out until we carry her out and it doesn't seem to me necessary that such should be the case."[55]

Inspections revealed desperate circumstances at the schools. Special Physician H. V. Hailman, for example, visited the Marsh Pass School in the summer of 1922. He found the dormitories "in bad condition and overcrowded with children"; fifty-two children had been placed in an area that could accommodate thirty. Hailman did not mince words: "The plant as a whole is terribly run-down and dilapidated and the dormitories are not kept in proper sanitary conditions as regards beds, bedding, and ventilation. The same thing applies to the lavatories, wash rooms, and toilets, they being at this time entirely out of commission, because of the lack of water and disarrangement of the sewage system." The doctor provided more unwelcome news: "The bath tubs are of sheet metal, are broken, unpainted, or without enamel, and when the children are bathed at all, water is carried by hand, placed in the tubs and children bathed seven at a time in the same water." Hailman called the school "a disgrace."[56]

Cultural differences made treatment of tuberculosis, trachoma, and other diseases highly problematic. Most physicians who came to Diné Bikéyah disliked the traditional healers and the ceremonies they conducted. The superintendents almost always shared these sentiments. Paquette, for example, issued a solemn pledge: "I intend to stop the practice of Medicine Men on this reservation and I hope to bring this about by a slow, persistent yet firm attitude of opposition to it." Lacking words in their language for "germ" or "bacteria," the Navajos had difficulty understanding how these diseases were contracted and how they were spread. The physicians who came to Diné Bikéyah were rarely the best or the brightest, and most Navajos avoided them whenever possible. Minimal government funding also hampered efforts to treat the diseases. Trennert summarizes the condition of the Navajos at the start of the World War I: "Tuberculosis and trachoma remained unchecked, hospitals were inadequate and underfunded, and employees' living conditions remained primitive."[57]

The story of Dr. Albert Wigglesworth, however, suggests that a good physician with cultural sensitivity could make a difference. He came to Diné Bikéyah and remained for twenty years, working under difficult circumstances. Wigglesworth cared for patients across 160 square miles, assisted only by a "nurse" with no medical training and a team of mules to transport him. He actually made an effort to understand the traditional Navajo belief system. Wade Davies recounts one memorable episode when a patient, a Navajo policeman named Betahne Nez, complained of chest pains. Wigglesworth's diagnosis of mild angina did not satisfy Nez and did not alleviate his pain. The policeman concluded that a witch might have put a coyote's tooth close to his heart. Upon hearing this conclusion, Wigglesworth pulled out one of his own loose teeth, sterilized it, and made "a small incision in Nez's chest" and passed "his tooth off as the coyote's. 'He nearly collapsed, but was cured from that moment,' said Wigglesworth." Davies notes that the superintendent disapproved of this sort of creativity as he strongly opposed traditional Navajo healing, but the doctor's patients respected him all the more for his action. Navajo singer Frank Mitchell later termed him "the very first good doctor the People ever had."[58]

The Diné did gain more hospitals during this era. In addition to a hospital that had already been constructed at Fort Defiance, other hospitals were built at Tuba City, Leupp, and Shiprock.[59] A "Save the Babies" campaign launched during Cato Sells's term as commissioner achieved slight success. "INDIAN MOTHERS. SAVE YOUR BABIES," blared one brochure. "Many Indian babies die before they are 2 years old because they do not have the right kind of care."[60] The brief publication provided clear instructions in regard to nursing, bottle-feeding, solid food, water, and bathing. But since few Diné women spoke or read English, the brochures probably had a minimal effect. The old fears about hospitals still prevailed and, with rare exceptions, the physicians who came to work in Navajo country remained antagonistic toward traditional healing. A bilingual, bicultural program would have to wait for another day.[61]

SCHOOLS

Inspector H. J. Traylor completed his tour of the San Juan School in the spring of 1916. He could barely contain himself. The federal government rarely rewarded candor, but he had to risk it. Something had to be done about Miss Loomis, the head teacher, just as something had to be done about Mr. Shelton. The children deserved better. He owed it to them to speak up. Traylor proceeded to characterize Loomis as "a perfect trainer of parrots. Every student under her is trained like a parrot. All individuality and personality have been submerged or destroyed by the indomitable wills of this woman and Supt. Shelton. All the students are so metallic that they ring, and the ring is always the same—certain, accurate, and monotonous." As a result, Traylor contended, "They are over-trained, over-worked and over-controlled. In fact, ambitions and aspirations have been destroyed and all have been cast in the same mold and weighed by the same scale."[62]

Traylor observed that the industrial education at the school had been directed and supervised by other teachers "who are not as Miss Loomis." In this realm, the school had done "very superior work."[63] The San Juan School thus mirrored the curriculum introduced in 1901 by the new superintendent of Indian education, Estelle Reel. Reel believed in "low expectations and practical lessons," and the approach taken by federal Indian schools, not surprisingly, embodied this stance. Many onlookers applauded Reel's "practical" emphasis, but former Commissioner of Indian Affairs Thomas Jefferson Morgan sharply criticized Reel's agenda. He asked a fundamental question that observers continued to ask as the twentieth century progressed: "Why should the national government offer to its wards so much less in the way of schooling than is offered by the states to the pupils of the public schools?" He added, "The Indian child has a right that he shall not be hopelessly handicapped by such an inferior training as from the very beginning condemns him to failure in the struggle for existence." For the former commissioner, it was clear that this philosophy simply ensured that the next generation of Native peoples would be condemned to living on the fringes of American society. Reel did not feel at all apologetic about the vocational-technical emphasis of the Indian schools. She believed hers to be a practical perspective that would encourage Navajos and other Indians to take pride in the value of labor. "A civilization without the elements of labor in it rests upon a foundation of sand," she emphasized. "Labor is the basis of all lasting civilizations and the most potent influence for good in the world. Whenever any race, of its own volition, begins to labor its future is assured."[64]

Few Navajo parents had the opportunity to read and ponder Reel's sentiments, but if they had been given this chance, they might well have been puzzled. Reel implied that the schools would introduce Native students to the world of work. But Navajo children had looked after livestock and had labored in the fields. Some had woven rugs or fashioned bracelets. Wasn't that work? What about building a hogan or shearing a sheep? What about hauling water or breaking a horse? Shouldn't those activities be considered work? If adults had done their jobs properly, their children should know all about the fundamental importance of work. Children didn't need to be introduced to labor as though it were some foreign concept. They did need to be prepared to live in a rapidly changing world. Too often the Indian schools, like many other educational institutions, appeared determined to prepare their students for the previous century rather than the current one; they kept churning out tinsmiths rather than teachers.

The early twentieth century witnessed a significant increase in school construction and operation on the reservation. The federal government built schools at Tuba City, Leupp, Tohatchi, Shiprock, and Chinle during the first decade of the century and added schools at Crownpoint, Toadlena, and Fort Wingate in the 1920s. Many Navajo children continued to avoid school altogether or enrolled briefly and departed, never to be seen again. The reasons pupils and parents disliked the schools in the 1890s were the same reasons they still detested the schools in the early 1920s. Dormitories were still crowded, the food still bad, and the health care still appalling. Even without such problems, many Diné children would not have willingly enrolled in these schools.[65] According to Robert W. Young, this educational system simply did not meet Navajo needs. "Within the traditional society, an educational process was carried on at home," he writes, "designed to teach children the traditional techniques of agriculture and stock raising, the legends, the tabus, and the practices of Navajo culture. Reading and writing an alien language and assuming the ways of alien people" were not important.[66]

Running away offered the most dramatic and effective way a student could express dissatisfaction with a boarding school. When Carl Gorman refused to respond to a teacher at Rehoboth Mission School and instead insulted him in Navajo, the principal locked him in a basement room and chained him for a week against a wall with nothing but bread and water to sustain him. "Now, perhaps you'll be obedient," he told Gorman when the week finally came to an end. Gorman resolved to run away and finally did so in February 1920, accompanied by his uncle Frank (who was his own age) and his younger brother, Wallace. It took them three days, their journey made more complicated and taxing by snow and rain. Famished and exhausted, they made it home at last. When Nelson Gorman heard his son's story of the mistreatment he received, he refused the principal's entreaties that his son must return. A year and a half later, Carl Gorman returned to school in Albuquerque, where he graduated. Gorman went on to become one of the original Code Talkers and a distinguished artist and educator. Years later he visited with a Rehoboth physician who tried to tell him that Rehoboth had made a man out of him. "No," Gorman replied, "the Marines made a man out of me."[67]

By the time Carl Gorman ran away from Rehoboth, abuse of children was less likely to go unnoticed, in part because of the presence of watchdog organizations, such as the American Indian Defense Association, a newly formed outfit with which the reformer John Collier was associated. On November 9, 1923, Stacher wrote to Commissioner of Indian Affairs Charles H. Burke about a complaint made to "Mr. Collier, the paid agitator for some organization." A seventeen-year-old girl had run away from the school on half a dozen occasions. "We have no jail," Stacher noted, "and the only thing I felt that we could do to keep her was to put a hobble on her, though I told her I did not like to do it but that she would not keep her promise and behave herself like two or three days." After three days, Stacher said he took the hobbles off, and two days later she was gone. The superintendent would not admit he had erred: "[W]e do not feel that we have been unjust or unnecessarily harsh in having put hobbles on her. . . ." Stacher also admitted, "[W]e have had to hobble boys who were chronic runaways but only as a last resort to keep them here, when kindness and persuasion had no effect." He did not want to bring criticism upon the school: "If the Office objects to this method, I should like to be so advised."[68]

Burke did not hesitate to furnish counsel. "This method is regarded as especially objectionable," he informed Stacher, "in the case of a girl who has about reached the years of maturity." The commissioner concluded, "Whenever occasion has arisen, I have tried to make it plain that we cannot justify putting pupils in irons. Every school management should make the effort paramount to maintain conditions sufficiently interesting and attractive to hold pupils without resorting to corporal punishment or to means felt by them to be degrading."[69] Burke believed ardently in assimilation. He issued an order that required Indian children in boarding schools to attend Christian church services on Sunday. Elsewhere, Burke outlawed the Sun Dance. He determined that Pueblo Indians in New Mexico had entirely too many ceremonies and attempted in vain to limit how often they occurred. Yet even Burke knew Stacher had gone too far.[70]

The Navajo schools also frequently failed to retain teachers. Isolation, low salaries, and difficult working conditions made it difficult to maintain a stable staff. Aneth, Utah, for example, did not appear to be the top choice for newly hired instructors. Traylor's report in 1916 about the school and community explained why. The Aneth School "is located on the most barren, desolate and desert looking spot one could find anywhere. . . . It is indeed far away from the world," he commented. "I know of no place which has less connection with the outside world than this." Traylor said that if he had "wanted revenge upon any one I would seek employment for them in the government school at Aneth, Utah. . . . Any employee who will be satisfied here will in truth have the true missionary spirit."[71]

Older Diné students who wished to obtain a more advanced education in the federal Indian schools had to resign themselves to leaving the reservation to attend one of the large boarding schools in Albuquerque, Phoenix, Chilocco (Oklahoma), Haskell (Kansas), or Riverside (California). A relatively small number also attended Carlisle (Pennsylvania) and Hampton (Virginia).

Jacob C. Morgan moved on from Grand Junction, Colorado, to Hampton. He continued to develop his skills as a musician and appeared to enjoy his time at the school. Morgan never lost his belief that formal education furnished a key to a better future for the Diné. Writing to Charley Day, the son of trader Sam Day, he responded to Charley's query about his violin playing by saying, "My lessons are getting hard." Morgan then sketched in two lines of a score, noting "by these examples you can how I am getting on with my violin now." He added, "I am very glad you are still at your cornet practice. Don't give it up, but keep it up. Work on your scales every day if you possibly can, for that is [the] only secret of becoming a successful cornetist." Morgan signed the letter with a flourish: "Good-night from ever your friend, Jake C. Morgan."[72]

Morgan enjoyed his time in Virginia, but looked forward to returning home. Several years later he wrote to Dr. W. H. Harrison at Fort Defiance: "Last June I resigned from the Government work and have come back to live among my own people. . . . In order to show them what an education really means to them, I have started this trading post with Mr. Perry's consent."[73] Morgan assisted a missionary at Rehoboth, near Gallup, and worked on a Navajo translation of the Bible. Seeking a position as a teacher at Crownpoint, he practiced his violin and cornet, "bought quite a lot of music," and asked Stacher for a list of any instruments the school might already own.[74] By the summer of 1914, he had secured a position as disciplinarian and music teacher. He played a cornet solo at the Pueblo Bonito July 4 program, which also included Stacher speaking on "The Glorious Fourth," and recitations by Marion Napa ("The Brown Thrush"), Pahe Padilla ("Don't Kill the Birds"), Tom Largo ("A Mid-Summer Song"), Kenneth Antonito ("The Swing"), Eskey T. Martin ("The Boy and the Sparrow"), Earl Holio ("Who Likes the Rain?"), and Johnson Biocitty ("Twinkle Little Star").[75]

Holidays such as the Fourth of July or Washington's Birthday gave the schools the opportunity to emphasize patriotism. Pueblo Bonito School observed Washington's Birthday in 1913 with a program featuring recitations and songs with a patriotic theme. The employees also performed, presenting "Columbia, Gem of the Ocean" and the "Star Spangled Banner" to supplement various student exhortations to "be like Washington" and students singing about the "Dear Old Flag." This kind of celebration reflected a clear goal of the schools. One commissioner of Indian affairs expressed the objective: "The Indian youth should be instructed in their rights, privileges, and duties as American citizens; should be taught to love the American flag; should be imbued with genuine patriotism, and made to feel that the United States, not some paltry reservation is their home."[76]

Years after they left the schools the students could still hear the bells that awakened them and moved them through the day. Federal employees saw Indian life as undisciplined and unregulated and they were determined to instill in each pupil a deeply rooted sense of punctuality and purpose. Thus, what Riney terms "the tyranny of the bell" and the sound of the steam whistle governed the typical day.[77] The 1921–1922 school year at Pueblo Bonito featured a daily program representative of the era:

Morning:

4:30–5:30	Fires to be started in the School Bldg, the Employees' Club Kitchen, School Kitchen, and furnace by Night Watchman
5:30	Fires started by the boys detailed to Homes, 1, 3, 5, 2, 4, Hospital, and Industrial Bldg.

5:45	Rising Bell, Reveille
6:00	Setting-up Exercises
6:25	Assembly and Roll Call
6:30	Breakfast in the Dining Hall
7:00	Care of rooms, bed, and house work
7:30	Assembly for Details—Bell Call—
7:45	Sick Call and Clinic at the Hospital
8:00	Recall boys from Physical Exercise
8:20	First Call for Academic Division
8:30	Assembly. School Academic work begins.
8:30–11:30	Applications in Industrial Departments
10:00–10:15	Recess at school
11:30	Recall from classrooms
11:30	Industrial Departments close (whistle)
11:50	Assembly, Mess Call
12:00	Dinner bell

Afternoon:

12:55	First work call
1:00	Assembly for School
1:00	Work begins in Industrial Departments (whistle)
2:30–2:45	Recess at School
4:00	Recall bell Academic Department
4:00–5:00	Physical Training for girls Academic Division
5:00	Recall signal from industrial departments
5:25	Assembly, Mess call, Flag Salute, Roll call
5:30	Supper bell

Evenings

6:00–6:50	Free play time
6:55	Call to quarters, little folks
7:00	Roll call in all dormitories
8:30	Taps
9:00	Taps (Party nights and special occasions)

Sunday Program:
Morning:

5:45	Rising Bell and first call
6:20	Mess Call
6:30	Assembly and roll call (Salute to flag)
8:30	Assembly call for inspection of quarters
9:30	First call for regimental inspection
9:45	Regimental inspection
10:00	Sunday School. (Assembly Hall)
11:50	Mess Call

Afternoon:

Games Strolls, rest and quiet.

Evening:

5:30	Supper
6:50	Chapel Call.
8:00	Call to quarters
8:30	Taps[78]

In such a highly regimented environment Diné students longed for a life less blessed with bells and with more opportunity for activities of their own choosing.

Those who attended off-reservation boarding schools also contended with a heightened sense of homesickness because they could be gone for years at a time. "It has been two years since I came back and I would like to come home this summer," requested Katherine Atencia.[79] Alice Becenti said, "I want to go home and get well. I am asking this with my tears."[80] Having a sibling attending the same school helped reduce that longing. Lilly Julian wrote from Sherman Institute: "I like this school very much and I want my sister to come to school if I can get her."[81]

Letters from students attending such schools reflect several other concerns. Students inquired about how various family members were doing, often worrying about their health. They also often commented on their own struggles to stay healthy. "I always have to be sick," wrote Alice Becenti. "Last year I was sick all summer. This year again."[82] And they were always short of money. Although some of these concerns are typical student concerns of any era, they should be understood in the context of their society and of the boarding schools. Students who addressed such matters were not whining about conditions at exclusive prep schools. As the Pueblo Bonito schedule makes evident, they were trying to do the best they could under the most difficult and regimented of circumstances. Even as they faced the problems of health and homesickness, they projected an air of steadfastness, as if to say: "Don't worry about me even though there are reasons to worry about me. I am fine. I will make it." John Charles said he was "trying my best to learn all I can while I am at Haskell."[83] Grace Padilla professed, "Yes, I hope I will make a better girl."[84]

The messages and letters sent to these students sounded consistent themes. Students were advised not to worry about their families, to remain in school, and to recognize that a better future could only be obtained through education. The authors of such epistles may have wished to sound firm, but they appear as cold and unyielding dismissals, often lacking in sensitivity. Students could learn about tragedies in their families by means of a terse letter that conveyed no sense of sympathy or regret. The entire text of one such letter, from Stacher to Eske Pahe, a student at the Albuquerque Indian School read:

Dear Sir: Your father Hosteen Beal, wishes me to advise you that your oldest sister died last week. Her name is Eske Despah, wife of Sloppy. The rest of the family is well, and her father is here to attend the Yabechi dance. Please write your father, Hosteen Beal as he is anxious to hear from you. I hope you are getting along fine in school."[85]

When they needed to transfer from a reservation school to attend the higher grades only offered off the reservation, candid assessments from their past principal accompanied them. The following quotations in a letter to the Albuquerque superintendent in 1916 illustrated how varied these judgments could be: "to[o] nice a girl to while her life away in a hogan"; "she is ambitious and wishes to further prepare for the battle of life"; "has been rather wild and has been a rover and rather worthless but wants to go to school"; "has lived with two women since he left school but says he wants to go to school and learn things that will help him to do something worth while. Says he wants to be a good man."[86]

Additional options began to appear closer to home. The Navajo Methodist Mission School began with thirteen students in 1899. First located in Hogback, twenty miles west of Farmington, by 1912 it had relocated to Farmington to a site it would occupy for many years.[87] St. Michael's Indian School opened its doors in 1902 with twenty-one Navajo students who ranged in age from eight to twelve. Anselm Weber traveled to many parts of the reservation to recruit students as well as to gain permission from parents to provide religious instruction to children attending government boarding schools. St. Michaels placed a strong emphasis on music and the arts.[88] "We have a literary society and every month we have a little play," Gertrude Lynch noted in 1915. These "help us learn the English language better, as we talk in English every day but it is quite hard."[89] In Ganado, the Presbyterians initiated classes in a missionary's home in 1902 and started regular classes at Ganado Mission in 1906. Near Gallup the Christian Reformed Church established Rehoboth Mission in 1898, with six Navajo children enrolling in the school when it opened in 1903. By the time Carl Gorman enrolled in the first decade of the twentieth century, the school's enrollment had grown and there were six or seven teachers. Some students would remember them as strict; Carl Gorman recalled them being "as mean as scorpions."[90] Since public schools did not begin on the reservation until the 1950s, these four schools were all the more important during the first half of the twentieth century. Students' memories of the mission schools were not always happy, as Gorman's experience so graphically illustrates. Yet others had more positive recollections and there were families for whom going to one of these schools became a pattern followed by one generation after another.

The end of the school year was a day enthusiastically anticipated by students, teachers, and staff. Many students had been counting the days. "There are only nine more weeks till vacation," one St. Michaels student wrote in 1915.[91] The schools tried to finish with a flourish, often featuring athletic competition, musical performances, and other activities. Often an individual school would simply conduct its own program, but as more schools began to operate and roads began slowly to improve, students from several schools could gather. The closing program of the 1922–1923 school year at the Fort Defiance school, for example, included two days, June 7 and June 8, filled with basketball, baseball, band concerts, an "operetta," and a recitation and vocal contests for students from Fort Defiance, St. Michaels, Chinle, Crownpoint, and Tohatchi. Employees from St. Michaels took on Fort Defiance employees in a baseball game. The schools exhibited their best work from academic and industrial classes. Those who remained at or returned to Fort Defiance on June 9 had the opportunity to see a motion picture, *Suds,* starring Mary Pickford, with music between reels by the Fort Defiance Glee Club.[92] Regardless of such finales, more than a few students in any given year had already decided not to return. The St. Michaels student who had been counting the days had actually written a longer sentence: "There are only nine weeks till vacation and then I am not coming back any more."[93]

GAMES AND FAIRS

In the midst of difficult economic times and all the demands of an assimilationist era, Navajos continued to emphasize community. The ability of the Diné to incorporate ideas or institutions initially imposed from the outside could be witnessed in such activities as baseball and rodeo as well as the early fairs. The importance of doing something well and of competing well against others may be seen in the arena of athletic competition.

At this time baseball truly did live up to its name as the national pastime. Although it did not become incorporated into Navajo life in the manner of rodeo or, later, basketball, baseball did matter to a number of the Diné. The Franciscans clearly liked baseball, for St. Michaels embraced the sport in the early 1900s. "We are playing base ball every day," wrote Patrick Dinéaltsini in April 1915. "The big boys lost one game and beat the Fort boys one game." Like other communities in early twentieth-century America, St. Michaels also recruited outsiders to play for its community team, especially if they could pitch. In 1921, for example, the St. Michaels Ball Team, as it called itself, carried on a spirited rivalry with the Gallup City Team. The two teams had already played each other fifteen times by early June, with St. Michaels winning thirteen of the games. But Samuel E. Day, Jr., of the St. Michaels team was concerned about an improving Gallup team and asked Father Leopold Ostermann in Chinle to see if Harry Price would be available to pitch in an upcoming game. Ostermann tracked down Price, who initially "seemed somewhat disinclined to go," as "he had not yet done his planting and had other work on hand besides." However, "after some talking, he reconsidered."

This pleased Ostermann, who reaffirmed his wish "to see your team as strong as possible, and the Gallup team get properly walloped."[94]

Agents and superintendents started versions of the county fair on various reservations as a means to encourage Indian farming and to publicize Native productivity. Cato Sells also pushed for Indian exhibits to be entered in county and state fairs. By 1916, Sells observed gleefully: "A large number of prizes were won by Indians on agricultural products in open competition with the exhibits of white farmers, which is gratifying evidence that our work in behalf of the industrial uplift of the Indians is accomplishing substantial and permanent results." Sells ordered the fairs limited to three days, prohibited "the old-time dances entirely," and restricted horse races to two per day. "If evening entertainment is thought advisable," the commissioner added, "stereopticon talks on suitable topics, band concerts, etc., might be arranged. In this connection, representatives from the State Agricultural College were present at a number of the fairs the past season and delivered instructive addresses to the Indians." He added, "Superintendents should endeavor to make these addresses a regular feature of the fair each year."[96] If federal employees happily envisioned a procession of potatoes and uplifting lectures on lettuce, the enthusiasm by Indians accelerated when they realized that horses as well as horticulture could be featured at fairs. In time, Indian fairs included not only agricultural exhibits but rodeos and horse races as well; in time Native people rather than the local superintendent ran the fairs.

William Shelton initiated the first regional fair at Shiprock in 1909. His autocratic approach did not endear him to the traders any more than it did to other groups. An incident at the 1911 fair nearly put an end to this fledgling enterprise. H. B. Noel, the founder of the trading post at Teec Nos Pos, remembered that the weather had not been good prior to the fair. There had been quite a bit of rain that year in mid-October, but it did not deter the traders who "brought the best of their blankets and silverwork, camping on the river bottom among the cottonwoods just east of the old wooden bridge. The exhibit booths were set up in a large rectangle, on slightly higher ground, where the agency buildings are located today." That night the San Juan River rose and the traders relocated to the hill near Bruce Barnard's post. "In the morning," Noel recalled, "I went down to the exhibit grounds where my horses were tied and found them in water up to their backs, stretching their necks up to keep from drowning."[96]

The traders, not surprisingly, wanted to move their exhibits, but Shelton commanded them to stay where they were. Noel became just a little anxious; he had brought along $5,000 worth of blankets and silverwork. Later in the morning, Harry Baldwin called from the Hogback Trading Post, eight miles upriver. He passed along a bit of rather useful information. The river was cresting, Baldwin informed them, and regardless of what Shelton said, the traders had better retrieve their goods without delay. Shelton, rather predictably, still did not want the traders to move. The traders defied the superintendent and moved all of their materials to higher ground. Then, Noel remembered, "The river crest hit Shiprock a few hours later, swept away the San Juan bridge and exhibit booths, and filled the bottomland to the eaves of the houses. It was the worst flood in the valley's history."[97]

So, the Shiprock Fair experienced a somewhat inauspicious chapter in its early history. The fair was not held from 1915 to 1918, but then Shelton's successor, Evan Estep, helped revive it in 1919. Samuel Stacher established the Eastern Navajo Fair, which started in 1916. The first Navajo fairs featured competition in regard to "farm and garden products" (oats, alfalfa, corn, cabbage, potatoes, beans, onions, squash, or pumpkin), sheep (Cotswold ram, Merino ram, Persian Merino ram, improved ewes, improved lambs), cattle (yearling steer, milk cow, calf, range cow), horses (team, draft mare, sucking colt, yearling colt, saddle horse), and poultry (rooster, hens, pullets, gobbler, and turkey hen).[98]

"Native art and other handicraft" offered another highlight. Entrants sought to present the best blanket, saddle blanket, moccasins, hat band, woven sash, Germantown blanket, braided bridle and reins, string of turquoise beads, braided lariat rope, set of six teaspoons, silver-mounted bridle, string of silver beads with crescent pendant (the squash blossom necklace), string of coral or red beads, silverware, and wedding basket.

The chicken pull, forerunner of Navajo rodeo. Photograph
by Leo Crane. Mary Riordan and Robert Chambers Collection,
Arizona Historical Society, Flagstaff. Neg. no. AHS.0020.00200

Traders seized this opportunity to showcase the latest work from their areas. At the 1920 Shiprock Fair, for example, more than four hundred rugs were displayed.[99]

Prizes also were awarded for the "best dressed and cleanest" man and woman in the parade, and the "best looking, cleanest, and best dressed" baby, and boy and girl, two to eight years old (part of the "well baby" campaign orchestrated from Washington). Schools competed in classroom exhibits, with categories such as "best general display," "best general school industrial exhibit," and best display of sewing, laundry, and fancy work. Cooking and baking categories encompassed best loaf of wheat bread, loaf of cornbread, layer cake, "6 gems," baking-powder biscuits, pie, and half-dozen doughnuts. Finally, schoolgirls competed to see who had produced the best blanket. The prizes included agricultural tools and cash for entrants in farm and ranch categories. Depending on the category, winners in Native art and other handicrafts could take home a post-hole augur, a Dutch oven, an axe, a hayfork, a currycomb and brush, or cash. A washboard and tub or washing machine awaited victors in the competitions for laundry.

"Field sports" leavened each day of the fair. On the first day of the fair in Crownpoint in 1916, competitions included a hundred-yard dash, sack race for boys, three-legged race, tug-of-war (ten men on a side), standing broad jump, half-mile horse race, and chicken pull (where men on horseback raced by and pulled a chicken from the dirt). The tug-of-war, horse race, and chicken pull took place again on the second day, along with a half-mile run, high jump, running broad jump, horse-harnessing and hitching-up contest, and greased pole. The third day was limited to the chicken pull and a relay race, where entrants changed horses and saddles four times. For these events, cash prizes were awarded, with the first-place winner gaining from $1 up to $10 for the relay race.[100]

Stacher chaired the Eastern Navajo Fair committee, but Platero, Juan Etcitty, Sam Grey, Werito Jesus, Hoska Woods, and Heschessi served as vice presidents and as judges for farm, stock, and handicraft exhibits. J. C. Morgan helped evaluate industrial school exhibits. White judges predominated at the first fairs, but Navajos participated as well. Approximately 2,500 people attended the first two fairs at Crownpoint, and about 4,000 people came to the Shiprock Fair in 1920.[101] Navajo Nation residents and residents from reservation border towns, such as Gallup, Flagstaff, and Farmington, enjoyed these occasions. A photograph taken at one of the first Eastern Navajo fairs shows an absolute sea of hats, as people mill around in a considerable crowd. Superintendents worked hard to publicize these events, sending posters and writing letters encouraging attendance. "You, your friends, and your Indians are cordially invited to be with us and take part," Shelton wrote to Stacher in the fall of 1914.[102] Given the amount of work, Stacher recommended that the agency fairs be halted and a central fair be established.[103] Although that idea did not win acceptance, the appeal of the fairs did help to encourage the establishment of the Gallup

There is always competition in Navajo society, even between
mules and horses. Photograph by Leo Crane. Philip Johnston
Collection, Special Collections, Cline Library, Northern
Arizona University, Flagstaff. Neg. no. NAU.PH.413.4

Inter-Tribal Ceremonial in 1922 and the Navajo Tribal Fair in 1937. The
Diné did not see the patronizing correspondence of federal officials and
employees. They appreciated in their own terms the value of such gatherings. In time they made the fairs, too, their own.[104]

WEAVERS AND TRADERS

By the time of the first fairs, Navajo weaving was already well into a particularly rich period of invention, adaptation, and revitalization. Weavers
created extraordinary new work. At the turn of the century, "Oriental"
rugs had become enormously popular in the United States. Traders, such
as John Moore of Crystal—better known as J. B. Moore—played a pivotal
role in introducing design elements of weavings from the area of the
Caucasus into rugs woven by the Diné. As with the case of the squash
blossom necklace, the source of the initial inspiration soon ceased to matter. Marian E. Rodee notes that weavers from the two regions "used similar looms and techniques." She adds, "It is not surprising, that similar
patterns emerged—for example, the serrated diamonds are common to
both cultures. Moreover, the bold angular patterns, in both knotted pile
and flat woven techniques, would have been relatively easy for Navajo
weavers to understand, interpret, and adapt."[105]

Navajo weavers at Crystal, Two Grey Hills-Toadlena, and Teec Nos Pos all quickly fashioned rugs bearing the unmistakable stamp of their own creativity and, at times, genius. Ed Davies at Two Grey Hills and George Bloomfield in neighboring Toadlena both took over their respective posts in 1912 and labored to market what became known as the Two Grey Hills rug, even if Toadlena actually was the heart of the weaving area. As Rodee observes, "Because of their stylistic similarity, a connection seems probable between early Crystal rugs and those from Two Grey Hills." The border, the use of hooks, and a central medallion combined with "floating motifs" form a look that has had lasting appeal. Two Grey Hills rugs began to be known and prized for their technical refinement, with impressive weft counts that evidenced a particularly tight weave. H. B. Noel built the post at Teec Nos Pos in 1905. The Teec style also was influenced by "Oriental" patterns and included a wide border; Teec rugs used aniline-dyed, handspun yarn.[106]

"Yei," "yeibichai," and sandpainting rugs first made an appearance during these years. A trader from Gallegos Canyon, Dick Simpson, promoted weavings that included ceremonial figures. These textiles were controversial. Many Navajos disapproved of preserving ceremonial images from sandpaintings, customarily destroyed at the ceremony's end. The commercial appeal of the rugs could not be denied, however, and that value helped reduce friction, although it did not eliminate it altogether. The Lukachukai and Shiprock areas became important centers for the creation of yei rugs.[107]

Marketing, of course, was of central importance during this period of transition from blanket to rug. Moore certainly ranked as a master in this regard. His colorful and engaging catalogs from the Crystal trading post in 1903 and 1911 gained enormous circulation and helped boost regional and national interest in Navajo weaving. Moore also pioneered the idea of identifying the individual weaver of a particular rug. This practice not only gave credit and recognition to an outstanding artist but also helped increase the prices that a Daisy Taugelchee or Bessie Many Goats (two Toadlena weavers of the next generation) could command. Moore stood out for his influence over each stage of the overall weaving process. He did not hesitate to tell weavers what to do, how to do it, or when to do it. He could be criticized for being heavy-handed, but he also helped weavers achieve unparalleled results.[108]

If imitation is a form of flattery, then Navajo weaving began to receive perverse compliments early in the twentieth century. J. Capps and Sons of Jacksonville, Illinois, started to produce and market what they termed "Indian blankets." Capps shamelessly blended the vanishing Indian theme with stereotypes of the romantic Indian, partaking of the old American tendency to place an image from one people into the land of another Native community, and the ability of modern technology to create a superior product. "Are You Romantic?" their advertisements asked.

a hasty departure. J. B. and Marion Moore turned over the post to their clerk and left Crystal, never to return.

OIL AND THE NAVAJO TRIBAL COUNCIL

Albert Bacon Fall chewed cigars, did not like the presence of the federal government in the West, and held American Indians in something other than high regard. He was, therefore, the ideal person to become secretary of the interior during the administration of Warren G. Harding. Fall had figured out why Texas was wealthy and New Mexico poor; Texas had little federal land and New Mexico had a lot of it. He had no patience with environmentalist perspectives. "I stand for opening up every resource," he said.[118]

Fall had his detractors, but some Navajos were willing to try out some of his development schemes. The Diné were poor and the United States needed oil. Commissioner of Indian Affairs Charles Burke assisted oil companies in their quest for oil on Indian lands. Midwest Refining Company, Western States Oil and Gas, E. T. Williams, and Kinney Oil and Gas surveyed Navajo lands and sought permission from the Diné to proceed, but at this time no reservation-wide council existed to approve or disapprove this kind of development. After a council of San Juan area Navajos rejected applications, Burke demanded that Superintendent Estep convene another council. This time, after extended discussion, Midwest Refining Company won a 4,800-acre lease. Dissatisfied, other companies kept pounding on the Diné door. Burke once again insisted that Estep call another council, which once again turned down additional exploration. Eventually, in September 1922, a final San Juan council approved a lease for Producers and Refiners Company at Tocito, twenty-five miles south of Hogback, but the Department of the Interior decided not to approve it because of concerns over drilling in this area.[119]

In the fall of 1922, the Department of the Interior decided that any oil and gas royalties, bonuses, and rentals from any part of the Navajo reservation belonged to all Diné, not just to the Diné in the immediate vicinity. This conclusion mirrored Dodge's views but ran contrary to the perspective of Jacob Morgan. In the meantime, pressure had been building for development within the Southern Navajo agency area. Chee Dodge, Charlie Mitchell, and Dugal Chee Bekiss formed a business council to consider future applications. According to Kathleen Chamberlain, Dodge "believed all Navajos should share royalties, and everyone, not just the San Juan Navajos—should approve leases. Conversely, pro-oil Navajos in the San Juan area claimed that consent and revenues belonged solely to them."[120] This business council really could not represent all Navajos; a larger and more fully representative council still had to be created. In the meantime, an oil strike by the Midwest Company at Hogback increased pressure for further development.[121]

Fall turned to Herbert J. Hagerman, a former New Mexico territorial governor, to become a special commissioner, charged with the responsibility of negotiating with the Diné. Anxious to expedite oil development, Fall also created a Navajo tribal council that would represent the entire reservation and, he assumed, dutifully sign off on leases brought before it. The appointment of Hagerman did not win universal applause from the Diné. Jacob Morgan and others from the greater Shiprock area opposed the appointment.[122] By contrast, Chee Dodge supported the choice. On March 2, 1923, he wrote to Burke to assure him that most Navajos supported the appointment: "[W]ith the exception of a few misguided Navajos in the immediate oil section of the Shiprock jurisdiction, all the Navajos feel that this appointment is a great boon for them and that it is the only move on the part of the Government which will safeguard the rights of the Navajo tribe as a whole." Dodge blamed the opposition from Shiprock on the influence of "some interested Whites whose plans of grabbing the best leases for little or nothing have been overthrown by this recent appointment."[123]

By the time the Navajo Tribal Council met in Toadlena on June 7, 1923, Albert Fall had been forced out as secretary of the interior. Hagerman had already demonstrated his independence by refusing to go along with Fall's shameless suggestion that the entire reservation be leased for oil exploration and development to one company, Midwest, which just happened to be headed by one of Fall's old pals. Fall's replacement, the Postmaster General Hubert Work, asked Hagerman to stay on in his position. Hagerman worked with the various agency superintendents to fashion the Tribal Council. The council would consist of twelve delegates, divided by agency based on population. Navajo (Southern) claimed four delegates, San Juan (Northern) three, Western two, Pueblo Bonito (Eastern) one, Leupp one, and Moqui one. Chee Dodge became the first chairman; the first delegates were Robert Martin, Deshna Clah Cheschillige, Jacob C. Morgan, Todechene Bardony, Hosteen Usahelin, Louis Watchman, George Bancroft, Zagenitzo, Hosteen Begoiden Bega, Hosteen Nez, Becenti Bega, and Hosteen Yazzie Jesus. Frank Walker and Morgan served as interpreters.[124]

In some ways, the powers of the first Tribal Council were very limited. It could only meet at the request of Hagerman, and Hagerman had to be present when it met. It is likely that the various superintendents had more than a little to say about who became a Council delegate. It is certainly fair to conclude that the Council was created not to protect or to assert Navajo sovereignty, but to provide a stamp to approve leases and other forms of exploitation. Nevertheless, the creation of the Council is a significant landmark—not so much for what the Council did as for what it would become. The first meeting constituted another important landmark—not so much for the decisions made as for the potential for assertion that resided just beneath the contemporary political surface.[125]

Like the 1911 Shiprock Fair, the Navajo Tribal Council may have initially appeared to be a washout. Organized and manipulated by outsiders, it struggled to find its own identity and to believe in its own voice. At the same time, its membership consisted of some of the strongest political forces in Diné Bikéyah. In addition to Dodge, two other men—Deschne Clahchillesge and Jacob Morgan—later served as chairmen of the Navajo Nation. Others, such as Robert Martin, would become active participants in the workings of the Council. Despite its limitations, the Council represented a vital step toward a more cohesive approach to Navajo issues, a centralized authority that could examine the larger picture and consider how developments in one area might affect all the Diné.[126] Dodge had written to Cato Sells in 1918 that all Navajos could make "equal progress, but I am sure that is only possible if we have one man at the head of the tribe, an active, strong, energetic, and capable man. Then the whole tribe would advance as one unit."[127] Although Dodge does not go so far as to describe himself as active, strong, energetic, and capable, it is reasonable to conclude that he is not talking about Jacob Morgan. Atsidi Nez of Crownpoint had expressed a similar view in 1920. "All the Navahos in every direction want to have but one boss, and him located at Ft. Defiance," he wrote to Anselm Weber.[128]

At the first meeting of the Navajo Tribal Council, the delegates considered a proposal by Acting Commissioner E. B. Meritt. This proposal gave Commissioner Hagerman the power of attorney "to sign on behalf of the Navajo Indians all oil and gas leases which may be granted covering tracts on the treaty part of the reservation." This power remained the commissioner's until the tribe eventually rescinded this authority. The Council voted for this measure for the same reason it would vote for controversial proposals during the 1930s: The Council had been promised an expansion of the reservation if it would go along with this notion.[129]

In the small community of Toadlena something important had happened. However small that first step, a new journey had begun for the Diné. As Robert W. Young notes, the Council was not a governing body. On the other hand, "it did bring together a group of influential men from all parts of the Navajo Country, and it did provide a forum for discussion of matters of tribal, rather than local, interest." Young concludes, "The annual meetings were perhaps too brief, and Federal officials utilized a disproportionately large share of the available time."[130] Nevertheless, Diné delegates began to demonstrate an interest in central questions that faced the people. They began, in many instances, to take a broader view of particular concerns. They began to see how the Council eventually might become a vehicle to express their views and to work for the benefit of all Diné. They began to realize that ambitious and regional division could prove divisive.

During the half-century prior to 1923, American Indians lost two out of every three acres of land they possessed. They were harassed for practicing traditional ceremonies, and were hounded into sending their children to distant schools. They struggled with hunger and with despair. They were not sure things could get much worse and it appeared that it would be a long time before they got better. Although less affected than those Indian communities who lost most or all of their land, the Navajos could understand the terrible emotions of the time. There remained land to be claimed and injustices that demanded remedy, but despite everything, they had made their way through an era of repression and fear. They had even survived a day in July 1920 that a traditional healer had identified as the moment when the world would come to an end.[131] Now, they would have to summon new courage and new determination to confront yet another man who thought he knew what was best for them. His name was John Collier.

5

"Our People Cried": 1923–1941

I think my people really got hurt by the livestock reduction program because they are really close to their animals. . . . Our people cried. My people, they cried. They thought this act was another Hwééldi, Long Walk. They asked the government, "Why are you doing this to us? What are you doing? You gave the animals for us to use, and now you are turning around and killing our livestock."

—*Marilyn Help, 2001*

MORGAN VERSUS DODGE

"I grew up in the midst of sheep herds," Buck Austin remembered. "The first things of which I became aware were my mother's and my father's flocks and herds. . . . But all these things that we once raised have been taken from us," he said. The Blind Man's Daughter added: "When I had a husband and a lot of sheep I was happy. Then when it came my sheep's turn to be acted upon, they were all driven away from me. . . . [M]y husband said, 'You people are indeed heartless. You have now killed me. You have cut off my arms. You have cut off my legs. You have taken my head off. There is nothing left for me. . . .' It wasn't long before my husband fell ill . . . and at the beginning of spring he died. These two events, the loss of my sheep and the loss of my husband, made me feel terribly unhappy. I was despondent, and I am still so today."[1]

The sweeping program of livestock reduction caused massive trauma within the Navajo world. Dan Phillips called the Collier program "something akin to the dictatorial systems of government across the sea."[2] Stock reduction influenced Diné attitudes toward not only land use, but also tribal government, education, health care, and religious observance. Nothing would ever be quite the same again. Conflicts between Chee Dodge and Jacob Morgan and their respective supporters helped shape the political agenda of the period.

Morgan strongly opposed the idea of using royalties from oil development to purchase land for Navajos in the checkerboard region. He argued that investing within the existing reservation had to take priority. Morgan contended that too much attention was being paid to obtaining more land. He said he favored "not more land, but more education and good homes for the people to live in where they can be happy." Morgan also advocated water development, more sawmills, new trachoma and tuberculosis hospitals, more physicians, better roads, "well equipped schools where useful trades and domestic could be taught," and placement of Navajo children in public schools "where they can learn twice as fast as they do in Government schools."[3]

As Morgan emerged as a prominent politician, he attracted criticism as well as attention. Opponents of Morgan complained about his off-reservation residence and his missionary activities. They chastised him for not owning any livestock and for his approach to land policy. Hola Tso and Kenneth Kirk wrote to the Farmington newspaper saying that they had heard Morgan wanted to become chairman. "We know that the majority of the Navajo people do not want him," they retorted. "We believe that the Council should be free to act for our benefit and not be influenced by any missionary."[4]

Such criticisms angered Morgan, who believed Chee Dodge was orchestrating a campaign to discredit him. Morgan did not hesitate to return the favor. He questioned Dodge's use of power and even denied that Dodge was a Navajo. In a letter to Hagerman on May 20, 1927, he charged that "Chee Dodge and his friends" were trying to "put some of the educated Navajos out of the Council." Morgan acknowledged that he worked out of Farmington but that his work took him all over the reservation, where he spent "more than three weeks out of every month." Then he went on the attack: "I am a full blood Navajo and therefore I have the right of the tribe, and to help my people in every way I can, and I do not wish to see my people to be put under the thumb of a person who is not a Navajo. Chee Dodge has been trying to make himself a kaiser and try to have an absolute power over the people."[5]

Morgan and Dodge differed on a number of important points. A member of the Christian Reformed Church, Morgan did not care for the Catholic Church or for the Native American Church. Dodge had personal and financial ties with the Franciscan Fathers and was more tolerant of the peyotists. Morgan married once; Dodge married eight women, four of them sisters. Morgan owned no livestock and had little money; Dodge was a major stock owner and the wealthiest of all Diné. More of a regionalist than a nationalist, Morgan believed that oil revenues should go to the area that produced that money; Dodge was dedicated to Navajo nationalism and sought to centralize Navajo political authority. Such contrasts explain why the two men symbolized conflicting tendencies within Navajo life and why they and their opponents clashed so bitterly over the course of a generation.

PRELUDE TO LIVESTOCK REDUCTION

Concerns about the status of the Navajo range escalated as the 1920s progressed. Observers had ample grounds to articulate their fears. A series of events prior to the actual beginning of the "Indian New Deal" clearly indicated that the federal government was preparing to launch some kind of drastic initiative to counter soil erosion on Navajo terrain. However, for the average Navajo, the rumors of catastrophic alteration to the Diné way of life remained distant and speculative. No one could quite believe or imagine that the government would suddenly impose this kind of draconian plan that would have such a devastating effect on everyday life within the Navajo Nation. As Assistant Solicitor for the Department of the Interior Felix Cohen later emphasized, no real attempt had been made to significantly curtail grazing on the reservation. "On the contrary," Cohen noted, "the chief motive of Government work with the Navajos had been to increase herds (originally introduced by the Government in an effort to turn the Navajo away from their raiding propensities), and the phenomenal increase of the Navajo herds from a few thousand head in the 1860s to over a million in 1933 is largely a consequence of the Government's own efforts." Moreover, as Cohen realized in retrospect, "no white man really knew the Navajo institutional patterns of livestock ownership and land occupancy." The situation was made all the more challenging "by the difficulty of securing good prices for the livestock the Navajos were willing to sell and the difficulty of altering a whole pattern of life based on family flocks supplying meat and wool to a tribe of weavers and meat-eaters."[6]

During the 1920s, the federal government made several attempts to reduce Navajo livestock holdings. Through a program to eradicate sheep scabies, an effort to cut the number of horses, and the introduction of supposedly better-quality sheep, Washington tried to change Diné practices and beliefs. Some of the superintendents also objected to sheep dipping and the introduction of new breeds because they believed it unnecessary and even potentially harmful. They worried that new sheep would be more susceptible to disease. The Navajos generally resisted these imposed "improvements," although they objected less strenuously to dipping sheep on the public domain if they thought their chances for greater control of the land would be enhanced. After much energy and more than a little money had been devoted to these attempts, little "progress" had been realized by decade's end. Federal officials concluded that more drastic, less voluntary action would be necessary.[7]

At the same time, Navajo hopes for additional land went largely unfulfilled. Members of Navajo communities circulated petitions expressing their strong support for adding land to the reservation, but to no avail. Ninety-five Diné from the St. Michaels area, for example, sent a petition to the president of the United States in support of the drive to extend the reservation in the eastern Navajo country. The petition argued that "this extension is necessary for us that we may continue to make progress."[8] However, unyielding opposition by Anglo stock growers doomed efforts to increase the reservation land base. McKinley and San Juan county ranchers continued to circulate the same petitions. Superintendent Stacher informed Special Commissioner Hagerman in 1924 that "Governor Hinkle is unalterably opposed to the extension of the Navajo reservation and will not listen to any argument, no matter how just or plausible it may be."[9]

The lack of sufficient grazing posed problems on all borders of Navajo country. After an extended consideration of the matter, additions were made to the Navajo land base in Arizona and Utah. Areas around Lupton, Dilkon, and Cameron became part of the reservation in Arizona in 1934, while the "Paiute Strip" and additional land near Aneth were stitched to the reservation in Utah earlier in the 1930s. The Arizona additions heightened existing tensions between the Navajos and the Hopis. In 1926, for example, C. I. Walker, superintendent for the Western Navajo Agency in Tuba City, reported increasing friction between the Diné and the Hopis in his jurisdiction. The proximity of the Hopi village of Moenkopi to Tuba City presented a problem. With the continuing growth in the livestock holdings by both peoples, Walker noted, "there isn't sufficient grazing land for all." He added, "We have tried to settle arguments amicably, but it appears that neither side can be satisfied." The prescient superintendent concluded that the matter was "likely to be one of long standing." Without definite boundary lines, he noted, "disputes will come up from time to time and bring about serious trouble later."[10]

The Hopis vigorously campaigned for extension of their own lands, which would have had the effect of evicting thousands of Diné. At a Congressional hearing in 1932, Senator Carl Hayden asked what should be done with the approximately twelve thousand Navajos whom the Hopis wanted to force off lands they had occupied for an extended period of time. Hopi statements reflected early mastery of the "small, peaceful, settled, hard working Hopi versus the large, aggressive, nomadic, lazy Navajo" theme. Chief Saloftoche replied, "Clear them out to whatever territory you lay aside for them because we cannot breed right here in that little hole there with our stock, cattle, and farm in the district here. There is Navajos here, and there are Navajos on this side and all around." Otto Lomavitu of Oraibi read a prepared statement in which he maligned the neighboring Navajos. The government needed to find other land for the Diné. Lomavitu appeared unlikely to emerge as a cultural broker between the two communities or as an advocate of short sentences. He asserted, "It is more than we can bear . . . to have these indolent and lazy people come prowling and congregating around our choice fields when we of miniature stature have stood the brunt of sandstorms, cutworms, drought, and burning sun with aching and blistered backs to nurse one stalk of corn to maturity in this desert waste while these tall and muscular people have spent time in visiting hogans, their groups of wives (for the Government does not seem to mind that these people live in polygamy), and gambling while feasting at their host's expense having forced their infant children no sooner out of the cradle to tend their sheep and cattle while their women weave rugs to support their men."[11]

The federal government began to employ a kind of carrot-and-stick approach in its dealings with the Diné on the land question. It exploited the Diné's need for more land in order to gain backing for more extensive efforts to reduce livestock holdings. Federal officials started to say, in essence, we will try to get the land, but the price you must pay for our campaign is to go along with stock reduction. News of this arm-twisting did not go much beyond the members of the fledgling Tribal Council. Knowing how wildly unpopular any attempt at reducing livestock numbers would be among their constituents, Council delegates made a logical, politically expedient decision. They decided to say little, if anything, to the people about these strange new demands coming from Washington. In the short term, it did not matter. In the longer term, it meant that the Diné were not prepared in any way for the more intrusive, more sweeping attempts at livestock reduction that would be imposed in the following decade.[12]

Although the government sought to expand the Navajo reservation, it also transformed the Canyon de Chelly area into a national monument in 1931. The lands within the monument remained Navajo land, but the existence of the monument drew tourists who, initially at least, seemed far more trouble than they were worth. It also meant potential trouble, when park superintendents did not fully recognize that there were limits to their authority.

Charlotte Frisbie notes that the Navajos did express approval of the notion at a Tribal Council meeting held at Fort Wingate in 1925, but later there was considerable local concern about the boundaries and about grazing rights in the vicinity. The designation encouraged more outsiders to come to Canyon de Chelly and Canyon del Muerto. These individuals might purchase a rug or a necklace, but their presence disrupted the flow of everyday life and endangered sacred sites. Subsequent federal efforts to curtail soil erosion within the monument in the 1930s prompted the planting of tamarisk in Canyon de Chelly and Canyon del Muerto. The decision did not bolster the Navajo faith in the scientific prowess of the outsiders, for the tamarisk over time proved to be an environmental disaster— becoming a kind of gigantic weed that competed for precious water resources and crowded out indigenous plants.[13]

As the government called on the Navajos to reduce their herds and flocks, it also assisted the Diné in developing new water sources for the livestock. One hundred sixty-six deep wells with pumps, windmills, and storage tanks represented a significant addition. The government also helped the Navajos take more advantage of hundreds of springs and funded the construction of twenty-one reservoirs during the 1920s. Although such assistance provided positive assistance to the livestock industry and aided the overall battle against soil erosion, it also sent a rather mixed message to the average Diné livestock owner. Why would Washington pay us to construct all these things if it really wanted us to get rid of our livestock? It did not make much sense, but then Washington did not always make sense.

Prior to the arrival of John Collier as commissioner of Indian affairs, federal observers were increasingly dissatisfied with Navajo range conditions and the reluctance of the Diné to cut back on the number of livestock they owned. The social and cultural significance of the animals worked against any significant reduction and the Navajo perspective on ownership did not coincide with that of Washington bureaucrats. In 1928, Little Silversmith explained to the ultimate D.C. bureaucrat, E. B. Meritt, that although it may have appeared that he owned two thousand sheep, this ownership actually was divided among his wife, seven children, and three grandchildren. The Council delegate thus argued that if Washington wanted to impose a tax on owning more than one thousand sheep, he would be exempt. So, for that matter, would everyone else among the Diné. Undeterred by such reasoning, Meritt lobbied vigorously for such a penalty. The seven-to-five split among Council members over a symbolic tax anticipated the kind of division that would greet subsequent proposals.[14]

Marsha Weisiger emphasizes that critics of Navajo livestock holding did not understand the priorities within Diné culture. Big herds "brought status as much as prosperity or the prospect of commercial gain," she notes. "They signified an owner's hard work, careful management, and ritual knowledge, and it was these qualities, as much as the numbers of animals themselves, that earned respect." The social obligations of wealth "helped enmesh the Diné in networks of economic reciprocity that linked spiritual life with family and kin."[15]

The Navajos only elected men to the Council during this era, but the men understood what Weisiger terms the "largely matrilineal terrain" of Diné sheep and goats. By contrast, the government men who received paychecks from Washington never appreciated the role women played in Navajo society. They underestimated the kind of social and cultural havoc that livestock reduction would create. They saw soil erosion as a practical problem, created by people (they would say "caused by man"), which people could and indeed must solve. They had no long-term grasp of local climate or indigenous tradition. Grass was grass. Sheep were sheep. Soil erosion was soil erosion. Or so they assumed.[16]

There could be no question by the dawn of the 1930s that hard times had arrived. Superintendent Stacher sent "Order No. 2" from Crownpoint on December 3, 1930, declaring, "Hard times are upon us with no work for the Indians, no market for lambs, no demand for Indian blankets or rugs which brings about a critical situation among the Indians of this tribe, and we already find it necessary to issue subsistence supplies and, in some cases, clothing to some of the families who are almost destitute."

He appealed for help in letting his office know of families who needed medical assistance or other relief.[17]

The calls continued for something to be done about the Navajo range. Foresters William Zeh and Donald Harrison completed extensive surveys in 1930 documenting damage to the land; E. A. Johnson followed with another survey in 1931. Despite the efforts made in the 1920s to improve water resources, Zeh determined that lack of sufficient water for stock "unquestionably" presented the primary reason for the current situation. More water sources had to be developed, rodents had to be controlled, and surplus horses eliminated; otherwise, the range would continue to deteriorate "rather steadily and more rapidly each year." Johnson said that everywhere he traveled in Western Navajo, he "found a deficiency or a total lack of range forage. The grass is almost entirely absent from broad areas in the vicinity of Tuba City, Gap, Cameron, and Red Lake." Moreover, "[t]he region around Cow Springs and Shonto Canyon, White Mesa, Wild Cat Peak, Red Mesa, the region north of Bodiway to Lee's Ferry and great areas near Kayenta have only a sparse covering of vegetation and there is only a fraction of the amount of forage normally present in these places."[18]

Johnson estimated the Navajos had 50 percent too much livestock, including thousands of "wild and worthless horses in excess of domestic needs." He suggested that similar conditions had developed in the past because of the combined impact of drought and overgrazing, but that the current situation must be considered a departure from prior developments. "The principal difference now," he concluded, "is that the raising of sheep, by Indians as well as others, is subject to more acute economic influences than those prevailing formerly when market requirements were less exacting, economic losses due to faulty methods of range management were less costly and less keenly felt, fewer numbers were grazed, the need of care for the condition of the range and forage was not so evident, and the preservation of future values was not so important."

Therefore, Johnson urged that immediate action be taken in regard to the "overstocked and overgrazed" land. Numbers of livestock had to be reduced "to conform to a limited forage supply." He doubted the capacity of "the Indians" to "take the necessary steps to voluntarily regulate the use of the range or adjust numbers of stock to the existing forage resources." However, the chance to establish "range control" had been heightened by the desperate nature of the current situation, even if such a program would not be greeted "with much favor."[19]

Superintendent Walker from Tuba City responded to the commissioner after Johnson's visit. He called upon the government "to compel" the Navajos "to sell off a lot of the surplus sheep and cattle."[20] By contrast, Superintendent E. R. McCray wrote to the commissioner of Indian affairs to argue against reducing the number of goats, given the goats' versatility and the Navajos' appreciation of goats' milk and meat.[21]

McCray's perspective remained an isolated one. When John Collier became commissioner of Indian affairs in 1933, he heard one main message: Act now without delay to implement a sweeping program of livestock reduction. Although Collier differed from his predecessors in his commitment to cultural pluralism, he soon demonstrated that he could act just as arbitrarily and just as forcefully. Collier and his associates saw their heavy-handed means as justified by the good ends they intended to achieve and the crisis before them. Years of bureaucratic reports suggested both the need for stock reduction and its inevitability. The superintendents had been talking about the matter for years, so some kind of major initiative would not surprise them. However, few Navajos had been a part of these conversations. It has been said that people can deal better with the unanticipated if they just have a little advance warning. Most Diné had not received any kind of alarm.

The Congressional hearings held in Navajo country in the spring of 1932 did serve notice to those who attended them, but a great many Diné never heard about the hearings, could not be present at them, or chose not to testify at them. The hearings that gave livestock interests in New Mexico a forum to express their continuing opposition also served notice that livestock interests in New Mexico remained vigilant in their opposition to any extension of the reservation. Floyd Lee of the New Mexico Woolgrowers Association reeled off the usual charges that the Navajos were unproductive ranchers who really did not need additional acreage. If the Diné received more land, he contended, they would overgraze it in the same fashion as they had with the terrain already reserved for them.[22]

Navajos in the checkerboard area agreed something had to be done, but their prescription, not surprisingly, differed from that offered by Lee. Smith Lake, New Mexico, residents decided to take matters right to the top. Even though Superintendent Stacher had tried to prevent it, they decided to bring their problems to the attention of President Herbert Hoover. Tom Ration wrote to the president and received no response. He tried again with the same absence of a reply. Ration had hoped that his ability to use the English language to communicate with others might lead to some kind of a job, but obviously his chances for employment would be improved by presidential notice. "This is the 3rd time now. So please answer this," Ration requested. He emphasized that they did not want Stacher and others to speak for them. They wanted to speak for themselves.[23]

A "PLUMED KNIGHT" BECOMES COMMISSIONER

The Navajos did not want John Collier to speak for them, either. An outsider turned insider, John Collier went from being the BIA's fiercest critic to being its boss. His success as a critic may have made him too confident about what he could achieve as a bureaucrat. If federal officials underestimated the Navajo capacity to undermine their programs, then Collier gave insufficient credit to the power of the Congress to gut his plans. Senator Dennis Chávez carried out a successful one-man crusade against additional Diné land in New Mexico; the Indian Reorganization Act eventually passed by Congress in 1934 bore relatively little resemblance to the legislation Collier had initially proposed. Fueled by a desire to turn the BIA away from the gospel of assimilation, Collier brought a unique vision to the commissioner's office. His commitment to cultural pluralism resulted in innovative approaches to education, health care, and religious worship; some positive achievements would be recorded in Navajo country during his administration. But Collier's passionate support for livestock reduction encouraged him and key administrators on the Navajo reservation to impose their will on the people. This imposition inspired an angry rejection of the stock reduction program by most Diné as well as a narrow defeat of the Indian Reorganization Act. Navajo resistance prompted violation of Diné civil rights by Bureau administrators that in some ways surpassed the worst excesses of the previous half-century.

In the end the Navajo backlash against Collier reduced gains previously achieved in education, health care, and religion, denied the people a tribal constitution, and left a bitter legacy. At the same time, somewhat paradoxically, the battles over livestock reduction and the imposition of administrative authority fostered a greater sense of Navajo nationalism. As at Fort Sumner, an increased sense of shared identity rose from the common experience of opposition. The shared sense of outrage also propelled outspoken opponents such as Jacob C. Morgan to even greater prominence on the Navajo political stage.

Diné opposition to livestock reduction stemmed in part, of course, from rejection of the basic premise that the Navajos had too much livestock. But the opposition intensified because of form as well as substance. Collier and his cohorts simply went about it the wrong way. Convinced of their correctness as well as their virtue, they moved far too quickly to impose an idea whose time had definitely not come—at least from the vantage point of most Diné. Various forces hammered on Collier to proceed precipitously: The national concern over soil erosion, concern over silt runoff that could compromise the effectiveness of the newly constructed Boulder (later Hoover) Dam, the plummeting price for wool and mutton, and Collier's own concern that overgrazing endangered the future of Navajo life all helped accelerate the process.

Collier did not believe he had the luxury of time to allow this foreign notion to percolate and brew; he opted instead for instant livestock reduction. The commissioner came to meet with the Navajo Tribal Council at Fort Wingate in the summer of 1933. The chairman of the Council, attorney Thomas Dodge, introduced him. Dodge praised Collier as "a man who had consistently raised his voice in behalf of the Indian nations" and one who "has continued to fight for the rights of the many Indian tribes." Dodge expressed his "hope and trust that at last the Indian will get not only a new deal but a new square deal." He called Collier "the 'Plumed Knight' of the Indian cause."[24]

No one had ever called Collier a plumed knight and no one ever would again. Robert Ingersoll had employed the phrase when nominating James G. Blaine as the Republican candidate for president in 1884. Blaine turned out to be something other than a knight in shining armor. Indeed, he had taken a bribe while serving in the House of Representatives. Blaine had been given $64,000 by the Union Pacific Railroad to encourage him to lobby on their behalf. He managed to fight off the allegation in 1876, using portions of documents supplied by James Mulligan, a key witness. However, eight years later copies of letters received by Mulligan were released, including one from Blaine that concluded with clear instructions that had not been followed. The postscript said: "Burn this letter." •

The "Plumed Knight" began with a tribal tribute, a flowery sentence with eleven commas that set the stage for the first part of a larger plan. "This Navajo tribe," he said, "is the one, which, among all of the large tribes, stands on its own work, supports itself, does its own thinking, and this is the tribe, this Navajo tribe, among all the other large tribes, which has shown the greatest capacity to take up new ideas, to deal with the modern world in an efficient way while at the same time remaining truly Indian and faithful to the Indian traditions and to the great Indian ideals." The federal government and the Navajos had to work together. Collier stated, "[I]t is our intention in the case of the Navajo tribe to do nothing of importance out here except in consultation with you and in line with your own expressed views and wishes. . . . There is no doubt at all that the most interesting problem in the whole Indian country is the problem which is being faced by the Navajo tribe." That problem involved how the Navajos, with an increasing population, "can remain an intact tribe, living together on a solid area of land; of how you can multiply the productivity of the land which you know and diversify your industries so that you can make one acre do the work that five acres once did."[25]

To demonstrate the capacity of the land to regenerate, the commissioner proposed a soil conservation demonstration project near Mexican Springs, New Mexico. He hastily assured his listeners that "there is not going to be any loss on the part of the families occupying that area" and that "no step will be taken except with complete consent not only of the Tribal Council but of the local chapter and the families on the land in question." Of course, Collier knew that the government was poised to proceed with or without Navajo approval and he knew the Council members knew it, too. The Diné response revealed something other than overwhelming enthusiasm for the scheme. Albert G. Sandoval suggested that the idea "be laid aside and let us hold a recess on it because there is going to be a lot of confusion among the spectators if we act on it at once." He added that he favored a recess because "it seems to be the nature of the Navajo tribe that he is always suspicious. No matter if a man is going to save him he is always suspicious that he is going to kill him." However, on the second day of its two-day meeting, the Council acceded to Collier's request and approved the station at Mexican Springs.[26]

COLLIER IMPOSES STOCK REDUCTION

From October 30 to November 1, 1933, Collier met with the Navajo Tribal Council in Tuba City to present the first stage of his program for livestock reduction. Before Collier assumed center stage, Tom Dodge addressed several matters, including what he termed "erosion control." He spoke straightforwardly and with considerable candor. "I know from my own observation that the reservation as a whole is very much over-grazed," the chairman stated. "We Navajos should organize in some way or other to at least stop the process of erosion," he continued. "We ourselves should take the lead in dealing with this question of erosion. We should not be driven to it by outside people. We ourselves should take the initiative. We should not hold back hoping that the conditions will better themselves without our help. Certainly the conditions will not be improved if we graze our sheep as we have been doing in the past." Dodge called upon "those who own livestock" to "take the lead."[27]

Dodge had opened the door to the possibility of a federal-Navajo partnership. Had Collier been astute enough to take advantage of this fleeting opportunity for genuine cooperation and a significant degree of self-determination, the course of livestock reduction might have been quite different. This process would have taken more than a little time and initially, at least, might have yielded minimal results. But in the longer term, it might have produced a very different outcome. Collier did not believe he had the luxury of allowing democracy to run its course. He slammed the door Dodge had opened by insisting upon immediate action. Immediate action meant imposition, confusion, resentment, and resistance.

Collier came away from Tuba City with what he had sought: formal Council approval to begin an initiative to reduce Diné livestock holdings. In the process he had lived up to the reputation of white men as beings who talked too long and wanted too much. Collier tended to use ten words when four would do and the transcript of any Tribal Council meeting he attended included a generous amount of testimony on his part. Moreover, Collier generally would be accompanied by other bureaucrats who also could not resist a relatively captive audience. The whispers had begun among the Navajos concerning this little white man with the glasses who kept coming out from Washington to see them. Curiosity got the best of Ben Morris. He rode all the way from Crownpoint to Tuba City just to have a look at John Collier. "He was not a very handsome white man," Morris later recalled. "[H]e was kind of skinny, he was wearing black, he stepped out of the car like a big, black crow."[28] In other words, he was not exactly a plumed knight.

In the spring of 1934, Collier journeyed again to Fort Defiance in March and Crownpoint in April to meet additionally with the Council and to gain approval for more sweeping efforts. His remarks at the Crownpoint meeting clarified the basis for immediate federal intervention. Key officials from Washington, including President Roosevelt's advisor, Rexford Tugwell, had come to Navajo country to see conditions firsthand. Tugwell had told him "unless erosion could be stopped, then the Government ought not to do anything looking toward permanence on the Navajo reservation; ought not to spend money looking to the future unless it could convince itself that erosion was going to be checked."[29]

There is no other word than blackmail for this approach. Collier's words in Crownpoint help us to understand why in the world the Council went along with this ill-fated initiative. The commissioner threw the obligatory bouquet. He said that Secretary of the Interior Harold Ickes, Secretary of Agriculture Henry Wallace, and he had "complete confidence because we know what the Navajo Indians are like. We know that the Navajo Indians are thinking people. We know that they are not in the habit of allowing anything to defeat them. We know that the Navajo Indians will take hold of their own life problems and will solve them." But without acquiescence on soil erosion, there would be no federal aid. Collier explained: "[I]f it is not going to be done, then the Government ought not spend money on other improvements. There is no use in putting two million dollars into day schools in areas which five or ten years from now, the way things are going, will be desert area and there will be no one there to occupy the schools. We are going to build these schools because we believe in the future of the Navajo country. We are going to build the roads for the same reason, and we are going to try to get you the additional needs because we believe those lands can be protected from erosion. We do not want to buy any more land to provide more silt for the Boulder Dam."[30]

The commissioner reminded the delegates that "the Government has the authority to limit the grazing, to hold it down, to put the entire force of the Federal Law back of its orders, and the orders are obeyed." However, he added, "We do not intend to issue orders to you about your range." Collier emphasized, "I think it is a matter of life or death to you. . . . [S]till we are not going to go ahead with that program except as helpers to you, helping you in the way you want us to help you, and we are not going to use compulsion on you even though it might look like we ought to." Employing words he would later regret, Collier pledged: "As long as I am Commissioner we are not going to use compulsion on the Navajo tribe." The government used compulsion, time and again. Someone should have provided clear instructions: "Burn this speech."[31]

If Collier had listened to Felix Cohen, he and the Navajos would have been spared considerable angst and agony. On June 1, 1935, Cohen furnished extended commentary on the proposed grazing regulations. He objected to cloaking the imposition of new regulations in the guise of "aiding the Indians in the management of their own affairs." Cohen believed that "[t]he 'aid' offered very much resembles that which Japanese advisers render the government of Manchukuo." The assistant solicitor stated fundamental objections to the proposed regulations: "Regulation by the Office of Indian Affairs of the number of livestock which Indians may graze upon their own lands is, I believe, unauthorized and illegal." Cohen had been "unable to discover any statutory authorization for such regulation." He added, "This is not to say that an individual has the right to do as he pleases with his land, but rather that his right is subject to *restrictions imposed by law* [Cohen's emphasis], and not to restrictions imposed by third parties without statutory authority, even if they are high officials of the Government who are much better informed than the Indians themselves about the best interest of the Indians." If federal personnel are *"inadequate for the task of education which this procedure involves,"* Cohen stressed, *"it is more obviously inadequate for the task of coercion"* (Cohen's emphasis).[32]

Cohen foresaw the problem of imposed livestock reduction: "The requirements of law, as well as sound policy," he asserted, "require that control over a matter loaded with personal and intangible values, as is the ownership of domestic animals, should not be invested in an irresponsible technical agency." He concluded, "I do not think such an agency, even if it has proper authority in the form of regulations, can actually restrict the size of a man's flock and herds which he is pasturing on his own land, except at a tremendous expense, and with an intolerable amount of snooping and a certain amount of bloodshed." Although Cohen's remarks were specifically addressed to allotted or assigned lands, he said "the same principles govern the use of tribal land by members of the tribe under common agreement or tribal custom."[33]

The idea of grazing units or districts, Cohen argued, "exemplifies professionalism run wild." It constituted part of a more general problem—that professions tended to establish technical standards "which are illicitly substituted for a standard of human welfare." Cohen believed it the "task of statesmanship to subordinate standards of technical efficiency to more comprehensive social ideals." This would be a test that Collier failed. Collier chose what Cohen termed "benevolent despotism" rather than democracy. He made that choice in the interest of quick results rather than wait for "the slower processes of democracy." In the end, Collier would lack confidence in the Navajo ability to establish "wise measures of social control to prevent the exploitation of their resources." Cohen predicted correctly that Navajos and other Indian communities would "not endure being made the nation's guinea pigs for experimentation with types of coercive control that we would not dream of applying to their white neighbors." After all, Cohen reiterated, referring to the federal initiative to reduce crop surpluses, "When the Government wants a white farmer to reduce his herds or crops, it *pays him"* (Cohen's emphasis).[34] Of course this point would not be lost on the Navajos. Roger Davis made it, for example, in an impassioned speech to the Tribal Council in 1940. How, indeed, could the federal government treat the Navajos so differently from other American farmers and ranchers?[35]

In 1934, Henry Taliman and other delegates pleaded with the commissioner for more time. He stressed things were going in the right direction. Because of hard winters, Taliman said, the number of sheep and goats in the southern Navajo jurisdiction had declined from 580,000 to 373,000. The younger generation was gaining access to the best lands and these Navajos were beginning to employ fencing. But these matters took time. "Our people back home do not know the whole situation. They do not realize. They are just so afraid that this thing is going to be carried out so they begged me especially not to accept this program until it has been considered later on." A few Navajos who lived near the agency towns could turn to wage work, but for the rest, livestock reduction spelled disaster. "Without livestock," Taliman declared, "we cannot be individuals. . . . With livestock we can make a living under the most

This delegation came to Washington, D.C. in the 1920s to protest the diversion of Navajo tribal funds by the federal government to help pay for the Lee's Ferry bridge. From left to right: Maxwell Yazzie (Tuba City), Hosteen Bikin Lichai (Indian Wells), Goldtooth (Tuba City), Deshna Clah Cheschillige (Shiprock), unidentified (perhaps Supt. Duclos, Fort Defiance), Chee Dodge (Crystal), Herbert Hagerman (special agent to the Navajos), Little Silversmith (Sanders), Samuel F. Stacher (Supt., Crownpoint), John Perry (Crownpoint), Becenti Begay (Crownpoint). Courtesy of Canyon de Chelly National Monument.

adverse circumstances." And if they could not have more time to adjust, they at least wanted more time to speak during the Council meetings. Jim Shirley of Ganado was sufficiently irritated at Collier's tendency to ramble on that he finally complained in the spring of 1934 about it. Shirley expressed the quaint idea that since this was a meeting of the Navajo Tribal Council, Navajos should do most of the talking.[36]

Collier could not be deterred. Livestock reduction became a reality. And that reality, like Fort Sumner, turned out to be even worse than the Diné could have possibly imagined. Years later, the Bureau's main administrator for the Navajo reservation, E. R. "Si" Fryer, vigorously defended the program he had overseen as of 1936. Armed with a variety of Milton "Jack" Snow photographs of the livestock and the land, he argued that despite its bad name the campaign had actually been a success. Reduced numbers of sheep, goats, horses, and cattle allowed the range to improve. Individual animals tended to weigh more. The sheep generally produced more wool. As quality improved, prices got better. When coupled with continuing improvement to water resources, more miles of fence, and other alterations, the land began to make a modest comeback. Boulder Dam continued to function, too. The dangers to its future had been exaggerated.[37]

A COLONIAL MENTALITY

Anthropologist William Y. Adams understood this mentality. In "Growing Up in Colonial Navajoland," a paper presented at a Navajo studies meeting in the early 1990s, Adams related how as a nine-year-old boy he had moved to the new community of Window Rock in 1936. His mother, Lucy W. Adams, had been named director of the consolidated Navajo, Hopi, and Southern Ute school systems for the BIA. Adams summarizes stock reduction's legacy: "Though conceived with good intentions, the program was carried out so clumsily and highhandedly as to generate a Navajo resentment that has hardly subsided to this day. The purely economic consequences of stock reduction were not as severe or as long-lasting as is sometimes claimed; when I was trading at Shonto in the 1950s, animal populations were once again at or above their pre-reduction levels. But the forcible seizure and destruction of the Navajos' sheep, without their consent, was a symbolic affront that would not soon be forgotten."[38]

Adams lived in Window Rock from 1936 to 1940, precisely at the time when emotions ran their highest in Diné Bikéyah. "Yet it is amazing to recall even now," he says, "how little most of us at the agency were affected by or even aware of developments 'out there' in the world of the hogans." Even those most directly involved in stock reduction—the range management and soil conservation people—were naively convinced that Navajo opposition was a passing thing, that the range would soon recover its productivity, and that The People would then recognize that it was all for the best." The white people in Window Rock "were a privileged ruling elite," who "never thought it necessary to ask the Navajos' permission for anything we did on anyplace we went, because we thought of the reservation as being as much ours as theirs." He concluded, "The whole colonial enterprise and mentality were underpinned by an ideology of paternalism."[39]

This colonial mentality, one that Adams aptly describes as "at once progressivist and primitivist," prevailed in the face of overwhelming evidence to the contrary. The isolation of the little BIA communities combined with a sense of privilege and mission to prevent a thorough understanding of how or why Navajos would respond as they did to the livestock reduction program. The administrators just could not imagine that ultimately the Navajos would not go along with this initiative.[40]

One of the rare examples of demonstrable concern in the Window Rock-Fort Defiance community during the 1930s had nothing to do with the trauma of livestock reduction. Rather, in a scene reminiscent of the final days of the British Empire in India, the residents circulated a memorandum to Fryer in May 1938 expressing their severe displeasure. The tennis courts, they informed him, were "in a deplorable state." The Navajo Service employees maintained a ranking board and conducted a tennis club tournament in August, so proper upkeep of the courts mattered. They cited four shocking examples of neglect:

1. There are no protecting backstops at three corners of the courts, and no side stops on each side.
2. The concrete is badly cracked and missing in many places.
3. The courts are so directionally faced that it is almost impossible to play because of the sun striking the players directly into the eyes at a time when the courts are mostly used, namely, in the evening after the dinner hour.
4. The condition of the nets which were very poor and dilapidated was remedied by the general contribution of the individuals of the Community whose private donations have enabled the purchase of new ones.

A total of forty-eight people, including several Diné, "cordially" invited Fryer's "personal inspection of the above mentioned courts."[41] Fryer's formal response is missing from the National Archives.

CARRYING OUT LIVESTOCK REDUCTION

Within Navajo country itself, concerns were of a somewhat different sort. Members of the Tribal Council, under duress, may have agreed to the principles of stock reduction, but they did not condone the way in which the program was carried out. Federal officials called community meetings to try to explain the rationale behind the program and to attempt to clarify how it would be carried out. As anthropologist Edward T. Hall later recalled in his memoir, *West of the Thirties,* the Navajos witnessed "the government in sheep's clothing." The federal officials' "logic was unassailable," Hall concluded, "provided you were used to an Aristotelian paradigm and accepted the assumptions that logic was based on." These men spoke in English and then the translators assigned to these sessions would gulp and, fearing the possibility of a riot, often would soften the blow by furnishing a vague and occasionally misleading translation. Then federal employees would come out and demand so many animals out of a flock or a herd. From the vantage point of most Navajos, these demands were capricious and arbitrary, unfair and unnecessary. Hall realized something the federal officials did not understand: "Sheep and money were not interchangeable. Sheep were not a commodity as they were for us. Each sheep was known individually. Any Navajo with a herd could tell you how many lambs each ewe had dropped and could identify every lamb's mother." Stock reduction decimated "the ongoing relationship between the herd's owner and every sheep in the herd."[42] Moreover, the Depression had not lost its grip on the interior West and market prices remained abysmally low. With no substantial market available for Navajo livestock, the federal men would seize animals, take them over a hill or down into a canyon or into a corral, and shoot them and leave them to rot.

Howard Gorman said such "incidents broke a lot of hearts of the Navajo people and left them mourning for years. They didn't like it that the sheep were killed; it was a total waste." To many Navajos, Gorman emphasized, "livestock was a necessity and meant survival. Some people consider livestock as sacred because it is life's necessity. They think of livestock as their mother." Gorman added, "The cruel way our stock was handled is something that should never have happened. The result has left the condition of the land and stock the way it is today. What John Collier did in livestock reduction is something the people will never forget."[43]

Marilyn Help explained: "I think my people really got hurt by the livestock reduction program because they are really close to their animals. . . . [T]he government came and took the cattle and the sheep and they just shot them. They threw them into a pit and burned them. They burned the carcasses. Our people cried. My people, they cried. They thought that this act was another Hwééldi, Long Walk. They asked the government, 'Why are you doing this to us? What are you doing? You gave the animals for us to use, and now you are turning around and killing our livestock.'"

Today she understands there was overgrazing, but bemoans the impact of the era on a later generation. She notes that the younger people "are not as interested as they used to be in raising animals. The older people wanted the land to raise sheep. But now, the younger generation, it seems like they don't want to herd sheep. Therefore, there is a lot less shepherding now."[44]

Navajo Tribal Council Chairman Henry Taliman and Commissioner John Collier. Photograph by Milton Snow. Courtesy of the Navajo Nation Museum, Window Rock, AZ. Catalog no. NO9-98

For the purposes of administration, the government divided the Navajo and Hopi lands into eighteen land management districts, with the Hopis occupying district six. Within each of these districts, federal officials ascertained what they deemed the carrying capacity of the range and then tried to work toward that combination of livestock. The grazing regulations and their attendant definitions became the source of endless discussion, confusion, and debate. It all began with a sheep unit, defined as the amount of forage needed to support one sheep. A goat counted as one sheep unit, a cow counted as four sheep units, and a horse as five sheep units, much to the bewilderment and bemusement of the Navajos. A "family group" consisted of "a single home economic unit, living closely associated in one or more grouped hogans or houses, which shares its livestock and agricultural income in common and recognizes one individual as the family head." The "family head" was "the person who exercises control of a family group either because of the responsibility placed on him by blood relationship, moral or economic obligations, or otherwise." Grazing permits would be issued to family heads. The superintendent of each agency determined the total stock in sheep units. Before reduction, the "sale of non-productive, unserviceable and cull animals (including excess horses, scrub cattle, wether sheep and goats, and old ewes)" would be encouraged. The superintendent also had primary responsibility for making sure that Diné livestock were dipped annually to reduce the likelihood of contagious diseases, assessing and collecting trespass fees, and regulating the fencing of range and agricultural lands. The grazing regulations listed four objectives, including "[t]he protection of the interests of the Navajo and Hopi Indians from the encroachment of unduly aggressive and anti-social individuals who may or may not be members of the tribe." The call Dodge had issued for Navajo responsibility had been ignored. So, too, had the role of women.[45]

Collier and his colleagues paid a severe price. When the time came for the Navajos to vote on their acceptance of the Indian Reorganization Act's provisions, the matter of stock reduction centrally influenced the ultimate result. Under the terms of this legislation, Indian communities had the right to develop constitutions, were encouraged to form representative tribal councils, and had access to certain federal loans. But by the time the Diné voted in June 1935, the Diné vote had become a referendum on the current state of Navajo affairs. Morgan campaigned tirelessly against the act; Chee Dodge offered only lukewarm support. The Navajos voted 8,197 to 7,679 against being included in its provisions, with Shiprock's overwhelming vote against inclusion—2,773 to 536—making the difference. After the vote, Tom Dodge alleged that Morgan and Robert Martin told Navajos "that if they voted for the acceptance of the Act their reservation would be allotted, their sheep and goats taken away from them, and their property, tribal and individual, made subject to taxation."[46] Collier had anticipated victory; the results startled and deeply disappointed him. While it is too simple to say that livestock reduction offered a means to pay the Navajos back, it is reasonable to conclude that he never regained his earlier sympathies for the Diné.

The tribal constitution also failed to become a reality in large part because of guilt by association. The proposed constitution, according to

Scene from the livestock reduction era. Photograph by
Milton Snow. Arizona Historical Foundation, Tempe.

Robert W. Young, "was very similar" to those adopted by tribes that had
voted in favor of the Indian Reorganization Act. "Most importantly," he
states, "for the first time in the history of the Tribal Council," it "included
a statement of powers to be exercised by the Tribal Government." And
these powers were considerable. The Council would be able to "veto the
sale, encumbrance, lease or disposition of tribal lands and other assets

(including trust funds of the Tribe on deposit in the U.S. Treasury), and it could authorize mission sites on tribal lands." With the secretary of the interior's approval, the Council could do a great deal more, including the regulation of trading, collection of license fees, employment of legal counsel, the levying of taxes, the regulation of inheritance, and other centrally important matters. The Council now could meet without so much federal control staring at them. Now a federal official would not have to be present at all Council meetings and would not have to keep the minutes.[47] However, the secretary of the interior did not approve the constitution for a variety of reasons, including his concern over the opposition to it by Morgan and his allies and the consequent likelihood of long-term factionalism within the Navajo Nation. The Navajo Tribal Council instead came to operate under a series of rules and regulations.[48]

As the livestock reduction program began to be enforced, the Navajos became increasingly polarized. The anger felt by many Diné about the heavy-handed tactics of the government naturally encouraged a groundswell of popular support for Morgan and antagonism toward federal officials. Chee Dodge and Tom Dodge could not have been unhappier. Chee Dodge wrote to James Stewart of the Bureau's Land Department on April 20, 1936, to warn him to anticipate the most "serious trouble" the Diné had encountered. Dodge believed the Navajos would be best served by the removal of Fryer, Soil Conservation Service (SCS) Director W. G. McGinnies, and the SCS's chief engineer Arthur Fife. Dodge charged Fryer did not know how "to get at things" and lacked good judgment; he certainly did not seem to recognize all that the two Dodges had done to represent the Diné. McGinnies and Fife thought the Navajos did not "have any rights at all" and "continuously want to run over them."[49]

Tom Dodge felt especially betrayed by what had transpired. On May 7, 1936, he resigned his position as chairman of the Navajo Tribal Council. Dodge also had been serving as assistant superintendent under Fryer and he realized that under current circumstances he could not continue to hold both positions. His letter informing Collier of his decision furnishes a searing indictment of the "Indian New Deal." "The Navajos as a tribe have become disappointed and disillusioned by the New Deal policies applied to them," he wrote. "To them, the entire Navajo program is so complicated and involved that no amount of explanation will begin to make them see any rhyme or reason in it. This utter confusion in their minds has had the effect of convincing them that the program was purposely made complicated and involved so that they would not get wise to the plan to rob them of their resources and their livestock." Most Diné believed Fryer had been chosen as superintendent "for one purpose only and that is to completely crush the Navajos." Most Diné were so angry about livestock reduction that they were now "determined to reject the entire Navajo program."[50]

THE RISE OF JACOB C. MORGAN

For Tom Dodge, the saddest thing about recent developments was its elevation of J. C. Morgan's political prospects. Morgan and his allies, he informed Collier, had "seized this confusion as their golden opportunity, and the net result is that practically the entire tribe has joined the opposition camp with no hope of getting them back even to neutral ground." As a result, "the entire Navajo program has gone by the board as far as the tribe is concerned" and in the process, Tom Dodge's chairmanship had gone by the board, too.[51]

Jacob C. Morgan c.1940. From the Fern Morgan Collection.
Courtesy of the Farmington Museum. 1989.50.18

Dodge had written to Secretary of the Interior Harold Ickes in the summer of 1935, leaving no doubt about his estimation of Morgan and his longtime political ally Robert Martin. In Dodge's view, from the Council's first days, they had "opposed and tried to destroy everything held valuable by the people themselves." He added, "They always depended for their opposition upon misrepresentation of facts and half truths and fraud." Morgan and Martin, Dodge asserted, "can always be depended upon to represent just the opposite of anything that's true and worthwhile." He urged Ickes to remove them from the Tribal Council, but Ickes refused to do so.[52]

As Navajo resistance stiffened, federal officials' attitudes became more resentful and rigid. Morgan became the focal point for this frustration and anger, but as the movement to reject livestock reduction spread, other Diné came under increased scrutiny. More Navajos began to refuse to dip their sheep, to confront range riders, and to call for noncompliance.

Speaking to a land management conference in Flagstaff in March 1937, Fryer concluded: "The future of the Navajo is in our hands. His very economy is dependent upon our successful solution of his land problems. We believe that we have found that solution." In the past, Fryer suggested, the government had sought "the muffling of Indian complaints"; now it had developed "a constructive and aggressive policy of working out their problems in a manner most beneficial to the land and the people." He ventured an unfortunate but revealing analogy about a crying child: "Where formerly the parents placated the child with a stick of candy when it cried, now the parents are attempting to find the cause of the tears and to take such corrective measures as are necessary," even though "[t]he youngster will not always understand why a dose of castor oil may sometimes be more efficacious than a stick of candy." Fryer admitted that "[i]n all honesty, the Navajos have every reason to misunderstand land management," given an unfair prior system whereby large owners had more room to maneuver than owners of relatively few livestock. He lashed out at "the creators of misunderstanding, . . . the impassioned demagogues who, without any regard for the truth, grab the nearest soap box from which to condemn the government." Fryer charged that "[t]heir usually irrational speeches are so hidden behind bombastic oratory as to appeal to the emotional and less intelligent Indian, and are accepted in lieu of sounder, yet less spectacular ideas."[53]

Fryer and his associates were not inclined to compromise with Morgan nor go out of their way to do any favors for him. For example, when Morgan asked the government to give one of his sons a job and requested permission to use the Kirtland Day School for religious education, William W. McClellan, Shiprock area supervisor, informed Fryer he had told Morgan "we would consider these favors he was asking but thought he might reciprocate by promoting a better future in the field." McClellan said, "I am not much in favor of giving Jake any help whatever," unless he would "reciprocate." He added, "If we could get him down here where he had to herd sheep he would probably have a better attitude."[54]

A worried Henry Taliman, who had followed Marcus Kanuho, Dodge's replacement, as chairman of the Council, telegrammed Ickes on July 23, 1937, to express his concern about the current situation. Although Ickes acknowledged that Morgan "has brought about a certain amount of confusion in the eastern portions of the Reservation," he expressed his preference on August 2, 1937, "to rely upon the practical common sense of the Navajos rather than upon the compulsions of law." If Morgan and his followers became a majority, then their practice of "distorting facts" and their "impracticable" and "wild" program might evoke a different response.[55] Twelve days later, Ickes issued a public statement addressed to the Tribal Council. "A few individuals are attempting to incite" the Navajos to resist sheep dipping and "to provoke the use of violence against government employees," the secretary observed. He blamed Jacob Morgan and attorney Paul Palmer for "being chiefly responsible for the campaign of resistance."[56]

Palmer had a significant role in the livestock reduction era. A member of the Church of Jesus Christ of Latter-day Saints, Palmer was a well-known attorney in the Navajo area and county chairman for the Republican Party. He and Morgan both had offices in Farmington, New Mexico, a border town approximately thirty miles east of Shiprock. Although of different religious denominations, the two men shared the same antigovernment attitude and both detested John Collier. Fryer's status as a "jack Mormon," or nonpracticing member of Palmer's church, probably did not help matters. After one confrontation between Palmer and Fryer, Palmer penned a letter to the superintendent in which he simultaneously apologized for losing his temper and reiterated his opinion that Fryer's remarks "were untrue and uncalled for." Fryer tried to persuade church leaders to intercede and demand Palmer stop what the superintendent termed his "malicious revolutionary tactics," but apparently those efforts were fruitless.[57]

THE GOVERNMENT COUNTERATTACKS

Ickes's public statement and Fryer's maneuverings formed part of the government's counterattack against Morgan and his allies. Writing to BIA administrator Walter V. Woehlke on August 5, 1937, Fryer spoke of taking "the offensive—'and how.'" The government began to keep files on leaders of the opposition such as Morgan and Palmer. The Bureau authorized an undercover investigation of Palmer. A federal investigator posed as an investor interested in engaging Palmer's services to obtain a piece of privately held land also sought by the federal government. Palmer made a number of statements condemning the government but did not make the kind of self-incriminating statements the government had anticipated.[58]

On September 16, 1937, in a memorandum to district supervisors that he labeled "confidential" and "not for general circulation," Fryer asked that they "report immediately the existence of any evidence you learn in your district along the following lines":

1. What is being said by Morgan, Palmer, et al? Preferably all that is being said should be reported. In many cases there is no one available to make such a complete report. Therefore you should pay particular attention to false statements of existing or past facts; requests for money; statements as to why the money is being collected, and with regard to how this money will be used. Have whoever makes these reports sign them, and if possible, have them witnessed.
2. Who makes contributions; how much each Indian promises to pay; to whom it is paid; Indians who promise to make payments, and how much and when; how payments are made, that is, whether by cash or traders checks, etc.[59]

Thus, Fryer commissioned a network of reporters, or perhaps more accurately, spies, to document various community meetings and meetings of the Navajo Progressive League, an organization Morgan had established. These accounts no doubt provided helpful details to Fryer, but the process also contributed to the "us versus them" siege mentality that Window Rock had adopted. Moreover, the district supervisors knew enough to report what they assumed Fryer wanted to hear. For example, when McClellan suggested that at a July 21–22, 1938, meeting of the Navajo Progressive League "[n]othing constructive was said or done at the meeting for the good of the Navajo," Fryer assuredly felt reconfirmed about the wisdom of his decision to counterattack.[60]

On another front, Lucy Adams wrote to superintendents, school principals, SCS employees, and others requesting the names of five "most prominent anti-government leaders" in their respective areas. She also asked for information about their schooling, their age, knowledge of English, and the extent of their livestock holdings. A. G. Hutton, the superintendent at the Hopi agency in Keams Canyon, replied that he had "had practically no contacts with the Navajos in the past two years and I am unable to give you the information requested,"[61] but others had no trouble nominating a quintet. Rudolph Zweifel, an SCS employee based in Shiprock, named Slim Yabeney, Ellis Denet Sosie, Hosteen Hoshkay Benally, Natonie Pahe, and Slocum Cash.[62]

Land management district supervisors and employees furnished most of the responses. From Tohatchi, District 14 supervisor H. H. Smith listed Charles Damon, James Becenti, Clarence Denet Claw, Dewey Etsitty, and Bob Lee,[63] while his counterpart in Chinle (district 10), Willard Brimhall, thoughtfully provided five leaders in ranked order of importance: Zhealy Tso, John Gorman, Reed Winny, Notah Tayah, and Etsitty Begay.[64] District 12 supervisor, William W. McClellan, Jr., responded from

Shiprock with the names of Slim Todachine of Aneth, Aaron of Sanostee, Todachine Tso of Sheep Springs, Bob Martin of Shiprock (who, like Morgan, had attended Hampton), and James Manuelito of Newcomb.[65] M. J. Bedwell of Kayenta singled out Salt Water, Hugh Black, Slim Redhouse, Whiskey Badoni, and Lawrence Luna.[66] E. G. Stocks from Dilkon cited Murphy Spencer, George Nells, Honigothney, Begeshe Begay, and Roger Davis,[67] and William Thomason of Leupp mentioned Hosteen Tso, Hosteen Chahe, Hosteen Sonni, Charley Thompson, and Little Singer.[68] Crownpoint Boarding School principal Hugh Carroll put forth Jim Largo (Little Water), Fred Tsosie (Torreon), Eski Martin (White Horse Lake), Charley Damon, and Castiano (Pueblo Alto).[69]

These lists demonstrate that by 1938, the year Morgan achieved his goal of becoming chairman of the Navajo Tribal Council, opposition to the Collier program could be found in all sectors of Navajo society. Individuals who had received eight or ten years of schooling combined with those who had never been to school. Christians mixed with traditional ceremonial leaders. Large-scale stock owners joined with those who had only a few sheep. Present and future Tribal Council members allied with the apolitical. This diverse collection of people had been united by a common dislike for the form and the substance of livestock reduction.

Writing a personal letter to Fryer, Tom Dodge expressed his outrage at

Reading about the federal program at the
Shiprock Fair. National Archives, Seattle.

Morgan's ascendancy. "The Navajo situation has become quite critical," Dodge concluded. "The Navajo Hitler (Jake) has pulled off a coup and made a sudden conquest of the tribe. . . . Now many Navajos including those who were always known to be sound and reasonable are telling us they will not give up a single animal under the Navajo range program. . . . Some of them even go so far as to say that they will die first before any animal is taken from them." "Keep your chin up!" Fryer responded. But he also admitted that "[c]onditions on the reservation are worse than I thought. I did not realize Morgan would be able to stir up so much trouble."[70] Recognizing the need to get the message out more effectively, Fryer assigned Lucy Wilcox Adams and John C. McPhee to develop "[a] program of Education, Public Relations, Propaganda, and Publicity that will acquaint Navajo Service Personnel, Traders, Missionaries and other important groups with the total Reservation program and problem." Included in his list of suggested activities were "[b]etter use of the Tribal Fair as an educational medium," "[t]he purchase of a recording machine to record for the use of the schools and at Navajo meetings," and "[o]ffensive, rather than defensive, newspaper releases."[71]

MORGAN BECOMES CHAIRMAN

Morgan assumed the chairmanship in the fall of 1938. The consummate outsider suddenly found himself playing a very different part, and as had Collier, he found it a difficult transition. Morgan recalled the recent past in his inaugural address to members of the Council. "What I have tried to do to protect your rights and your interests in the past four years, I did not do alone," Morgan said, "but you, my Navajo people, have a large share of the credit. I am proud that in spite of much misunderstanding, confusion, disappointment and discouragement, we are still happy people and still marching on, and, my friends, we will not retreat."

Morgan called this session of the Council the first in tribal history where delegates assembled "as free and progressive people." He praised his people for being "hard workers" and "industrious." The new chairman said that it was "too bad that our sheep are causing much trouble"; however, the "tribe needs kindly encouragement rather than abuse by all kinds of threats." He added, "It must be realized that no people of any nation has ever become happy and prosperous by abuse and threats. . . . I believe I have been abused in many ways already, not because of my crimes but because I have stood for the rights of my people." Nevertheless, he professed that he had "no hard feelings against any person."[72]

Morgan served one four-year term. Defeated in 1942 by Chee Dodge, he decided not to continue an active political career. After all the emotion and clamor that preceded his chairmanship, the term seemed almost anticlimactic. Morgan came to realize as chairman the need to find what he termed "some common ground of understanding" between the Navajos and Washington. In a radio broadcast on March 7, 1939, for example, he said, "The Navajo program includes some tremendous problems. . . . These conditions cannot conscientiously be worked out to some satisfactory result overnight unless the Navajo people and the Indian Bureau employees, who are acting as the guardian, come together on a common ground of understanding." Morgan added, "A great deal of these pernicious misunderstandings would have been avoided if the rights of the Navajo had been recognized and respected. . . . I believe that in order to untangle some of the wrongs inflicted upon the happiness and dignity of the Navajo people there should be a change of attitudes on both sides."[73]

Under the rules governing Navajo elections at this time, the candidate who finished second in the balloting for Tribal Council chairman became vice chairman. This arrangement had not worked out very well when it had been tried in U.S. presidential elections, as Thomas Jefferson could attest, and it did not prove ideal in Navajo country in 1938 either. Howard Gorman had sought the chairmanship and came in second, so he had the unenviable assignment of serving as vice chair for a chairman with whom he frequently disagreed. Although Morgan preached sweetness and light at the start of his administration, he was willing to make an exception in Gorman's case, as this exchange during a May 1939 Council meeting suggests:

> Gorman: "Mr. Chairman." Morgan: "Are you a delegate?" Gorman: "I am vice chairman." Morgan: "Then you have no right to speak." Gorman: "I have every right to speak." Morgan: "According to the rules the delegates must discuss matters. I am asking them for discussion." William Goodluck: "Mr. Chairman—." Gorman: "I have the floor." Morgan: "The Chair did not recognize the Vice Chairman just now. I wish the delegates to get a chance to discuss these resolutions. I think that is only proper." Charlie Damon: "When the President of the United States is in a session of Congress, the Vice President has nothing to say. He goes fishing."[74]

The discussion continued, but Morgan never did recognize Gorman—not on that morning and not very often during his four-year term.

VIOLENT RESISTANCE

Violence flared on a number of occasions in 1940 and 1941. In Navajo Mountain, Shiprock, Aneth, Toadlena, and other locations, Navajos refused to go along with the mandates of stock reduction and for their trouble ended up spending time in the next generation's version of Shelton hotels.

Some of the activists were also federal employees. Their participation in protests angered Bureau administrators who adhered to a particular definition of loyalty. Navajo employees joined other area residents to meet with Julius Bainbridge and other Toadlena chapter officers in Shiprock on January 17, 1940, to discuss effective means of protesting current conditions. Supervisor William McClellan dutifully reported to Fryer on what he called this "outlaw meeting" and then summoned employees for another session the next day to express his displeasure. He conceded that they had "a right to attend a meeting of this sort." He emphasized, "But, when Government employees attend meetings of this kind, and vote for action to be taken against the Administration and its personnel, and make cash donations to carry on agitation work, while they are receiving their living and salary from the Government, I can see no place for them on the Government payroll. You should be 100% for whom you are working."[75]

The next week the "Shiprock uprising" erupted. People in the Shiprock area had been told to bring in their horses in December for branding. Bainbridge and other protesters urged noncompliance. They found a ready audience among the owners of sizable herds. McClellan decided to file complaints against some of those refusing to brand their horses in order to pressure them and others into following this requirement. On January 22, 1940, warrants were issued for the arrest of Fred Begay, Kitty Blackhorse, Short Hair Begay, Frank Todecheeny, Clizzie Clonie Bega, and Delewoshie.[76]

The following day Navajo judges Sam Jim and Slow Talker heard the cases of these individuals. Fred Begay and Clizzie Clonie Bega reiterated their refusal to comply with the regulations. Both were ordered to brand their horses within ten days and sentenced to six months in jail. Frank Todecheeny then indicated he would comply and was given six months probation. Kitty Blackhorse was then called. According to McClellan, "When he was asked to take the stand, he pulled off his coat, threw it down on the floor, and sat down in front of the judge and stated before the judge had time to say anything: 'I don't want to hear what you have to say, but sentence me right now.' At this point his three sons took seats along side of him, and they began calling to each of the police, who were in attendance, to handcuff them." Then the sons asked the crowd for help. "There was quite a bit of commotion," McClellan observed. "All at once a number then got up and started making speeches of all sorts." The supervisor recorded, "One asked that the supervisor be thrown out of the room at once. There was much disorder. . . ." After things quieted down the prisoners escaped and headed back to their homes.[77]

The following day, Kitty Blackhorse and his associates received instructions to return to the Shiprock Agency jail. About forty Diné marched toward the Agency buildings. McClellan stepped out and spoke to the crowd, warning them not to be "an accessory to mob rule" and reminding the prisoners to return to jail. The crowd did not budge and the prisoners refused to surrender. Federal officials took one long look at the throng and decided to postpone calling for immediate justice.[78]

Navajo dissidents continued to seek assistance from members of the U.S. House of Representatives and Senate. Scott Preston, Julius Begay, Frank

Goldtooth, and Judge Many Children wrote in 1940 to complain about Collier's failure to live up to his promises of more work to offset the costs of stock reduction. They argued that the Bureau had transformed a "self-sufficient and self-supporting" tribe to one that had "become dependent upon charity for our subsistence."[79] Deshna Clah Cheschillige sent a letter to Senator Dennis Chávez of New Mexico on December 8, 1940, to reassert Navajo grazing rights. Cheschillige helped fan the flames of resentment and resistance in northwestern New Mexico now that Morgan was perceived as part of Window Rock and therefore part of the problem, and used his considerable organizational and oratorical skills to preach noncompliance. He pledged to New Mexico senator Chávez that he and his allies would fight in "the American way for our rights." He added, "We have organized to protect our rights and to see that accused members of our tribe be given a fair trial."[80]

This organization was the Navajo Rights Association. For a one-dollar membership fee, those who joined belonged to an organization with an ambitious and wide-ranging agenda. The association pledged to work for the right of a trial by jury, for better education, range conservation, natural resource development, improved medical care, protection of personal property, "the maintenance of adequate herds from which the Navajo tribe can make a living and for the promotion of Indian crafts and arts and for protection against imitation of Navajo arts and crafts." Although the list was largely symbolic, it did clearly suggest areas of particular concern as the 1940s began.[81]

The arrival of World War II ultimately provided far more clout to the battle against livestock reduction than could any fledgling association. Yet the organization did matter as a means to express outrage and to articulate and vent the extraordinary emotions that accompanied this extraordinary time. Although it was difficult to perceive the transition at first, the tide, in fact, had started to turn in the Navajos' favor. Cohen helped bring about a change of heart in Washington's attitude by his criticism of how stock reduction had been applied to the small-scale owner. As of 1941, the Bureau decided to issue temporary permits allowing smaller livestock owners "to graze stock in excess of the number originally assigned them under the 1938 regulations."[82] The decision meant the beginning of the end for livestock reduction, an initiative that was still trying to find its way. Only the year before federal employees met in Window Rock for a planning and policy conference. Among their topics: "possible principles of livestock reduction."[83] Possible principles? The Navajos thought it a little late to be searching for them.

COMMUNITY CONCERNS

This era is noteworthy for a heightened sense of community. That sense found expression in many ways: through the newly established chapter system, through petitions and community meetings, through weaving, and through responses to schools. Opposition to the stock reduction program increased a sense of community solidarity by emphasizing a common grievance and promoting a kind of siege mentality.

Leupp Superintendent John Hunter initiated the chapter system in 1927. The chapter provided an opportunity for discussion and in some instances governance at the local level. Each chapter represented a particular, defined community. Within six years the system had become institutionalized throughout the Navajo reservation. Howard Gorman said in 1962 that Navajos thought the chapter "was a good idea for it built upon what was already present, that of organized group meetings." Chapters formalized that custom, adding officers, majority-rule voting, and a version of *Robert's Rules of Order*. Chapters quickly became a vital forum for settling local disputes over the land. Chapters could decide which individual or family had the right to graze animals within a specific area based on prior land use. Grazing permits, however, continued to be issued through the federal government.[84]

Navajo communities shared many concerns during this period and community members often circulated petitions as a way to rally support for and bring attention to particular priorities. An examination of these petitions brings out several areas of widespread interest. These included livestock reduction and land use, employment, education, roads, medical care, and personnel matters. The typed or handwritten petitions ended with

Ganado Trading Post, the base of the J. L. Hubbell empire. Photograph by Leo Crane. Leo Crane Collection, Special Collections, Cline Library, Northern Arizona University, Flagstaff. Neg. no. NAU.PH.658.976

signatures and thumbprints. In their own way, these appeals furnish eloquent testimony not only to needs and wants but also to community itself.

Chapters often used petitions to complain about livestock reduction or about restrictions or limitations placed on their use of the land. Kinlichee residents tried the ploy of meeting on Christmas day in 1937 and then asking that their Christmas wish be granted. They wanted livestock reduction halted.[85]

People from the Toadlena area used petitions to ask for wage work and a doctor to serve their community. They noted that the nearest physician resided fifty miles away in Shiprock and that the closest hospital also could be found there. Especially in the case of an emergency that was simply too great a distance. Greasewood chapter officers requested a new boarding school because "there are only a few well-educated Navajos on our reservation." Rock Point chapter members had come to know and like range rider Ernest Eaves; his planned transfer to Teec Nos Pos evoked a protest from the community.[86]

Diné also employed petitions to call for changes in federal personnel. Fred Nelson, Billy Pete, and Paul Williams signed one such appeal as representatives of Navajos living near Keams Canyon. They cited Doctor Cecil C. Shaw for refusing to see patients. The trio asked that this "no count" physician be transferred and that a new doctor "always willing to help us" be hired. In addition, Nelson, Pete, and Williams charged chief clerk John D. Keeley with not doing satisfactory work and requested his transfer as well.[87] Such requests constituted a vital early step in the effort to achieve self-determination.

Improving the roads within the Navajo Nation became a high priority. Better roads opened up the Navajo world. A rug weaver might not be limited to selling a rug to the local trader. Needed goods and services could be obtained more easily and in a more timely manner. Shonto residents circulated a petition speaking to the need for a new road so that trucks could make their way into the community. A petition from Lukachukai in 1937 offered a common sentiment. The community asked the federal government "to repair our roads so that we will have at least one outlet during the winter months. At the present time, in disagreeable weather, we have no outlet," the petition stated. "This makes medical treatment from outside our community practically impossible."[88] Although some improvements were realized, major improvements to Navajo roads would have to wait until the passage of the Navajo-Hopi Long Range Rehabilitation Act in 1950.

WEAVERS, SILVERSMITHS, AND TRADERS

The Depression obviously affected the course of Navajo weaving during this period. Adverse economic times did not encourage the market. Nevertheless, the Santa Fe Railway, the Fred Harvey Company, and other boosters of Southwest tourism continued to bring new and return visitors to the region. The founding of the Gallup Intertribal Ceremonial and the development of museums in Arizona and New Mexico furnished important venues for the display of high-quality work.

Trading posts struggled in the wake of the Depression. One major figure, J. L. Hubbell, passed away in 1930. Enthusiastic newcomers, such as Bill and Sallie Lippincott, arrived at Wide Ruins. In certain areas, traders played a significant role in promoting particular regional styles. For example, Cozy McSparron of Chinle, the Lippincotts, and others helped promote the use of vegetal dyes. In addition to Chinle and Wide Ruins, Pine Springs emerged as another significant center for rugs made with vegetal dyes.[89]

When the young anthropologist John Adair ventured to the Pine Springs area to do research on contemporary Navajo silversmithing, he captured on film artists, such as silversmith Tom Burnside and weaver Mabel Burnside (Myers), the latter a recent graduate of Wingate High School. Nearly half a century later they would be included in a memorable film portrait of Navajo life, "A Weave of Time." In his classic work, *The Navajo and Pueblo Silversmiths*, Adair would provide wonderful descriptions of how Tom Burnside fashioned a ketoh and a tobacco canteen.[90]

Even under these difficult circumstances, Navajo weavers continued to create extraordinary work. Daisy Taugelchee of the Toadlena-Two Grey

Conversation at the Tuba City Trading Post. Photograph by
Philip Johnston. Philip Johnston Collection, Cline Library,
Northern Arizona University, Flagstaff. NAU.PH.413.694

Hills area, arguably the greatest of all Navajo weavers, came into her own as a remarkable artist. Other area weavers, such as Bessie Manygoats, contributed to an outpouring of weaving that established Toadlena-Two Grey Hills weaving as the premier Navajo regional style. The completion of the Museum of Navajo Ceremonial Art, also known as the Wheelwright Museum after its patron, Mary Cabot Wheelwright, provided a permanent home for the master works of weaver and sand painter Hosteen Klah.[91]

Although it appeared on the surface that it was business as usual for the operators of trading posts, in fact, Navajos began to raise questions during this era about how trading posts were operated. These questions set the stage for the serious reexamination of trading on the Navajo Nation that took place in the late 1940s, when more Navajos had access to cars and trucks and thus to other choices, when the Diné had legal counsel, and when more generally a new sense of Navajo rights had emerged.

Tom Dodge had urged the Tribal Council to consider the issue when he served as Council chair. He stated that "within recent years the trading business as a whole has been slipping, I might say, from bad to worse." Traders bristled at Dodge's descriptions of their situation. Nevertheless, it could not be denied that most Diné still lived in isolated locales and remained closely tied to a particular trading post. If a person had been badly treated by a trader, he or she often did not object, even if he or she might complain to family members. Yet just as the behavior of school officials came under closer scrutiny at this time, so too did the actions of traders. Tom Dodge called for trading post prices to be strictly regulated and for the trading business to be "aired out and reformed."[92] Given the financial, social, and cultural investment of traders into their operations, this movement to demand greater accountability did not always evoke positive responses from them. They started to become more defensive and they resented and resisted attempts to regulate more fully how they did business.

Traders collectively took pride in their relationships with the Navajo communities and the literature on this subject is dominated by warm, paternalistic memoirs in which trouble between trader and client very rarely surfaces. That relationship, however, involved pride and status as well as dollars and cents and it should not be altogether surprising that there was friction from time to time. Indeed, there is evidence in the archival and oral historical record that verifies that traders on occasion acted violently against their Navajo customers. Traders usually justified the use of force in much the same way as school officials rationalized it. They portrayed such behavior either as an aberration or as regrettable but necessary action provoked by the subject. Violence was clearly the exception rather than the rule, but it should also be understood that not all violent behavior was reported. The economic stress of the late 1920s and the 1930s, the demands of the job, the difficulty of living in a culturally different environment, isolation, weather, alcoholism, and poor medical care all could contribute to the possibility of inappropriate behavior.

In 1930, for example, Superintendent B. P. Six of Shiprock reported four separate cases of violence within his jurisdiction. These involved members of prominent trading families: Hugh Foutz, Joe Hatch, Arthur Tanner, and Roy Burnham. Foutz got into an argument with Joe Jack over the extension of credit; he acknowledged striking Jack and admitted that "he might have kicked" him, as Jack had charged. Joe Hatch pleaded guilty to assaulting a Navajo at his post. Arthur Tanner attacked a Navajo at his post, but the superintendent let him off with a $100.00 fine paid to the person he had attacked because Six judged Tanner "to be genuinely sorry." Roy Burnham admitted that he threw a Navajo man to the ground and kicked him, but contended that Silent Man's Brother was "bent on making trouble" and was trying to make his customers "suspicious of me" because of a prior incident when Burnham had inadvertently shortchanged him by a dollar. Silent Man's Brother kept coming into the post and taunting Burnham about the matter and finally one day the trader lost his temper. Burnham also noted that he had been in the trading post business for fifteen years and this incident was the first of its kind. Nevertheless, Six concluded that the Navajos were "going to stand for just so much mistreatment of this kind and then someone is going to have some serious trouble to settle. In the case of Joe Hatch, the Indians were very much incensed and there was a large amount of hard feelings in the case of Roy Burnham."[93]

By the end of the 1930s, white men operated almost one hundred trading posts in the Navajo Nation. The decade had been a difficult one for them and the few Navajos who attempted to enter the business. Hard economic times and the critical attitude of the new Bureau officials toward past practices on the reservation, including trading, inspired considerable disgruntlement. M. L. Woodard, secretary of the United Indian Traders Association, complained to Senator Burton K. Wheeler of Nebraska about Bureau attitudes, including their willingness, indeed eagerness, to support the Mexican Springs chapter in its bid to buy a trading post. Woodard argued that this constituted unfair assistance and would lead to unfair competition. In regard to prices, Woodard argued, "If the Indian Service would give traders reasonable assistance in collecting legitimate accounts prices could be lowered."[94]

Moreover, in Woodard's judgment, the government did not appreciate sufficiently the kind of role played by traders nor had it done as much for the Diné. "Rather than Government it has been the trader, who has been doctor, lawyer, confidant, undertaker, and relief agency for the Navajo Indians," he wrote. "They have known the Navajo more intimately, speak their language and deal with them in everyday realities rather than in fanciful theories. Traders extend the Navajo credit beyond all reason in hard times and relieve the needy with outright charity in innumerable cases. Traders have done more than the Indian Service so far to give the Navajo his present economic independence."[95]

Despite Woodard's argument, more Navajo voices were being raised about trader business practices. An individual trader's monopoly over a sizable area came increasingly into question, especially if that monopoly meant higher prices. Diné in the greater Pinon area, for example, expressed their dissatisfaction with Lorenzo Hubbell's stranglehold on the market. Hubbell had a post at Pinon and used his location to both control trade and fight livestock reduction. Howard Gorman reported in 1939 that Hubbell "would not extend credit to the Navajos unless they took a firm stand against the Stock-Reduction Program." He also noted that wealthier Navajos received better treatment.[96]

Occasionally, Navajos attempted to gain a trading post for themselves. A Navajo woman, Betty Rogers, was one of very few women to try to gain such an enterprise. Rogers had been raised by Louisa Wetherill, so she grew up around trading. Rogers had two strikes against her. She was married to a white man and she was a woman. Superintendent Fryer argued that the real question centered on "whether or not she is going to run the store herself or whether there are white interests in back of her." After a delegate charged that white interests supported her, Rogers replied, "I have no white people behind me and I am not doing it for a white man. I am doing it for myself." Nevertheless, council delegate Glownizen charged that there were such interests present. "I have no white people behind me," Rogers retorted. The Council delegates were not persuaded. They voted to revoke her license. Nevertheless, Betty Rogers eventually became a trader, even if the men of the 1930s Council had not yet been ready for such a notion. It is perhaps telling that immediately after the Council voted to revoke the permit, a delegate rose to propose a resolution that would have made it illegal for Navajo women to marry white men. The resolution was never introduced. Morgan did not recognize its author, either.[97]

THE "LITTLE HERDER" YEARS

In the 1940s, a Navajo child enrolled in school could read about a family returning home from a traditional ceremony:

We have listened	Dadighinii bighiin
To the Holy Songs.	dasidiits'ą́ą́
We have walked	Dadighinii be'atiingóó
On the Holy Trail.	ndasiikai
It is finished.	Nitít'i'.
Our hearts are good.	Nihighí yá'ádahoot'eéh.
All around us is good.	Nihinagóó yá'adahoot'ééh.
We ride along	Nihighan bich'ii 'atiingóó
On the home trail.	néiikah
It is finished.	Ninít'i'.[98]

Written by Ann Nolan Clark, illustrated by the Navajo artist Hoke Denetsosie, a recent graduate of the Phoenix Indian School, and translated into written Navajo by Robert W. Young and Navajo linguist William Morgan, the Little Herder series included four volumes, one for each season of the year. Although Young later acknowledged with his characteristic modesty that such passages in English proved "difficult to make into effective Navajo," it was evident from the beginning that the Little Herder series represented a real breakthrough in bilingual, bicultural education.[99] Here, at last, were beautifully illustrated, culturally sensitive materials that offered a true opportunity for Navajo students to learn to read in both English and Navajo.

As this passage demonstrates, the books were supportive of Navajo culture. The emergence of these volumes may be in part attributed to a response to the sweeping criticisms offered through the Meriam Report and they were helped along by the Bureau's greater commitment to cultural pluralism during the Collier era. But they also resulted from a shift in organization. When Lucy Wilcox Adams arrived in Window Rock to assume her position as director of Navajo education, she had charge of a reservation-wide educational system. The schools within this system included older day schools at Cornfields, Nava (Newcomb), Sanostee, Teec Nos Pos, Pinedale, Klagetoh, and Lukachukai, and newer day schools from Aneth, Baca, Beclaibito, Burnham, Cañoncito, Cove, Crystal, Denehotso, Greasewood, Huerfano, Hunter's Point, Iyanbito, Crystal, Kaibeto, Kayenta, Kinlichee, Mariano Lake, Mexican Springs, Pine Springs, Pinon, Pueblo Pintado, Red Lake, Red Rock, Rock Point, Rough Rock, Seba Dalkai, Shonto, Standing Rock, Steamboat, Naschiti, Navajo Mountain, Pine Springs, Torreon, White Horse Lake, and Wide Ruins, as well as a number of boarding schools.[100]

As the Diné discovered with their livestock, they could count on the federal government to try to evaluate something on a numerical basis. Federal officials wanted the day schools to become community centers. They did attract some individual Diné into the school buildings. Navajos used the schools to repair cars, chains, shoes, tires, trucks, harnesses, plows, guns, sewing machines, furniture, oil cans, lanterns, sewing machines, tools, and shovels. Even more would have taken advantage of the new school buildings had it not been for the animus against livestock reduction.[101]

The Little Herder readers reflected a more general transition away from heavy-handed assimilationism at the schools. Schools now were supposed to utilize Navajo culture in their efforts to teach Diné children. The military uniforms and the military drills eventually disappeared. Schools began to teach weaving and silversmithing and the Navajo language. The high school at Wingate, New Mexico, in particular emerged as an important center for instruction in silversmithing and weaving.

However, student attendance still lagged at most schools for the reasons it had always lagged. Many parents continued to take their children out of school or keep them out of school. "Hello school teacher," wrote Lucy Harvey in March 1938. "You have ask me to send my children back to school." But, she said, her wagon was broken and so they needed to "just stay at one place." She concluded, "I like for my children to go to school, but it's like that."[102]

Collier had initially envisioned a more radical approach to education. Like many intellectuals of his day, the commissioner recognized the importance of formal education but also worried about the tendencies of school systems toward conformity and uniformity. He hoped the day schools would be a major step in a more progressive direction. But a different setting and an altered curriculum did not change automatically or dramatically the time-honored approaches employed at certain schools. Collier discovered that the schools were resistant to sweeping change. For that matter, many Navajo parents were suspicious of too rapid a transition away from what they had known, regardless of their varying degrees of dissatisfaction with it.

So, Navajo schools continued to present holiday programs that seemed to belong to another time. For example, Crownpoint students in 1936 participated in a Thanksgiving "playlet" in which two children, Robert and Patience, get lost in the forest and barely escape being sacrificed to appease the Indians' war gods. The Indians are frightened away by the sight of the Pilgrims' shotguns and all is well. School officials did not hesitate to cast Pablo Chavez as Robert Allen, Esther Norberto as Patience Allen, and Tony Castillo as Miles Standish.[103]

Children had to endure not only bad playlets but also the indifferent fare provided. The meals at the schools continued to be unimaginative and often inedible. The fundamental motto in Navajo school kitchens seemed to be "when in doubt, fry it." During a typical week Eastern Navajo students encountered a variety of delicacies that had shared this common fate, including fried carrots, fried cabbage, fried hominy, fried potatoes, and fried rabbit.[104]

A PRINCIPAL'S CHALLENGES

Administrators and teachers encouraged continuing attendance and school loyalties through activities, athletics, and school songs. Basketball already had become popular in Navajo country and tournaments helped keep more than a few students in school. School principal Paul Schmitt had graduated from the University of Kansas and so he appreciated basketball. He encouraged students to participate in the sport and helped get them to one game or tournament after another. He also took the opportunity to write "alma mater" hymns to the tune of "The Crimson and the Blue" for each of three schools in which he served as principal during this period. The songs did not necessarily improve as he moved from Fort Wingate to Keams Canyon to Toadlena, but they remained consistent in their emphasis on a brighter tomorrow. An excerpt follows:

Lofty snow-clad Colorado's
Grace the northern skies.
East our stalwart sentinels,
Two Grey Hills arise.

Chorus: We shall ever sing thy praises
Love and honor, too.
Hail to thee our Alma Mater,
Toadlena, true.

Far removed from all discomforts.
In our work and play.
Toadlena leads us onward,
To a better day.[105]

Any principal in Navajo country had to deal with problems relating to staff and transportation and endure the never-ending demands from Window Rock. Schmitt wrote to Lucy Adams in August 1939, for example, to express his hope that one "unprofessional" couple "be either kept at Klagetoh or assigned to some other area than Toadlena." He concluded, "I think it is time that they be made to realize that the Indian Service has other needs to fulfill besides their purely personal ones." In addition, classes would soon start, but "the position of beginner teacher is still unfilled, and although we appreciate very much Mrs. Schmitt's assignment last year, we should very much prefer having the vacancy filled in some other way." He had to administer five area day schools at Nava (Newcomb), Burnham, Sanostee, Red Rock, and Cove. Even with his reliable Oldsmobile, purchased from Rico Motors in Gallup, the roads often did not allow him to reach his intended destination. He wrote in January 1941 to his daughter: "[T]he snows and the rain continue. Roads are impassable. I have not been to Cove, Red Rock, and Burnham since before Christmas. Only Nava is accessible and only Nava has operated its bus since the holidays. Sanostee has 25 or 30 pupils walk in. The other schools are closed until the snows melt and the roads improve."[106]

Schmitt had known from the day of his arrival that he would have his hands full. A memorandum entitled (in capital letters), IMPORTANT WORK THAT SHOULD BE ACCOMPLISHED BEFORE A GREAT WHILE, welcomed him to Toadlena. It informed him that Toadlena School needed loads of heavy soil to be brought in to be placed next to one building; Nava needed doors hung at the wash house and the heat plant in the classrooms needed attention; Burnham needed a stove installed in the assistants' quarters; Sanostee had problems with drainage, a stove needed to be purchased for the teachers' quarters, and desk tops needed to be sanded and mended; Red Rock needed a coal bin, buildings needed painting, teachers' quarters needed to be redecorated, and school desks should be sanded and varnished; and at Cove, the two hogans constructed for assistants were beginning to crumble and fall apart.

More interested in the writings of John Ruskin than the rudiments of coal bin construction, Schmitt did the best he could to deal with such concerns. From time to time, however, he would remind Window Rock that it should be more concerned with treating good people properly than about the current state of the coal bins. He, too, realized Window Rock's preoccupation with technical efficiency rather than social ideals. In one of his final reports from Toadlena, he chided George Boyce for the government's failure to try to retain the person who had been in charge of the school's small power plant. "He has been given no word of encouragement other than mine, no substantial promise or expression of appreciation." We cannot do our work under these circumstances, he said. In the absence of "conscientious men on adequate salaries in charge of such plants, there will be no light, heat, and power, even with coal-bins overflowing."[107]

Waldo Emerson appreciated some of the limitations of life at such schools. A student at the Charles H. Burke Indian School (later Wingate), "Wild" Emerson studied agriculture, played basketball, and worked on the school newspaper and yearbook. But by the fall of 1935, he had had it. The problem involved a girl that he really cared about and the harassment she was receiving from school matrons because of that attention. "She is being scolded and blamed all because I can not keep away from her and she can't keep away from me," he wrote. It was time to move on. Emerson asked for help in finding a job driving a truck or a school bus.[108] He got his wish. A Navajo Agency survey for 1939 included him as a driver for one of the day schools in the area.[109]

Although conditions at the schools improved in some ways in the 1930s, Navajo public opinion remained divided. The day schools continued to be suspect. Many Diné rejected anything to do with John Collier—and that included educational reform. As the Navajo Nation became increasingly immersed in the outside world, the pendulum of popular opinion on the reservation began to swing toward a more supportive attitude for formal education. The experience of World War II would underscore the need for better schools, marking the beginnings of a demand by the Diné for more access to better education.

SEEKING HÓZHǪ

Navajos continued to seek hózhǫ́, that sense of balance, beauty, and harmony, during these turbulent times. The cultural pluralism that Collier espoused and sometimes practiced should have resulted in more significant breakthroughs in medical care and freedom of religion.

Although some progress was achieved, the bitter response to stock reduction limited what might have been accomplished.

The Meriam Report's publication in 1928 signaled once and for all that Native communities confronted major crises in health care. In this period, federal doctors recorded one significant victory. They finally gained the upper hand in their ongoing campaign against trachoma. A sulfanilamide treatment developed by a physician on the Rosebud reservation in South Dakota began to be administered and produced impressive results. However, tuberculosis remained an elusive foe. In spite of screening and educational materials, many Diné were not reached and the disease continued to be widespread.[110]

The arrival in 1927 of Dr. Clarence Salsbury to serve as the medical director of the Presbyterian mission hospital in Ganado and the dedication three years later of the Sage Memorial Hospital at the mission both ranked as important developments. The dedication opened with Howard Gorman conducting the Mission Brass Band's performance of a composition by Handel and closed with the band's rendition of "America." Chee Dodge and John Hunter provided greetings on behalf of the Navajo Tribe and the Indian Service and, of course, Salsbury had a few remarks. With the advent of the new facility, Salsbury inaugurated a training program for Navajo women who wanted to become nurses. Ganado became the leading hospital on the reservation and was used more frequently than federal facilities, even given its antagonistic stance toward traditional Navajo culture.[111]

In W. W. Peter, Collier found an impressive person to head the federal medical efforts in Navajo country. Less antipathetic than most Christian missionary doctors toward Navajo ceremonialism, Peter attempted to encourage a more pluralistic approach to healing. He emphasized that the Navajo healers had much to contribute to the overall healing process. Peter said that the Navajo healer "understands the language and the customs of the patient and the patient's family. . . . He is the beneficiary of tradition." The "Navajo Health Plan" he developed sought, according to Trennert, "to improve professional standards among doctors and nurses, train Navajos for medical jobs, and create a Navajo Board of Health to directly involve the Diné in understanding their health needs and cooperating with the government." Peter brought in new doctors and nurses, tried to equip them at least minimally for cross-cultural understanding, and labored valiantly, even with the usual lack of sufficient funding, to allow Navajos access to better medical treatment.[112]

At the same time, other voices spoke out against Collier's approach. A medical missionary at Rehoboth Mission Hospital, Dr. Richard Pousma, lashed out at Navajo ceremonies, for he believed that Diné attendance at such ceremonies helped spread disease. "I think people who encourage Indians" to attend them "are idiotic, exceedingly stupid, and ignorant of conditions among the Indians," he contended.[113]

Collier truly believed in freedom of religion. The Native American Church came into Navajo country at this time and its growing number of adherents hoped to be able to encourage still more people to attend. Peyote attracted some individuals and drove away some others, but its emphasis on Indian brotherhood, its message against alcoholism, and its ability to bring people together encouraged widespread attendance. Collier was dismayed at the Tribal Council's unwillingness to support freedom of religion, but believed he had no other choice than to back its decision in June 1940 to ban Native American Church services. Even with official sanctions against it, the Native American Church had gained a sufficient foothold to show promise of becoming a major new cultural presence in future years. David Aberle's thesis that the trauma of live-stock reduction had driven individual Diné to peyotism may be debated, but it appears not entirely off the mark. Surely the unsettling nature of the time helped encourage Navajos to look for new answers. For a growing number of people in the Navajo Nation, peyotism had started to become an integral and essential part of their lives.[114]

Collier's stance on religious freedom had another significant and often overlooked effect. Mainstream Protestant denominations and the Catholic Church had gained what amounted to Christian monopolies in different parts of Indian country, including the Navajo reservation. The commissioner thought that practice unfair to other Christian churches and made it clear that those other denominations could also construct churches and attempt to convert Navajos or other Native communities to their particular congregation. The full impact of this perspective would not be felt until the late 1940s and the 1950s, but the origins of a wider variety of Christian services may be traced to this time. The Church of Jesus Christ of Latter-day Saints (the Mormons) and various Pentecostal churches especially gained large numbers of new adherents in the years that followed.

A MATTER OF PATRIOTISM

President Franklin D. Roosevelt issued a declaration in 1941 that required all men over the age of twenty-one to register for the Selective Service on July 1. This order affected the Navajos as they, like other American Indians, had been made full citizens of the United States through the Indian Citizenship Act of 1924. Citizenship did not guarantee the right to vote in state and national elections, however, and in 1941 state law in Arizona, New Mexico, and Utah still prevented Indian reservation residents from voting.

The Diné hoped to gain the franchise in the near future. In the meantime, they did not need any prompting about the likelihood of war nor of the importance of their contribution to the war effort. On June 3, 1940, the Tribal Council passed the following resolution:

WHEREAS, the Navajo Tribal Council and the fifty thousand people we represent cannot fail to recognize the crisis now facing the world in the threat of foreign invasion and the destruction of the great liberties and benefits which we enjoy on our Reservation, and

WHEREAS, there exists no purer concentration of Americanism than among the First Americans, and

WHEREAS, it has become common practice to attempt national destruction through the sowing of seeds of treachery among minority groups such as ours, and

WHEREAS, we may expect such activity among our people,

THEREFORE, we hereby serve notice that any un-American movement among our people will be resented and dealt with severely, and

NOW THEREFORE, we resolve that the Navajo Indians stand ready as they did in 1918 to aid and defend our Government and its institutions against all subversive and armed conflict and pledge our loyalty to the system which recognizes minority rights and a way of life that has placed us among the greatest people of our race.

PASSED BY UNANIMOUS VOTE OF THE NAVAJO TRIBAL COUNCIL AT WINDOW ROCK, ARIZONA, THIS THIRD DAY OF JUNE, NINETEEN HUNDRED AND FORTY.[115]

In July, President Roosevelt acknowledged the resolution. He said it filled him "with the warmest gratitude." The president added, "I have long been aware of the fact that our Indian tribes have been among the most devoted to our American way of life of any group within our borders, and this fact has been more striking in view of the long history of struggle and hardship through which so many of our Indian tribes, your tribe not excluded, have had to pass. These hard days are now behind us, and I am confident that the future will bring a better time for the Indians." Roosevelt concluded, "I sincerely hope that it may never be necessary to call upon the Navajo Tribe to take up arms against a common enemy, but I shall always remember that it stood ready in these times of uncertainty."[116]

As chairman and vice chairman of the Navajo Tribal Council, J. C. Morgan and Howard Gorman, respectively, had signed the resolution. On this matter, at least, the two men agreed. They knew that the Diné had to be ready to fight, not only for America, but also, once again, in defense of the sacred mountains. And, once again, they did not have long to wait.

6

"We Have an Opportunity": 1941–1962

Fellow Councilmen, we must understand that here we have an opportunity for development of our human resources as well as our material resources. . . . [W]e have reached a capacity where we cannot increase our grazing. . . . [W]e must look for other means for our future generations.
—Ned Hatathli, 1955

Hundreds of Navajo men learned these words during World War II. They are the verses to a familiar song.

Wááshindoon Be'akał Bik'osí Biyiin
Nikin, niík'e, anaa'á lá
T'áá'ałtsogóó nahosiilkáá'
Ts'ídá t'áá'aaníinii
Éí bee nihééhózin
Wááshindoon be'akał bik'osí lá
Jílįįgo baahózhǫ́

Nihidahnaat'a'í lá
Yilk'oołgo e'e'ááh.
Deení t'áá ałtsogóó nidashiijaa'
T'áá ałtsogóó nidasiitą́.
Hak'az dine'é bikéyah
Áádóó t'áá ahééháshį́įh.
Doo nídindáahii óolyé.
Wááshindoon be'akał bik'osí

Hózhǫ́ǫgo naildeehdoo
Anaa'í bik'eh deedlį́į'.
Nihik'eh didlíínii t'áá ádin.
Yéé' wolyéii nihee ádin.
Siláołtsooi dóó tałkáá' siláo

Yá'ąashgóó dazdéez'į́į́'.
Wááshindoon be'akał bik'osí lá
Hózhǫ́ǫgo kééhat'į́.

The song speaks of pride in defending our country, in fighting for right and freedom, in never losing our nerve. It is the hymn for the United States Marines.[1]

When the war came, countless Diné men volunteered to fight for the United States. When the war came, countless Navajo women and men left the reservation for the first time. When the war came, the hard-earned education of those who had endured the long years of boarding school suddenly took on new meaning. When the war came, the old values continued, but new ideas and new possibilities also emerged.

When the war ended, the Navajos had gained new perspectives that challenged the status quo and encouraged self-determination. In the 1950s, the Diné experienced rapid economic growth as well as noteworthy political change. The Navajo government evolved into a far more ambitious and wide-ranging enterprise. The Navajo "tribe" started to become the Navajo Nation.

John McPhee (seated) registering Navajos for Selective Service, February 26, 1941. Photograph by Milton Snow. Courtesy of the Navajo Nation Museum, Window Rock, AZ. Catalog no. NH1-22

The original twenty-nine Code Talkers are sworn in at Fort Wingate.
National Archives, Pacific Region, Laguna Niguel, Calif.

THE WAR YEARS

Soon after the attack on Pearl Harbor, Sidney Bedoni decided to enlist in the Marines. He hitchhiked sixty miles, walked another thirty-four miles through a rain storm, gained the approval of his parents, and then made the return journey of nearly one hundred miles to sign up at the recruiting station. Nor was Bedoni alone. Navajo men by the hundreds started coming to Window Rock, determined to enlist in the armed forces. Diné women also enlisted in the Women's Army Corps. Even though Arizona, New Mexico, and Utah had denied the right to vote to residents of Indian reservations, these men and women reaffirmed their dual loyalties to the Navajo Nation and to the United States and their commitment to fight to defend both homelands. They shared other Americans' anger at what had happened in Hawaii and they wanted to do their part to protect the sacred mountains.

Code Talker Cozy Stanley Brown stated, "My main reason for going to war was to protect my land and my people." Within the first year after the beginning of the war, 1,400 Navajos had joined the armed forces, including 350 as volunteers. They often brought guns, bedrolls, and food to the selective service registration. The men called Hitler "mustache smeller" and Mussolini "gourd chin." They proclaimed themselves ready to go after Hitler and shave off Hitler's mustache. Eventually, over 3,600 Navajos served in the military.[2]

Navajo patriotism soon found a special outlet. Philip Johnston, the son of missionary William R. Johnston, had grown up in Navajo country. When he heard about the American need for an effective code that could be employed in the Pacific campaign, he immediately thought of the Navajo language. The idea of employing Indian languages for code purposes, however, did not originate with Johnston. He knew that the Choctaw language had been used on one occasion in World War I. Its employment had befuddled the Germans. The journal of the Society of American Indians proudly reported the incident, headlining its story, "Played Joke on the Huns."

Marine Corps officials at first responded skeptically to Johnston's proposal, but events in the Pacific demanded that new approaches be tested. In a trial run at the Los Angeles Coliseum, Navajos demonstrated their facility with the language, and the results impressed the attending Marine Corps personnel. So began the Code Talkers. The term "Code Talkers" came from an early stage of the program when an officer demanded an explanation of how Carl Gorman and Bill McCabe had been able to communicate so quickly and effectively. Gorman replied and referred to McCabe and himself as each being "a talking code machine."[3]

Thirty men formed the initial Code Talkers unit. One did not complete training, leaving twenty-nine in the original group: Charley Begay, Roy Begay, Samuel Hosteen Nez Begay, John Ashi Benally, Wilsie H. Bitsie, Cozy Stanley Brown, John Brown, Jr., John Chee, Benjamin H. Cleveland, Eugene Roanhorse Crawford, David Curley, Lowell Smith Damon, George H. Dennison, James Dixon, Carl Gorman, Oscar B. Ilthma, Allen Dale June, Alfred Leonard, Johnny R. Manuelito, William McCabe, Chester Nez, Jack Nez, Lloyd Oliver, Joe Palmer (also known as Balmer Slowtalker), Frank Danny Pete, Nelson S. Thompson, Harry Tsosie, John W. Willie, and William Yazzie. One of the twenty-nine, Harry Tsosie, died in battle, as did twelve Code Talkers who enlisted at a later date: Paul Begay, Johnson Housewood, Peter Johnson, Jimmy Kelly, Sr., Paul Kinlacheeny, Leo Kirk, Ralph Morgan, Sam Morgan, Willie A. Notah, Tom Singer, Alfred Tsosie, and Howard Tsosie. Many Navajo men and women attributed the survival of so many Navajo soldiers to ceremonies conducted "to protect us and bring us home safely." About four hundred men eventually joined the group, although not all of them, including future tribal chairman Peter MacDonald, actually participated in battle. Regardless of the length or nature of their service, however, all the men took great pride in their affiliation.[4]

The original Code Talkers enlisted at Fort Wingate and then traveled by Greyhound bus to San Diego. As they adjusted to their surroundings, they had to endure the seemingly inevitable "hey, chief" salutations. With one notable exception, people generally seemed to be on their side. However, their drill sergeant, a Texan, went well beyond the customary boundaries of his assignment. The Navajos were used to adversity and equally resolute about not letting him get to them. Finally, one morning the sergeant had them line up and he began moving down the row of men, punching each one in the face. At first, the astonished Diné offered no resistance. Then the sergeant came upon Carl Gorman, who had seen more than enough Southern hospitality for one day. Moreover, Gorman knew how to box. He ducked the sergeant's punch and flattened his adversary with a one-two combination. The other Navajos laughed in relief and with appreciation, the sergeant filed no report, and Gorman avoided a court-martial.[5]

Johnston may have come up with the idea of a code, but its development rested with the Navajos. They employed Diné words for military terms, foreign countries, and other subjects. A bomber plane now was *jeeshóó'* (buzzard), a submarine *beeshłóó'* (iron fish), and a battleship *łóótsoh* (whale). Britain became Tóta' (between the waters), India Éé' (white clothes), and Germany Bééshbich'aahí (iron hat). Each letter of the alpha-

Code Talker Carl Gorman, Saipan. National Archives, Washington, D.C.

bet underwent a similar transformation. In the code *wólachíí'* (ant) stood for "a," *shash* (bear) for "b," and *mosí* (cat) for "c." Thus, the Diné produced a code within a code and they were able to transmit it far more quickly than the usual codes could be sent. The Japanese would determine that the code was in Navajo but they never broke it. After eight weeks basic training ended and the Diné began to be sent overseas. Marine Corps officers continued to express doubts about the new method, but the Code Talkers demonstrated time and again their competence and their courage. They played a key role at Guadalcanal, Tarawa, Peleliu, and Iwo Jima. During the first forty-eight hours on Iwo Jima the Code Talkers sent eight hundred messages without error.[6]

Although the initiative remained cloaked in secrecy, more than a few people knew of its existence. One of them, James M. Stewart, the superintendent of the Navajo Agency, wanted to share his pride in the Code Talkers and their achievements. He authored an article for *Arizona Highways* about the Navajos' contributions to the war effort. The interested Japanese reader or American reader learned through this essay that the Marine Corps had "organized a special Navajo signal united [sic] for combat communication service." Stewart wrote, "A platoon of thirty Navajos was recruited in the spring of 1942." By year's end he could report that "Navajo Marines performed their duties so successfully that the plan was expanded, a recruiting detail was sent back to the Navajo Reservation, and by early December 967 new boys were enlisted." Marine Corps officials were not enthusiastic about this article, but its publication did not lead to the abandonment of the code.[7]

Code Talkers essentially worked as part of an assault team or as part of an intelligence team that would land, go behind enemy lines, and relay back vital information about the Japanese fortifications and location of troops. This highly dangerous work was the stuff of nightmares ever afterward for many of the survivors, even after Enemy Way ceremonies had been conducted.

After he returned, Code Talker King Mike dreamed of being chased by a Japanese soldier brandishing a bayonet. He had participated in the assault on Okinawa's Sugar Hill, which he termed "the bloodiest and the dirtiest fight in the South Pacific." The assault claimed the lives of 2,662 Marines—the most fatalities of any battle in the history of the Corps. The thirty-six days of hand-to-hand combat on Iwo Jima also furnished an ultimate test. The Code Talkers ultimately won over the skeptics through their bravery, fortitude, and skill. They were American heroes. "Without the Code Talkers," one major commented after the war, "the Marines would never have taken Iwo Jima."[8]

However, in the aftermath of World War II, the Code Talkers received essentially no public praise for their endeavors. The Marines ignored them. They received no promotions or special medals. When they returned home, the Code Talkers had no welcoming parades. The Diné

Code Talkers Frank and Preston Toledo.
National Archives, Washington, D.C.

obtained no promotions or special medals from the Marines for their accomplishments. They returned home uncelebrated by non-Navajos and undecorated by the military, despite their important contribution. The military kept the code a classified matter until 1968. Within the Navajo Nation, however, the Code Talkers were known and honored and the memory of their achievements would continue to be cherished. But decades would pass before the Code Talkers began to receive the more general recognition they so richly deserved.[9]

Navajo participation in the war, of course, was not limited to the Code Talkers. Diné men and women enlisted in the other branches of the armed forces. About ten thousand worked in war-related industries and two thousand more worked for the railroads. Hundreds of Navajos worked in the Navajo Ordnance plant in Bellemont, near Flagstaff, and at the Fort Wingate Ordnance Depot near Gallup. These employees faced discrimination, but earned significantly higher wages than they had received on the reservation. In 1943, Navajo workers earned $1 million at the Fort Wingate Ordinance Depot; two years before, the combined total income of all Diné working both on the reservation and away from it totaled $150,000.[10]

Tribal Council members spoke out about Diné sacrifices, despite the imposition of livestock reduction and the existence of prejudice. Dan Keyonie, for example, contended that Navajos and other Indians were fighting to protect John Collier and Collier was doing nothing but harm to the Navajos. He wondered aloud "how many boys Mr. Collier has fighting in the armed forces. . . ." Many Farms chapter members petitioned for an end to livestock reduction: "Why are we sending thousands of young Navajo people overseas to fight a war. What are they fighting for? They are fighting so we can be free, free to talk, free to do what we like about our own affairs. . . . [Y]et . . . every Navajo stock owner is compelled to reduce their stock, threatened with a jail sentence if they did not do it."[11]

Navajo men and women serving in the military had ample reason to ponder why they fought and to reconsider inequality and inequity at home. Those who belonged to the Native American Church observed the dichotomy between the American ideal of freedom of religion and the harassment that church members continually confronted. Private First Class Jack Jones, for example, wrote to Superintendent Stewart in 1944, noting that the world needed what the church had provided for him: "moral imagination," an "understanding heart," and "the willingness to forgive." He and other Native American Church members complained that their meetings were disrupted, even when they were praying for President Roosevelt.[12]

The denial of the right to vote particularly angered Navajo soldiers. Private Ralph Anderson called on tribal leaders "to use every power to push this /the right to vote/ through. . . ." Noting that Congress in 1924 had granted all Indians citizenship but that two decades later Navajos were still not able to vote, Anderson said he and his fellow soldiers did "not understand what kind of citizenship you would call that." They were "fighting for their country just like anybody else" and "should be recognized as a full citizen."[13]

Although World War II blunted the federal government's crusade for livestock reduction, it did not end the campaign. Navajos continued to protest the imposition of this program. The most dramatic example of this resistance took place in Teec Nos Pos in January 1945. District range supervisor Rudolph Zweifel had refused to issue a grazing permit to Slocumb Clah because he had been grazing too many sheep. Instead, Zweifel issued a trespass order against Clah. Clah protested that the sheep actually belonged to his son, Henry Salt. Clah, Herbert Clah Brown, Moses Clah, Harry Lee Benally, Capiton Benally, Mrs. Benally, Adakai, Evan B. Tsosie, Chee Yabeney, Ned Yabeney, Walter Yabeney, and Ellis Coalminer kidnapped Rudolph Zweifel, Mrs. Zweifel, and range rider Roy Palmer from an office, beat Zweifel with a blackjack, tied up the three persons, cut the telephone lines, commandeered a government truck, and took the trio to a hogan in an isolated location. Navajo police promptly rescued the Zweifels and Parker and eventually several of the protesters served time in jail for their actions. Stewart blamed the incident and the general refusal to go along with federal edicts on the Navajo Rights Association and its attorney, Paul Palmer of Farmington.[14]

The war severely curtailed educational opportunities for Navajo children. Lack of vehicles and gasoline as well as a labor shortage caused enrollment to decline in the day schools. Eight large boarding schools—Chinle, Crownpoint, Fort Defiance, Shiprock, Toadlena, Tohatchi, Tuba City, and Wingate—plus fifty day schools existed at war's end. An increasing percentage of Navajo parents had been persuaded that Diné children needed more formal education in order to survive in a rapidly changing world. Experiences in the armed forces and in off-reservation employment had underlined the utility of English language proficiency. Some Diné began to speak to the need for more public schools and greater educational opportunities. However, funding limitations delayed efforts to try to build a public school network on the Navajo Nation.[15]

AFTER THE WAR: A TIME OF TRANSITION

The end of the war marked a key transition in Diné life. New schools, new roads, new health care facilities, and new or revitalized forms of economic development all signaled the start of a period in Navajo life that furnished innovation and change. The trauma of the livestock reduction remained and it was clear that raising livestock would sustain a progressively smaller percentage of the Diné. Many individuals started to imagine a world in which livestock remained socially and culturally important but in which other possibilities for economic, social, and cultural sustenance could be realized. A diversified and expanding economy had to be created and sustained in order for young people to remain within the Navajo Nation rather than be forced to live elsewhere. In 1955, Ned Hatathli thus reminded his fellow delegates that the Council had "an opportunity for development of our human resources as well as our material resources." The Diné needed "a far-sighted, future-planning Council which our people will be proud of in time to come." The Navajos had "reached a capacity where we cannot increase our grazing . . . so we must look to other means for our future generations." Hatathli certainly understood the challenge, accepted it, and looked forward to meeting it. He knew full well that Navajo life had entered a new day.[16]

During this period, both in response to their own desire to gain greater control over their lives and lands and to combat attempts by the states to exercise greater authority over Indian lands and peoples, the Navajos began the transition from "tribe" into "nation." In so doing they increasingly took charge of the world in which they resided. They wanted county, state, and federal governments not to take advantage of them but to take them seriously. "What is the land," asked Ned Hatathli, "if you do not have anything to say about it?" He added, "If we fight for a land, why is it not our privilege to improve the land we fought for?"[17]

In 1946, the Navajo Tribal Council outlined major problems facing the people and made a series of requests to the federal government in order to address these matters. Education emerged as a foremost priority. "Education is our greatest need," the Council declared. "There are no schools for over 14,000 of our children. Our people are now very poor. Our children must have a good education if they are to learn to support themselves." By building more schools and adding more dormitories to existing schools, more Diné students could be accommodated and many adult Diné could be employed. The Navajos sought viability and visibility in the marketplace, but "without education we cannot compete with the white man anywhere."[18]

Health care constituted a second significant crisis. "Sickness is our greatest fear," the Council stated. The Diné needed more physicians and nurses, more centrally located and larger hospitals, and more effective treatment of tuberculosis. They hoped for health care professionals who would be more culturally sensitive. Inadequate health care restricted the ability of many Navajos to find work. Inadequate roads also hampered the Navajos in their efforts to reach clinics and hospitals, trading posts, and other destinations.

Empowered by their experiences in wartime, the Navajos sought more political and legal authority as well as full participation in the American political system. The Council asked for "fuller authority" to be vested in it and for the right to vote to be granted all Navajos. "Our people were subject to Selective Service," the Council reminded the federal government. "Before this, our people volunteered to fight for the United States more frequently than the white man. About 3,600 of our people were in the armed forces fighting all over the world. Our people worked hard in every way in war work, in donating money to the Red Cross and in every way to win the war." The Navajos also sought resolution of the conflict with the Hopis over contested terrain and resources.[19]

Economic development constituted another priority. The Navajos appealed for more land, an end to livestock reduction, support for their recently established arts and crafts guild and for their artists, and a greater return from their natural resources. "The livestock program has been harassing the Navajo people for more than ten years," the Council reiterated. Council members advocated that "grazing regulations be suspended and that we be allowed to increase our livestock by at least twenty-five per cent." They also spoke out in favor of closing the plots of land where the federal government had been attempting to demonstrate the benefits of its approaches. The people wanted this productive land back under local control.[20]

During the 1940s, the Navajos worked with the federal government to put together an economic development plan. In 1950, the Congress passed the Navajo-Hopi Long Range Rehabilitation Act, an $88-million package, with primary attention given to road construction ($38,237,680); school construction ($24,997,295); soil and moisture conservation and range improvement ($7,097,175); irrigation projects ($6,616,775); hospital and health facilities ($4,750,000); resettlement on the Colorado River irrigation project ($3,449,750); a revolving loan fund ($1,800,000); and agency, institutional, and domestic water projects ($1,356,670). In 1958, Congress added another $20 million for road construction. When combined with the effects of massive new revenues from oil and the acquisition of legal counsel, it constituted a time of transformation.[21]

Road construction illustrated the change. Other than the highway that ran north from Gallup to Shiprock, route 66 to the south, and the highway north from Flagstaff that skirted the western edge of the reservation, paved roads were nonexistent. The possibilities for inconvenience only slightly exceeded the chances for disaster. A point on a steep hill on the road to the Ganado trading post symbolized the problem. Locals had labeled it "The Place Where the Mexicans Cry." Mexican teamsters hauling goods to Ganado from Gallup invariably had gotten stuck at this place and then cried out in frustration at their inability to move their wagons forward out of the mire. Years later the situation had not improved. The absence of good roads discouraged industrial development as well as access to public schools and hospitals and clinics. By the end of fiscal year 1961, almost three hundred miles of bituminous-surfaced highway had been completed.[22]

In his inaugural address in 1959, Paul Jones spoke of "a Divine providence" that had made possible the "unexpected wealth" derived from the "natural resources not known to be there in our earlier history." He declared, "We are now making rapid strides in the management of our own affairs, in freeing ourselves in an orderly manner from the past paternalism, and in dedicating our resources to the betterment of Navajo life, and the unfolding of unlimited opportunities for every young Navajo in search of education and advancement toward the fuller exercise and enjoyment of rights, privileges, and duties of American citizens." He added, "Our purpose is and ought to be to make secure the legal right of the Tribe to govern itself . . . to control all of the business activities on the reservation, and to administer the affairs of the Navajo people according to our notion of propriety. . . ." In *Navajo Studies at Navajo Community College*, Ruth Roessel writes, "During the 1950s, a great people were awakening and rising to the challenges and opportunities facing them." It is this time that marked "the birth of the Navajo Nation."[23]

NEW SUPPORT FOR EDUCATION

A resolution passed by the Tribal Council in the closing days of the war dramatically illustrated the degree to which Navajo perspectives on schooling had changed. Education now had become the way out of widespread poverty and the means through which greater self-sufficiency could be gained once again. Only through education could central goals be achieved. The resolution noted that only six thousand of twenty thousand Navajo children from six to eighteen had access to schools, that existing schools were overcrowded, and that day schools were too distant and too inconvenient. In addition, the resolution observed, "[T]he Navaho tribe is handicapped with poverty, poor health, limited resources, inability to speak English, and lack of training for improving our condition. . . ." However, "our record of military service and war industry, together with our wish to be self-supporting," the resolution continued, "are evidence of our desire to progress as citizens of the United States." Moreover, "our people are realizing that education like the white man's is needed to learn better farming, to learn how to improve livestock, to learn to improve health, and to learn trades."[24]

In the year after the war ended, twenty-three Navajo representatives made the long journey to Washington, D.C. to voice such sentiments to congressional representatives. Tribal Chairman Chee Dodge, Vice Chairman Sam Ahkeah, and Tribal Council members Scott Preston, Billy Norton, and Joe Duncan testified before the U.S. Senate Committee on Indian Affairs, chaired by Senator Carl Hatch of Utah. Dodge testified first. He described education as "our gravest need." The experiences of Diné in military service and in industry had prompted this changed perspective. Education should be compulsory, Dodge said, and facilities had to be improved. At Shiprock and in other locations, children attended "worn out" schools in buildings "ready to fall apart." Dodge specifically called for schools to be constructed or expanded at Fort Wingate, Crownpoint, Toadlena, Tohatchi, Fort Defiance, Chinle, Kayenta, Tuba City, Leupp, Indian Wells, Greasewood, Tanner Springs, and Oak Springs. The chairman emphasized the need for Navajo pupils to be taught English and "to be educated to such an extent that when they are through with schools on the reservation they will be able to compete with the white people." Dodge called upon the federal government to live up to the provisions in the 1868 treaty.[25]

Sam Ahkeah followed Dodge. Ahkeah pointed out still more areas that needed improved educational facilities, including the Utah portion of the reservation and Lukachukai. Access to education would "enable us to help ourselves along better," the vice chairman declared. Ahkeah and several other Navajo representatives advocated boarding schools rather than day schools and spoke to the benefits of a practical, vocationally oriented education.[26]

In subsequent meetings of the Tribal Council, delegates continued to revisit these themes. Although Dan Keyonie reminded his listeners that unlike white people he "did not have to rely on paper" to remember something, he still realized the importance of schooling. Roger Davis criticized the federal government for failing to insist that Diné children

A teacher who means business at a day school.
National Archives, Pacific Region, Laguna Niguel, Calif.

attend school. In effect, the government had said "we are just children, we are wards of the Government and can do as we please." The first woman elected to the Tribal Council, Lilly Neil, reiterated that the Navajos wanted to be "self supporting, self reliant, well educated citizens, not "dependent on the ones who neglect us the most." She added, "When the government is making all these big loans to foreign countries and bragging about what they are doing so fine and noble for the countries who try to ruin us, it seems as if they would try to do something for their poor neglected children or wards at home . . ."[27]

The Navajo record in war, the troubled Navajo economy, and the vocal support by the people for education combined to encourage a greater federal commitment to education for the Diné. A study of contemporary Navajo education carried out by University of Texas faculty member George I. Sánchez, offered needed publicity to the poor roads, outmoded facilities, and teacher shortages on the reservation. Not all Navajos would have posed the issue as a "battle for acculturation," as had Sánchez, but at least his analysis, printed at Haskell and distributed by the Interior

Department, helped build support for passage of the Navajo-Hopi Long Range Rehabilitation Program. So, too, did a report issued by Secretary of the Interior Julius A. Krug, which also attested to the hurdles standing in the way of adequate education for all Navajo children.[28]

Funds from the act began to provide more classrooms. For a six-year-old beginning school, the new facilities allowed him or her a better chance of recording steady progress. But for the twelve-year-old to eighteen-year-old who had never been to school or who had attended school for only a limited amount of time, new facilities did not by themselves make up for lost time. These individuals with minimal schooling could not be expected to enroll in first or third grade.

The federal government thus devised what it termed the "Special Navajo Program" to offer these students five years of vocational education designed to improve their chances for living and working off of the reservation. From 1946 through 1959, slightly more than 50,000 Diné students enrolled in a version of the Special Navajo Program at eleven off-reservation boarding schools. Of this number, over 20,000 attended Intermountain, a new institution created out of a remodeled hospital in Brigham City, Utah. Nearly 10,000 Diné enrolled at Sherman Institute in Riverside, California. Chemawa (Oregon), Chilocco (Oklahoma), Albuquerque, Phoenix, and Stewart (Nevada) each enrolled several thousand more, while three other schools in Oklahoma—Concho, Riverside, and Fort Sill—plus Haskell in Kansas took in smaller numbers of students.[29]

The Special Navajo Program mirrored the age in its unapologetic emphasis on vocational training and assimilation. A history of the program was entitled *Doorway Toward the Light*. L. Madison Combs and other BIA administrators of the era had no doubt that the Navajo future lay off the reservation. Intermountain Indian School embodied these sentiments. George Boyce, who had succeeded Lucy Adams as director of Navajo education, served as its first principal. In 1950, the school distributed a glossy, heavily illustrated, bilingual publication promoting itself as "a new opportunity for Navajo children." Boyce employed the same style he had adopted in his annual reports about the state of Navajo education. Rather than "talking down" to the people, Boyce insisted, he employed "detailed precision." In the introduction, Boyce said, "We wish every parent could visit Intermountain Indian School. They would see one of the finest schools in the United States. It is even better than most white schools." A caption accompanying one photograph read, "These boys are well clothed. They are neat. They are healthy. They are well behaved. They are eager to learn. They are getting good schooling at Intermountain Indian School." Another caption of a cook in the school kitchen read, "There is plenty of good, clean food at Intermountain Indian school. The children can have two helpings when they are hungry. They can have all they want to eat." Other captions advised Navajo parents that "[t]he sleeping rooms in the dormitories are like the bedrooms in a white man's house" and that "[e]ach pupil will be trained for a job according to the number of years he can spend at Intermountain Indian School."[30]

Such powerful and effective messages inundated Navajo country in the late 1940s and early 1950s. Parents were informed, again and again, that they would be doing the right thing by sending their children away to boarding school. Before the massive school construction program funded through the 1950 act got underway, thousands of Navajo children left the reservation in search of schooling. A listing of children in the 1948–1949 school year attending such schools continued for thirty-four single-spaced pages. From Teesto, for example, two young boys headed off to Chilocco. Dean Jackson would go on to become president of Navajo Community College; Jack Jackson would become a member of the Arizona State legislature.[31]

The Long Range Act eventually made it possible to replace the old BIA school structures with new ones, construct new schools, and add some trailer schools at more remote sites. Almost four thousand more Diné students attended on-reservation boarding schools in 1960 than in 1950. In

Practice makes perfect; penmanship exercises at a day school.
National Archives, Pacific Region, Laguna Niguel, Calif.

Flagstaff, Holbrook, Snowflake, and Winslow in Arizona, and Albuquerque, Aztec, and Gallup in New Mexico, as well as Richfield, Utah, Navajo students attended high school and lived in new dormitories. In New Mexico, Crownpoint, Huerfano, Magdalena, and Ramah dormitories were expanded.[32]

Many students who left home to attend boarding schools on or off the Navajo Nation believed that they paid too great a price. They disliked going to sleep in the dormitories. They could not stand the food. They hated being removed from the daily lives of their families. They missed ceremonies, birthdays, holidays, and other special occasions. They did not have the same opportunity to learn from their elders. Those who went to distant institutions sometimes complained about the effect their absence had on their Navajo language skills. Some contended in later years that they were less prepared to assume parental responsibilities. These individuals thus remembered their school days with enormous sadness or great bitterness.

Yet, as in the previous generation, not all Diné students had entirely negative experiences. Students who were orphans or who came from unfortunate home situations or out of dire poverty expressed gratitude for places that furnished food and shelter each day. More than a few boys relished the chance to participate in football, basketball, baseball, or track and field. Others took pride in their performances in the school band or choir. Some saw the whole experience as a necessary gauntlet that they had to run in order to achieve certain things in life. As they made their way through school, they wondered about what would happen to their peers who had taken a different path.

Alice John Bedoni of Phoenix Indian School pondered the fate of those young people who did not avail themselves of such opportunities. "Out of a family of eight children," she wrote, "about half will herd sheep, sleep in crowded quarters and become poorer because our economy can no longer support them." She added, "What could these talented young people do in our present civilization if introduced to the best in books, music, art, science, and economics? Who knows but what a Charles Curtis, Will Rogers, a Curie or a Toscanini roam the desert herding his sheep, guiding his lead goats or seeking the companionship of his sheep dog." She concluded, "We must educate our parents to send our brothers and sisters to school so that they may move forward with the rest of the young people of this great country of ours. We are called the First Americans. But we are among the last Americans educationally."[33]

Development of a Navajo public school system began to make it possible for more children to remain at home. Passage of Public Law 815 and Public Law 874 in 1953 provided funds for the construction and operation of public schools within the Navajo Nation. These laws were modeled after the kind of federal support given to school districts with military bases. Since military personnel did not pay taxes on their property, the government contributed funds to make up for that shortfall. Thanks to this support, by 1960 public elementary schools were constructed at Chinle, Crownpoint, Fort Defiance-Window Rock, Ganado, Kayenta, Shiprock, Tohatchi, and Tuba City, and junior high schools or high schools at Chinle, Fort Defiance, Shiprock, and Tuba City. Public schools in border towns in Arizona (Page) and New Mexico (Bloomfield, Cuba, Gallup, Kirtland, and Thoreau) also benefited from this aid.[34]

Not all Navajos agreed about the kind of education children should receive, but during a time when nearly all Diné children arrived at school speaking Navajo, many influential Diné advocated that schools stress the speaking of English. Tribal Council delegates worried aloud about the Navajo Nation being "behind." They believed students had to be compelled to go to school and that the schools should not "waste time" on Navajo history and culture. Hoskie Cronemeyer spoke for many in 1952 when he argued, "The teaching of Navajo customs should be done away with so that only school work will be carried on for our children." Children already knew their culture; what they needed to know was how to compete in and with the larger society.[35] A student council member at Intermountain in 1952, David Lee, advocated "speaking English all the time. In the dormitory, in the classroom, and everywhere you are, speak only English, not Navaho. If you learn it now, you can make a living much easier. When we get out of school, it is important that we know how to talk English well because we will want a job." This perspective linked with another that held little hope for the reservation economy. Sam Gorman in 1953 conveyed a common sentiment in his contention that "there is no hope of making a decent living under any circumstances" on the reservation. If Navajo children received sufficient training and education, then they would be equipped to survive in the world beyond the Navajo Nation.[36]

As more Diné students began to complete high school, more attention began to be devoted to their enrollment in colleges and universities. Sam Ahkeah helped lead the campaign for higher education. In 1953, the Tribal Council established a special fund of $30,000 to support Navajos who sought post-secondary training. The Navajo Tribal Scholarship Program gave thirty-five grants in this first year. By 1957, the money available had nearly quadrupled to $115,000 and the grants now reached two hundred students. Revenues from the Four Corners oil field made possible a tremendous expansion of this initiative. In 1958 and again in 1959, the Council deposited $5 million into the program. This infusion of money dramatically increased both the number and the amounts of the grants. A Navajo child could now perceive a college education as a real possibility.[37]

The development of the fund proved particularly satisfying to Ahkeah. In 1953, he addressed the Council and asked them to tell young people to prepare for this kind of education. Ahkeah emphasized the need for Navajo doctors, nurses, and other professionals. "We need conservationists," he said, "who would see our land is given proper care." Now, he observed, "the whites are holding these positions," but he looked forward to the time when "we would not have to depend on white people all the time."[38]

At the beginning of the 1960s, Dillon Platero, chairman of the Education Committee for the Navajo Tribe, expressed his optimism about recent developments. By 1956, he observed, only five thousand of the twenty-nine thousand Navajo children remained out of school. The Diné realized that education is "a coming thing." Education, Platero concluded, "is and will be the livelihood of the Navajo people in the future." Moreover, he commented, "[s]ince the Navajo people have realized the importance of education, they want to be part of it."[39]

ANNIE WAUNEKA AND THE PUBLIC HEALTH SERVICE
A shortage of personnel and frequent budgetary constraints plagued the federal government's attempts to provide better care to Navajo individuals and communities. The war years had been disastrous. The nursing staff at the Fort Defiance hospital dwindled from thirty-eight to thirteen and other facilities suffered similar depletions. Hospitals at Fort Defiance, Kayenta, Leupp, Toadlena, and Tohatchi closed their doors. So, too, did the Kayenta Sanatorium. Collier even let go his longtime medical director, W. W. Peter, because of budgetary constraints. Congress kept slicing federal appropriations for the Health Service; the federal government seemed unable to authorize sufficient money. With Peter's departure and then Collier's resignation in 1945, the government's commitment to providing better health care seemed very much in doubt. In the meantime, the Diné struggled with an ongoing epidemic of tuberculosis, distance from hospitals, and the intolerance of non-Navajo physicians about traditional healing ceremonies.[40]

In the winter of 1947–1948, the Navajos endured an unusually severe series of storms. The blizzards stranded countless Diné, with many lives endangered in the process. The national publicity that attended search and rescue efforts also exposed the existence of malnutrition, tuberculosis, and high infant mortality. The Navajo rate of tuberculosis had reached fourteen times the national average. More than half of all Navajo deaths were recorded in children under five years of age. Concerned outsiders who knew of the Navajo contribution to winning the war seized the opportunity to call for a stronger federal commitment to the well-being of the Diné. This criticism helped prompt Krug's report, which presented the evidence necessary to pass the Navajo-Hopi Long Range Rehabilitation Act: "Tuberculosis and infant mortality have reached what is believed to be the highest rate in the United States. There are relatively high over-all birth and death rates; a high incidence of diarrhea, dysentery, pneumonia, dental caries, skin disease, and venereal diseases." The Navajos still suffered from trachoma. The situation had become intolerable.[41]

Funding from the Rehabilitation Act began to allow the federal government to build new hospitals at Gallup and Shiprock and new clinics at Chinle, Kayenta, and Tohatchi. By 1955, when responsibility for Navajo health care was transferred from the BIA to the Public Health Service, the number of physicians had reached twenty-three, an increase of seven since 1950; by 1960, that number had risen to forty-three, spurred in part by physicians now being drafted.[42]

As Wade Davies observes in his important study of Navajo health care in the twentieth century, *Healing Ways,* the transfer to the Public Health Service must be understood in a more general context.[43] During the late 1940s and the 1950s, a drive began in Congress to terminate federal trust responsibility for Indians. The termination movement, as it was generally known, gained the support of both Democrats and Republicans, but given the perpetual Republican interest in cost cutting and more limited government, it is not surprising that Republican Senator Arthur Watkins of Utah and Representative E. Y. Berry of South Dakota assumed leadership in this crusade. Although termination is recalled primarily for ending reservation status for certain Indian communities, it affected all Native peoples.

Many Indians were not entirely unhappy with the idea of termination. They had grown weary of federal mismanagement and control. The Navajos were hardly alone in calling for the government to allow them to assume more control over their own affairs. However, the absence of federal protection gave rise to a new specter: intervention by state, county, and private interests. This prospect raised new alarm because these interests were so often antithetical to those of the Indians. On the other hand, the threat of intervention also galvanized Navajos and other Native communities to move aggressively to safeguard their interests and renew their efforts to gain a more significant degree of self-determination. Thus, somewhat ironically, the termination movement helped inspire a Navajo nationalist movement representing something very different than the full assimilation of American Indians into mainstream American society. The period from 1945 to 1960 thus should be understood as a foundation for the more visibly activist phase that we customarily associate with the 1960s.[44]

Enter Annie Wauneka. Wauneka sought to continue the work of her father and her brother, both of whom had pushed the Tribal Council to become more involved in the attempt to gain better health care for the Diné. The youngest of Chee Dodge's children, Annie Dodge was born in 1910. She attended several schools, including Albuquerque Indian School, where she met George Wauneka. They were married in 1929 and soon came to live and work on the Dodge ranch at Tanner Springs, south of the Klagetoh-Wide Ruins area. She learned about politics firsthand from her father and often accompanied him to political meetings in the vicinity. In 1951, four years after her father passed away, she decided to seek a seat on the Tribal Council, representing Klagetoh and Wide Ruins. Wauneka won and proceeded to serve on the Council for the next thirty years.[45]

Lilly Neil had not run for reelection because of a serious automobile

Annie Dodge Wauneka, Navajo leader.
Courtesy of Rough Rock Community School.

accident, so the number of women on the Council remained constant at one. Within her first term, one of the male delegates said, as Wauneka recounted it, "Where's the lady? You women can take care of the sick far better than we men can. So let's appoint her and get her to work." Just like that she had become the chair of the Health and Welfare section of the Community Services Committee.[46]

In this new assignment, she worked with area physicians to tackle tuberculosis. She demonstrated her dedication to fighting this terrible disease and her ability to communicate effectively to Navajos who had contracted it. Slowly but surely more and more Diné became convinced that the doctors actually could help them. It took years, but by the late 1950s, the Tribal Council finally empowered the tribe to confine and isolate individuals with communicable diseases. The battle had entered a new stage, due both to the unflagging efforts of the indefatigable Wauneka and a more pluralistic perspective on the part of some of the newly arrived doctors in Diné Bikéyah.

Health care entered a new era in 1955 when the Public Health Service assumed responsibility, displacing the BIA. The newly established Indian Health Service (IHS) unit had access to more funding as well as the Rehabilitation Act funds. By the end of the decade, new hospitals had been constructed in Tuba City and Shiprock; health centers were built in Chinle, Kayenta, and Tohatchi; and field stations built at Cornfields, Pinon, Pueblo Pintado, Round Rock, and White Cone. In 1961, the Gallup Indian Medical Center opened its doors. A project in the Many Farms-Rough Rock area, sponsored by Cornell University with significant funding from the Public Health Service, demonstrated from 1955 to 1962 that with more attention to cross-cultural communication and more respect being given to the Navajos by non-Navajo personnel, Diné satisfaction and usage of hospitals and clinics could realize dramatic increases. Tuberculosis rates dropped by 60 percent from 1952 to 1960, and the infant mortality rate was cut in half between 1955 and 1959. Patient and outpatient numbers increased substantially. From 1955 to 1960, the number of Navajo women giving birth in hospitals rose by 46 percent.[47]

These developments represented hard-earned victories. Wauneka always knew more remained to be done and that honest disagreements could erupt over where a particular facility might be constructed. Ever the pragmatist, she acknowledged that the medical center would be built in Gallup not because the town offered a central, convenient location for Indian patients, but because the commissioner of Indian affairs, Glenn Emmons, just happened to be from Gallup. From the outset, Wauneka cajoled and countered, prodded and pleaded to achieve results. "Mr. Commissioner," she told Emmons in November 1953, "our people are not getting the kind of medical service we were promised under the Long Range Program." She called on the Bureau to transfer its responsibility to the Public Health Service because "[t]oo many Bureau doctors are not working to make people well. At Window Rock, two doctors and a dentist sit at desks." She challenged Navajo traditional healers to demonstrate they could cure more people of tuberculosis than the IHS doctors. Wauneka said she was eager to have them succeed, so that Navajos would not have to go to distant sanitariums. However, she added, "I asked Scott Preston if he can cure tuberculosis and he says he can't do it." Preston acknowledged that although there were some diseases that only Navajo singers could cure and there were others where both doctors and singers could achieve results, there were "diseases that we medicine men have given up on. We know that you white doctors have better cures than we do. One of the diseases of that sort is tuberculosis."[48]

By decade's end, non-Navajo health care providers were also gaining a clearer sense from the outset about Navajo cultural perspectives. One orientation guide published in 1959 counseled, "With sincere effort, some skill, and a little luck, the public health worker may earn for himself a place with the Navajos as a potential friend; and not a person who is always in a superior role."[49] Navajo nurses, aides, and interpreters all made a difference in this process. White physicians still showed up with imperious attitudes; missionary physicians still thundered about the foolishness of traditional healers. The sign outside of the Ganado Mission school and hospital still read, "Tradition is the Enemy of Progress." But progress, in fact, had been achieved.

VOTING RIGHTS AND FREEDOM OF RELIGION, 1945–1962

Superintendent Stewart kept returning to Private Anderson's letter. Deeply moved by Anderson's plea in regard to Navajo voting rights, he tried to summon appropriate words. "There should be no question," he began, "that you, who are making such great sacrifices for your country should be governed. Your patriotism is not denied, your devotion to duty is beyond question. . . . [T]here can be no denial that you are entitled to the same right of suffrage as other citizens." Stewart vowed to help achieve the goal. "While you are fighting on the battlefront," he asserted, "a fight must be waged here on the homefront to obtain for you the right accorded all free peoples." He expressed the hope that "the fight here will be as successful as your fight there so that upon your return you can take your rightful place in the peaceful army of citizens, kept free through your efforts, and cast your vote with theirs."[50]

Indian voting rights had been a matter of contention for decades. After the passage of the Indian Citizenship Act in 1924, two Pima men attempted to exercise their right to vote in the presidential election of 1928. The state of Arizona claimed they could not vote because the federal government acted as guardians for them and the state constitution prohibited any person under guardianship from voting. The Pimas were denied the franchise and took the issue to court. In *Porter v. Hall*, the Arizona Supreme Court ruled in favor of the state, again citing the question of guardianship.

Guardianship was a code word for the real objection—that Indians who resided on reservations did not pay state property taxes. Although Anglo residents of counties such as Apache in northwestern Arizona did not always prove forthcoming on this question, there remained another vexing concern. If the Navajos were able to vote in Apache County, their numbers suggested that they might hold the balance of power in a close election. They might even be emboldened to seek a seat in the legislature, on the county board of supervisors, or on a local school board. This was not the happiest of prospects, so registrars started digging in their heels. There the question remained until the 1940s.[51]

Then Navajos in the service and on the home front, together with Stewart and other allies, decided enough was more than enough. Navajos started to vote by absentee ballot in the 1944 election, even if they were not formally registered to cast their ballot. In San Juan County, New Mexico, a grand total of four Diné were registered and they had one thing in common: they were all named Morgan. But, district supervisor Clyde Hunter informed Stewart in February 1945, Jacob C. Morgan, "Mrs. Jacob C. Morgan," Wilbur E. Morgan, and Irvin Morgan had been registered for years and had voted before. They were taxpayers; they owned real estate.[52]

However, the dam showed signs of giving way. Navajo Tribal Council delegate Robert Martin of Shiprock had voted in a local election, presenting only an automobile tax receipt as evidence of his status. His ballot had not been challenged. Moreover, many others had cast absentee ballots in that election. In addition to Wilbur Morgan, they included four residents of Farmington (Hugh Dempsey, Taylor Jones, Ben Lopez, and George Yazzie), three residents of Toadlena (Keeyah H. Begay, Kee D. Jackson, and Hugh S. Johnson), two residents of Bloomfield (Allen Thompson and Joe B. Charley), and eleven residents of the Shiprock area (Roland N. Begay, Daniel Benally, Clah Ben Nez, Fred Blue Eyes, John Chee, Willie Frank, LeRoy John, Joe Kee, Frank D. Pete, Norman Yazzie, and Woody Yazzie). San Juan County officials were reported to be ready to acknowledge the Navajo right to vote. Yet when a number of Navajos came to the Shiprock Public School on May 6, 1946, to try to register to vote, they were denied permission to register. John Dayish, Harry Denetclaw, Julia Denetclaw, Jimmie K. King, Howard H. Nez, and other Diné filled out affidavits stating the length of their residence in the state of New Mexico, the county of San Juan, and the voting precinct. "Fifty-three years, 53 years, 53 years," certified Dayish. Of course, it could have been 153, 153, and 153 and it would not have mattered.[53]

In the meantime, other Diné tested Arizona's resolve. William Ashley, Theodore R. Dawes, Tom Irving, James Charlie Manuelito, Salago Nez, Robert Perry, and Alvin Wilson all attempted to register on May 3, 1946. Ashley confessed to being a Democrat, acknowledged that he weighed 145 pounds, assured one and all that he could read the Constitution in the English language, and recorded that he had served in the army. In the space labeled "color," the clerk decided to type in "Indian." Ashley could have been a Republican weighing 350 pounds. It did not matter. Following the instructions of Apache County attorney J. Smith Gibbons, the justice of the peace refused to permit Ashley to vote.[54]

At the McKinley County Courthouse in Gallup, a rather similar scene unfolded. At two o'clock that afternoon, Watson Watson, Jimmie Largo, and Frank Peralta came in and asked to see the county clerk. Along the way the clerk learned that Gibson was a veteran, that Largo was twenty-nine years old, and that Peralta did not speak any English. She also verified that they paid no property taxes on any land in New Mexico.[55]

In response to a letter from R. E. Karigan, Levi S. Udall wrote to "Dear Friend Bob" on April 11, 1946. The judge expressed his opinion that given state law then in place, this time around the Navajos would not be allowed to vote. In order for things to change, the Arizona Supreme Court would have to reverse the decision rendered years ago. But, Udall reminded Karigan that he was running for the supreme court. "Maybe there will be something I can do."[56]

Several different incidents could have employed to force the Arizona Supreme Court to rule, but it turned out to be the denial of the right to vote to two Yavapais that gave the court the chance to "back up" and change the law. Maricopa County registrar Roger G. Laveen did not allow Frank Harrison and Harry Austin to vote. After a Maricopa County judge supported Laveen, the Arizona Supreme Court reversed and remanded this decision. "The right of American Indians to vote in Arizona elections for state and local officers," the court declared, "has after two decades arisen, like Banquo's ghost to challenge us." The court answered the challenge with the majority opinion being written by a newcomer, one Levi S. Udall. In 1948, New Mexico Indians gained a comparable victory in the state supreme court. Utah Indians finally reached their objective in 1953.[57]

In addition to voting rights, a second issue continued to raise major questions. The Native American Church had gained an increasing number of adherents and, as has been suggested, the question of its nature, purpose, and influence had become a hotly debated topic throughout Navajo country. A few Tribal Council members were members and some other Council members believed in the church's right to hold services without harassment. However, those with strong ties to traditional Navajo beliefs or evangelical Christian beliefs heatedly objected to its very presence. In the 1940s and 1950s, therefore, the rights of church members became the matter of vigorous debate and dispute.

A meeting with Department of the Interior officials on May 13, 1946, afforded ample opportunity for an exchange of views. Scott Preston criticized peyote as "causing a lot of trouble among the Navajos." He said, "It began to cause trouble, particularly dividing the people in two factions. . . . In many, many cases it has split families, where some members use it while others are against that practice." He contended that peyote was not needed because "we have our own ceremonies and the prayers that are connected with it." Preston labeled the use of peyote "a money-making scheme" but conceded that "[t]his peyote thing has made quite an inroad on the Navajo reservation." Sam Ahkeah disputed claims that peyote should be considered medicine. He called it "a narcotic." He said he did not oppose the right of people to join the church but concluded, "[W]e do not want that church on the Navajo reservation."[58]

Native American Church member David Clark disputed these conclusions. Church meetings offered prayers in the same way that prayers were offered in traditional ceremonies. Peyote healed "a good many sick people," Clark averred. It had also been used to offer prayers for Navajo servicemen. "[W]e offered prayers that our boys be saved, and that our enemies' weapons be turned to water." Although it is said that peyote kills our people, Clark continued, alcohol is really what is killing our people. Traditional Navajo ceremonialism often was "not effective" in this regard, but peyote had helped many individuals.[59]

The Tribal Council maintained its stance against peyote through this period. Eventually, the Native American Church on behalf of William Peter Tsosie, Shorty Duncan, and other Diné, sued the Council, as represented by Chairman Paul Jones and Council members Joe Duncan and Sam Garnez, to overturn the ban against possession or use of peyote on Navajo land. In *Native American Church v. Navajo Tribal Council* (1959), the Tenth Circuit Court of Appeals ruled in favor of the tribe, declaring that the First Amendment did not apply to Indian tribes because "[t]hey have a higher status than that of states. They are subordinate and dependent nations possessed of all powers as such only to the extent that they have expressly been required to surrender them by the superior sovereign, the United States."[60]

An increasing number of Navajos had begun to participate in Native American Church meetings. The church's appeal appeared to be the same within Navajo country as its appeal elsewhere. It encouraged brotherhood and furnished an effective means to battle problems with alcohol. During the 1950s, even as more Diné were arrested for violations against the tribal ordinance, more Navajos who did not become church members became more tolerant of its presence. Support of church members and their allies played a key role in supporting Raymond Nakai in his bid to become chairman of the Tribal Council in 1959 and in electing him in 1963. Nakai did not belong to the church, but made it clear that he opposed the kind of official sanctions that had been imposed on it. With Nakai's election, the issue of peyotism did not disappear, but did enter a different phase.[61]

AN EXPANDING GOVERNMENT AND THE ACQUISITION
OF LEGAL COUNSEL
In 1947, Navajo political life ventured into uncharted terrain. Chee Dodge had regained the tribal chairmanship in 1946, with Sam Ahkeah elected as

the vice chairman. However, Dodge passed away before serving another term. Dodge had literally been a bridge for his people. As David Brugge phrased it, his life spanned "the years of war, exile, expatriation, and the emergence of tribal government among the Navajos; years when Navajo society was transformed from semi-sedentary bands and local family groups into the largest tribe living on the largest reservation in the United States."[62] Although he was about eighty-six years of age at the time of his death, it remained difficult to believe that he was gone and it seemed almost impossible to imagine Navajo life without Adiits'a'í Sání.

A high requiem mass preceded burial at the veterans' cemetery between Window Rock and Fort Defiance. Speaking in Navajo at the memorial service, Father Berard Haile, a longtime friend, reminded the hundreds who had crowded into St. Michaels how Manuelito and other Navajo headmen had enabled the young Dodge to become an interpreter, how Dodge had become friends with Father Anselm Weber, and how "he made all things clear to the Navajo people." An observer counted nearly one hundred cars and pickups at the service—an appropriate tribute in and of itself to a man who had always loved motor vehicles and had been one of the first in the Navajo community to own one. Then on a clear, cold early January morning, with hoar frost covering the sagebrush and piñon, the mourners made their way to the cemetery and said good-bye to "Old Mister Interpreter."[63]

Sam Ahkeah followed Dodge as chairman and served two full terms before Paul Jones's election in 1955. Born in the final years of the nineteenth century, he spent his early childhood, as did most children of the time, listening to the elders and learning some of life's lessons while looking after the sheep. From his boyhood home in the vicinity of Rock Point, he made the long journey to Fort Lewis, Colorado, where at the age of eight in 1904 he first enrolled in school. At Fort Lewis, he became "Sam Ahkeah," with the school principal altering the Diné word for boy, ashkii, and arbitrarily tossing in "Sam" to complete the process. Ahkeah, as previously mentioned, later attended school in Shiprock, where taking in one of the first of the Shiprock fairs became a far happier memory than enduring Mr. Abbott's monologue. Although tuberculosis abbreviated his days as a student, his nearly eight years of formal education were unusual for the time and provided a good foundation for his life and career. Ahkeah regained his health in southern Colorado, while breaking horses and milking the fifteen cows of the Broadhead ranch near Alamosa. He then moved on to more lucrative employment as a foreman in the Telluride area, where he supervised forty Navajo miners. The collapse of a mine ceiling one day reminded him how much he loved ranching. Ahkeah returned to the reservation and scraped together the beginnings of a small ranch north of Shiprock, then left the fledgling operation in the care of his sister and signed on as a foreman for a maintenance crew at Mesa Verde. After sending money home for fourteen years and having the satisfaction of seeing

Portrait of Sam Ahkeah, Window Rock, Arizona.
Photograph by Milton Snow. Courtesy of the Navajo
Nation Museum, Window Rock, AZ. Catalog no. NO9-63

his herd of sheep expand to 550, he returned. However, the stock reduction program decimated the holdings his sister and he had labored so hard to develop. His herd dwindled to thirty-nine.[64] Ahkeah's outrage inspired him to pursue a career in politics, where his articulate manner and dedication to the people won him a wide following. Elected initially as vice chairman in 1942 and reelected in 1946, he was ready in 1947 to assume the mantle of leadership.

One of the most significant decisions of the Ahkeah chairmanship came during its first year when he selected Norman Littell as the Navajos' first attorney. The Tribal Council formally endorsed the choice on July 10, 1947. The two men had met at a conference in New York City on February 28 and March 1, 1947, in which some of the issues currently facing the Navajos were being addressed. The creation by Congress of the Indian Claims Commission pushed the Navajos to hire an attorney. As linguist and veteran BIA administrator Robert W. Young noted, the Council also "was convinced of its need for a person to whom it could look for guidance—someone outside the Federal Government in whom it could place full confidence to assist in the development of the rehabilitation program and to counteract a renewed effort on the part of the Department and the Bureau to resume the stock reduction program of the prewar period."[65]

Littell's work on the Navajo claim thus occupied only part of his time. The commission reviewed Native claims for compensation for a variety of wrongs inflicted on them by the federal government, especially in regard to more appropriate payments for territories relinquished through treaties and agreements with the United States. The commission had not been established because of liberal hand-wringing of guilt for past injustices but because of conservative desires to terminate federal trust responsibilities for Indian affairs. But the process of hearing Indian claims turned out to be a very extended one. Even though Littell served as the Navajos' attorney for nearly two decades, he would not be around in 1970, when the decision finally emerged.

In the meantime, Littell moved quickly to maximize his power and influence within the workings of the Tribal Council. A graduate of Wabash College and the University of Washington law school, Littell had been a Rhodes scholar, had been associated with two Seattle law firms, and then had worked in Washington, D.C., as assistant solicitor in the Department of the Interior and assistant attorney general. From 1939 to 1944, he had headed the Lands Division for the Department of Justice, dealing in part with issues involving the public domain.[66]

The situation in Navajo country in 1947 enabled Littell to assume a position of considerable authority. Robert W. Young later recalled that the circumstances confronting the Diné "drove the Navajos right into Littell's arms" and permitted him to become "the sparkplug of Navajo economic development."[67] The Navajo-Hopi Rehabilitation Act funds, the royalties from mineral resource development, the anger the Diné felt about livestock

Norman Littell, general counsel. Photographed
by Milton Snow. Courtesy of the Navajo Nation
Museum, Window Rock, AZ. Catalog no. NO9-185

reduction, and the termination era all combined to change what the tribal government could do and could become. Littell was a quick study; he soon learned that criticizing Collier and supporting equal rights for the Navajos furnished a message that the Diné wanted to hear. He knew the Navajos were eager to take charge of more of their own affairs and he became determined to help them achieve that objective. He appreciated the central role played by the general counsel. In 1951, he commented, "Legal advice not only gave the Tribal Council and officers confidence as to the meaning of resolutions and knowledge of tribal authority and power over lands and resources, but also expedited the work of the Bureau of Indian Affairs in transacting business with the tribe."[68]

Littell did not succeed in bringing in compensation to the Navajos through the Indian Claims Commission, but he did succeed in helping to make the tribal government a far more ambitious and independent presence. Through the late 1940s, the 1950s, and into the early 1960s, the ubiquitous Littell acted in meetings of the Tribal Council as though he was being paid by the word. Almost no issue escaped his scrutiny and almost no matter avoided his commentary. Littell's hand could be seen in most of the resolutions passed by the Council and his presence surely encouraged more resolutions to be crafted and approved. From 1947 to 1957, the Council approved 2,300 resolutions, nearly ten times as many as it had passed in the previous two decades.[69]

Littell's successful battle against the livestock reduction program solidified his influence. Eventually, the federal government essentially abandoned the fight, turning over the matter to the tribal government. The Tribal Council devoted a great deal of time and emotion to the subject, before finally in 1956, it adopted grazing regulations that were sufficiently vague that the Navajos believed they could live with them. Many credited Littell with this outcome.[70]

The Navajos' commitment to greater self-determination received a noteworthy test in the final days of 1947 when the federal government attempted to reappoint E. R. "Si" Fryer as superintendent of the Navajo reservation. When he heard the news of the impending appointment, Chairman Ahkeah sent forty telegrams protesting the action to congressmen, other officials, and newspapers. "We do not want Fryer back," he said. "Mr. Fryer was the one who forced stock reduction on the Navajo" and "thousands of innocent Navajos went to jail right here on the reservation because they were trying to take care of their sheep." Council delegate Joe Duncan looked at the calendar and observed, "This is not a very nice Christmas present for the Navajos." The Interior Department chose not to return Fryer to Window Rock.[71]

In addition to *Native American Church v. Navajo Tribal Council*, Littell won a second significant legal triumph in 1959 in *Williams v. Lee*. A non-Indian trader on the Navajo reservation had sued a Navajo in state court in an attempt to receive $281 for goods sold on credit. The Arizona

Supreme Court ruled in favor of the trader, but the U.S. Supreme Court reversed this decision. Justice Hugo Black's majority opinion declared, "There can be no doubt that to allow the exercise of state jurisdiction here would undermine the authority of the tribal courts over Reservation affairs and hence would infringe on the right of the Indians to govern themselves." Prominent Chemehuevi attorney Fred Ragsdale labeled *Williams v. Lee* "the first modern Indian law case," for it ushered in a period of legal efforts to defend and expand tribal sovereignty.[72] The decision also signaled the beginning of the end for the terminationist movement, even if, for the time being, proponents of termination stubbornly refused to concede the fight.

When Howard Gorman announced the results of *Williams v. Lee* to the Tribal Council, he encouraged and received a round of applause for the efforts of Littell and his associates to defend Navajo jurisdiction. However, Littell was not immune from pointed criticism. Annie Wauneka echoed Ahkeah's theme about the need for trained Navajo professionals so that the Diné would not have to depend on outsiders. Speaking to the Council in 1956, Wauneka commented about the general counsel: "Now when he tends to his job on the Claims in behalf of the Navajo Tribe and gives us a specific instance at least one time showing that he is actually on the job and gives us some return on our hiring to represent us on the Claims, then we can get some assurance that . . . we have hired the right person to do a good job for us. So far he has not given us a definite showing and brought us some money here." Wauneka continued, "Our attorney is a white man. If we had an attorney from our own tribe to tell us these things which we have had told us by this white man, we would give it our hearty support but there is a doubt about the present attorney's ability, or lack of it, to help us."[73] When Ahkeah attempted to wrest the chairmanship back from Jones in 1959, he criticized Littell for not achieving any results in the claims case and for becoming too dominant in tribal affairs. These criticisms eventually took a toll on Littell's support and weakened his ability to withstand the kind of campaign Raymond Nakai waged against him in the 1960s.

There may have been debate about Littell, but there could be little disagreement that the Navajo tribal government significantly expanded its role and mission in the 1950s. Positions within the government became full time or essentially full time. The escalation of the chairman's salary offers a case in point: from $200 a month in 1940 to $5,000 a year in 1950, to $9,000 a year in 1956, and $13,000 for the final year of a first term. The number of days a Council delegate had to invest grew from just a small number per year to about one hundred. The tribal budget tripled from $1,022,647 in 1954 to $3,254,325 in 1957 to $12 million in 1958, including the $5 million appropriated for the College Scholarship Program.[74]

With an unprecedented amount of money at its disposal, the Council resisted the siren song of per capita payments, realizing that the size of the Navajo population would mean that individual shares would be too small to make much of a difference. Instead, the Council tried to develop programs that benefited all the people. It expressed a particular interest in long-term development, both economically and culturally. Delegates took seriously "the rare privilege," as Paul Jones phrased it in his inaugural address of 1959, "of participating in one of the most significant developments in Indian tribal government in the history of the United States."[75]

Some of the new money went to revitalize the chapter system, which had become moribund during the livestock reduction era. An infusion of money allowed for the building or reconstruction of chapter houses and to provide per diem payments to officers. In 1957, the start of the Emergency Work Relief Program employed the poor through small-scale construction or repair projects. By 1960, the Council was putting $5 million into this program. Dispensing these funds began to give chapters a new focus and new reason to be. "Public [w]orks," concluded anthropologist Mary Shepardson, "meant the full institutionalization as part of the political system." The chapters furnished "the means by which a traditional society with its traditional problems is channeled into the modern Tribal Council system." In 1957–1958, the chapters of Chinle, Crownpoint, Fort Defiance, Shiprock, and Tuba City met a total of 283 times, with 14,560 in total attendance.[76]

By the early 1960s, more than half of the chapter houses were of new construction. These facilities provided a place for community gatherings and local decision making. Chapter meetings, nevertheless, were not for the weak nor the faint of heart. Irene Stewart served as secretary of the Chinle chapter during this period and she recalled meetings that could "become very tedious, with long drawn-out talks of the old ways, how old leaders used to give talks, and control the people."[77]

At the Navajo national level, Paul Jones followed Ahkeah as chairman and also served two terms, from 1955 to 1963, when Raymond Nakai defeated Jones in his bid for a third term. Jones's terms coincided with the rapid increase in the revenues being generated by the exploitation of Navajo mineral resources. He thus helped oversee the continuing expansion of Diné government as the Navajos responded to the threat of termination.

A contemporary of Sam Ahkeah, Jones was the last Navajo Tribal Council chairman to be born in the nineteenth century. He was born on October 20, 1895, just south of Naschitti, New Mexico, and spent his first years herding sheep and living a traditional lifestyle. Then the principal of the local school at Tohatchi dispatched a Navajo policeman to bring in Tł'aashchi'i Biyé' (or Klass Chee Begay—the son of Klass Chee) to be enrolled and gave him the name of Paul Jones. Tohatchi also was the site of a Christian Reformed Mission church, where medical missionary Dr. Lee Huizenga lived. Huizenga heard of Jones's growing facility with the English language and took an interest in him.[78]

Jones's association with Huizenga eventually allowed him to go east

Paul Jones, Navajo Tribal Council Chairman.
Courtesy of Rough Rock Community School.

with the physician and his family and live with them while attending high school in Englewood, New Jersey. When Huizenga moved to China, Jones moved on to Grand Rapids, Michigan, in order to complete his high school education through classes being offered in a division of Calvin College. Since Jones had not begun his schooling at the age of seven, he was now twenty-two years old and eligible for the draft. The army drafted him and Jones served in Europe. After the war concluded, Jones returned to Tohatchi and worked for a year at the Tohatchi school, saved money, and then returned to Grand Rapids, Michigan, to enroll at McLaughlin's Business College. Following the completion of his education, he worked as an assistant shipping clerk for the National Tea Company. In 1933, Jones finally returned to the Navajo Nation. He worked as an interpreter for the Tribal Council, quickly earning praise for his skill with both the Navajo and the English languages, and also worked as a district supervisor in Pinon.[79]

Ahkeah and Jones ran against each other for the chairman post in 1955 and again in 1959. As a two-term incumbent, Ahkeah had to defend his record, while Jones in 1955 could be seen as a new voice, yet one who knew the business of the Council because of his work as interpreter. Thus, Ahkeah had to defend himself against versions of "Sam lied to us; he said he'd get us back our sheep," while Jones benefited from perceptions that he was better educated and more worldly. Jones's popularity certainly attested to the kind of transition that had occurred in general Navajo attitudes about education. He and his running mate Scott Preston won the election, receiving 10,211 votes to 6,700 for Ahkeah and Adolph Maloney.[80]

Four years later Jones had his own track record to defend. Ahkeah hammered away at Littell's salary ($35,000), his control of the Council, and his failure to achieve results in the claims process. Peyote also captured a good deal of attention, with Jones opposing it, and Ahkeah and a third candidate, Raymond Nakai, leaning toward legalization. This contest promised to be closer than the election of 1955, but Jones emerged as the nominee of the four electoral provinces and thus was the only name on the November ballot. A good deal of unhappiness accompanied this development, but under the rules of the election, Ahkeah could not appear on the ballot and Jones thus won an uncontested victory in the fall. Voters also elected an unprecedented number of younger men to the Council. The Diné electorate's willingness to entrust responsibility to younger people augured well for Raymond Nakai if he chose to seek the chairmanship in 1963.[81]

Both Ahkeah and Jones took an active interest in the revitalization of Navajo chapters. They realized that a more viable network of chapters could contribute in a valuable way to the overall viability of the Navajo political system. So, too, did the development of a court system, encouraged by Diné interest in self-determination and their realization that without such development, the Navajos risked judicial invasion by the states of Arizona, New Mexico, and Utah. Congressional approval of Public Law 280, which granted states more authority on Indian reservations, underlined the need for a timely Navajo response. In 1959, the Tribal Council approved the expansion of its judicial system to a three-tiered operation. It included six trial courts and a court of appeals. In addition, recognizing the needs of individual Navajos for legal assistance, it also created in 1958 a legal aid services program in Window Rock. This modest program furnished a foundation for a more vigorous and far-reaching legal services program to be started in the late 1960s, funded by the federal government. The Tribal Council in 1959 also established the Navajo police so that the Navajo Nation could assume responsibilities for law enforcement rather than the federal government. Police stations opened in Fort Defiance, Tuba City, Shiprock, and Crownpoint, with another added in Chinle in 1962.[82]

THE CONFLICT WITH THE HOPIS INTENSIFIES

Disagreements intensified with the Hopis over occupancy and land use. During this period this simmering conflict entered a crucial phase. Ongoing complaints about trespassing, growing populations, the acquisition of legal counsel, and the mineral resources contained within some of this disputed ground all influenced the evolution of the conflict. Although individuals on both sides continued to hope that a solution could be found, the end result of the era brought heightened tension and disagreement rather than resolution.

Many Navajos continued to blame John Collier for the difficulties the Diné faced in their relationship with the Hopis. Council delegate Eugene Gordy, for example, on December 8, 1954, named Collier as "the cause of trouble with the Hopis, because he made the land divided for the Hopis as well as the Navajos." He argued, "We do not complain about them, but they start the complaints about the Navajos." One of the persistent Hopi complaints concerned "trespassing" Navajo horses. In 1954, 150 to 200 Navajo horses were captured and held until redeemed for a fee. The Navajos suggested that in the absence of a natural boundary or artificial barrier, livestock would "drift" back and forth, "chiefly into the Hopi Reservation because of better grazing conditions." They also complained about the Hopis hauling off wood from Navajo land.[83]

This kind of back-and-forth had gone on for years, with a degree of unhappiness but without major confrontations. However, in the mid-1950s this picture began to change. The presence of two entities—attorneys and coal—helped ratchet up the rhetoric. The existence of vast coal deposits in the 1882 executive-order area had long been known. But at this time, there emerged a market for coal and an insistence on the part of major utilities in California and the Southwest that they have access to this resource. The presence of legal counsel escalated the existing conflict and made some kind of showdown almost inevitable. Norman Littell was not about to back off from a fight. Neither was the attorney for the Hopis, John Boyden.

Boyden had applied to become the general counsel for the Navajos and been passed over in favor of Littell. He never forgot nor forgave that slight. Nor did the Salt Lake City attorney care much for Littell, whose more flamboyant personality severely contrasted with his own more conservative approach. At an early stage, observers could anticipate that the conflict between the two Indian nations might be linked to a clash between these two men hired to represent them.[84]

In 1956, the Hopis filed a brief with the Department of the Interior claiming all the minerals within the 1882 reservation area. Littell advised the Navajos to contest this move. Scott Preston and other Navajos expressed more concern about the possibility of Navajos in the disputed area being forced to leave than a possible loss of tribal revenue from mineral resources, but eventually the Diné agreed with Littell's recommendation. A bill that attempted to resolve the matter eventually passed Congress in 1958. The act permitted each tribe to sue the other in the U.S. District Court "for the purposes of determining the rights and interests of said parties in and to said lands and quieting title thereto in the tribes of Indians establish such claims pursuant to such Executive Order as may be just and fair in law and equity." And so the battle began.

In September 1960, in Prescott, Arizona, the two sides met in court. Each nation had prepared extensive testimony in regard to its occupation and use of the territory in question. The Navajo research team consisted of Lee Correll, Dave De Harport, and David Brugge. The night before the court convened, an anxious Brugge discovered in his hotel room "not only the *Gideon Bible* but a *Book of Mormon* as was usual in hotel and motel rooms throughout the Southwest at that time. As the Hopis' attorneys were known to be Mormons," Brugge opened the Mormon volume and "was rewarded with a long text berating lawyers as avaricious hypocrites."[85]

The next morning, Littell and Boyden made their initial statements. Boyden, Brugge thought, "relied heavily on oratorical ability and had a melodramatic style in court" that reminded him "of an old-time preacher." Brugge observed that Boyden worked "to make the Hopis appear as impoverished saints and the Navajos as nomadic aggressors." Testimony followed from non-Indian scholars and Hopi and Navajo witnesses. Navajos testifying included James Cook, Joe Kabinto, David Bitsillie, David Benally, John Reed, John Tsosie Nez, Emil Kanuho, George Nells, Slow Horse, Ashiihii Ts'osie, Lester Benally, Yellow Hair Bedonie, Scott Preston, Jacal Badaanee, Oscar Yonnie, Hastiin Bedoni, Moses Dijoli, Maurice McCabe, Clarence Ashby, Edward O. Plummer, Wilbur E. Morgan, Clifford Beck, Donald Mose, and Annie Wauneka. Most of these individuals were elders from the disputed area.[86]

Healing v. Jones, announced on September 28, 1962, turned out contrary to Navajo expectations. The Hopis retained all of land management district 6 and "joint, undivided and equal rights and interests" with the Navajos to the rest of the 1882 reservation. Although the judges recognized Diné use and occupation, they concluded that the Hopis had been presented rights to the entire acreage in 1882 and that they had not abandoned nor lost that interest. Of course, the Navajos appealed the decision to the Supreme Court. At the end of 1962, they awaited its response.[87]

THE TRADERS FACE CRITICISM

Another important confrontation involved the role and place of traders and trading posts. During the late 1940s, the Tribal Council tackled this complicated but highly important matter. Criticism had been expressed about certain traders before the war, but just as the movement for Navajo suffrage received a boost from veterans' expectations and demands, so, too, did the drive for reform of the trading post system.

The war had delayed the movement for reform of the arrangements through which the traders did business. Now the pent-up feelings of many Diné erupted in a campaign that startled many of the old-time traders, who had grown accustomed to minimal regulation or accountability. They had also become complacent about an association that anthropologist William Y. Adams labeled in 1963 as "reminiscent of the parent-child relationship." According to Adams, "Each particular behavior pattern, whether it be joking, sincerity, condemnation, threat, or advice, emphasizes in its own way the superordinate authority of the trader and disparages independence, initiative, and counter-authority on the part of the Navaho." He concluded, "Trading post customers are expected to receive condemnation with humility, reward and praise with gratitude, threats with fear, and advice with attention and assent."[88]

That may have remained the ideal from the average trader's perspective, but many Navajos came out of the war years no longer willing to play the role of "the Navvies," as some of the old-time traders persisted in calling them. Within the Council chambers, delegates became quite outspoken in their demands for major changes in the relationship between traders and the Diné. Council delegates Dewey Etsitty and Roger Davis, speaking on June 26, 1948, expressed widely shared sentiments. Etsitty argued, "The reservation is our home. . . . [W]e should have our own people do the trading business on the reservation." Davis contended, "[T]he people want something done about the traders. . . . They pay us but not enough. They get all the money. We pay everything. . . . I think we should get a fair rental on the land. . . . I feel that twenty-five dollars a year for trading on the Navajo and getting rich on the Navajos, sucking the Navajo life is unfair. I think it is time the Navajo Tribal Council get down to business and do something."[89]

This reexamination occurred in the context of the widespread publicity given to the Navajos' postwar economic woes and the hardships brought on by both blizzards and drought. Consultant Max Drefkoff completed a study commissioned by the Department of the Interior that called for significant investment in industrial development, the establishment of a Navajo credit union, the taxation of missions, and a fee being levied on the traders based on a percentage of their sales. Secretary of the Interior Krug endorsed Drefkoff's analysis. In turn, the Tribal Council passed a resolution on March 20, 1948, supporting Drefkoff's main recommendations: price controls on goods, increased rents through a tax on gross sales, and much more extensive bookkeeping.[90]

This resolution remained subject to federal approval and rather than bowing their heads and going quietly into the night, the traders counterattacked. Many blamed Littell and Drefkoff, above all. They lampooned Littell as someone from Washington and depicted Drefkoff as un-American. Writing fully a half-century after these events, Sallie Lippincott Wagner could not bring herself to mention Littell or Drefkoff by name. She remembered, "Changes were afoot all over the reservation. The Tribal Council was coming under the domination of a man from Washington and a strange little Russian. He was, confusingly enough, born in Georgia, Russia, and had lived in Moscow, Idaho. Under their domination, rules and regulations were passed that were insupportable by the traders."[91]

The traders lobbied vigorously before the Tribal Council and before the Congress. William J. Lippincott, who had operated a trading post at Wide Ruins for a decade, protested that the resolution would limit traders "so drastically that they face the prospect of being forced out of business." Superintendent Stewart believed that the acting commissioner of Indian affairs would approve the resolution. "There is no earthly reason why that resolution will not be approved," he reassured the Tribal Council's Advisory Committee. "We just have to keep pushing them." Instead the traders' push caused Acting Commissioner William J. Zimmerman to cave in; he did not approve the resolution, but rather called for a study of trading on the reservation. The study carried out by Bonney Youngblood, an experiment station administrator for the Department of Agriculture, produced a compromise document that irritated both sides and did little to resolve the dispute.[92]

The traders won the battle and lost the war. They succeeded in the short term in blocking meaningful change to how they did business, but their statements and attitudes would be remembered and held against them in the early 1970s when trader business practices came under far more unrelenting scrutiny. Trader intransigence, moreover, could not stonewall a changing marketplace. Access to automobiles by the Navajos and improved roads on the reservation made possible by the Long Range Rehabilitation Act paved the way toward an end to isolation. The trader monopoly began to evaporate and the old pattern of dependency was disrupted. Nor did the Navajo Nation entirely back down. It formed a trading committee in 1950, and by 1955 had succeeded in gaining federal approval for a modest but still more substantial body of regulations of the trading business. In the meantime, some of the traders decided to call it a day, including Bill and Sallie Lippincott, who sold the Wide Ruins post in 1950, and left Navajo country for good.[93]

MINERAL DEVELOPMENT

The impact of livestock reduction and the experiences of Navajos in the war continued to push more Diné into the wage-work economy. Livestock remained important in the workings of traditional Navajo culture, but a progressively smaller percentage of the population could rely on raising livestock as economically viable. The full implications of this transition would not be evident for some years to come, but it contributed to the steady movement into the wage-work economy.

Traders helped recruit workers for the railroads and other off-reservation employers looking to recruit Navajo laborers. Such employment benefited not only individual Diné households but also the trader, for it brought more cash spending money into the local economy. At Shonto, for example, Adams reported: "The combination of wages and unemployment compensation from the railroad accounted for just over half the community's total income, in 1955." Shonto's workers on the railroad generally worked for a two- to three-month period in the fall. They worked together as laborers, helping to repair or lay track, usually for the Santa Fe Railway. Their supplementary income made a significant difference in their lives and the lives of their families.[94]

The experience of veterans and defense workers during the war enabled many of them to move off the reservation in search of employment. The BIA aided and abetted such efforts because federal employees believed that individual Diné had much more of a chance to become self-sufficient if they moved away from the reservation. Despite confronting considerable discrimination, problems with housing, and other dilemmas, the tradeoffs still seemed worthwhile to more than a few Diné.[95] Sam Ahkeah's experience in the mines of southwestern Colorado was not atypical. Mines in the region employed hundreds of Navajo workers, who endured housing segregation, lower wages for the same work, poor housing, and racism. Even with all of the indignities they confronted, Navajos were eager to work in places like Grand Junction because it had earned a reputation for offering higher wages. However, they did not want to become permanent or even long-term residents of the area where their employment was situated. They tended to work for a few months, save some money, return home for a time, and then leave to start the employment cycle again.[96]

The Tribal Council took an active interest in the welfare of off-reservation workers. Council delegate Frank Bradley chaired a committee charged with safeguarding the interests of these laborers. He reported to the Council in 1947 that although some Navajos were earning more money than they would at home, their living conditions were often "deplorable." He said, "In some places we found the Navajos are living in chicken coops." Bradley also expressed concern for the children of agricultural workers. There were hundreds of Navajo children who had not returned to school. The Tribal Council or the Bureau needed to do a better job of tracking what happened to these families. "Nobody goes around and sees about these things," he concluded.[97]

A different kind of tracking did not take place for those Diné who found work in the booming uranium industry of the postwar years. When Paddy Martinez, a Navajo, discovered uranium deposits in the checkerboard area in 1951, the find triggered a boom. Timothy Benally, director of the Navajo Uranium Workers office in Shiprock, recalled: "Right after World War II, when the government found out what uranium can do, they decided to mine some of those areas and a lot of it was found on the reservation. People just went crazy looking for uranium, prospecting all over the reservation." He added, "The Vanadium Corporation of America and Kerr-McGee were the principal owners of these mines and they have taken advantage of the Navajo workers. Not only with paying low wages but by not informing the workers about the hazardous effects that uranium has on their lives."[98]

Hundreds of Navajo men worked in these mines. A man left home in the morning, not always eager to confront a hard day of labor, but glad to have a job. He worked in a mine without proper ventilation. When he got thirsty, he might scoop water from a dust-covered puddle on the mine floor. He came home wearing clothing covered with material that endangered other family members. Children played in and around the mines, coming into contact with tailings. No one knew the deadly price to be paid from this association. From 1952 to 1963, Kerr-McGee operated uranium mines near Shiprock. Red Rock Council delegate Harry Tome looked back in 1979 and remembered this time. "No one ever told us of the danger in it. . . . It was the only employment that was ever brought to our part of the reservation." The jobs brought in "quite a lot of income. Then the mines closed. They went away. Now the people are dying."[99]

Uranium produced about $6.5 million in royalties and coal brought in a fraction of that amount during the 1950s. The Navajos possessed considerable coal reserves, but they were not fully developed during this era. Coal brought but a few thousand dollars a year into the Navajo treasury, but promised to bring more. Utah Mining and Construction received a permit in 1953 to explore for coal and four years later the Navajos approved a lease with the company. The lease yielded royalties of fifteen cents a ton for "as long as coal is being produced in paying qualities." The royalties paid for coal in 1960, 1961, and 1962 totaled $24,320 each year.

Navajo uranium miners near Cameron, Arizona. Fronske Studio Collection, Cline Library, Northern Arizona University, Flagstaff. Neg. no. NAU.PH.85.3.94.188

These actions offered a foundation for the boom that would take place in the subsequent decade. By signing for a fixed amount, the Navajos did not take into account either inflation or the workings of the marketplace. As the 1960s made increasingly evident, the lease amounted to a bad deal of rather colossal proportions.[100]

Oil revenues amounted to more than ten times that of uranium—a total of $76.5 million. The discovery in 1955 in southern Utah, near Aneth, turned out to be very substantial and oil revenues increased markedly during the latter half of the decade. Oil royalties in 1955 were just under $50,000. This sum more than doubled in 1956 ($114,000), more than doubled again in 1957 ($257,797), more than tripled in 1958 ($800,000), and then in 1959 increased to more than twelve times the previous year's total ($9,752,317). When rents and bonuses entered the picture, however, 1957 and 1958 stood out as the two most lucrative years—netting the Tribe in sum $34,819,482 and $28,793,053, respectively. For 1960 to 1962, the comparable totals were $15,323,950, $11,684,046, and $15,139,135, respectively.[101]

Livestock continued its largely imperceptible decline. Livestock reduction had achieved one of its goals: In 1956, Navajos owned less than a third the number of sheep units they had in 1931. In 1931, Navajos earned about half of their individual income from livestock; twenty-five years later that percentage had dwindled to slightly less than 10 percent.[102] Grazing issues continued to occupy a considerable amount of time in Council sessions, with delegates pondering for years what exactly to do about livestock numbers and soil erosion.

Livestock owners appealed to the Council and to Washington in an effort to preserve a way of life. The federal government responded by calling on the Navajos to devise an appropriate land management plan. Such a directive inspired many extended discussions in the Council chambers. Former Councilman Dewey Etsitty seized upon the Republican capture of the White House in 1952 to echo the Republicans' "time for a change" theme. "We are looking with renewed faith and hope to you, our new Republican administration," he wrote Interior Secretary Douglas McKay, "to give us a new business understanding and leadership. . . . These Democratic regulations have caused us too much trouble and should be dumped in the arroyo." We need, he said, to get "rid of the donkey that is still kicking us and give us the elephant to pull us to a more confident living." Commissioner of Indian Affairs Glenn Emmons received a letter from land management district 14, clearly authored by Etsitty, complaining about regulations that "bind us too tight." The people had "many years of experience with and without grazing regulations," the letter informed the Commissioner. The letter concluded, "[W]e are sure we can now handle this grazing matter locally without being bound fast by outside regulations."[103]

A CHANGING ECONOMY

However, by the end of this era it seemed evident that it did not matter too much which animal dominated the District of Columbia. The shrinking percentage of the Navajo population that participated actively in ranching and farming mirrored a regional and nation pattern. Although one thought of the Navajo Nation in rural terms, it was becoming increasingly urbanized. Robert W. Young concluded in 1961 that "the degree and extent to which the Navajo people depend on livestock has declined dramatically during the past 20 years." Those who attempted to continue to raise livestock were well on their way to becoming "a new minority."[104]

In a vote of 58 to 12, the Tribal Council approved the revised grazing regulations on January 27, 1956, and these new rules were approved in Washington on April 25, 1956. Adoption of the regulations hardly served to close debate on the subject. Rather, the regulations became one more thing to discuss. The federal government kept pressing the Diné to enforce Washington's will to impose a new round of livestock reduction, or as the BIA preferred to phrase it, to adjust livestock to the permitted numbers.[105]

Drought prevailed in Diné Bikéyah throughout this era, making it all the more difficult to obtain approval for any kind of "reform." Nevertheless, at the end of the 1950s, few objective observers could see anything other than disaster. A BIA report dated June 15, 1959, reported an unhappy situation. Two million acres lacked sufficient forage, 9.3 million acres possessed limited forage, slightly more than 3 million acres had adequate forage, and only half a million acres contained abundant forage. About half of the land management districts were seriously overgrazed.[106]

The lumber industry began to become a more significant component in the overall economy. The Navajo Nation's forests, including substantial stands of ponderosa pine, comprise a 458,457-acre area, primarily located in the southern Arizona portion of the reservation. The Navajos worked with the BIA to develop a sustained-yield approach, to modernize the old mill at Sawmill, and to work toward creating a more commercially viable program. These efforts helped bring about a new tribal enterprise, the Navajo Forest Products Industries. A management board made up of retired business executives and able Navajo managers oversaw the process. Board members in 1961 included four non-Navajos (Charles L. Wheeler, Louis Gervais, Herbert Jensen, Jan Oostermeyer) and four Diné (J. Maurice McCabe, Ned Hatathli, Sam Day III, and Henry Gatewood). A new planned community, named Navajo, began to be constructed near Red Lake, 13 miles north of Fort Defiance. It would be the site of a new mill that promised to employ four hundred workers and generate a substantial amount of income for the Navajo Nation.[107]

The BIA promoted industrial development as a central feature of reservation economies in the late 1940s and 1950s. Drefkoff and other consultants cited some advantages the Navajos had in attempting to attract industry: (1) the existence of coal, limestone, and volcanic ash; (2) the absence of taxation; (3) a market for building materials; and (4) funds available through the Long Range program. However, the disadvantages were considerable: (1) a workforce with limited training and limited command of English; (2) lack of housing, sanitation, roads, water, and electricity; (3) the expense of developing more electrical power; (4) the cost of transportation; (5) the isolation of the Navajo Nation from other markets; and (6) the lack of an organization capable of making prompt, knowledgeable decisions.[108]

According to Robert W. Young, the emphasis changed after 1954 from promoting small enterprise development to trying to lure major industries to the edge of the reservation, where some of the liabilities mentioned above would be less pronounced. The Babyline Furniture Company factory at Gamerco became the first industry to be imported through this new approach.[109] This initiative began with high hopes but as of 1962, it had only been marginally successful in luring new industries to the Navajo area.

Three major construction projects, however, did furnish employment to Navajo workers. The construction of Glen Canyon Dam started on October 13, 1956. The dam was completed in September 1966. The town of Page developed adjacent to the dam on land the Navajo Nation ceded to the federal government. This massive dam created Lake Powell, which, in turn, brought a significant number of tourists to the region. Two major power plants at Page and at Fruitland, New Mexico, also began to employ workers during their construction phases.

Even with this emphasis, relocation continued to be promoted in the name of economic opportunity. Urban relocation formed the primary component in this strategy, but some Navajos also resettled along the Colorado River through a new program developed by the federal government. Part of the Colorado River Indian Community acreage was set aside for this purpose. Indian colonists from the Navajo Nation and elsewhere began to come to the site in 1945. Eventually, 116 Navajos, 29 Hopis, and 3 Havasupais migrated here, but the program could only accommodate a small number of people because of second thoughts by the Colorado River Tribal Council about this project. The Council brought suit over the matter and the ensuing extended legal process essentially halted the program.[110]

Tourism in Navajo country also started to figure more prominently in economic development strategies. Canyon de Chelly and Monument Valley had become world-famous destination sites, with both locations promoted through the pages of *Arizona Highways* and the latter promoted additionally through the films made by John Ford. Ford had first come to the area in the late 1930s. Local trader Harry Goulding helped encourage him to choose the area as a site for filmmaking and helped facilitate Navajo acceptance of and eventual participation in this enterprise. *Stagecoach* was released in 1939. Following the conclusion of the war, Ford employed Monument Valley as the setting for seven films, six of them completed during this era: *My Darling Clementine*, 1946; *Fort Apache*, 1948; *She Wore a Yellow Ribbon*, 1949; *Wagon Master*, 1950; *The Searchers*, 1956; and *Sergeant Rutledge*, 1960. Given the presence of John Wayne, Ford's talent as a director, and the spectacular backdrop that Monument Valley yielded, it is not surprising that the films were generally very successful. If nothing else, they helped create international interest in the spectacular sandstone scenery on the Arizona-Utah border.[111]

People from around the world began to travel to Monument Valley to "say hello to John Wayne." Visitors also sought out Canyon de Chelly, Rainbow Bridge, and other remarkable sites. The advent of paved roads encouraged many motorists to seek out more remote locations. Tourists discovered they could eventually get there from here, generally with some difficulty, especially in the case of inclement weather. The Gouldings constructed a motel in 1953 next to their trading post and helped welcome countless guests to Monument Valley. Thunderbird Lodge helped beckon people in the direction of Canyon de Chelly. The creation of a Navajo parks

On the road to Monument Valley. Photograph by Bill
Belknap. Bill Belknap Collection, Cline Library, Northern
Arizona University, Flagstaff. Neg. no. NAU.PH.96.4.24.5

commission by the Tribal Council in 1957 helped produce more information and materials about such destinations and led to the first Navajo tribal park being created at Monument Valley in 1960.[112]

Navajos, like other Westerners, wished somehow to have tourist dollars without tourists, but generally recognized the kind of contribution that tourists could bring to the economy. For the time being, traders—almost of all of them non-Navajo—profited more from this invasion than did individual Navajos or the Navajo Nation, although weavers and silversmiths did benefit as well. In the summer months, a growing number of Diné positioned themselves in small stands along the highway leading to tourist destinations, including the Four Corners, where four states met. The Diné did find it a bit peculiar that tourists would drive a long way in order to place their left arm in Utah, right arm in Colorado, left leg in Arizona, and right leg in New Mexico, but they concluded this was just one more thing about white people they would never quite understand, any more than they could figure out why they said "cheese" when they took pictures of each other. They gradually became more accustomed to answering in their own way the odd questions that the tourists somehow managed to concoct. They wondered why these people were so eager to wear clothing that made them look foolish. Navajos saw balding men who usually did not have sense enough to wear hats and who wore strange-looking short pants that revealed even stranger-looking legs. They shook their heads at the sight of older women with unnatural hair colors who tried but failed to look like much younger women. These white people had time but they always seemed to be in a hurry; they had money and privilege yet they rarely seemed to be happy.

Navajo artists enjoyed mixed success, despite the growth in tourism. Silversmiths and weavers continued to create extraordinary work. Kenneth Begay became recognized as a master silversmith. Daisy Taugelchee of Toadlena, arguably the greatest Navajo weaver of any period, continued to produce tapestries of incredible beauty, noteworthy for the fineness of the weave. Regional styles continued to evolve, with weavers from particular areas primarily limiting themselves to variations on a specific, localized stylistic theme. Gilbert Maxfield identified in 1963 the following area or regional styles: Shiprock-Red Rock, Lukachukai, Teec Nos Pos, Red Mesa, Two Grey Hills, Crystal, Gallup, Chinle, Wide Ruins, Ganado, Keams Canyon-Pinon, west reservation, and Coal Mine Mesa. Sandpainting, pictorial, two-face, and twill rugs added still greater diversity, while saddle blankets remained popular. Maxwell sounded the traditional note of inevitable doom. He wrote, "The native crafts are disappearing, and there is no reason to believe Navajo weaving will be any different. . . . Simply stated, it doesn't pay to weave a Navajo rug."[113]

Painters as well as weavers and silversmiths would benefit from the renewed interest in Indian life that characterized the next period, but this era also saw artists, such as Harrison Begay, Gerald Nailor, Quincy

Tahoma, and Andy Tsinajhinnie, gain considerable recognition for their work. Begay's placid images fit the 1950s and he enjoyed great popularity. Unfairly criticized by later observers as creating Disney art, Begay marshaled his considerable talent to provide a more wide-ranging depiction of Navajo life than has been generally realized. Nailor and Tahoma showed great promise before their untimely deaths, while Tsinajhinnie delighted many patrons with his portrayals of familiar scenes. Even if limited by the conservative, if not rigid tastes of white patrons, Navajo artists began to expand their horizons by the end of this time. Some artists benefited from instruction at more distant locations or came into contact with other Native artists or non-Indian artists whose vision often inspired or encouraged them. They, too, established a kind of foundation for the innovations of the 1960s and beyond.

CONCLUSION

As campaigning began in earnest for the elections of 1962, the electorate and the candidates could look back on a remarkable period in Navajo life. The Long Range Act had had a dramatic effect on the Navajo Nation. Oil revenues had help transform the size and scope of Navajo government. The battle against termination had been won. Questions remained, of course, about the consolidation of these gains. Pressing issues still faced the Diné in regard to education, health care, rights, sovereignty, and economy. Could Navajo control over their own schools be realized? Could more comprehensive health care be provided? Could individual Navajos have their rights more fully protected? Could the appropriate role of the general counsel be determined? Would new leadership come forward? What would be the outcome of *Healing v. Jones*? Could economic growth be sustained and at what cost? These and other vital questions confronted the Diné as another era began.

7

"We Stand Together": 1962–1982

We are one, because we are on the reservation. . . . We are one, because of our religion. . . . [W]e stand together as one tribe: the Navajo! We are one!

—*Deenise Becenti, 1977*

Spring should have arrived over three weeks ago, but in Window Rock it never seemed to be in any hurry. The 6,880 feet of elevation discouraged a prompt or extended visit by the most elusive season in Diné Bikéyah. On the morning of April 13, 1963, however, Raymond Nakai was less concerned about the weather and more anxious about the political climate. Today he would deliver his inaugural address as the new chairman of the Tribal Council. He had so anticipated this moment that now he could not fully believe it had arrived.

Nakai made his way over to the ceremony, greeted some friends, and waited to be introduced. Then, as the assembled crowd grew quiet, he walked up to the podium, and began to outline the goals of his administration. "Today," he said, "as every four years, the Navajo people, their friends, well wishers and the seekers of their favor assemble for the inauguration of a new Council and Chairman—a new Legislature and executive—in the undimmed hope that newly installed officers will lead America's largest Indian Tribe toward the varying goals of their hearts."[1]

Now that, listeners thought, is Raymond Nakai. His abilities as an orator had made a critical difference in the recent campaign. Among those who had served as chairman, perhaps only Tom Dodge rivaled Raymond Nakai in his employment of the English language. Veteran observers testified that in his command of Navajo, Nakai was in a class all by himself. Years of radio broadcast experience had only sharpened his natural skills. Only forty-five years old, Nakai brought a youthful optimism to the enormous responsibilities he now assumed.

THE FIRST MODERN LEADER

Raymond Nakai appears to be somewhat forgotten three decades after his chairmanship, but he is likely someday to occupy a more prominent place in Diné history. He was the first modern Navajo political leader. Nakai had a more complete understanding of how to use modern media and he redefined the power and meaning of the chairman's office. Nakai believed in a powerful and independent chairman. Even given the controversies and conflicts that permeated his administration, he demonstrated the potential of the position and boosted the movement toward Navajo nationalism.

Nakai's very success, however, paved the way for his political demise. Peter MacDonald returned home to the Navajo Nation to head one of the important new programs, the Office of Navajo Economic Opportunity(ONEO). The effectiveness and impact of the ONEO provided MacDonald with a political base from which to challenge the incumbent chairman in 1970. MacDonald thwarted Nakai's bid to become the first person to serve three consecutive terms as chairman; he then proceeded to serve three consecutive terms before Peterson Zah defeated him in 1982.

In 1963, Nakai knew full well the challenges ahead. His inaugural address revealed some of his priorities: greater access to and achievement in education, reduction of the high unemployment rate, further development of the Navajo economy and tribal government, and improved relations with the federal government and the surrounding states. Nakai understood that the average Navajo citizen felt removed from the Navajo tribal capital of Window Rock and believed the general counsel, Norman Littell, had too much power and made too much money.

He put Littell on notice. "I will spend less money in my administration on monuments and white elephants," Nakai pledged, "and more for the direct and lasting benefit of the Navajos in the hogans." He continued, "I will trim exorbitant retainers and expense allowances to persons on contract with the Tribe and evaluate their Services by the visible results, rather than their own self-serving boasts." Then came the real applause lines: "I will seek advice from our non-Indian consultants, but not take orders from them, nor permit them to give orders to the personnel of my administration. I will engage economists to give economic advice, engineers to give engineering advice, and lawyers to give legal advice. For political advice, I will go to the people."

Nakai concluded, "Now as new workmen, we enter the great unfinished edifice of the Navajo Tribe. We must repair the damages we find, but the great task of building leaves no time for inquests over every crooked board. It is a better world we have to build, the one where every Navajo shall stand erect beside his fellow American as an equal among equals. Councillors and friends, the tools are ready and the task is enormous. Now let us go to work together."[2]

Raymond Nakai, Navajo Tribal Council Chairman.
Courtesy of Rough Rock Community School.

Raymond Nakai was born October 12, 1918, in Lukachukai, the fourth of eight children. Like Ahkeah and Jones, he had spent his early childhood herding sheep and did not enter school until the age of eight. After a brief stint in the day school in his home community, he transferred to Fort Wingate. There he developed a love of reading and became a member of the Catholic Church before moving on to the BIA boarding school in Shiprock. He graduated from Shiprock in 1942. Nakai served in the Navy during World War II and participated in the campaigns on Guadalcanal, Attu, Makin, and Tarawa. After the war, he worked at the Navajo Ordnance Depot in Bellemont until his election as chairman. Nakai's daily program on radio station KCLS in Flagstaff made him well known to Navajo listeners from the western portion of Diné Bikéyah.[3]

Nakai defeated incumbent chairman Paul Jones and Sam Billison, a former Code Talker and a college graduate. His electoral success may be traced in part to his skills as an orator and his lack of political baggage. Since he had not held elective office, he did not have a record to defend. In addition, Nakai took three stances that proved very popular: (1) he would let the Native American Church alone, (2) he would fire Norman Littell, and (3) he would disregard grazing regulations. In the election, he received 11,190 votes, a nearly 2,000-vote margin over Jones (9,296), and well over 3,000 more than Billison (7,422).

In his inaugural address, Nakai placed significant emphasis on working together with other individuals and groups. The new chairman clearly believed that in unity there was strength. Navajos certainly subscribed to a common cultural identity. Eighth-grader Deenise Becenti of Tohatchi wrote a poem in 1977 in which she expressed this sentiment:

"Navajo people . . . together we are one . . . because we are on the reservation . . . because of our religion . . . we stand together as one tribe: the Navajo! We are one!"[4]

Cultural identity was one thing, political unity quite another. Chairman Nakai may have sought to bring people together, but the issues of the 1960s combined to make consensus as elusive as spring. Nakai observed before the Governor's Interstate Indian Council in 1964 that "getting together is a beginning, keeping together is progress, working together is success." Nakai envisioned a "day of glory" for the Diné in their economy and their society. But for a "place of honor" to be realized, people had to be committed to forging consensus rather than promoting conflict. For Nakai, thinking together contributed to working together. He believed that "the mind is the bootstrap and the only bootstrap with which the people can lift themselves to a higher station in life." Nakai wanted the Navajos and other Native peoples "to substitute brains for brawn, skill for sweat, and power for the muscles of man."[5]

"Ours will be a trying life ahead but it will be an exciting and interesting one," Nakai predicted in 1964.[6] His two terms as chairman of the Tribal Council certainly fulfilled that forecast. Nakai helped encourage greater cultural pluralism through his support of religious freedom for the Native American Church. During his administration, the *Navajo Times* could run a story about recognition awards being presented to members of the Native American Church. He also advocated Navajo self-determination in education. Nakai was an early and firm supporter of the Navajo Community College. Perhaps because his own education had been delayed, he took special interest in elementary and secondary education. Nakai did not want young adults pushed off the reservation in search of employment. Developing natural resources would make it more likely that they could stay as well as furnish badly needed revenue to the tribal treasury. Finally, Nakai wanted to decrease the power of the general counsel.

NAKAI FIRES LITTELL

He knew it would not be easy to fire Norman Littell, for the attorney had four years remaining on his contract, did not want to leave, and enjoyed considerable support within the Tribal Council. However, Nakai decided he must take this step. Littell had become too central a figure; he cast too long a shadow over the Diné political stage. For the chairman to be viewed as a truly independent figure and for the Council to fully come into its own, Littell had to depart.

As Nakai had assumed, Littell had no intention of leaving that stage. He fought his exit every step of the way, labeling Nakai a "stooge" and a "puppet" of Secretary of the Interior Stewart Udall and referring to Udall as a "knife wielding" bureaucrat bent on character assassination. Littell considered himself as the champion of the Diné and contended that he was being persecuted because of his success in safeguarding Navajo interests.[7] The general counsel filed suit in U.S. District Court to obtain an injunction against Nakai. Littell claimed Nakai tried to have him removed from his post, kept him from coming to Council sessions, had him "forcibly ejected from the Council Chamber," and blocked payment of more than $10,000 owed to him. The Ninth Circuit Court of Appeals ruled against him, citing *Williams v. Lee* as an important factor in its decision. Did this situation constitute a matter "demanding the exercise of the Tribe's responsibility for self-government"? "Here," the Court concluded, "we believe that requisite is met. Indeed, the very heart of the dispute appears to center on Nakai's authority as Chairman."[8]

Nakai's authority as chairman had also been challenged by a group known as the Old Guard, a faction featuring such political stalwarts as Howard Gorman and Annie Wauneka. The Old Guard went along with the chairman on some issues, including grazing. It remained ambivalent about the Native American Church. But it did not approve of his firing Littell. Nakai went around the full Council and turned to the Council's Advisory Committee, where he had stronger support. The committee requested that Secretary of the Interior Udall "investigate, audit, and terminate" Littell's contract. Udall did just that. Littell attempted to reverse his dismissal, but eventually the court system ruled against him.[9]

This protracted controversy persisted throughout Nakai's first term, finally concluding in the early months of 1967. By that time the Navajo electorate had returned Nakai to office and voted in a Council more sympathetic to him. Nakai and his running mate, Nelson Damon, defeated Sam Billison and Paul Jones in a rather close race, 13,941 to 12,381. Native American Church members provided strong support for Nakai and the chairman also benefited from widespread Navajo dissatisfaction with the prior Council.

Nakai chose Harold Mott to be the new general counsel. Mott was a graduate of the Georgetown University law school and had worked in private practice in Washington, D.C., for more than twenty years, yet he lacked a truly thorough knowledge of Native American law and did not have any appreciable background in Navajo history and culture. The Tribal Council took five months to confirm Mott and finally did so by a decidedly split majority, 39 to 28. Mott preferred to work behind the scenes and assumed a much lower profile than his predecessor. He generally took a much less confrontational stance than Littell. However, he did not like the newly established legal services program at all and this animosity probably reinforced Nakai's growing antipathy toward this program. Mott also played a key role in urging the chairman to support industrial development as a means of boosting tribal revenues and reducing unemployment.

INNOVATIONS IN EDUCATION
The BIA remained a significant presence in the schooling provided to Navajo children. It constructed three new large boarding schools at Chuska, Many Farms, and Toyei. Some two thousand Navajo students attended Intermountain and still more were enrolled in other off-reservation schools. Diné parents had never liked sending their children away to school, but now they became more openly critical of this practice.

Here is what one witnessed in autumn during this era. The cottonwoods in Canyon de Chelly have yet to change color, but the nights are beginning to turn cold. A Navajo parent wakes up this morning, and in a split second she realizes that this is the day the bus will come and take her daughter away to Intermountain. She walks slowly over and wakes her child, gathers her belongings, and they make their way to the bus stop. There are other parents and other children there. Some parents and some children are not speaking; some speak softly and briefly and then look away. It grows even quieter before someone sees the bus coming in the distance. Then she and her daughter exchange hurried final words; the mother gives instructions, advice, and reminders. The bus brakes to a stop, her daughter clambers on board, and the bus pulls away. The mother looks at her through the window, then watches the bus depart, then squints, holds her hand to shade her eyes, and watches the vehicle become smaller and smaller. She keeps peering into the distance, even after the bus has vanished from view. She returns home to a too quiet home, perhaps drinks some coffee. She remembers the sound of her child's voice, as the silence wraps around her, for she will not see her daughter again for months. Later that fall, she reads a report by a special Tribal Council committee that confirms her worst fears about Intermountain. It mentions widespread vandalism, poor attendance, fighting, drinking, and glue sniffing at the school. She grows all the more determined to work with others to bring about change. "It is time," she says half aloud. "It is time for her to come home."[10]

The children themselves joined in this campaign. Fannie Chee, a sixth-grade student at the Crownpoint boarding school, wrote to New Mexico Governor David Cargo in 1969. She asked, "Why can't the Navajo reservation have all day schools rather than boarding schools?" Attending boarding school meant that "we Navajo students are away from our families for months at a time." She asked, "Is this fair? Why can't we have all public schools like the white and black men?"[11]

The period from 1963 to 1970 marked a major transition in the direction of Navajo education. The era began a transition toward greater self-determination. It could be seen as both the last chapter of a book that was already too long and the first chapter of another book that had been anticipated for some time. Two institutions, Rough Rock Demonstration School and Navajo Community College, and two men, Robert A. Roessel, Jr., and Ned Hatathli, figured prominently in the crusade to change Navajo education. These schools and these individuals had an impact not only within the Navajo Nation but also throughout Indian country. The Diné's efforts would help inspire other Indian nations to establish their own educational institutions.

Rough Rock Demonstration School rose from the ashes of a short-lived effort at educational reform within the school at Lukachukai. Nakai had been enthusiastic about the Lukachukai initiative. He spoke at the dedication of the project on April 30, 1965, calling on the school to "develop programs which will make the community and parents a vital force in Navajo education" and to "make the Navajo children proud of who they are and knowledgeable about their community, tribe, and history." However, the attempt at Lukachukai failed because the school had already hired its faculty and staff and not all had been persuaded about this different approach. A new school had just been constructed at Rough Rock, but no teachers and staff had been employed. At Rough Rock the reformers could start with a clean slate.[12]

Rough Rock thus became the first successful contract school in the United States. Through this arrangement the board contracted with the BIA to run the school and the BIA passed along the funds it normally would have allocated for that purpose. Guy Gorman, Ned Hatathli, and Allen

Students leaving from Fort Wingate, NM on a Greyhound bus to Intermountain School in Utah. Photograph by Milton Snow. Courtesy of the Navajo Nation Museum, Window Rock, AZ. Catalog no. NF18-162

Greyhound bus leaving Tuba City, Arizona to Intermountain School in Utah. Photograph by Milton Snow. Courtesy of the Navajo Nation Museum, Window Rock, AZ. Catalog no. NF18-304

Yazzie took the lead in establishing a corporation they dubbed Demonstration in Navajo Education (DINE) in order to forge that contract with the BIA. DINE turned to Bob Roessel to serve as principal. Roessel, an Arizona State University professor of education, had taught and served as principal at several Navajo schools. He was married to Ruth Wheeler, a Navajo from the Round Rock area. The Rough Rock community elected a new board for the school. By 1968, Roessel had departed to help start Navajo Community College and Navajo educator Dillon Platero had taken his place at the helm of the Rough Rock institution.

An outside evaluation team headed by education professor Donald Erickson from the University of Chicago questioned how much control the community really had over this experiment, but most community members seemed pleased with Rough Rock Demonstration School. Other observers praised Rough Rock's emphasis on Navajo history, culture, and language. This focus necessitated the development of the Navajo Curriculum Center to publish appropriate materials for use in the school.[13]

Rough Rock Demonstration School inspired other communities to follow its example. Moreover, Navajo parents began to take a more active interest in the local public schools. As the 1960s concluded, Navajo parents were seeking and gaining positions on school boards. They were beginning to exercise unprecedented influence on hiring and curriculum.[14]

Down the yet unpaved road to Many Farms, Navajos launched another significant educational institution. In 1967, Raymond Nakai had summoned BIA officials and business leaders to a meeting to share his goal of creating the first Indian-controlled college. After he concluded his remarks, a BIA bureaucrat dismissed the idea. "My god, Mr. Chairman," he exclaimed, "you don't mean to tell me that you Navajos think you can run a college." Nakai replied, "We're not asking for your permission but rather telling you what we are going to do." The first college to be established by an Indian community, Navajo Community College (later renamed Diné College) opened its doors to 301 students in the spring of 1969. It shared facilities during its first years with a new BIA boarding high school. The college attempted to serve students from throughout the Navajo Nation and it began its efforts with what by now constituted a familiar cast. Roessel took the reins as the college's first president, with the clear understanding that he soon would relinquish them to a Diné replacement. Dillon Platero, Roessel's successor at Rough Rock, was appointed to the board of regents. Guy Gorman became president of that board. Ned Hatathli and Allen Yazzie both surfaced as vice presidents, with Hatathli the heir apparent to succeed Roessel. Other members of the board included Carl Todacheene (vice president), Chester Yellowhair (secretary-treasurer), Yazzie Begay, Timothy Benally, Howard Gorman, Larry Isaac (student representative), Raymond Nakai (ex-officio), and Wilson Skeet.[15]

The college recruited faculty from within the Navajo Nation and from around the United States. It succeeded in hiring many talented Diné to assume important positions. Navajo studies were featured at the heart of the curriculum, with Kenneth Begay (silversmithing), Mike Mitchell (history and culture), William Morgan (language), Mabel Myers (weaving), Ruth Roessel (director, history and culture), and Atah Chee Yellowhair (basketry) among the instructors. Teddy Draper, Mike Etsitty, Nathan Silversmith, and Erwin Wayne taught in adult basic education. Other initial Navajo faculty members included Elouise Jackson (English), Grace McNeley (English), Priscilla Mowrer (sociology), Paul Platero (sciences), and Rudy Sells (mathematics). Key Navajo staff members included Tommy Begay (comptroller), Margaret Etsitty (counselor), Dean Jackson (federal programs), Jack Jackson (dean of students and basketball coach), and Agatha Yazzie (registrar).

The college achieved noteworthy successes on several fronts, but its nonacademic environment limited its ability to attract and keep students. Those who lived on campus were sentenced to reside in Dormitory Nine, with no rugs on the floor, no carpeting in the hallways, harsh overhead lighting, and paper-thin walls. The high school furnished the cook, the food, and high school students whose presence extended the lines in the cafeteria. The cook obviously regarded pepper as a dangerous spice and his concoctions lacked imagination, variety, or taste. Students complained constantly about the food. One expressed his unhappiness in the student newspaper: "My socks have absorbed so much starch they walk by themselves!" Those enrolled at the college played basketball in a high school gym, saw movies in a high school auditorium, checked books out of a high school library, and attended class in high school classrooms. It is not surprising that they wondered about whether they were attending "a real college." Many Farms' centrally isolated location did not aid those who needed a change of scenery.[16] In sum, by the early 1970s, the future well-being of the Navajos' own college remained very much in doubt, despite the need for a Diné institution of higher education.

IMPACT OF THE OFFICE OF NAVAJO ECONOMIC
OPPORTUNITY AND THE DNA LEGAL SERVICES PROGRAM

The ONEO was not a Navajo idea. The office emerged because of money available through the federal government's "War on Poverty" during the 1960s. The Navajo Nation brushed aside the BIA's request to administer a local program sponsored through the Office of Economic Opportunity (OEO) and decided to run the program itself. An initial grant of $920,000 from the OEO in January 1965 launched ONEO. By May 1965, Peter MacDonald had become executive director of ONEO. He remained at the helm until he resigned to run for chairman.[17]

In one way or another, different ONEO programs soon affected the lives of most Diné. The Legal Services, Home Improvement Training, the Navajo Culture Center, the Neighborhood Youth Corps, Local Community

Navajo Community College weaving instructor
Mabel Burnside Myers as a young woman. Don Dedera
Collection, Arizona Historical Foundation, Tempe.

Development, Alcoholism, Head Start, Migrant and Agricultural Placement, Recreation and Physical Fitness, and Operation Medicare Alert programs soon engaged many Diné. By 1967, 23,382 people had been served by the ONEO.[18]

The federal government's generous funding of the ONEO made possible a wide-ranging program. The Navajos once again found a way to take an idea from the outside and make it work within their society. Nearly all of its top administrators were members of the Navajo Nation and the benefits of the program resonated throughout the reservation, with residents of more distant communities seeing immediate benefits through new employment or help for young children.

The Local Community Development (LCD) and Child Development (CD) programs exemplified the ONEO's value. LCD projects often resulted from ONEO partnering with other government agencies for funding and assistance. This program enabled residents of Aneth, Utah, to construct a much-needed medical clinic, members of the Teec Nos Pos chapter to improve a local road and expedite the delivery of water for irrigation, Red Mesa residents to construct a utility building, and Nenanezad chapter members to build a hay shed. By early 1970, the CD program furnished preschool activities for more than two thousand children. Through this initiative, many children gained medical and dental care to which they otherwise might not have had access. Hundreds of children received physical examinations, skin tests, immunizations, dental treatments, hearing screening, and other tests. These initiatives gave the ONEO a kind of concrete reality that Window Rock- or Washington-based innovations often lacked. The ONEO combined adequate funding, local involvement and support, and visible and viable programs that mattered.[19]

Little controversy attended most components of ONEO, with one notable exception: Diné Bee'iiná' Náhiilnah Bee Agha'diit'aahii (or "Attorneys Who Contribute to the Economic Revitalization of the People") Legal Services, soon shorthanded to DNA Legal Services, attracted opposition and animosity from the outset, even as it also demonstrated its value to thousands of Diné. Debate over the program, soon to split off from the ONEO, began in the waning days of 1966 when DNA's board decided to hire Theodore ("Ted") Mitchell as its executive director. A 1964 graduate of Harvard law school, Mitchell had grown up in Phoenix, and had also attended Phoenix College and Brigham Young University. He had worked as an attorney for the Navajo Tribal Legal Aid Service from January 1965 to March 1966. At the time of his appointment to head DNA, he was working as legal services director for an OEO regional office in Austin, Texas.[20]

Not all of the Diné welcomed Mitchell's return. The brash, outspoken young lawyer had displeased some powerful Navajo politicians, including Sam Billison and Annie Wauneka, because of his disagreement with Littell. They protested his appointment. Their opposition also reflected their antagonism toward Nakai. Mitchell expressed pleasure at his appointment and declared, "[T]he prime objective of the program will be to provide justice for the Navajo who cannot afford to hire a private attorney to advise and represent him."[21]

DNA hired attorneys from leading law schools and set up offices in Chinle, Crownpoint, Shiprock, Tuba City, and Window Rock. Thousands of Diné flocked to its offices to seek assistance on a variety of matters, including sales contracts, grazing rights, misdemeanors, pawn, and state and local welfare. This list indicated that DNA had to deal with key institutions and influences in the Navajo area. By defending individual Navajo rights, DNA began to take on vested interests and long-standing concerns, as the following example demonstrates.

A Navajo man travels from Newcomb to Farmington in order to buy a used pickup truck. He visits Farmington Vehicles and a fast-talking salesman sells him the least desirable vehicle on the lot. The customer wonders how such an old-looking truck can have such limited mileage on it, but he speaks only limited English and does not feel comfortable asking about it. The salesman pressures him into signing the papers, including one that calls for 25 percent interest. The new owner starts toward Newcomb. He doesn't like how the truck sounds, but drives west out of Farmington hoping for the best. Then he turns off the main highway and heads down toward the river in order to pay a brief visit to the Hatch Brothers trading post in Fruitland. As he begins to drive away from Hatch's, the truck begins to go into some kind of nervous shock. It shakes, shudders, and dies. He is furious about being sold this lemon. What can he do? He calms down, walks back to the trading post and asks Stewart Hatch to call the DNA office in Shiprock. Eventually, he gets his money back and some additional compensation, given how he has been treated. He becomes a booster of DNA legal services. Farmington Vehicles does not.

This fictional but representative example helps to illustrate why a variety of businesses resisted this challenge to their customary way of doing business and why DNA became so popular. The Tribal Council's general counsel, Harold Mott, concluded that the DNA attorneys made his life more complicated and difficult. He viewed the young lawyers with disdain and they tended to return the favor. One named his two dogs after the general counsel and his wife, christening them Harold and Louise Mutt.

ANNIE WAUNEKA RESPONDS TO TED MITCHELL'S LAUGH

In Gallup, DNA attorneys tackled conditions in the local jail, abuses of the pawn system, and poor working conditions. Mitchell called jail conditions "so intolerable that even for a man to spend one day there is indefensible." The Gallup city manager called DNA's critique "a last dying gasp at obtaining a little publicity." Gallup residents complained about DNA's criticism hurting the image of the community. A suit against contemporary pawn practices received the following headline in the Gallup newspaper: "DNA Complaint May End Indians' Pawn Privileges." The owner of Virgie's Café, Virgie Chavez, responded unhappily to a DNA attorney's complaint concerning her payment of low wages and lack of overtime pay. She said such criticism demonstrated "this agency's gross incompetence and disregard for ethics" and labeled DNA lawyers "long-haired, irresponsible and ill-manner[ed] clerks" and an "inferior group of rabble rousers" with a "pernicious empire."[22]

Trading post operators on the Navajo Nation echoed these emotions about the intent and impact of the DNA program. Brad Blair, a member of a well-known trader family, wrote to Commissioner of Indian Affairs Louis Bruce to register his objections. He likened DNA to John Collier in being "racist and totalitarian in nature." Blair urged the BIA to "exercise its proper function to protect the individual rights and property rights of all citizens of Indian reservations." He told Bruce to "bear in mind that historical evidence shows that the most notorious of rights [abusers] has always been government—for example: Hitler's Germany—and in case of the Navajos—John Collier's livestock reduction program during the Roosevelt administration."[23]

Nor did DNA in general and Mitchell in particular escape continuing criticism from some members of the Navajo Nation. The most publicized instance involved Annie Wauneka. In August 1968, during a meeting of the Tribal Council's Advisory Committee, Duard Barnes, the acting associate solicitor on Indian affairs, was being questioned about whether the Navajo Nation could exclude people from the reservation under the terms of the 1968 Civil Rights Act. Responding to a question from Barnes, Wauneka said, "I do not have anyone particular in mind." Mitchell laughed out loud because "everyone in the room knew she was talking about me."

A furious Wauneka confronted Mitchell on the following day. She asked, "Ted, are you ready to laugh some more?" Mitchell responded, "No more, Mrs. Wauneka. I apologize." Wauneka said, "I don't need your apologies," and began to hit Mitchell on the head. Wauneka's biographer, Carolyn Niethammer, observes, "The pummeling was not as spontaneous as it might have seemed. Two decades later Annie would confess to a newspaper reporter that she had wrapped her hand around a penknife before hitting Mitchell. 'I told myself my hands were too soft because I hadn't handled a calf in years,' she said."[24]

The confrontation had significant consequences. The Advisory Committee supported Wauneka by voting to exclude Mitchell from the reservation. Mitchell drove the short distance to exile in Gallup. Mitchell remained nominally in charge of DNA, but his ability to provide effective leadership had been permanently compromised. Even though he eventually emerged triumphant in the suit filed against his exclusion, *Dodge v. Nakai* (1968), he could not continue to serve as head of DNA. Mitchell resigned his position in February 1970, and moved to Micronesia to head its legal services program.[25]

Peterson Zah, head of DNA Legal Services.
Peterson Zah Collection, Labriola Center,
Hayden Library, Arizona State University, Tempe.

Mitchell's departure also expedited the assumption of leadership positions in DNA by Navajos. Leo Haven and Peterson Zah became the new leaders for the program. Although DNA continued to receive sharp criticism from the same quarters, it survived various efforts to halt or severely curtail its funding. MacDonald's election in 1970 signaled its survival. The new chairman eventually rued his support for an organization that provided the same kind of political base for Peterson Zah that the ONEO had once offered him.

PEABODY COAL AND BLACK MESA

The Nakai administration embraced industrial development as a central element in its overall approach to economic growth. Nakai believed that the Navajo Nation had to demonstrate its support for industrialization, and the Tribal Council backed up his wish by allocating $1 million to help lure industry to the reservation. But as happened again and again in Indian country during this period, the industries drawn to reservations often did not prove themselves worthy of the money and trust invested in them. The Armex Corporation and the Westward Coach Corporation operations quickly collapsed. Fairchild Camera and General Dynamics Corporation also jumped to take advantage of Navajo and federal investment and the presence of cheap labor. They both lasted for less than a decade, employing far fewer people at far lower wages than their supporters initially had envisioned.[26]

In common with the governors and legislators of Western states, Navajo chairmen and Tribal Council delegates hoped that development of natural resources would bolster the overall economy. Oil and gas, uranium, and coal thus figured prominently in the Nakai administration's plans. Oil and gas revenues continued to play a major role in the workings of the Navajo economy. In the year after Nakai's election, in fact, oil and gas revenues accounted for $31 million, the second highest total ever obtained. From that pinnacle, oil and gas revenues had nowhere to go but down, to slightly more than $18 million in 1965, $13 million in 1966, and from 1967 to 1970, an average of $8 million annually. Both oil and natural gas production declined, with corresponding declines in royalties. Navajo uranium miners persisted in their deadly work, but the Navajo Nation, again, did not realize an appropriate level of financial return for this labor. The Diné, like other Indian nations, kept paying the price for long-term leases, which had locked in low royalties.[27]

Coal also constituted an environmental hazard, but the members of the Tribal Council were often not fully informed about the kind of ecological price that would be paid for coal mining. Moreover, industry consultants told delegates and Nakai himself that with nuclear power just around the corner, coal might soon become obsolete. Federal representatives worked closely with industry executives to encourage Navajo participation in a regional process that would accelerate delivery of electrical power to a rapidly growing region. Most Council members had not traveled to Appalachia; they could not predict the ravages that the strip mining of coal would inflict on the Navajo landscape. Energy company officials also minimized the amount of air pollution that a power plant like the Four Corners facility would emit.[28]

During the 1960s, Black Mesa symbolized the problems inherent in Western coal mining. Environmentalists took out full-page ads in major metropolitan newspapers to publicize the kind of environmental, social, and psychological damage caused by the strip mining of coal in this location. They compared the overall process to tearing apart St. Peter's in Rome in order to salvage the marble used in its construction. Reporters for leading newspapers and news magazines journeyed to the area to assess the damages. The seventy-eight families who resided within the lease area on Black Mesa never saw the advertisements nor read the accounts. Fifty-three of these families had homes directly on the coal deposits. They would be "compensated" for moving away, but they said again and again there could be no appropriate compensation. They could not imagine living elsewhere. Their world had been turned upside down by two leases signed with the Peabody Coal Company in 1964 and 1966.

The more significant lease of 1966 encompassed 64,000 acres, 24,000 entirely within the Navajo Nation and 40,000 in the area claimed by the Diné and the Hopis. Peabody anticipated mining 400 acres per year. The lease called for the company to pay twenty cents per ton for coal destined for the Navajo Generating Station at Page and twenty-five cents per ton for coal employed at more distant sites, such as the Mohave Generating Station at Bullhead City. The Hopis and the Navajos each expected to gain about $2 million a year from the thirty-five-year lease and at least this amount annually in wages paid to tribal employees who worked at the mine.[29]

By 1970, the concrete consequences of the operation at Black Mesa had become far more apparent. Dan Benally voiced a common complaint of local residents. "We were not informed by the coal company or our leaders that the strip mining will take place here," he said. "I did not approve of this. I did not sign anything," Benally added. "When our land and homes are destroyed there is nothing left for us. . . . I was taught and raised to make a living with sheep. Sheep is worth more than money." Many Mules' Daughter commented, "Where they are mining now is my land. My father is buried there. His grave was torn up in the strip mining." Florence Leonard claimed that local residents "cannot get jobs at the plant. Jobs are made available only to outsiders."[30]

Area residents also faced the prospect of long-term damage to their water supply. According to the terms of the lease, Peabody was entitled to slurry coal the 275 miles to the Mohave Plant through a pipeline eighteen inches in diameter. Five deep wells were planned to obtain the water. Perhaps 2,310 gallons of water per minute would be pumped from the Navajo sandstone beneath Black Mesa. Although the contract stipulated that the wells could not deplete supplies of surface water, area residents continued to be skeptical about the company's commitment to this provision.[31]

A final element in the overall story surrounding Black Mesa surfaced years after the negotiations over the lease. Cherche Prezeau, a research assistant for University of Colorado law school professor Charles Wilkinson, discovered incriminating archival evidence about the Hopi attorney, John Boyden. Based on his review of this material, Wilkinson writes, "There is no longer any question" that Boyden "violated his high duty to the Hopi by working concurrently for Peabody Coal during the decisive years of the 1960s." The general counsel for the Navajos, Norman Littell, did not know about this arrangement. Neither did anyone else representing the Navajo Nation. Such an arrangement guaranteed that the final details of the lease would be as advantageous as possible to Peabody Coal.[32]

The Navajo Forest Products Industry (NFPI) provided a welcome economic success story. During these years, it experienced consistent growth and presented consistent profits to the Navajo Nation. Retired or senior members of the industry worked with able Navajo representatives, including Maurice McCabe, Ned Hatathli, Sam Day III, and Leigh Hubbard, to offer skilled management. A sustained-yield program allowed for proper harvesting of timber. Nakai and members of the Tribal Council resolutely stayed out of NFPI business, allowing the enterprise to be run on a nonpolitical basis. In a volatile industry, the NFPI's future remained in doubt, but as of 1970 it was a tribal enterprise in which all Navajos could take considerable satisfaction and pride.[33]

CELEBRATING THE TREATY OF 1868 AND DECLARING NATIONHOOD

Raymond Nakai presided over the Navajos' centennial observance of the treaty of 1868. The yearlong celebration took "a century of progress" as its theme. Speaking at the opening of this centennial year, Nakai expressed his hope that the next century would be called "a century of achievement." He said, "We are, indeed, on the threshold of great achievements for our people in the fields of education, industrial development, and economic well-being. The next decades will witness giant strides forward in these areas."

In his preface to a volume commemorating this anniversary, Nakai noted the "drastic and far-reaching changes" the Diné had experienced "in their economy, self-government, social status, education, and living conditions." The chairman acknowledged persisting problems: "poverty, land depletion, lack of modern utilities, and chronic unemployment." The Navajos would be pausing during the year to "honor their heritage" and to prepare "to make this the start of a bold new era of progress, growth, self-sufficiency, industrial and economic development for our beloved country."[34]

The Diné combined memory, present challenges, and a look toward the future in a resolution passed in the following year, 1969. The Council's Advisory Committee through the resolution called for "the Navajo Nation" to be employed as the official term for the Diné. The resolution read in part:

The Diné—the Navajo People—existed as a distinct political, cultural, and ethnic group long before the establishment of the States of Arizona, Colorado, New Mexico, and Utah, and

The Government of the United States of America recognized this fact and entered into treaties with the sovereign Navajo Tribe, and down through the years both the Congress of the United States and the Supreme Court of the United States have recognized the inherent right of the Navajo People to govern themselves, and

When the geographical area occupied by the Navajo People was incorporated into the Union of states of the United States of America, no one asked the Navajo People if they wished to be so included, and

It is becoming increasingly difficult for the Navajo people to retain their identity and independence, and

It appears essential to the best interests of the Navajo People that a clear statement be made to remind Navajos and non-Navajos alike that both the Navajo People and Navajo lands are, in fact, separate and distinct.[35]

This articulation of a nationalist statement in no way refuted Navajo patriotism nor the Navajo identity as Americans. Some years later, in response to a question about Indian participation in World War II, Nakai said, "Many people ask why we fight the white man's war. Our answer is that we are proud to be Americans. We're proud to be American Indians. We always stand ready when our country needs us." This resolution testified again to the Diné status as a part of and apart from the United States. It delineated the wrongs of the past, underlined the problems of the present, and looked with characteristic optimism to the future.[36]

THE ELECTION OF PETER MACDONALD

Nephie Cody anticipated the election of 1970. Writing to the *Navajo Times* in February of that year, Cody suggested that a "new man" could win the chairman's position. Nakai had served two terms and appeared to have become isolated in Window Rock. Moreover, the Diné had always been reluctant to approve an additional term for a two-term incumbent. Sam Billison had been away from home, enrolled in a doctoral program at the University of Arizona. In any event, he had had his chance. Someone who could "represent the local people" could carry the day, especially if he had some association with the ONEO or DNA—organizations that really had a positive impact.[37]

This description fit Peter MacDonald. Born December 16, 1928, in the area of Teec Nos Pos, MacDonald had grown up in traditional surroundings. He dreamed of being a truck driver, but, as he later recalled, his "dreams were always cut short by my parents telling me that I have not done my chores." At school, his father's name reminded others of the name of McDonald in the old song, "Old McDonald had a farm." Just thirteen years of age at the time of the start of World War II, MacDonald enlisted before his sixteenth birthday, and became a sort of last-minute member of the Code Talkers—never actually serving with the group but still associated with it. Discharged as a corporal in 1946, he moved to Oklahoma to attend Bacone High School and then Bacone College in Muskogee. After he earned his associate of arts degree, he transferred to the University of Oklahoma, where he obtained a B.S. degree in electrical engineering in 1957. MacDonald found work as a project engineer and technical staff member for Hughes Aircraft in southern California. Then in 1963, he came home to accept a gubernatorial appointment to join New Mexico's economic advisory board and a post in Navajo government as head of the Management, Methods, and Procedures division. Two years later he became head of the ONEO.[38]

MacDonald and his colleagues at the ONEO learned as they went along, or as he once phrased it, they had to start sailing the ship while the ship was being built. Nakai initially gave the ONEO and MacDonald high marks. After the ONEO's first year Nakai called it "one of the most successful and imaginative anti-poverty programs on any Indian reservation." Nakai added, "Mr. MacDonald and his employees deserve the praise of all the Navajo people."[39]

However, the ONEO's independence from political control as well as MacDonald's free-wheeling administration of the program made both the ONEO and MacDonald himself into controversial subjects by the summer of 1966. In June, the Tribal Council voted 30 to 29 to allow the ONEO to administer the new Neighborhood Youth Corps (NYC) program. Annie Wauneka charged that MacDonald, his secretary, and others had already drawn on NYC funds for $2,000 in personal expenses. MacDonald responded by accusing his critics of spying on him and denying the charges against him.[40] Most of the Diné did not seem especially bothered by these reports. They perceived them as political smears by his opponents or else had such a low opinion of politicians that it did not matter. MacDonald knew how to get things done, most concluded, and that mattered more than the rumors.

In 1970, MacDonald gained the chairmanship, defeating Nakai in the fall election. Sam Billison, Joe Watson, Jr., Donald Dodge, and Franklin Eriacho had also sought election. Billison's candidacy had been hurt by his absence from Navajo country. The other three candidates only commanded limited followings. Billison obtained nearly 20 percent of the primary vote and toyed with the idea of running a write-in campaign. He waited until the final week before the fall election to endorse Nakai. Billison said he preferred Nakai because "it's silly to think you can replace eight years of experience and leadership with a candidate who is being investigated by the FBI." Such an endorsement proved too little, too late; MacDonald again denied the charges and won a convincing victory at the polls, 18,334 to 12,069. The Teec Nos Pos native proved to be a born politician. He matched Nakai's eloquence and did not have two terms in Window Rock to defend. The traditional reluctance of the Navajo electorate to support an incumbent for more than two terms, an escalating concern over the land dispute with the Hopis, dissatisfaction with the limited results of Nakai's industrial development strategy, and the popularity of MacDonald's running mate from Bread Springs, New Mexico, Wilson Skeet, with New Mexico voters all contributed to the resounding victory.[41]

Peter MacDonald, Navajo Tribal Council
Chairman. Photograph by Monty Roessel.

MACDONALD'S FIRST INAUGURAL ADDRESS

Peter MacDonald's inaugural address in January 1971 offered a clear call to action. The new chairman demanded that bold, new steps to be taken. MacDonald set forth three primary goals for his administration: "First, what is rightfully ours, we must protect; what is rightfully due us we must claim. Second, what we depend on from others, we must replace with the labor of our own hands and the skills of our own people. Third, what we do not have, we must bring into being. We must create for ourselves."

The speech included a stirring appeal for self-determination as well as a stinging attack of his predecessor's record. MacDonald promised not to "barter away the Navajo birthright for quick profit that will cheat our children and their children after them." He specifically pledged to work toward realization of the irrigation project from San Juan River water that had long been promised to the Navajos. The new chairman also insisted the Diné must no longer "depend on others to run our schools, build our roads, administer our health programs, construct our houses, manage our industries, sell us cars, cash our checks and operate our trading posts." He called upon Navajos to discard "the bonds of forced dependency." He asserted, "We must do it better. We must do it in our own way. And we must do it now." MacDonald observed that the Diné had land, labor, and some sources of capital; what they needed to do was to "move from a wage and welfare economy to an ownership economy." In perhaps the most applauded and quoted line from his address, he stated, "Every time someone says how good we Navajos are with our hands, I want to ask: 'Why not give us a chance to show what we can do with our minds?'"[42]

MACDONALD AS CHAIRMAN (1971–1982)

"He is the best damn Indian politician I have ever seen," said a prominent Native scholar at the conclusion of MacDonald's very successful first term.[43] The chairman knew how to reach people. He seemed to be able to speak to all age groups. Most elders appreciated his reaffirmation of tradition. Adults admired his outspoken belief in what the Navajo Nation could become. The young valued his support of education and his energy. MacDonald spoke to Navajo veterans as one who had volunteered during World War II. He reminded those who owned sheep that he had grown up herding sheep. He addressed a collegiate audience as one who held a degree in engineering. MacDonald articulated common grievances and concerns about economic development, racism, and ongoing, unresolved issues, such as the land dispute with the Hopis. He pushed the Diné electorate to believe in themselves and in the capacity of the Navajo Nation to reach new heights.

If politicians might be divided up between those who played slow pitch softball and those who played real baseball, MacDonald definitely would have been assigned to the hardball side. His willingness, even eagerness to be combative initially constituted a real political attribute. The Navajos generally liked the fact that he would not let anyone push him around. For example, they appreciated his response to Barry Goldwater after Goldwater had complained about MacDonald opposing him. MacDonald replied that certain politicians had taken the Navajo vote for granted and liked the Diné as long as they were content to assume the centerfold role in *Arizona Highways*.

MacDonald instinctively understood how group identity worked. He realized that Navajo identity had been formed through contact and conflict and knew this identity continued to be influenced by those who were perceived to be opponents. Part of Diné identity was rooted in opposition; part of who the Navajos were was who they were not. These opposing forces would vary, of course, over time. In 1864, it had been Kit Carson; in 1914, it had been William Shelton. In 1942 it had been the Japanese, and in 1972, it might be the Hopis or the traders or Peabody Coal or the state of Arizona. MacDonald knew how to take advantage of past and present antagonisms.

When MacDonald stood up for Navajo rights or defended Navajo claims, he frequently employed an "us versus them" strategy. Thus, for example, in 1977, he addressed the matter of energy resource development at a conference on "The Rise of the Southwest." MacDonald reminded his audience that Indian nations with energy resources needed to be treated with fairness and equity, but these elements had usually not been present in past negotiations. He added, "The first conference on growth in the this country occurred when the Pilgrims landed in New England and invited the Indians to a conference on growth. Such conferences have been held with great regularity as the nation expanded westward. But we were not normally the luncheon speaker; more often than not we were cooking the lunch." MacDonald concluded, "Every time a coal gasification company like WESCO and El Paso or a uranium company like Kerr-McGee or Exxon or United Nuclear invites me to come talk about growth, I know whose growth they are talking about. And whose resources will fuel that growth."[44]

MacDonald hardly invented "us versus them" politics. It is a time-honored technique and it is fair to say that most politicians use a version of it at one time or another. Such an oppositional strategy is well suited for an election campaign, for example. It lacks subtlety; it hits home. The senior George Bush's use of Willie Horton in the 1988 presidential campaign furnishes an instructive example. By employing the specter of a prisoner prematurely released and let loose to do harm, Bush skillfully placed himself with those who saw themselves as endangered by violent individuals. This maneuver also did double duty politically, for it allied Bush with whites who were hostile to African Americans and saw African-American criminals as being coddled by the law.

Such a strategy helped elect George Bush, but it created a rather major problem for him once he was elected. Most African Americans had been sufficiently antagonized by this tactic that they were extremely reluctant to work with the president.

MacDonald's reliance on "us versus them" ultimately proved similarly divisive. He used it masterfully in gaining election in 1974, 1978, and again in 1986. But its employment made it all the more difficult to forge some kind of agreement with the Hopis, for example, or to construct some kind of compromise or alliance with any party who had just been pilloried. This strategy galvanized the Navajo into initial action. It took advantage of long-standing and perfectly understandable animosity toward the BIA, the IHS, state and county officials, corporate representatives, and other entities to promote the general notion of Navajo self-determination. In MacDonald's first administration, it worked splendidly to delineate problems and to express the need for Navajos to be in charge.

The problems came later on, after criticism and after the assumption of responsibility. It was one thing to argue for control over schools, but quite another to forge consensus over curriculum once control had been achieved. It was one thing to go after Peabody Coal, but quite another to find alternative bases for economic development. And it was one thing to criticize one's opponents in an election, but quite another to earn their cooperation and contributions when the votes had been counted.

As time went on, MacDonald not only did not let go of "us versus them," he added "me and us versus them" to his political repertoire. That is to say he tended to portray criticism of his own actions or inactions as criticism against the Navajos. This variant on another time-honored tactic, usually labeled "divide and rule" or "divide and conquer," exacerbated already existing internal divisions among the Diné. Almost any questioning of MacDonald came to be cast in an anti-Navajo guise. It tended not to allow for any shade of gray in political discussion. Things were all black or all white. One was either with MacDonald or entirely against him.

Finally, there was the matter of personal integrity and the possibility of corruption. Given MacDonald's eventual political fate, the early warning signs about financial irregularities appear all the more troubling. Journalists who follow politics are fond of remarking about any long-term rumor concerning a politician that where there is smoke there eventually is found to be fire. In MacDonald's case, a four-alarm fire would not be reported until the late 1980s, during what turned out to be his final term as the elected leader of the Diné. But signs of smoke had been detected a long time before that terrible conflagration.

GENERAL COUNSEL AND DNA LEGAL SERVICES

The choice of the Phoenix law firm of Brown, Vlassis, and Bain as the new general counsel constituted one of the important early decisions of the new MacDonald administration. A partner in the firm, George Vlassis, became the primary representative of the firm to serve MacDonald. Lawrence Ruzow, a young Harvard law school graduate who had previously worked for Navajo Community College, assisted Vlassis. Vlassis and Ruzow played a central role in MacDonald's life. They helped draft the many speeches the chairman was called on to give and advised him on a variety of matters, including economic development. Eventually Vlassis split off from the firm in Phoenix to serve as general counsel. By 1980, his general contract had reached $552,000.

As Harold Mott had discovered, the proposals for economic development did not always come from the most reliable of companies. Ruzow bluntly asserted, "There is flake proposal after flake proposal. There aren't many good reasons for a company to come, and most outfits are not resource-oriented but rip-off inclined." Vlassis and Ruzow struggled with the same dilemmas that had confronted Mott. Any time they sided with industrial development they could count on harsh criticism from a variety of quarters, including the DNA attorneys. Ruzow asserted that it was easy for those employed through DNA to express such opposition because "they didn't have to work for a living, that is to say, produce income." Vlassis and Ruzow prided themselves in being "pragmatists," working for "incremental progress," in contrast to "reformers who want to make speeches and write for the *New Republic*," but "who are not interested in following things through." Ruzow, however, later parted company with Vlassis and became openly critical of his former colleague, labeling him in 1981 as "a banking lawyer from New York" who had failed "to get high quality law firms for water rights issues, mineral lease negotiations and things like that. You can never undo all the harm that's been done up till now."[45]

The DNA Legal Services program survived a variety of challenges to its continuing existence and made its presence felt throughout Diné Bikéyah. It mounted a full-scale assault against the trading post operators. This crusade helped prompt significant changes in the ways in which traders did business. DNA's critics charged the program with deliberately running many traders out of business. Through its newsletter and by following through on the many complaints they continued to receive about consumer issues, DNA attorneys actively sought to change the established order. For example, in Pinon, Robert Hilgendorf and John Silko not only filed a class-action suit against the Pinon Trading Post but also helped advise the founders of a competing concern, the Diné-Bi-Naa-Yei Cooperative of Pinon.

Some of the victories won by DNA had national consequences, including *McClanahan v. Arizona State Tax Commission* (1973). This case started in 1968, when Rosalind McClanahan, an employee of the Great Western Bank in Window Rock, challenged the right of the bank to withhold Arizona income tax from her pay. She asked for a refund, arguing the state did not have the right to tax her. After the bank denied her request, she went to court. She lost three times in a row: in the local Arizona Superior Court, the Arizona Court of Appeals, and the Arizona Supreme Court. The federal government and the Navajo Nation both supported her appeal to the Supreme Court and the Court decided to hear the case and ultimately ruled in her favor on March 27, 1973. The decision meant that she, and other Indians, did not have to pay state taxes on income earned within the boundaries of reservations. In a broader sense, the Court's unanimous decision declared that Arizona had no jurisdiction over the Navajo reservation except where permitted by Congress. The decision represented an important reaffirmation of Navajo sovereignty, arguably the most significant such statement since *Williams v. Lee*. DNA attorney James Wechsler concluded, "If the decision had gone the other way, Indian independence from state control would have been threatened."[46]

In another significant case, DNA attorneys assisted seventeen Navajos to file suit against a proposed lease between the Navajo Nation and Exxon that the Tribal Council had approved in January 1974. The suit specifically cited concerns over the impact that uranium mining would have on the water table, grazing land, and health. Although the suit ultimately proved unsuccessful, it remained important for the issues it raised and the degree to which it publicized to many Navajos the inherent dangers in uranium mining. The resulting outcry by many Navajos and subsequent suits by DNA attorneys and other parties sharply curtailed new uranium mining on Navajo lands.[47]

DNA's significance ultimately could not be measured solely in terms of resolving consumer complaints or even in terms of its defense of Navajo sovereignty. The legal services program also mattered because, like the ONEO, it operated at the grassroots level and it achieved tangible results. These results boosted the political career of Peterson Zah. They also encouraged countless other Diné to go to law school, to run for the school board, and generally to stand up for their rights. The newsletter masthead reminded its readers of DNA's core: "Community Education, Preventive Law, Legal Services." DNA served as an advocate for individual Navajos and helped inspire Navajos to be their own advocates.

MACDONALD ATTEMPTS TO CONTROL THE JUDICIARY

At the start of the MacDonald administration the Navajo judicial system mirrored impressive stability. Chief justice Murray Kirk and justices Tom Becenti, Chester Hubbard, William Leupp, William Dean Wilson, and Chester Yellowhair had all been in their positions for at least ten years. The presence of DNA as well as a growing population prompted additions to the system. Prosecutors representing the Navajo Nation and court advocates representing individual Navajos were new components. The willingness and ability of the Diné to administer their own judicial system made one of the strongest and most effective arguments the Navajos could have possibly made against the intrusion of the states into internal Navajo affairs.

The Navajo courts confronted a variety of issues during the 1970s and early 1980s, none more problematic than that of reapportionment. In this era, the steady march of urbanization had continued and with it had come the demand for redistribution of Council delegates. Smaller communities pressed for continuing representation while larger towns argued for a larger share of delegates. Urban communities noted that LeChee, with less than five hundred people, had the same representation as Shiprock, with eight thousand people. The Court of Appeals upheld one plan for revision that consolidated rural representation, but eventually the Council decided to add more delegates from the largest communities rather than take away delegates from more lightly populated areas.

By the late 1970s, the judicial system had incurred MacDonald's displeasure for its decisions about reapportionment and several other matters, including payment to attorney F. Lee Bailey for his defense of the chairman against charges raised by a grand jury. The jury had indicted MacDonald for tax evasion and mail fraud. Bailey admitted to the court there was "unrefuted" evidence that his client had accepted $8,000 from Tucson Gas & Electric for airplane trips he had not taken. Even with this admission, MacDonald was acquitted when the jury could not reach a verdict. Bailey had earned his $70,000 fee, but many disagreed that the Navajo Nation should pay for it. Four Council members sued to stop payment and the Navajo Nation's highest court agreed.

Others, in addition to MacDonald, resented the judicial system. The Council passed a resolution declaring that their decisions should not be subject to judicial review. MacDonald, however, went one step better. He retaliated through the attempted creation of another court, dubbed the Supreme Judicial Council, comprised of five Tribal Council representatives (one from each agency), two retired justices, and the chief justice. The chairman had the power to appoint all but the chief justice to this new body charged with reviewing Navajo Supreme Court decisions, and the general counsel was designated as its advisor. Although the chairman already had the power to nominate justices to the Navajo Court of Appeals, justices tended to serve for a long time and no chairman was likely to appoint most or all of the members of the court. This new arrangement clearly gave the chairman a great deal of power to influence current judicial proceedings, which, of course, is exactly what MacDonald had in mind. Four of the eight people he selected were political allies from the Council and a fifth was a brother-in-law.[48]

Another instance concerned Donald Benally, the Shiprock chapter president and a foe of the chairman. The Navajo Board of Election Supervisors, all of whom had been appointed by MacDonald, took Benally's name off the 1978 Tribal Council election ballot because he was supposedly underage. Benally sued and got his name back on the ballot. The first case before the Supreme Judicial Council involved this very matter. The Supreme Council ruled against the decision of the Navajo courts. Benally's name exited the ballot again. In December 1978, MacDonald removed two judges from the Court who had voted for reapportionment and against paying his legal fees and appointed two people who sided with him on these and other issues.[49]

MacDonald and his allies earlier had succeeded in 1971 in revising the legislative and executive branches of Navajo government. The reorganization consolidated some Council committees and added others and gave the chairman the power to appoint members of all standing committees. The executive branch also was consolidated with five divisions—administration, business management, controller, operations, and program development—assuming a major share of the responsibility. The chairman appointed the head of each of these divisions. This reorganization clearly increased the chairman's power over the functioning of the Council and made it considerably less likely that MacDonald would face the same kind of blockade that had stymied Nakai so much of the time. The preamble to the Council resolution authorizing the executive branch revision attested to the growing emphasis on Navajo nationalism:

Whereas: (1) The People of the Navajo Nation are resolved that the Navajo Tribal Council shall exercise all powers of self-government necessary to attain self-sufficiency and self-determination, and prerequisite to protecting the rights and interests of the Navajo people and their possessions, and

(2) There are vested within the Navajo Nation certain attributes and powers of sovereignty that have neither been developed nor recognized due to inadequate executive organization within the Tribal Government, and

(3) A strong and united Tribal Executive branch is essential in developing both natural and human resources; in preserving and protecting what rightfully belongs to the Navajo People; and in planning and building a future for the Navajo Nation that will realize the goals and ambitions of the Navajo people.[50]

TRYING TO ACHIEVE SELF-DETERMINATION IN EDUCATION

Peter MacDonald often spoke about how crucial he believed it to be to gain full control over Navajo education. Members of the Tribal Council agreed. During MacDonald's first year in office, the Council established a Navajo Division of Education and called on it to become "the primary vehicle for assuring the preservation of the Navajo cultural heritage." The division represented a potentially a useful step in what MacDonald termed a total education system, one that would produce the kind of leaders and managers so needed by the Diné. The division helped initiate a program to increase the number of Navajo teachers, but overall progress toward true educational self-determination appeared intermittent and limited. When Dillon Platero was appointed in 1973 to head the division, many observers grew more hopeful about what might be accomplished. Platero brought considerable experience and insight to the job. However, his relationship with MacDonald turned out to be counterproductive. Bob Roessel judged it at best "uneven" and at worst "characterized by jealousy and vested interests." He believed MacDonald's office actively opposed the initiatives that Platero attempted to implement.[51]

Platero resigned in 1977, but before his departure, the division published a summary of hearings it had conducted in the Navajo Nation. Some of the key recommendations included giving more power to BIA school boards; hiring more teachers, especially more Navajo teachers; hiring more Navajo counselors; providing more programs in special education; providing more funding for preschools; providing more extensive funding for college students; and increasing offerings in adult education. Those who testified at the hearings understood that educational goals could not be realized without other changes. Improved housing, water delivery, sanitation, access to electricity, and better health care and related developments, they said, would have positive effects on student learning. In addition, Navajo parents recognized the need to reduce the long distances that many public school students had to travel by bus and to improve roads and highways so that students could get to school more quickly and easily. Although parents had no desire to return to the military regimentation that once characterized Indian education, they expressed concerns over the lack of student supervision and the increasing frequency of fighting, bullying, and other behavioral problems, often linked to problems related to alcohol and drug use.[52]

Schooling from kindergarten through twelfth grade in the Navajo Nation still resembled a crazy quilt. BIA, public, and contract schools remained separately administered and taught. The few contract schools struggled with inadequate funding. BIA and public schools had limited housing, low salaries, and difficult working conditions. Maintenance of schools at all levels continued to be an enormous challenge. Even at the beautiful new campus in Tsaile, college officials agonized over whether there would be enough money available to maintain the facilities. At the postsecondary level, more and more Navajo students were attending regional colleges and universities and the Navajo Nation offered a good deal of financial support to these individuals. However, the students coming out of reservation high schools continued to be inadequately prepared for higher education. Insufficient preparation, homesickness, racism, financial problems, and the needs and demands of relatives all combined to reduce the chances of Diné students earning bachelor's degrees.

Navajo Community College realized one dream in moving to a central, permanent campus in Tsaile, but new facilities did not solve the institution's continuing problems. According to its own self-study, the college did not work hard enough or cohesively enough in its recruiting, while other colleges and universities were beginning to devote more time and attention to seeking Diné students.[53] With the death of President Ned Hatathli in 1973, the college lost an outstanding leader. Hatathli's immediate successors struggled to cope with a frustrating and debilitating litany of woes. The Tsaile campus occupied a beautiful site, but it was arguably even more isolated than Many Farms. On the weekend, the campus was essentially deserted. Enrollments continued to fall far short of early projections. Low salaries and heavy teaching loads made it difficult to keep faculty. The entire picture in the early 1980s had become considerably cloudier than the sunny rhetoric of the previous decade had predicted.

Proponents of self-determination in education, nevertheless, could point to some impressive achievements. New contract schools at Ramah, Rock Point, and Borrego Pass offered exciting alternatives for area students. These institutions placed Navajo studies at the heart of their curriculum and, along with Rough Rock and Navajo Community College, produced innovative curricular materials, many of which are still being used in area schools. These materials reinforced children and adult's appreciation for Navajo history and culture. They are a valuable legacy from this period.

For example, Ethelou Yazzie's *Navajo History* offered an engaging and richly illustrated account of Navajo origins. Children had the opportunity in reading this book to learn about key cultural figures, important and sacred places, and central values within Navajo society. *Navajo Stories of the Long Walk Period* and *Navajo Livestock Reduction: A National Disgrace*, edited by Ruth Roessel and Broderick Johnson, brought together oral histories of two crucial eras in Navajo life. Also enhanced by remarkable illustrations by Navajo artists, these handsomely published volumes preserved the stories and the wisdom of Howard Gorman, Scott Preston, and many other elders. *Stories of Traditional Navajo Life and Culture* presented accounts by Descheeny Nez Tracy, Hoke Denetsosie, and twenty other Diné men and women about their own life experiences, from their first vision of a model-T Ford to singing "Ten Little Indians" in school.[54]

A slowly growing number of Navajo teachers, principals, and superintendents began to take their places in BIA and public schools. They were often the first person in their family to have had the opportunity to attend college and they understood the importance of role models. The best among them opened up new possibilities for their students. Public school boards began to gain more Navajo representation. In 1973, for example, Diné men and women occupied all five seats on the Window Rock School Board. The presence of Allen Begay, Joy Hanley, Wallace Hanley, Dan Smith, and Peterson Zah had a decided impact on school district priorities and approaches, but Window Rock schools were still restricted by financial considerations.[55]

In the early 1980s, the somewhat naive optimism of a decade before had been replaced by an understanding that true reform would take an extended period of time. Despite present difficulties, there were signs of hope. One of the most important could be found in the remarkable individual journeys of Diné women and men who left the Navajo Nation's boundaries in search of additional training and education and who then returned home prepared to contribute to the Navajo future. Glojean Benson Todacheene, for example, graduated from the University of New Mexico and came back to teach at Shiprock High School. Betty Reid graduated from the University of Colorado and began her career in journalism as a reporter for the *Gallup Independent* and the *Navajo Times*. Taylor McKenzie earned his medical degree and started work as a physician for the IHS. He maintained a strong respect for traditional knowledge and healing and began the challenging task of working for constructive change from within a bureaucracy.

Many students persevered to complete their education and then used that training to serve the Navajo Nation. Irene Nakai wrote, "I must be like a bridge/for my people/I may connect time; yesterday/today and tomorrow—for my people/who are in transition, also./I must be enough in tomorrow, to give warning—/if I should./I must be enough in yesterday, to hold a cherished secret./Does it seem like we are walking as one?"[56]

ADDRESSING HEALTH CARE NEEDS

Nurses Valerie Koster and Sandra Kramer had seen too many troubling things at the Shiprock Hospital to keep it all to themselves. They decided to go public with their criticism of conditions at the hospital. Koster and Kramer wrote a letter to the *Navajo Times* in 1974, complaining about a hospital staff that concentrated on "filling out forms, doing the least possible work with the least possible effort and just getting by." IHS administrators read the letter and decided to take direct action in response to it. They fired Koster and Kramer. The officials cloaked their action by accusing the two nurses of the use of profanity, "carelessness of dress," and "insufficient attention to duty." In other words, they had just written a letter that embarrassed the IHS administrators—not because it was false, but because it was true.[57]

The 1970s marked a time when more of the Diné grew more aware of the inadequate health care they were receiving and began to be in a position to do something about it. Reform of the system was desperately needed. Although the evidence is fragmentary, it seems certain that some Navajo women were involuntarily sterilized. The toll from uranium mining became more and more evident, with hundreds of miners discovering too late the full cost of their labor. Despite the efforts to increase cross-cultural understanding, new physicians and new nurses kept arriving with little, if any, understanding of Navajo life. Although a small percentage came to appreciate their surroundings, many appeared determined to remain isolated from their patients and remain ignorant about Diné history and culture. The prevailing hairstyles and dress of the era did little to increase Navajo respect for and confidence in these newcomers. The Diné tended to dismiss the newly arrived physicians as "interns."[58]

Richard Mike is today a prominent Navajo businessman, but at an earlier stage of his life, he taught mathematics, played in a country and western band, and drew the "SuperNavajo" comic strip for the alternative Navajo newspaper, *Diné Baa-Hani*. "Dr. Meanie" made a number of appearances in "SuperNavajo" and Diné readers took special delight in Mike's portrayal of the prototypical physician who kept six ugly, snarling dogs to drive away patients who dared to try to find him at home. When bronc rider Yazzie Manykids came rocketing out of chute 6 and promptly was bucked off, he waited in vain for IHS assistance. One spectator asked, "Where's the ambulance?" "Oh, yeah," replied another, "today is Saturday. The P.H.S. is off duty." A third wondered, "The P.H.S. has an ambulance?"[59]

The Navajo Nation took specific steps toward addressing health care needs by establishing the Health, Alcoholism, and Welfare Committee, the Navajo Health Authority, and the Department of Health Improvement Services (later renamed the Navajo Division of Health). The authority, a nonprofit, independent organization, was supposed to "foster, guide, and assist in the planning, development, operation and evaluation of a health service system for the Navajo people." Within this organization, Carl Gorman headed the Office of Native Healing Sciences, which put together a directory of traditional healers and the ceremonies they could offer. The Medicine Man's Association grew out of this effort. The MMA inspired a somewhat divided response. Not all healers joined it and Navajos who had moved away from traditional teachings also opposed it. As a result, the Tribal Council decided not to grant it an official charter, which would have allowed it to raise funds as a recognized nonprofit organization. Concern over the declining number of singers encouraged Rough Rock Demonstration School to inaugurate a project to train additional practitioners. This program received generous National Institute of Health funding and did succeed in preparing a small number of people for this vital responsibility. Taylor McKenzie headed an effort to explore the possibilities of starting an American Indian medical school. This notion never got beyond the discussion stage, but its very initiation, Wade Davies argues, marked a milestone in Navajo health care, for it showed an increased willingness on the part of the Navajo Nation to shoulder major responsibilities for health care.

The Navajo Nation Health Foundation of Ganado assumed responsibility for operating Sage Memorial hospital. Substantial grants from the IHS and the Navajo Nation permitted the foundation not only to run a forty-five-bed hospital but also to maintain a clinic in Wide Ruins and to offer outreach programs. Unlike many health care initiatives that would be announced with great fanfare but not last more than a few years, the foundation still existed in the twenty-first century and Sage Memorial

A Portfolio of Photographs
by Monty Roessel

Diné: A History of the Navajos

Diné: A History of the Navajos

Diné: A History of the Navajos

Diné: A History of the Navajos

Diné: A History of the Navajos

Diné: A History of the Navajos

Diné: A History of the Navajos

Diné: A History of the Navajos

Diné: A History of the Navajos

Diné: A History of the Navajos

Diné: A History of the Navajos

Diné: A History of the Navajos

Diné: A History of the Navajos

Diné: A History of the Navajos

Diné: A History of the Navajos

had become a far different place than a half-century before, when its officials considered tradition an enemy of progress.

The Navajo Nation continued its investment in the future through its funding of students wishing to pursue medical careers. Under the direction of Jack Jackson and aided by a Kellogg Foundation grant, the Office of Student Affairs helped make it possible for Marie Allen, Ellouise DeGroat, Mike Lincoln, Orville McKinley, and others to gain their training. These people, in turn, played central roles in health care delivery in the next generation.[60]

By the early 1980s, it appeared as though the Navajo Nation and the IHS were beginning to make progress in working together in the areas of environmental, preventive, and behavioral health. The new Navajo Division of Health (NDOH) absorbed the Navajo Health Authority. The NDOH project coordinator Peggy Nakai expressed the goal of assisting the IHS "do more for the people." A growing number of Diné employees in both entities improved communication.[61]

The dedication of the Chinle Comprehensive Health Care Facility on August 28, 1982, provided an indication of that progress. The need for a hospital for Chinle had long been apparent. Planning began in 1977 with the formation of the Chinle Hospital steering committee, chaired by Nelson Gorman, Jr. Committee members lobbied successfully for the hospital to be moved to the top of the Navajo and IHS priority lists. The spirit of cooperation was demonstrated when area residents Mary Bitsui, Charley and Bah Davis, Rosita Davis, Sarah Davis, Iris Garcia, Guy and Juanita Gorman, Joseph and Lillie Klade, Alice McCabe, Irene Nez, and Hosteen and Barbara Tso combined to donate over one hundred acres of traditional grazing land for the hospital and staff housing. That particularly generous act attested to community confidence in this project. The steering committee and the IHS unit for Chinle worked together to help plan and develop the hospital so that, as they phrased it, it could "better meet and reflect the needs of the people."

On the morning of April 28 all the hours seemed well spent. The program mirrored a more pluralistic approach. It included a blessing early in the day by Frank Begay; an invocation by Father Blane Grein; the presentation of colors by the Chinle High School Junior ROTC; the national anthem by the Navajo Tribal Band; music by the Rock Point Community Singers; remarks by IHS officials, Peter MacDonald, and Senator Dennis DeConcini; and a benediction by Chinle Chapter vice president Theodore Evans. Lunch, the program promised in large boldfaced type, would "be served immediately following the ceremony."[62]

THE DECLINE OF THE TRADING POSTS

For decades, the trading posts had been central to the workings of the Navajo society and economy. Diné entrepreneurs began to take over some of the posts just as they started their seemingly irreversible decline. In *Navajo Trading: The End of an Era*, Willow Roberts Powers sympathetically chronicles the decline and fall of the trading post system. She targets "radical" DNA lawyers for censure, contending that they deserved much of the blame for the disintegration of a network that had served the Diné well through the years. Powers depicts these attorneys as being more interested in annihilation rather than regulation of the trading posts. However, as Powers eventually concedes, while DNA attorneys may have expedited the process, they did not create the dilemma that confronted the traders. If Robert Hilgendorf had decided to return to Wisconsin or if John Silko had chosen to go home to Alaska after they had finished law school, the traders would still have been in trouble. Jim Babbitt, a Flagstaff businessman and member of a family who at one time operated a chain of posts in western Navajo country, blamed the situation on the increased mobility of the Navajos and the emergence of chains, such as Safeway, and later, K-Mart, and still later, Wal-Mart. These giant concerns spelled doom for the "little general stores scattered throughout the reservation" because they "could in no way compete on price or selection with larger retailers." Babbitt expressed sadness over this process, but saw it as inevitable.[63]

During the 1960s, the number of trading posts on the Navajo Nation declined from 137 to 100, 18 of which were operated by Navajos.[64] The traders were caught in the same financial vise that was choking the life breath from "Mom and Pop" stores across America. The Diné on this score were no different than other Americans; they went to shop where they got the best deal and the best deal rarely could be found at the Nazlini trading post. So, a Navajo who lived near Nazlini would drive past the Nazlini post to the FedMart store in Window Rock or one of the supermarkets in Gallup. By the mid-1980s, she simply drove to Chinle and shopped at the Bashas' store. More and more Diné did not raise livestock and a progressively smaller percentage of people were involved with weaving, so some of the old reasons to engage the services of a trader had vanished.

Most of the traders faced increasingly desperate financial circumstances and some of them did what some people tend to do in such a situation. They cut corners. They did not always follow the law in terms of the credit arrangements they made with their Navajo customers. In a 1999 interview, Jim Babbitt explained what happened. A trader would say to a credit customer who had a credit account, "When your check comes in, because we're the post office, we're going to hold that, and you have to pick it up in person." He continued, "Then when they come to pick it up, you have a pen ready and you say, 'Oh, by the way, you have a balance on your account of $300. This check is for $310. Sign it over to the trading post and we'll give you $10 change.'" This was, he concluded, "not a good way to do business" and it was "extremely common, extremely common." In addition, interest rates on pawn accounts "were probably legal, but they were very high. I mean, very high."

According to Babbitt, "There clearly were big credit abuses going on—widespread across the reservation." He added, "[T]he credit system, the pawn system, with this whole notion of having people's Social Security checks held at a trading post, and then signed over on the spot and taken as payment for accounts. I mean, all of that stuff was not good and it's good that they put a stop to it, I think."[65]

"They" were representatives of the Federal Trade Commission (FTC). Acting in response to complaints about trader practices, the FTC held public hearings from August 28 to September 1, 1972, at Window Rock, Shiprock, Kayenta, Crownpoint, Tuba City, Chinle, and Pinon. The hearing panel was comprised of the regional director and assistant director for the FTC in Los Angeles, the assistant executive director for the commission in Washington, D.C., the commissioner of Indian affairs, and the director of economic development for the BIA. Traders, DNA lawyers, an anthropologist, an economist, and individual Navajos testified, followed by MacDonald and Zah. Roberts concludes, "There was nothing balanced about the hearings; from every account, it appeared as political theater, pure and simple, and was clearly intended to be." Trader Jay Foutz compared the proceedings to a "circus in a circus tent." He called the whole thing a "total farce, a disgrace to the human mind, really." Many traders blamed the DNA attorneys for the hearings. They clearly resented outsiders coming in whom they believed knew little about them and even less about their heritage. By contrast, Babbitt argued that the hearings "were initiated in large part by the Navajo Tribe itself, by the people themselves." They would not have been held, he insisted, "unless there were widespread abuses going on. I just know there were abuses going on."[66]

The new regulations adopted in the wake of the hearings and other exposés of contemporary trading practices appeared to make all sides unhappy. On-reservation traders got out of the pawn business and off-reservation traders employed it very sparingly. Traders could not extend credit in the old way. Their customers found the new state of affairs one more reason not to bother with trading posts other than to buy gas, pick up a few groceries, or rent a few videos. If they had a rug to sell, they tended to keep driving to reach a larger business or to participate in the tribally organized auctions that had started to become popular.

In the mid-1970s, Thriftway arrived in Navajo country. This convenience store/gas station chain popped up all over the reservation through a special arrangement forged with the tribal government. Its presence cut additionally into the already thin base from which the traders operated. One by one, the trading posts continued to wither and die. When they went out of business, they tended to remain empty, over time becoming graffiti-scarred monuments to an increasingly distant and dimly remembered past. Those stubborn souls who remained in the business were likely to be either Navajo or married to a Navajo. Pride and a desire to continue a family business encouraged them to continue. Knowing no other home than Navajo country, they had no desire to move to Toledo or even to Tempe.[67]

The old Hubbell post at Ganado would have disappeared, too. It had continued to be operated into the 1960s by Roman Hubbell's widow, Dorothy. She was quite ready to turn over responsibility to someone else by that time, but there was no one to whom she could turn. Fortunately, federal officials recognized the historic value of the post and brokered a deal to have the post and its immediate grounds become a National Park Service site in 1967. Bill Malone joined the post as its manager in 1981 and did a great deal to sustain weaving in the Ganado area. He also initiated the idea of putting a Polaroid photo of the weaver together with the price tag on the rug, a personal touch that proved to be quite successful.[68]

In the meantime, a slowly increasing number of Navajo women and men had decided to open businesses. By 1970, Navajos owned or operated slightly more than half of the gas stations, nine of sixteen restaurants or cafes, and several other retail establishments. Fleming Begaye's Shell station at a strategic corner of Chinle generated significant revenues. Later in the decade, Mike Nelson opened Navajo Westerners shops in Tuba City and Window Rock. In 1978, Don Davis opened the first Navajo-operated car dealership in Tuba City. Tremendous problems still stood in the way of would-be entrepreneurs. Access to loans and land surely were two of the most important. Many Navajos applauded the idea of Diné entrepreneurs, but often it was difficult to accept the concrete reality. They still balked at taking land away from the community and relatives of owners were still known to expect special treatment. Such considerations made cooperatives a popular option. The ONEO and DNA both promoted this alternative. Co-ops offered food, dry goods, hay, feed, and gasoline. A credit union began. So, too, did several cooperatives emphasizing arts and crafts.[69]

Peter MacDonald continued Raymond Nakai's emphasis on industrial development, but, like Nakai, ran into opposition. Two undertakings for which the chairman had maintained great hopes were both derailed. Objections from the Sanostee chapter and a rapid decline in the uranium market slowed a joint venture between the Navajo Nation and Exxon to develop uranium reserves in northwestern New Mexico. Burnham residents bitterly protested plans for coal gasification that would have impacted their immediate area. Once again, the opposition carried the day.[70]

During the administration of President Jimmy Carter, MacDonald tapped into Economic Development Administration and Comprehensive Employment and Training Act (CETA) programs. Ronald Reagan's arrival in the White House spelled doom for the CETA, but the late 1970s had been marked by opportunities to work and to make improvements to water and sewers for many Navajo homes. MacDonald also established the Navajo Labor Relations Board, which insisted that contractors hire Diné workers for business done on the Navajo Nation, adhere to an appropriate wage scale, and furnish training so that workers could increase trade skills.[71]

Industrial development efforts were not assisted by a major disaster in the Church Rock, New Mexico, area in the summer of 1979. On July 16, the Rio Puerco carried more than 1,100 tons of uranium mining waste that had burst through a ruptured earth dam with a resulting level of radioactivity seven thousand times the allowable standard. This is considered the largest nuclear accident in the history of the United States, larger even than the one at Three Mile Island that spring, even though the media gave Church Rock scant attention by comparison.[72]

A confrontation at Aneth also did not encourage industrial development. MacDonald had helped establish the Council of Energy Resource Tribes and had gained considerable publicity for consulting with Organization of Petroleum Exporting Countries representatives. Those headlines did not help reassure Aneth residents. Oil in the Aneth area had been a significant component in the oil boom of the 1950s, so residents of the area were not unfamiliar with exploration and development. Yet it seemed to them that the benefits always went elsewhere and the local people and the land were left to absorb the damages. Residents blamed the oil companies for ruining their water, damaging sacred sites, and fouling their air; they chastised the Navajo Nation for ignoring them. They complained as well about the Utah Navajo Development Council, which they said had misappropriated trust funds. Finally, in 1978, urged on by a group known as the Coalition for Navajo Liberation, the people of Aneth decided to make a dramatic protest to dramatize their discontent. On March 30, forty to fifty Navajos assumed control of the Texaco pumping unit.

This action stunned not only Texaco officials but also the MacDonald administration. MacDonald hesitated before eventually coming to Aneth and deciding to close the area to non-Navajos. He declared that non-Navajo employees had been molesting local Navajo women and stealing livestock. At the end of his third term, MacDonald would look back and label his action "a dramatic assertion of sovereignty." However, in fact, a week earlier all of the oil companies in the area had already shut down operations and the employees were long gone by the time the chairman appeared. MacDonald gained positive publicity for appearing to stand up in support of the people from Aneth, but many of the people believed that the tribal government's main concern was in maintaining oil revenues rather than their welfare. In the compromise agreement eventually reached, local Navajos gained more employment and promises of greater environmental responsibility; revenue disbursement did not change and lease renegotiations did not occur.[73]

TRIBAL ENTERPRISES

The continuing success of the Navajo Forest Products Industry encouraged the Diné to establish or expand other tribal enterprises during the MacDonald years. The NFPI remained profitable and a vital source for employment. In 1977, for example, it employed over six hundred Navajos. However, the record of other enterprises was decidedly mixed. Most disappointing was the failure of the Navajo Agricultural Products Industries (NAPI) to become a viable operation. The Navajo Nation kept pouring money into this enterprise designed to develop irrigated farmland in conjunction with the irrigation project along the San Juan River. The Navajo Indian Irrigation Project (NIIP) had not been a very high priority for Raymond Nakai, who laughed scornfully about it. He told Shiprock Council delegate Carl Todacheene that such an undertaking was unimportant, except for Navajos who "only knew the tail of the sheep." MacDonald thought that the NIIP was more important, but other issues more fully engaged his attention. Mismanagement, administrative turnover, and the lack of progress on the irrigation system itself plagued the NAPI. The Navajo Tribal Utility Authority looked better on paper than in practice. It became a revenue producer for the Navajo Nation but did not really advance the cause of self-sufficiency because it remained dependent on outside corporate interests to generate and to sell back electrical power.[74]

In an effort to provide more adequate housing, the Navajo Nation expanded the powers and responsibilities of the Navajo Housing Authority (NHA) in 1972. Now known as the Navajo Housing and Development Enterprise, it was charged with creating and building more housing for the Diné and to make a profit while doing so. This initiative never succeeded and the NHA resumed its old name, with its primary responsibility resting with maintenance and management of existing properties. A scandal within NHA midway through MacDonald's second term ended any opportunity for revitalization. NHA director Pat Chee Miller pled guilty in March 1977 of attempting to defraud the government. Millions of dollars were involved in Miller's plan to use tribal money for personal investment purposes.[75]

A more positive story could be told about the Navajo Arts and Crafts Enterprise (NACE), renamed in 1972 from the Navajo Arts and Craft Guild. Lenora Begay Trahant concludes that the change in name involved "a fundamental change in the structure and nature of the crafts operation. Whereas the guild had been a tribal department that was confined by many tribal regulations, the enterprise could function more independently—with no direct involvement by tribal politicians." Politicians could influence the enterprise, nevertheless, and in 1972, MacDonald "conceived the idea for the enterprise to mass-produce Navajo jewelry." The enterprise hired one hundred silversmiths and waited for the current craze over Indian jewelry to bring in unprecedented sales.

The plan backfired. Raymond Smith, brought in as manager in 1977, looked back on the period from 1972 to 1977, and groaned. He explained that the managers "only cared about how much jewelry was being produced. As a result, the silversmiths got sloppy with their work. Later the price of silver began to rise tremendously." At one point, the enterprise took on a huge order from a New York City store and then could not fill it. The managers went over to Gallup and bought a lot of junk jewelry there. Smith recalls, "The department store had placed the order for quality Indian jewelry, but they found out it was junk jewelry. The jewelry was sent back to NACE, and that's when the enterprise took a nosedive. It lost its accountability, its integrity, and just about everything."

The Navajo Nation had lost about $1 million in NACE. The enterprise decided to bring in Raymond Smith. Smith had grown up in Lupton, graduated from high school in Sanders, and joined the Marines. Upon his return he opened a small grocery store. The construction of Interstate 66 eventually put him out of business, but he learned a lot about management in the process. Smith was elected as a delegate to the Tribal Council and served for twenty years, becoming chairman of the Budget and Finance Committee. He retired in 1975 to spend more time with his family, but when offered this position with the enterprise, he decided to accept it. "I knew it was going to be a great challenge," he said. "I wanted to prove that an Indian, a Navajo, could run the business successfully." Twenty years later he still held the position. Under his leadership the enterprise embarked upon the long and painful journey back to respectability and profitability. By 1982, NACE was headed in the right direction.[76]

THE CONTINUING CONFLICT WITH THE HOPIS

At some point along the way, the ongoing conflict with the Hopis over land both nations claimed had become labeled a "dispute." But that really was not the correct term. The "land dispute" was no more of a dispute than the "Long Walk" had been a walk. A dictionary observes that a dispute "is an oral contention, usually brief, and often of a heated, angry, or undignified character." The conflict with the Hopis was many things but it was not solely an oral contention and it surely was not brief. Moreover, labeling it the "Navajo-Hopi land dispute" made it appear as though the Navajos alone had caused the disagreement. Why not, for the sake of variety, let alone alphabetical order, at least occasionally term it "Hopi-Navajo"? "Conflict" is a more apt word, as it is defined as "a battle or struggle, especially a prolonged struggle."

The final act had not been played out but the ending of the drama now seemed clear. After all the debates, lobbying, and posturing, and all the delays, the outcome with the Hopis over land would not go as the Diné had hoped. The people from the affected area who would be forced to relocate waited and hoped against hope. A 1978 Princeton graduate, Roman Bitsui, observed, "I guess we all hope our prayers will be answered, that maybe Congress will see the process of destruction they're creating. We pray that although it's been mishandled, it will work out."[77] But despite their intransigence, despite their eloquence, despite how much they loved this land, the people realized what the judge's decision meant. It had been a battle and they had lost.

The judge was James Walsh of the U.S. District Court. In 1975, after a series of negotiations had failed and three different congressional bills had failed to win passage, a federal mediator had come to Walsh with a somewhat predictable solution. Divide the lands in half, the mediator suggested. It will mean that only a handful of Hopis, about 40 in all, will have to move, while 3,495 Navajos will have to do the same. In September 1976, Walsh decided to accept the mediator's suggestion, and in February 1977, he issued his decision, partitioning the joint-use area. The Tribal Council chose to appeal, even though Vlassis suggested the odds were against a reversal of Walsh's ruling. The appeal delayed the supposed effective date until April 18, 1979, and soon thereafter the date was pushed back once again, to April 1981.[78]

The Arizona congressional delegations had favored the Hopis. Morris Udall's mother had been a close friend of several Hopis and Udall continued that allegiance. Barry Goldwater also took the Hopi side. He had enjoyed a long association with both communities, but as he wrote to Secretary of the Interior Thomas S. Kleppe in 1976, "My feeling has always been that the Hopis are probably ninety-five per cent right and the Navajos about five." Goldwater sympathized with the smaller Indian nation. He wrote to Bess Arviso, a Navajo, in 1973, that he believed it "wrong for the Navajos because of their gigantic majority to use so much of the joint use lands." He later made the same point in a letter to President Ronald Reagan in 1982: "The Hopi Tribe is a poor tribe, a small tribe, while the Navajo tribe is the biggest in the nation, and, by far, the wealthiest." Goldwater visited Big Mountain in 1978, and got caught up in an angry shouting match with some of the Diné there, less because of his stance on the issue, and more because the Diné believed him less than fully informed. An enraged Goldwater stomped off, muttering to a *Navajo Times* reporter as he left, "I've lived here for fifty years, and I probably know this land better than most of the Navajos here today do."[79]

In his testimony before the Congress, anthropologist David Aberle had provided an eloquent, if depressing prediction. He said, "If 8,000 interrelated human beings, living where their ancestors have lived for centuries, are thrust from their homeland under these conditions, it can be expected that they will resist relocation. Such a reaction has nothing specific to do with Navajo culture or personality, it is an expectable human response." Aberle went on, "Deprived of livestock, crowded onto the reservation, moved into new territory that lacks what is needed to render it habitable, the relocatees will be impoverished, dislocated, disorganized and dependent. Those whom they crowd will be resentful and will also be economically impaired." He concluded, "The relocatees will lose their faith in their tribal government and be alienated from the Federal Government. Years of economic dependency, administrative problems, and waste of human potential can be seen."[80]

Aberle proceeded to critique the old, time-honored images and misconceptions. The Navajos are nomads. The Navajos fought the whites and the Hopis didn't, so the Navajos should be punished and the Hopis should not. He declared irrelevant "the size of the Tribes, their treasuries, and their total treasuries." The real question, he reiterated, was "whether or not the Navajos shall be displaced from their homes, their farms, and their pastures for the advantage of a smaller number of Hopis who want to use the land for range."[81]

THE START OF THE CROWNPOINT RUG AUCTION

The decline of the trading posts had important implications for most Navajo weavers. The very best weavers were only affected to a limited extent, or not at all. They did not take their work to the local trader. Rather they dealt with a gallery in a place like Santa Fe, Scottsdale, or Sedona. But most weavers did not have that option, so they had to drive a little farther or they had to develop alternatives. The growth of rug auctions can be directly attributed to the traders' fate. The door also opened wider for independent entrepreneurs, such as Steve Getzwiller of Benson, Arizona. Getzwiller brought a bulldog tenacity, high standards, and an uncompromising air to the business. He tried to reintroduce the old churro wool and attempted to encourage a return to classic design elements. By the early 1980s, this young, strong-minded operator was beginning to make some headway. Mark Winter, another young interloper, also began to become well known as a dealer. Winter prized the old blankets and the classic early weavings. He traveled to the New York auction houses or just about anywhere in search of a treasure and a deal. He preached to those who would listen (and those who would not) that the great Navajo weavings were masterpieces of modern art. Would he pay $25,000 for the right weaving? Winter did so without hesitation.

Most weavers could not even imagine receiving even a four-digit check for a rug they had created. In 1980, the average weaver may have earned about two dollars an hour for her work and about $2,500 per year altogether. Thousands of women and a handful of men still wove, but exactly how many remained anyone's guess. Certainly the impression held by most observers pointed to a declining percentage of the population, yet weaving continued to be an honored activity, one highly valued within the society. Despite its low return on an hourly basis, weaving still made sense as an activity because it could be done sporadically and at home. Income from weaving could still make a vital difference in a household's overall financial picture.[82] Weavers increasingly ignored the old regional boundaries to weave styles they liked or to create new styles.[83]

Pictorial rugs continued to surge in popularity. Isabell John of Many Farms was one of a number of weavers who enjoyed acclaim and a good income from her depictions of community life. She said she wanted her work to reflect "the way I live—the hogan, corrals, the livestock. Diné'é baghan, dine'é be'iiná—the Navajo philosophy of life, the way of life." She also saw it as a means to instruct a younger, more urban generation about "our traditional ways." John was a good example of a talented, skilled weaver who adjusted to changing market circumstances. In the 1950s and 1960s, she completed ye'ii rugs and rugs with geometrical patterns. At that time, Ann Hedlund writes, weavers from her area "all took their rugs to nearby trading posts where they exchanged them for groceries and supplies." As those posts began to close, she had to try something else and take her rugs somewhere else. Thus, in the early 1970s, "John became the first in her immediate area to put people, animals, and landscapes into her rugs." Hedlund notes, "Her example was quickly taken up by others."[84]

In the early 1960s, the decline of the posts and the minimal prices for most rugs at surviving posts alarmed weavers and sellers alike. Lavone Palmer, a trader in Crownpoint, had an idea. Why not start a rug auction? She helped organize the first one, donating fifty rugs to get things started. People from the immediate vicinity showed up. Then Bill Smith, the elementary school principal, suggested holding the auction in the school's gym. The auction grew from three to six or seven annually under the sponsorship of the Crownpoint Rug Weavers Association. Pauline McCauley and Martha Benally played key roles in the early years. Ena Chavez became the manager in 1981, a position she still held in 2001.

Mamie Begay was fifteen years old when the auctions began. She lived in Sweetwater, about ten miles south of Red Mesa. After hearing that weavers could set a minimum price for their rugs and would receive 90 percent of the sale price, she decided to give Crownpoint a try. Begay soon became a regular participant. She made the 150-mile trip to the eastern Navajo community on Friday, arriving generally in early afternoon. Begay checked in with the people running the auction, told them the minimum she would accept, left the rug, and then waited for early evening.

Around five o'clock all the rugs were brought out and placed on the tables at the back of the gym. Each rug had a small card with a number and the identity of the weaver placed on it. Begay watched the varied crowd that swarmed around the tables. She recognized some of the dealers or local BIA or U.S. Public Health Service employees who rarely missed an auction. Then there were others from the Four Corners region, drawn to the site by an article they had seen or by word of mouth. Auctioneer Herman Coffey eventually ambled on to the little stage. He asked the usual opening question, "Now, how many of you are here for the first time?" Coffey continued, "Anybody from outside the United States? Now, Texans don't count!" There was always laughter.

Mamie Begay never knew when her weaving would come up. They didn't go in numerical order. This wasn't Sotheby's. There was no fancy catalogue, nor buyer's premium. Perhaps they had some secret method of organization, but the method escaped her, just as it did the buyers. She did know she would get a better price for her work. As time went on, she noticed her weaving becoming more recognized and yielding a greater return. Mamie Begay kept coming back to Crownpoint.[85]

THE FIVE MAJOR SPORTS PROVIDE FRIENDSHIP AND COMPETITION

By the 1960s, both rodeo and basketball had become "traditional" sports and both enjoyed a substantial following in Diné Bikéyah. Rodeos offered an opportunity to celebrate community and reinforce family ties. Navajo rodeo cowboys and cowgirls understood at an early age that they represented their family and their area. Indeed, one of the reasons why they participated was because they wanted to follow the example of an older relative.

Rodeo also furnished a means to honor someone's memory or achievement. Michael Bia, a promising young bull rider, did not have the chance to compete during the 1968 season. Twenty-one years old and recently married, he was drafted by the military and sent to Vietnam on April 26. Two months later, Lieutenant Bia lost his life in an ambush. In September, Bia's best friend asked Lula Bia for his rodeo gear. At the Navajo Nation fair, he placed Bia's chaps and other gear on a bull that was released for the eight-second interval during the rodeo.

Rodeos provided a venue for competition and achievement. They "offered an opportunity for stories, anecdotes, lessons, exaggerations, and, now and then what some have been rude enough to label as lies." A particular arena would be associated with something that happened there. And the place itself became "the stuff of memories: the smell of fry bread, the struggle for meter and meaning within a country and western tune, a certain hue of the earth, the tentative light of early morning, the echo of a meadowlark's song."[86]

Dean Jackson, Jack Jackson, and Roy Spencer helped found the All Indian Rodeo Cowboys Association (AIRCA; later the All Indian Professional Rodeo Cowboys Association) in 1957. It began to sponsor rodeos as well as rodeo and judging schools. By the 1960s and 1970s, there seemed to be at least one AIRCA-sponsored rodeo just about every weekend in the summer. In July and August 1970, for example, rodeo contestants who wanted to compete in AIRCA-approved rodeos made the following circuit: July 3–5, Ahoohai Days (Holbrook); July 11–12, Tsaile; July 18–19, Lukachukai; July 25–26, Chinle; August 1–2, Steamboat;

August 8–9, Rock Point; August 22–23, Pinon; and August 29–30, Kayenta.

The competitors started out young. Various age-group competitions encouraged children to enter when they were four or five years old. Someone like Carole Jackson could not remember when she was not on horseback, not trying to win a particular event. She loved competing alongside her father and other family members. She didn't mind seeing her name in the *Navajo Times*. She was honored to represent the Navajo Nation at the first Indian National Finals Rodeo in 1976 in Salt Lake City. By the conclusion of the 1979 season, Jackson had won three national finals titles in barrel racing.[87]

Basketball players shared that love of competition. It seemed as though any home you visited in Navajo country had a basketball hoop. Future prospective National Basketball Association stars often learned to dribble on dirt and not to rely too much on a backboard when they shot the ball. Little kids went to high school games or tournaments, such as the annual Sheep Herders' Classic in the tiny Teec Nos Pos school gym. They closed

Two Navajo girls on a ferris wheel. Fairs and rodeos were often combined, adding to the appeal of either event. Photograph by Chuck Abbott. Arizona Historical Foundation, Tempe.

their eyes and imagined themselves at the free-throw line in a tie game with one second to go. They would dribble the ball once or twice, stop, take a deep breath, and aim just over the front rim. In their imagination, at least, the ball always went in and their team always won the game.

Urbanization contributed to the growth of basketball's popularity. Boys and girls were more likely to grow up in town, with easier access to a court, instruction, and teams. By the end of the 1970s, they were likely to have access to a television and watch the great college and pro players. When they reached high school, they looked forward to the possibility of their team competing in the state tournament. Since the schools were divided into different classifications depending on enrollment, even players on small school teams could dream of going to state. Like their counterparts in rodeo, they loved seeing their name in the paper, and relished defeating teams from other towns and other tribes. And like rodeo, it all started early. The March 23, 1972, issue of the *Navajo Times*, for example, featured a photograph of the Crownpoint Bearcats, participants in the second annual eastern Navajo peewee basketball league tournament. Jacob Willie, Peterson Francisco, Amos Billie, Larry Davis, and Leonard Yazzie posed with a trophy almost as tall as they. Basketball helped keep more than a few Navajo children in school during this era. A young man or woman might not like everything about Fort Wingate or Phoenix Indian School, but might stay enrolled in order to become a Bear or a Bearette, a Brave or a Bravette.[88]

ZAH DEFEATS MACDONALD IN 1982

Peterson Zah opposed Peter MacDonald in the 1982 election for chairman. Born in 1937 in Low Mountain, Arizona, Zah attended Phoenix Indian School, where he learned carpentry skills and played basketball. Teachers and counselors tried to discourage him from going to college, but Zah gained an athletic scholarship at Phoenix College and earned an associate of arts degree. He then transferred to Arizona State University and received a degree in education in 1963. Zah invited his teachers and counselors at Phoenix Indian School to his graduation from the university, but none came. He trained VISTA volunteers before helping to start the DNA Legal Services. In 1975, the home he had built in Window Rock burned down in a blaze that appeared to be caused by arson. Zah and his family escaped just before the roof collapsed. He then rebuilt the house.[89]

Zah's candidacy in some ways resembled the part that MacDonald had played in 1970. Through his direction of DNA Legal Services, Zah had become as well known as MacDonald had been as director of the ONEO. MacDonald carried the baggage of twelve years in office, whereas in 1970, he had been the new man. Zah was articulate, tough, and blessed with a good sense of humor. Like MacDonald, he was a college graduate. He had grown up in the area fought over by the Navajos and Hopis and that background increased his interest in resolving the conflict. Zah's friendship with incoming Hopi president Ivan Sidney, whom he had known since their days at Phoenix Indian School, also suggested that he might somehow forge an agreement.

MacDonald and Zah traded charges during the campaign. MacDonald kept saying that Zah had made promises he could not keep. Zah kept emphasizing that MacDonald had not solved the problem of high unemployment nor resolved the conflict with the Hopis. Many observers favored Zah to win, but they knew one should never count out the incumbent. Despite all of his problems and disappointments, MacDonald remained a formidable foe. He still commanded a solid base of support, especially in the Tuba City agency, the home area of his wife, Wanda, and in places such as Leupp, Cameron, and the Gap, where he had many clan relatives.

MacDonald emerged from the August primary with a slight edge in the totals, but in the November election, Peterson Zah won handily, defeating MacDonald by about 5,000 votes. MacDonald carried the Tuba City agency and the two candidates split the Eastern Navajo agency vote. However, Zah carried Shiprock, Chinle, and Fort Defiance agencies by substantial margins. In the community of Shiprock, Zah won by almost 700 votes. Zah did particularly well with young voters, who embraced his idealistic style. But he also did well across the board, demonstrating an impressive appeal with all sectors of the electorate. Many Diné voters responded enthusiastically to his goals of decentralization and a less imperial chairmanship. Many hoped a new administration would allow the Diné to truly "stand together." Overjoyed by his triumph, Zah declared it to be the end of "unbalanced, unresponsive government." With only about 1,000 absentee ballots remaining to be counted and Zah holding on to a margin of well over 4,000 votes, MacDonald refused to concede, but eventually he acknowledged his first electoral defeat.[90]

In late December, MacDonald provided the Council with a twenty-four-page, single-spaced statement on "the MacDonald years." In this document, MacDonald labeled the era as "the time of emergence" for the Navajo Nation. "Together we have built a nation," he told the Council. "We have become a sovereign people." MacDonald called it "an era of growth, of creativity, of development unmatched in all the annals of our people." In the first term, he declared, "we built, created, learned, and above all, expanded. We dreamed big; we reached for the sky. . . . The Navajo Tribal Government became the recognized model for self-determination."

During the second term, he recalled, "Despite the fact that we were being hit by everything from Hopi fomented range wars to FBI probes, grand juries, audits and investigations, we still kept going. We found out that our rate of growth as a nation had outstripped the capacity of our tribal government to deal with the sheer volume and complexity of what we were doing. So we used that second term, while we were under attack to put in place the management systems, the computers, the fiscal and accounting systems, the personnel system, the divisional organization and the internal monitoring mechanisms we would need."

The focus for the third term, MacDonald asserted, had been mostly "on economics." He perceived "two separate streams of development in our emergence as a nation": "a movement toward economic self-sufficiency" and "a movement toward governmental self-sufficiency." This term, he contended, had seen a "new developmental thrust," including the completion of shopping centers in Chinle, Tuba City, and Window Rock.

Following a fifteen-page review of his own administration, MacDonald proceeded to outline in nine pages "an agenda for the eighties." He presented a long list of challenges: "providing basic subsistence," "continuing the task of nation building," dealing with a series of issues relating to education, asserting Navajo preference, managing resources and creating economic growth, and asserting sovereignty.[91]

The document became especially emotional in its final pages. At one point it even appeared to borrow from *Star Trek;* MacDonald spoke of the Council "walking out in space, going where no tribal government has ever gone." These pages revealed how much Peter MacDonald had relished being chairman and how much he hated to leave this position of responsibility and power. On the last page he proclaimed, "[T]he end is only the beginning of a new journey."[92] This journey probably would not consist of riding quietly off into a political sunset. MacDonald's "agenda for the eighties" made evident that he had work he still wanted to do. Even before Peterson Zah gave his 1983 inaugural address, the 1986 electoral campaign had begun.

8

"We Survive as a People": 1982–2002

I will continue to be appreciative of and awed at the integrity and courage of my ancestors. Because of their love and bravery, their faith in the Navajo way, we survive as a people.

—*Jennifer Nez Denetdale (2001)*

"Ha'at'ísh yaa'ahályą́ą doo?" her mother asks. "Who will take care of the sheep?"

In 1999, this is a troubling question for Betty Reid, and her brother, William. Their mother, Dorothy, and their aunt, Jeanette, are both in their seventies. The two women have maintained a small number of sheep and goats in the Bodaway area, about thirty miles west of Tuba City. But they cannot look after the animals all the time. They hire a sheepherder occasionally; William, a biology instructor at Tuba City High School, or Betty, a reporter for the *Arizona Republic*, sometimes are able to provide assistance on the weekends.

The women continue to keep the sheep and goats for social and cultural reasons. They still like the idea of trading a sheep for firewood or being able to donate a sheep or a goat to one of their relatives for a Navajo healing ceremony. They like being reminded of the relatives who gave them sheep many years before. "Sheep are life to the women," Betty Reid writes. "Each morning the language of their prayers to the Holy People is laced with homage to the flock." But they realize this connection has become ever more tenuous. Her mother says, in Navajo, "I imagine my life and that of the sheep will end soon."[1]

In the 1960s and 1970s, the women had 400 head of sheep. In the early 1990s, they had 250. Now they have a total of twenty sheep and goats. Today a second question accompanies the query about who will take care of the sheep: How many sheep will there be? All across the Navajo Nation the numbers of sheep and goat have declined precipitously. Most people who have livestock now tend to prefer cattle, who require less work and who bring a better price in the marketplace.

However, few Diné now have livestock. Can there be a Navajo world without sheep?

At the beginning of the twentieth century, as we have seen, Americans assumed that Indians were a "vanishing race." The past hundred years demonstrated that Indians were not going to vanish, but they also revealed that Native communities would not remain the same. Over the course of the twentieth century, the Diné had defied the doomsayers who predicted or imagined their disappearance. When January 1, 2000, dawned, few non-Navajos asked if the Navajos were going to vanish. But many Navajos were asking themselves about their vanishing livestock and what it said about their identity and their future.

DIFFERENT JOBS, DIFFERENT RESIDENCES

Census data about the Navajos always used to bring to mind the old saying about lies, damned lies, and statistics. The 2000 census, however, appears more reliable. Arbin Mitchell, manager of the Navajo census office, insists, "We went down every road." The census takers used helicopters and all-terrain vehicles to get to places truly difficult to reach. In contrast to 1990, all of the census takers were Navajos. According to the 2000 census, 180,000 persons reside in the Navajo Nation, of whom 175,000 are Navajo. More than 100,000 Diné live away from the nation, primarily in border towns, such as Farmington and Gallup, and in the Phoenix, Albuquerque, Tucson, Salt Lake City, and Los Angeles metropolitan areas. The census reveals a young, rapidly increasing population, with the median age between eighteen and twenty-four. It also reflects an urbanizing people.[2]

Most Navajo towns grew substantially in the 1990s. A table for Navajo towns in Arizona clearly shows this changing picture:

Town	1990 Population	2000 Population	% Change
Tuba City	7,323	8,225	12.3
Chinle	5,059	5,366	6.1
Kayenta	4,372	4,922	12.6
Fort Defiance	4,489	4,061	-9.5
Window Rock	3,306	3,059	-7.5
Kaibito	641	1,607	150.7
Lukachukai	113	1,565	1285.0
Many Farms	1,294	1,548	19.6
Ganado	1,257	1,505	19.7
St. Michaels	1,119	1,295	15.7
Pinon	468	1,190	154.3
Tsaile	1,043	1,078	3.4
Teec Nos Pos	317	799	152.1
Dennehotso	616	734	19.2

Sawmill	507	612	20.7
Greasewood	196	581	196.4
Shonto	710	568	-20.0
Rough Rock	523	469	-10.3

Fourteen of the eighteen towns recorded an increase in population. The greatest growth occurred in smaller communities, such as Lukachukai, Greasewood, Kaibito, Pinon, and Teec Nos Pos. Pinon has received an influx of Diné from the land conflict with the Hopis; all had land available for home sites, whereas in larger communities land was much more difficult to obtain for that purpose. Lukachukai is also one of the most beautiful locations in all of Diné Bikéyah. It is near Canyon de Chelly and has a good road connecting it to Chinle. Town businesses will benefit additionally from the paving of the road over Buffalo Pass. This route will offer motorists a shortcut through the mountains into New Mexico. During 2000, almost three hundred home sites were requested and approved in Lukachukai. Its growth rate of 1,250 percent surpassed all other Arizona towns. Edward Bahe Harvey, an elder, is not pleased about such a rapid expansion. He expressed his displeasure with the transformation. "I could stretch my legs out and feel comfortable in 1940," the ninety-two-year-old said. "Today we're folded up on the land. . . . I can see into my neighbor's horse corrals. That's how much we've grown."[3]

Navajos have been moving from rural residence into reservation communities for a long time, but the past twenty years have truly witnessed a transformation of the Navajo social landscape. This change has occurred for essentially the same reasons that urbanization has taken place elsewhere in the American West. Navajos are drawn to town, not because they want to see into their neighbor's horse corrals, but because their economy today consists almost entirely of wage work, and the jobs, with a few exceptions, are in town. Moreover, proximity to town means easier access to the public schools and a variety of activities now based in a more urban setting, from shopping at grocery stories to participating in youth basketball. It doesn't always mean the promised land. There have been task forces on gang violence for more than a decade and they exist for a reason. "Gang Violence Leaves Two Dead" is not a headline one used to see.[4]

The major employers in the recent past and today include the Navajo Nation itself, the BIA, the public schools, the IHS, the National Park Service, and other federal, state, and county agencies. Much of this work involves clerical skills or demands some postsecondary education or training. The various Navajo schools, for example, employ a lot of teachers, but that option, of course, is only available to individuals who hold college degrees. This pattern of work has tended to be more advantageous for women than for men.

The development of natural resources, including coal, oil and gas, uranium, and timber, by contrast, has primarily been seen as male work.

However, this kind of employment has been more erratic and less pre-dictable. Within the past twenty years, the NFPI suffered major economic setbacks, forcing the tribal enterprise to close its major mill operation at Navajo, New Mexico. Employment in the uranium mines has been significantly reduced, both for economic and health-related reasons. Some employment has been possible through the coalmines at Black Mesa, for example, or the oil fields near Aneth, but such corporate ventures have been more important for their return to the Navajo treasury than their contributions to individual household incomes. Some Diné also have found employment in nearby border towns and have either moved there or commute to these locations. The proximity of Flagstaff, Winslow, Holbrook, Gallup, Farmington, and Cortez to the Navajo Nation has allowed for a significant number of the Diné to find employment in these locales.

A TRADITIONAL HOGAN BED AND BREAKFAST

Tourism continued to expand in Diné Bikéyah during this era and the Navajo Nation worked hard to take advantage of this market. The Navajoland Tourism Department published attractive brochures and newsletters promoting the sights and sites of Navajo country. "The Navajo Nation extends into the states of Utah, Arizona, and New Mexico covering over 27,000 square miles of unparalleled beauty," one publication trumpeted. "The Navajo Reservation is peppered with twelve lakes and ponds and is home to more than a dozen national monuments, tribal parks, and historical sites." The Official Visitors Guide published by the Navajo Nation included a map with sixty-three "scenic locations" within the four sacred mountains.[5]

The list of tour guide operators in the Navajoland Visitors Guide illustrates the growth of the tourist industry. More than two dozen operators are listed, including nine based in the Monument Valley area: Begay's Guided Tours, Bennett Tours, Bigman's Horseback Tours, Goulding's Tours, Homeland Horse and Van Tour, Jackson Tours, Roland's Navajoland Tours, Sacred Monument Tours, and Totem Pole Tours and Trail Rides. Located in Chinle or Canyon de Chelly or advertising tours to the Canyon are De Chelly Tours, Justin Tso's Horseback Tours, Navajo Nation Inn, Totsonii Ranch-Trail Ride, and Twin Trails Tours. The emphasis on Monument Valley and Canyon de Chelly is consistent with long-established tourism patterns. Chinle and Kayenta also benefited from that association, with each community claiming three motels (Canyon de Chelly, Holiday Inn, and Thunderbird Lodge in Chinle; Wetherill Inn, Holiday Inn, and Hampton Inn in Kayenta). At times, a particular enterprise stretched things a little bit to take advantage of that association. For example, the Many Farms Inn advertised itself as being "at the doorstep of Monument Valley," when it was close to one hundred miles away. On the other hand, that was no more misleading than labeling a vacant school dorm as an inn.

For $30 a night, most tourists traveling on a slim budget were not about to argue.[6]

Will Tsosie's Coyote Pass Hospitality shows there are new options to be tried. The Tsaile-based entrepreneur informs potential customers through his website that "[o]ff-the-beaten-track escapades are our specialty." He warns, "We pride ourselves in delivering more than views of passing scenery. You will need your time and attention. You may have studies assigned prior to your journey, so that you can appreciate and comprehend your stay among us." He encourages clients to call from JD's Convenience Store near the junction of Navajo Route 64 and Navajo Route 12, and he will meet them there. Tsosie advises: "If no one answers and you get the answering machine, no answer, and/or get lost, don't worry!" and "Try calling every thirty minutes if you can't get through—local telephone lines have been known to go down at times."

The opportunity to stay at a "traditional hogan bed and breakfast" has proven to be very popular. "The hogan, an octagonal structure made of pine logs and earth," Tsosie informs his readers, "is a single-room dwelling with earthen floors. They are well insulated and stay cool in the Summer

Tourists on top of Rainbow Bridge. Photographer unknown.
William G. Bass Collection, Cline Library, Northern Arizona
University, Flagstaff. Neg. no. NAU.PH.96.24.16.20

and are easily warmed in the Winter. Most are heated by a central wood stove and do not have running water." He quickly adds, "Out-houses are provided!" A night in the hogan, plus "a traditional Navajo breakfast," came to $85, nearly three times the fare for the Many Farms Inn.[7]

The very fact that Tsosie has guests calling from a convenience store rather than a trading post is yet another sign of the posts' continuing decline. In 1991, Monty Roessel bemoaned the rise of convenience stores that now pockmarked the reservation. Most of them bore the Thriftway label; some of the old trading posts, like the one Roessel knew as a child in Round Rock, had been transformed into Thriftway outlets. "About the only convenient thing about Thriftway," he wrote in an editorial published in the newspaper, the *Navajo Nation Today*, "is the way it makes money at Navajo's expense."

Roessel conceded that "not every post was honest and many a Navajo family lost their family jewelry in pawn," but there were also honest traders who dealt fairly with their customers and their establishments were "as much a part of the community as the chapter house." Moreover, each trading post was not identical to the next; each had its own character. But, he complained, "if you've been in one Thriftway, you've been in them all."[8] Thriftway became a small-scale Wal-Mart, driving one trading post after another out of business. Steamboat, Wide Ruins, Klagetoh, and other trading posts closed their doors.

CONTEMPORARY WEAVING

Once in a great while, a trading post could gain new life through new management and new money. In 1997, Mark Winter of Santa Fe obtained a twenty-five-year lease on the old Toadlena trading post in the heart of the Two Grey Hills weaving area. He hired Chuck and Phyllis Kinsey to run the place and began to make occasional trips out from Santa Fe in an effort to revitalize the great weaving tradition of the community.

Winter learned a fundamental truth. People were more likely to weave if they could count on someone being supportive of their work. His enthusiasm and appreciation for area weaving, his encouragement of older weavers to keep weaving and of younger people to begin weaving, and his ability to pay a more substantial price for the product he received had a dramatic effect. As he became more engaged with the community of Toadlena, Winter began to see connections in the weaving that he had not fully grasped before. He started to do genealogical research and started to chart who had learned to weave from whom. Over time he documented how weaving constituted a legacy passed down from one generation of a family to the next.

The Toadlena Trading Post became a place that honored the great weavers of the past, such as Daisy Taugelchee and Bessie Manygoats, but also honored the weavers of the present, from elders, such as Clara

Grace Nez, a weaving, and churro sheep. Photograph courtesy
of Gail Getzwiller. Getzwiller Collection, Benson, Arizona.

Grace Nez, weaver. Photograph courtesy of Gail
Getzwiller. Getzwiller Collection, Benson, Arizona.

Sherman and Elsie Lewis, to Lewis's granddaughter, Rose Blue Eyes, to children whose first rug he purchased. Winter used the old vault to start a museum in which he presented exceptional exhibitions, such as "Generations," which opened in June 2000 and featured more than three hundred rugs, including at least one weaving from every weaver in the community. He also entered the best work in shows, such as the Gallup Intertribal Ceremonial, and then hosted a celebration where weavers captured one award after another.[9]

Other entrepreneurs also demonstrated the continuing viability of the weaving industry as they promoted and encouraged the art. Bill Malone kept the Hubbell rug room going. Friends said he was limited by policies that restricted his options and reduced his maneuvering room, yet he maintained his reputation as someone who cared deeply about quality and fairness in his dealings with weavers.

Steve Getzwiller continued to make the long journey from southern Arizona to the Navajo Nation. Getzwiller brought a collector's eye to his business. He encouraged weavers to expand their dye pallets and to reach new heights in their artistry. In partnership with his wife Gail, he used the Internet effectively to promote his flourishing business in quality weaving. Getzwiller championed the use of churro wool, worked closely with Grace Nez and other members of the Nez family, a group of dedicated and talented weavers, and put together two memorable exhibits of historic and contemporary weaving at the Desert Caballeros Western Museum in Wickenburg, Arizona. The Crownpoint Rug Weavers Association's monthly auctions maintained their viability into the new century. Elderhostel buses still found their way north from Thoreau as the auctioneers cajoled and counseled, the vendors held forth in the hallways, and weavers made their treks from Burnt Corn and Blue Gap.[10]

These and other individuals and entities that promoted weaving or any of the Navajo arts did not always agree about form or substance. Opinions varied, egos clashed, and loyalties conflicted from time to time. In the fragile, fast-moving world of the year 2002, many observers simultaneously worried about the future of the arts and celebrated the many remarkable achievements of Diné artists.

GAMING AND KAYENTA TOWNSHIP

Two distinctive economic development projects received significant attention in this era. One involved gaming. During the 1990s, most Native communities in the Southwest took advantage of the opportunity to construct and operate casinos. Although gaming did not turn out to be equally profitable for all Indian nations, it did bring in tremendous revenues to more than a few groups, including Fort McDowell, Ak-Chin, Salt River, and Gila River in Arizona and several Apache and Pueblo communities in New Mexico. The Navajos and the Hopis balked initially at participation in this enterprise, but as time went on, more Diné had second thoughts about boycotting such substantial revenues.

The Navajos voted against gaming in 1994 and 1997. President Kelsey Begaye (the chairman's title was changed to "president" in 1989), who opposed gaming, decided not to veto a gaming ordinance approved by the Navajo Nation Council (the new name for the Navajo Tribal Council) on October 16, 2001, by a 45-17-1 vote. This ordinance approved proceeding with a one-hundred-thousand-square-foot casino within the Tóhajiileehí (formerly Cañoncito) chapter, twenty-five miles west of Albuquerque along Interstate 40. The casino will not serve alcohol, at Begaye's insistence. A consulting firm, Johnson and Associates, estimated that by the fifth year of operation the casino would realize a net profit of $55 million. Tóhajiileehí, an enclave separate from the main Navajo reservation, has supported gaming for some time. Area residents sought all the profits from this enterprise and then tried for 90 percent, with 10 percent going to the Navajo Nation treasury. The eventual percentage, no doubt, will be a good deal less than ninety, an outcome that would not have surprised Jacob Morgan. In December 2001, the Tóhajiileehí Band sent representatives to the fifth annual Southwest Gaming Conference and Trade Show. They presented a proposed design for their casino and sought advice from other Indian communities that have had casinos for some time. Tóhajiileehí would like to add a park for recreational vehicles and other related activities that will attract truckers, tourists, and families.[11]

Kayenta is the site of another intriguing economic development project in the Navajo Nation. For years entrepreneurs, such as Richard Mike and others interested in business development and civic management, spoke about how the lack of zoning, inadequate housing, and other limitations in the infrastructure of Kayenta made it difficult, if not impossible, to attract business. The BIA and Navajo government bureaucracies hindered development as well, with their seemingly endless supply of white tape. So, too, did the chapter system. Mike commented, "The chapter will have a meeting and ask if everyone says OK to your using a piece of land. If one person says 'no,' if one person makes a claim to using the land to graze sheep, then you're in trouble." If the land happens to be situated not far from a well or windmill, Mike added, "you've really got a problem, because ten families will say they used the land for grazing or to take their sheep to the water."[12]

On November 5, 1985, the Navajo Tribal Council agreed to withdraw 3,606 acres of Navajo trust lands to establish the Kayenta Township project. Two years of intensive work and advocacy by Kayenta area residents, including Council delegate Albert Bailey, provided the foundation for this action. Chairman Zah sent a memorandum to division directors in March 1985, urging them to support the project. In June, the Kayenta chapter passed a resolution formally supporting the Kayenta Chapter Planning Board. Gerald Knowles, an educational consultant residing in

Kayenta, was asked to write the concept paper for the township project. He drafted the paper in July, with the chapter furnishing its approval through resolutions passed in September and October, followed by the Tribal Council's authorization.[13]

Both local and Navajo national politics then intervened. Bailey and Zah both lost reelection bids in November 1986, and new opposition surfaced from within the Kayenta community. Bailey's successor as Council delegate, Elwood Seganey, helped lead the opposition. However, in 1991, project proponent Willie Begay defeated Seganey and won reelection in 1995. In 1991, as well, Knowles completed a lengthy five-year report for the Navajo Nation Council that clarified a number of issues and concerns relating to the initiative. Even with a series of changes in leadership at Window Rock, the Navajo Nation did not withdraw support. Finally, in January 1996, the Navajo Nation Council passed a resolution establishing the Kayenta Retail Sales Tax Project, and in November it authorized an election by voters living within the township boundaries to serve as commissioners. On March 5, 1997, Jimmy Austin, Jerry Gilmore, Yazzie Leonard, Richard Mike, and Charles Young won seats on the Kayenta Township Commission. They took their oaths of office in April, and by June the Commission began to levy a 2.5 percent sales tax on select local businesses.[14]

In the first eighteen months, the tax brought in $670,834. The commission projected revenues of $600,000 for fiscal year 2001–2002. Some concrete results have been achieved over the past few years. After local residents had waited for more than a dozen years, a post office was constructed. A huge dumping and trash problem has been confronted, with a new transfer station to collect waste also put in place. Dumping of trash in area ravines and gullies has been greatly reduced. More civic improvements are slated for the near future, including the completion of an almost three-hundred-home subdivision, which George Joe called "the first true middle-class housing" on the Navajo Nation. It is premature to evaluate the viability of the township, but Joe remained resolutely optimistic about it. "The outcome of Kayenta will reshape Indian country," he declared in the summer of 2001.[15]

Most Navajo livestock owners don't share Joe's optimism about their future. As the story about livestock in Bodaway makes evident, the last generation has experienced livestock reduction of a different sort. John Collier and E. R. Fryer are not the culprits this time around, although more than a few Diné still blame them for the devastation they caused and the long-term effects of their efforts.

However, at the end of the twentieth century, the Navajos heard their own government rather than the federal government promote livestock reduction. On two occasions, in 1996 and again in 1999, severe drought conditions prompted Navajo Nation employees to urge livestock owners to reduce their herds. In 1996, skeptical Diné doubted the drought warnings or saw them as a ploy to prompt reduction. As a result, ranchers had to sell animals that were nearly starving and lost hundreds of thousands of dollars in the process. In 1999, Elizabeth Washburne, director of the Navajo department of agriculture, advised Navajos to reduce the size of their herds. Eugene Guerito, director of the emergency management department, tried a novel approach. "We've been urging Navajo ranchers to reduce their herds so they won't have to work as hard day in and day out," he said. In Bodaway, however, ranchers may not have been very receptive to this message.[16]

Urban Diné, living on or away from the Navajo Nation, generally feel a sense of loss. They don't want to give up their careers or the other dimensions of life made possible by urban residence. However, they understand why their older relatives cannot imagine their bringing up a son or a daughter apart from the sheep. On the other hand, when they see their town-based grandchildren heading out to help with the sheep and goats, and they observe all that the young folks take with them on this assignment, they don't know whether to laugh or cry.

In the 1950s, Betty Reid writes, "a sheepherder wore a thin shirt, a jacket, canvas sneakers, jeans, and a simple scarf. They carried a rusty can loaded with pebbles attached to bailing wire" to use "when sheep or goats turned stubborn and refused to follow the main herd." They would take "one slice of day-old ash bread or cold frybread to nibble on" and "drink the muddy water from the earthen dam, together with the sheep and the dogs." In December 1999, Betty Reid and her two daughters headed out armed with "goosedown jackets, wool socks, thick sweaters, sunglasses, fleece-lined jeans, caps, gloves, Nike hiking boots, sun block, lip balm and a CD player with headphones." They do have a compact disc by Navajo singer Sharon Burch, but Burch is outnumbered by Tracy Chapman, the Grateful Dead, the Violent Femmes, and Fleetwood Mac. Reid's older daughter takes a copy of *Gone with the Wind* and her younger daughter has "a bag of coloring books and paper for doodling," Winnie the Pooh, Ernie, and another bear named Sniff. The grandmother takes a long look at all of this stuff and asks, "Moving somewhere?"[17]

Her question is meant in jest, but mobility is part of the force behind urbanization, just as it is with other families and other communities in the American West. Young Diné still care about their "home" chapter, and still have emotional ties to the place where they spent their childhoods. But new jobs, marriages and other relationships, and educational opportunities may move them in new directions and in the long run make it more likely they will live as adults in several locations. This is not to suggest that new traditions can't be established and that new foundations can't be set in other locales. It is not to say that having more choices about residence and career is somehow unfortunate. But it does mean that the world of children is likely to be more removed from the world of their parents and even more removed from the world of many of their grandparents. A woman from the Salt River Indian Community in Arizona once said she was wealthy, not because she had a lot of money in the bank, but because she could see her grandchildren each day. These days Navajo grandmothers understand that definition, just as they understand why it is not getting any easier to take care of the sheep.

PETERSON ZAH AND A DIFFERENT STYLE OF LEADERSHIP

Peterson Zah and Peter MacDonald dominated Navajo politics in the 1980s and 1990s. The animosity between the two men, the severe faction-alism that this rivalry provoked, and the eventual chaos and tragedy that marked the world of Navajo government constituted the central story of this era. In the year 2002, Zah will celebrate his sixty-fifth birthday and MacDonald his seventy-second. They remain larger-than-life figures. They remain in the center of the Navajo political stage, despite everything that has happened and because of everything that has happened.

Zah came into office determined to set a different tone and establish a different style. He ordered sedans purchased to replace the limousines that had been a hallmark of the MacDonald administration. Zah reduced the chairman's salary by $10,000, from $55,000 to $45,000. He appointed a Navajo law firm to take George Vlassis's place. Zah eschewed the three-piece suits that MacDonald had favored and instead opted for more casual attire, usually accompanied by a turquoise necklace or an old ketoh.[18]

The new chairman's term in office coincided with the high-water mark of the Reagan administration; Reagan had been elected in 1980, and was reelected in 1984. Reagan's ascendancy did not constitute particularly good news for Zah, a Democrat. Programs, such as CETA, were canceled and federal investment generally in Navajo country and elsewhere in Indian country plummeted. Moreover, he inherited a tribal treasury that had been depleted by MacDonald, particularly in his final months before leaving office, and as a result was unable to fund its commitments to the Navajo Agricultural Products and the Navajo Forest Products Industries and Navajo Community College. At the conclusion of his first year in office, Zah confronted a dismal fiscal situation. To partially remedy this situation, Zah pushed for the Navajo Nation to renegotiate its leases with energy companies. He initiated a trust fund with enormous potential to yield major dividends. But that was a long-term process and in the short run the Navajo budget was anemic.

Nor did Zah have positive news to report about improving relations with the Hopis. This failure to broker a better deal with the neighboring Hopis cost Zah dearly in the political arena. He had been confident he could work out a deal with his former classmate, Ivan Sidney, who had grown up not far from him. They had both attended Phoenix Indian School. Zah recalled, "We said enough of this nonsense about fighting and pumping all this money to the lawyers. So I decided to go visit the Hopi people. I drove over in my old pickup truck." Many disliked his willingness to make that seventy-two-mile trip. "They were ready to hang me," he said. "This is a hard, hard issue." Zah was found guilty of one of the ultimate political sins. He had raised expectations and then failed to deliver. Well before the election in 1986, he began to receive significant criticism from individuals whose hopes had been raised about a possible settlement.

Zah's political style also received mixed reviews. He maintained an open door for visitors at the tribal capital in Window Rock and generally attempted to make the government more accessible. Many Council delegates had grown so accustomed to MacDonald's more imperial style that they concluded that Zah was not acting sufficiently like a chairman. Although they liked the spirit of Zah's ideas, they often dismissed him as being naive or unrealistic. MacDonald picked up on this theme at an early point and continued to hammer away at it until the election in 1986. According to MacDonald, Zah was inexperienced, not sufficiently tough-minded, and naive. MacDonald insisted that the Navajos needed a leader and Zah was not a leader. The Diné needed "a skilled fighter," he suggested, and identified himself as that person.[19]

MACDONALD DEFEATS ZAH

The campaign for chairman in 1986 began early and only intensified as the election neared. MacDonald and Zah both thought the election of the other would truly bring disaster for the Diné. MacDonald contended that Zah was not tough enough in dealing with the Hopis, alleging that he had "caved in" on this issue. The former chairman clearly indicated he was not very interested in some kind of compromise settlement.[20]

Twelve people had crowded onto the Navajo primary election ballot in 1986. Eight of them received a small number of votes: Andrew Benallie (1,227), Raymond Nakai (531), Bobby M. Charley (468), Daniel Deschinney, Sr. (291), James Nahkai, Jr. (148), Kay Bennett (112), Raymond Hosteen Tso (69), Collier Greyhat (62), and Cecil Largo (58). Tohatchi businessman Larry Manuelito did somewhat better with 4,710 votes, although not as well as observers had generally anticipated. As all had expected, MacDonald and Zah received the lion's share of the ballots, with 22,330 votes for MacDonald and 15,742 votes for Zah. Although Zah indicated that he had not been able to run a full-time campaign because of his responsibilities as chairman, the November election loomed in the immediate future and it seemed rather unlikely that even with a full-time campaign Zah could overcome this kind of margin.[21]

That fall voters heard some of the most caustic and cantankerous commentary ever presented in Navajo country. The two men agreed to debate each other and the three-hour donnybrook at the Window Rock Cinema must have reminded the audience of a boxing or wrestling match. Several hundred onlookers who elbowed their way in heard the two go after each other on a number of issues, but especially the recent land purchase near the San Francisco Peaks and the conflict with the Hopis. The Navajo Nation had purchased in the previous summer 915 acres of land and obtained grazing rights to 174,000 acres of Forest Service land, which Zah hoped and anticipated that one day the Diné would also buy. *Albuquerque Journal* reporter Susan Landon recorded this vituperative exchange: "'Why do you lie to the Navajo people?' MacDonald said to Zah. 'You said you have purchased the San Francisco Peaks. You know you didn't, unless you were fooled. You only purchased 915 acres.' Zah responded that the tribe had purchased the peaks. 'I know you're a good liar,' Zah told MacDonald. 'We purchased grazing rights to the land, and you know it. It's land the Navajo people desperately need.'" Zah went on to say, "I want land that will benefit our children. You are more interested in Peter MacDonald. That's the main difference between you and me." MacDonald also pilloried Zah for not being firm enough on the battle with the Hopis over the contested land, especially in regard to those families who had been ordered to leave their homes and let the Hopis occupy their land. He argued, Landon said, that "the land never belonged to the Hopis and the Navajos shouldn't move."[22]

All campaigns feature promises made by candidates and this election was no exception. MacDonald had not lost his touch as a speaker, and his fiery rhetoric combined with lofty promises attracted both interest and support. Could he really produce a house for every Navajo veteran, fund a college scholarship for each Navajo who graduated from high school, and create at least a thousand new jobs each year? Were these just dreams, just ideals, rather than specific objectives? Were they just a way to get elected?[23]

MacDonald won by a narrow margin of approximately 750 votes. There had been hundreds of spoiled ballots and doubts expressed by some of his campaign staff about how the election had been carried out. Zah requested a recount but did not contest the election, a process that would have taken months, saying that the Navajo Nation had to move forward. Peter MacDonald was once again the elected leader of the Diné.[24]

MACDONALD SHUTS DOWN THE NAVAJO NEWSPAPER

On January 13, 1987, Peter MacDonald presented his fourth inaugural address. Speaking to a large crowd at the Navajo rodeo grounds, MacDonald said, "One hundred and twenty years ago, we Navajo people returned from the Long Walk to reclaim this land as ours. I feel that I, too, have completed a long and difficult journey to return home and serve my people." MacDonald emphasized employment: "The Navajo Nation is one of the last economic frontiers in the United States. . . . We must come out of our long hibernation to become self-sufficient and share in the bounty of America."

Ivan Sidney attended the inauguration, but his presence did not encourage MacDonald to alter his position on the ongoing struggle between the Hopis and the Navajos. He and the others in attendance heard MacDonald liken the Navajos being relocated from their lands to individuals in Afghanistan and South Africa who had been denied their rights. MacDonald repeated his vow to do all he could to allow them to remain rather than be forced to live elsewhere.[25]

The first major confrontation of the new administration involved freedom of the press. Freedom of the press is a perennial issue in Indian country. The people who work for tribal newspapers seek the liberty to be critical interpreters and reporters of the contemporary scene; tribal administrations rarely perceive such a forum as being in their interest. They want the papers to be "positive" in their perspective and supportive of what they are trying to achieve. When the *Navajo Times* began publication in 1960, it fulfilled that function, with the paper serving at the pleasure of the Tribal Council, but independent of the chairman's office. Raymond Nakai grew unhappy with the criticism in the *Times* and wanted to fire the editor, but could not. After the next election, he had enough support on the Council to have the editor removed. Then in the late 1970s, the newspaper again started to express more independent views and things really started to get interesting.[26]

It became, in part, the story of a man and a revolving door. Bill Donovan, an Anglo journalist serving as general manager of the *Navajo Times*, was fired for the first time in May 1979. The paper then hired him as a correspondent, but after a year and a half, the MacDonald administration fired him a second time for being too critical. The *Times* just didn't seem to be the same without Donovan, so it brought him back for an encore, this time, for good measure, as the editor. After about six months, the administration started to express anxiety about the paper's finances, and in due course arrived at what by then had been recognized as a traditional solution. It fired Donovan, who lobbied for his return through friends in the chairman's office. They were persuaded that he had not been involved with the financial side. After another Anglo was brought in as editor, the resilient Donovan resumed his increasingly familiar role as correspondent. Later in the 1980s, under the leadership of publisher Mark Trahant and managing editor Monty Roessel, the *Navajo Times* evolved into the *Navajo Times Today,* the first American Indian daily newspaper in the United States.[27]

During the Zah administration, the chairman decided to take an unprecedented stance in regard to freedom of the press in the Navajo Nation. Zah permitted the newspaper to be truly independent. If no good deed goes unpunished, then Zah's reward for unleashing the newspaper came in the form of editorials frequently criticizing him. MacDonald did not share this perspective about the need for the paper to be independent any more than a lot of other Diné. Freedom of the press still was a quite new and quite foreign concept. Monty Roessel later compared it to giving car keys to someone who has never seen a car. It takes a while, he said, for someone to figure out how to use them.[28]

A month after the inauguration, after giving two hours' notice, the MacDonald administration shut down the *Navajo Times Today*. The newspaper had supported Zah in the 1986 election, primarily because of his support for freedom of the press. It had not wasted any time in taking on the new chairman, criticizing him for spending too much money on a lavish inauguration ceremony. Loyce Phoenix, a staff member for MacDonald, bridled at the criticism and disapproved of the paper's financial circumstances. She decided to close down the paper. MacDonald went along with the decision, justifying the action on financial grounds. The chairman asserted that the money needed to make up the paper's debts could be better used for college scholarships or new jobs. Suddenly the Navajos were without a newspaper and all the staff members had to look for alternative employment.[29]

Trahant and two other staff members offered to buy the paper two weeks prior to its sudden closure. "If the finances were really the major concern, they would have sold it," Trahant said. Advertising revenues had increased by 46 percent in 1986, he reported. Trahant argued that MacDonald and his associates wanted to "put in people that will run the *Times* in their own image." Bill Donovan again took on the role of correspondent. Trahant and Roessel proceeded to establish *The Navajo Nation Today*, beginning in 1991. The paper, a mixture of critical reporting, attention to the arts, and storytelling, became a weekly, once again.[30]

THE BIG BOQUILLAS RANCH SCANDAL

The closing of the newspaper was followed on July 8, 1987, by the biggest land deal the Navajo Nation had ever concluded in its history. It purchased a ranch of nearly half a million acres, with access to almost another quarter million acres of state lease land. The ranch, known as the Big Boquillas, was just north of Seligman, Arizona, an old, Route 66-highway town. The Navajo Tribal Council by a 45 to 4 vote agreed on April 30 to put down a little over $8 million for the property. The total purchase price came to $33.4 million, or $68 dollars an acre. The Council decided in a subsequent 43 to 30 vote to employ tax-exempt bonds for this purpose.[31]

Two weeks after the completion of the deal, an anonymous individual gave *Gallup Independent* reporter Betty Reid a lead on a story. The informant told her through a written note that the Navajo Nation had purchased the ranch for $33.4 million at 9:55 A.M., five minutes after another party had bought it for $26.2 million. In other words, somebody had just made a profit of over $7 million in five minutes. Reid decided to check out the lead and called Flagstaff to get the information verified by the Coconino County assessor's office. The obliging folks at the office soon came back with confirmation that the deal had really happened just like that.[32]

Reid began to learn the details of this extraordinary transaction. The broker for the deal had been Byron T. "Bud" Brown from Scottsdale. Brown had known MacDonald for a number of years. He had worked for the Navajo Nation during the previous MacDonald administration, serving as general manager for the NAPI. Brown spoke with MacDonald about the possibility of this deal prior to his inauguration. In February 1987, the Navajo Land Administration Office in Window Rock heard from Tom Tracy of the Tracy Oil and Gas Company, using stationery with "Big Boquillas Cattle Company" emblazoned across the top. "We are willing to sell the ranch for sixty eight dollars per deeded acre under suitable and acceptable terms to purchaser and seller," he wrote. The Tribal Council agreed to buy the ranch. The Tracy Oil and Gas Company filed a "Certificate of Fictitious Name" at the Coconino County Courthouse, formally acknowledging their doing business as the Big Boquillas Cattle Company. This was a legal way of acknowledging a not-insignificant detail. The Tracy Oil and Gas Company did not yet own the ranch.[33]

Between May 15 and July 6, Tracy worked out final arrangements with the owners of the property, Tenneco West of Bakersfield, California. In the meantime, the word was starting to get out about the details of these transactions. A BIA official, Floyd Espinoza, heard about the proposed sale and wrote to MacDonald informing him that the ranch had been for sale for years and that the asking price had been $25 million, or $50 an acre. MacDonald would not be deterred. Tenneco sold the ranch to Tracy for $26.2 million and signed a warranty deed to that effect on July 6. Two days later, Tracy signed a similar deed to the Navajo Nation. The sale to Tracy actually was recorded the day after that, on July 9 at 9:50 in the morning. Five minutes later, the Navajos became the proud owners of the ranch and Tracy Oil and Gas made a profit of over $7 million. Bud Brown earned well over a million dollars for his role in the transaction.[34]

Betty Reid did not know all of these details when she wrote her initial article for the Gallup newspaper. She suspected that her people had paid over market value for the ranch and she realized some people had made a lot of money in the process. Reid had a clear sense of how MacDonald and his allies would respond to the story and how difficult her life was about to become. She went ahead, nevertheless, and the *Independent* published her article on July 24. As there is no word for reporter in the Navajo language, she would be called in Navajo a gossip and would be subjected to frequent harassment, especially when it became evident that her story helped begin the downward spiral of Peter MacDonald's career.[35]

More than a year passed, with rumors about a possible indictment continuing to circulate through Window Rock. Other events added to the growing controversy surrounding the administration. For example, in January 1988, MacDonald's choice of A&T Incorporated to plan the new $30-million Shiprock hospital came under fire. James Atcitty, a cousin and longtime political ally of the chairman, was president of A&T as well as a division director of legislative affairs for MacDonald. The Navajo Architectural and Engineering Evaluation board had A&T ranked in a tie for third out of six finalists.[36]

MacDonald's decisions about form and substance also came under increasing scrutiny. He spent $650,000 to remodel his office, including $4,800 for a new door; he spent more than $20,000 to fly to the 1987 Orange Bowl with his family in order to see the Oklahoma Sooners play in that game. MacDonald allocated $1.5 million for public relations and lobbying in Washington, D.C., at least five times the amount spent by Zah. MacDonald supporter Samuel Pete emphasized, "The image of our leader is important." Referring to Zah's preference for jeans and his 1966 International pickup truck, Pete commented, "You can't have a leader wear blue jeans and drive an old truck to meet businessmen in pinstriped suits."[37]

Independent Council delegate Percy Deal said, "The average Navajo in his or her hogan would not imagine what is going on here." The Hardrock representative alleged money and contracts regularly were funneled to MacDonald supporters on the Council. He cited a recent case in point when one delegate "was getting behind in payments on his vehicle" and the Advisory Committee "directed that a check (or loan) be issued to that individual so that he could make his payments." Deal also complained that many MacDonald boosters "have suddenly become businessmen," receiving consulting contracts for construction, schools, or roads. He expressed great unhappiness about how this pattern played out at the chapter level. Deal observed, "Each of the chapters call on social service workers to help identify the needy for things like housing, loans, and cash assistance." When these applications are submitted, "MacDonald has his handpicked people who know the loyalties of the councilmen. If a councilman is an outspoken supporter of Zah, all his chapter's applications are put aside."[38]

THE SKIRTS OF SOVEREIGNTY

Finally, hearings by the U.S. Senate Select Committee on Indian Affairs in February 1989 forced key participants in the ranch purchase as well as other persons who had conducted irregular financial dealings with the Navajo Nation to testify. The revelations registered well over a nine on the Navajo political Richter scale. The aftershocks are still being felt in Window Rock and throughout the Navajo Nation and no one knows when that ground will cease to move. The resulting turmoil in the summer of 1989 and the memories that remain from this troubled time are a bitter and lasting legacy of the most traumatic time in Navajo life since livestock reduction.

Senate investigator Eugene Twardowicz labeled the Big Boquillas ranch sale "a major fraud on the Navajo people." Twardowicz told the Senate committee that MacDonald had a $60,000 loan from the United New Mexico Bank in Gallup that was supposed to be paid off by December 1986.

Bud Brown spoke with bank officials, assuring that MacDonald soon would pay $25,000 of the sum. Tracy Oil proposed the sale of Big Boquillas to the Navajo Nation on February 20, 1987. Tom Tracy, like Brown, was an old friend of the chairman. Four days later a subsidiary of Tracy Oil and Gas, Reppel Steel, wired a transfer of $25,000 to MacDonald. Before May, he received an additional $5,800. Soon after MacDonald recaptured the chairmanship, Brown took him, his wife Wanda, and their daughter Hope MacDonald, to Hawaii at a cost of over $5,000. Two months after the Hawaiian vacation, Brown leased a BMW 735i sedan for $800 a month and gave MacDonald the car. When Brown met with MacDonald and his son, Rocky MacDonald, in early 1988, the Navajo chairman concluded that the car lease and the cash transfer did not look good. He urged his son to pretend that he had received the $25,000 and the BMW. Rocky MacDonald agreed to draw up a false promissory note for $25,000 from Bud Brown to himself and backdated it to January 1987.[39]

Brown and the MacDonalds saw each other again in early December 1988. Brown agreed to not deviate from this alternative story, even though it meant he committed perjury. Later, Rocky MacDonald tried to respond to questions about his actions. He had graduated from Santa Clara University law school in 1981, and recently had passed the bar exam after seven years and several tries. Although he knew he was risking his career, he believed he had no choice other than to accede to his father's request. Why had he participated in this scheme? "Because I love my father," he replied.[40] Rocky MacDonald also carried his father's requests for payment to Brown. Testifying under limited immunity before the Senate committee, he said he used the code words of "golf balls" in these communications. One golf ball equaled $1,000. Brown testified that Peter MacDonald stood to gain $750,000 from the ranch sale. To date in early 1989, he had received $50,000, or fifty golf balls. The chairman wanted to be paid incrementally so as not to raise suspicion.[41]

Brown's testimony proved all the more persuasive because he secretly taped telephone and personal conversations between himself and Peter MacDonald. Parts of these conversations were played for the Senate committee. The $25,000 wire transfer, the BMW, and other matters were included in the dialogue with the term "cover-up" specifically employed.[42]

In a speech given on February 9, 1989, at the dedication of a shopping center in Crownpoint, MacDonald acknowledged that he had received what he termed "gifts" from a number of different individuals seeking to do business with the Navajo Nation. "But that is not a crime," he told his audience and listeners over KTNN. After all, he said, gift giving was an old Navajo custom. MacDonald blamed the accusations on racism. "If you are white, you are all right," he charged. "But if you are red or brown or black, you are not all right." MacDonald added, "We are told there is nothing wrong with congressmen accepting contributions and honorariums from (special) interest groups . . . and congressmen certainly do not abstain from votes on matters simply because their vote may affect someone favorably who gave them a huge contribution." *Arizona Republic* correspondent Bill Donovan wrote, "MacDonald said he took the gifts because he wanted a decent lifestyle for his family, mentioning the fact that he put his children in private school. He said he will not sacrifice their education 'simply because I was elected chairman.'" Responding to the accusations of accepting free plane rides, MacDonald said, "[T]hey were no different from a Navajo standing alongside the road trying to hitch a ride."[43]

MacDonald blamed the furor in part on "fear of Navajo sovereignty. There is opposition. And there is fierce antagonism." He also blamed "sore losers" from the last election making "a particularly amoral effort . . . to boot me out of office." He charged, "They were more than willing to give our land away to the Hopis. They played the game of playing poor, helpless Indian. And so they became favorites of the media." MacDonald concluded, "We lose ground only when we allow outsiders to divide us. Together we can run as one. Together we can outrace the wind. United, we cannot lose." Zah replied, "In the face of overwhelming evidence of corruption, Peter MacDonald has chosen to try to mislead the Navajo people." He said, "Sovereignty, racism, and sore losers are points that are obviously intended to take attention away from the real issues. The real issues are the allegations that MacDonald accepted bribes and kickbacks; that he planned the purchase of the Big Boquillas before his inauguration and to split the profits with the middle men in the deal; and that, with his son, he planned to cover up the scheme to the point of asking others to commit perjury." Zah said it was "outrageous to compare bribes and kickbacks to traditional Navajo gift giving," and that it was time for him to stop "hiding behind the skirts of sovereignty" and to "tell the truth."[44]

In addition to Brown and Tracy, MacDonald had received gifts and loans totaling more than $100,000 from John Paddock of Marana, Arizona. Paddock had given Peter and Wanda MacDonald $35,000 as a personal loan in December 1987. He said, "I was in the chairman's office and he said he wondered if I could loan him some money, that he was in a bind, and needed $35,000." The money had not been repaid. Paddock provided the Senate with a list of fifty-eight separate payments and gratuities made to MacDonald or members of his family since July 1986. During his campaign, MacDonald had taken advantage of Paddock's offer to use his private plane and his pilot. After the election was over, MacDonald continued to ask for use of the plane. Wanda MacDonald was flown to Las Vegas on one occasion and she and two of her daughters flew to Houston another time. All told, Paddock furnished thirty-five flights at a cost of about $60,000. Paddock wanted MacDonald to win the election because Zah had decertified his company as being Indian-owned and he knew MacDonald would certify his Native American

Construction company as an Indian-owned concern, and therefore entitled to take advantage of Indian preference stipulations for various projects. A Navajo carpenter, Donald James, was named as owning all of the company stock, even though the company was merely a front for John Paddock Construction and another of his companies, FAITHCO. These two companies did more than $2 million in business in the Navajo Nation since the 1986 election.[45]

MacDonald also profited from connections with Pat Chee Miller, who had pled guilty in March 1977 to a kickback scheme to defraud the federal government, and had resigned from his position as director of the Navajo Housing Authority. Miller's company, PC & M Construction Company of Gallup, had partnered with Springer Construction Company of Albuquerque in order to get work through Indian preference contracts. Springer Construction controlled the partnership, but it was listed as 51 percent Indian owned. The combination received about $4.5 million in contracts, including the opportunity to build the site from which MacDonald spoke on February 9.[46]

REMOVING MACDONALD AND ENSUING POLITICAL CHAOS

The Tribal Council placed MacDonald on paid leave on February 17. MacDonald appealed to the Navajo courts and convinced Judge Harry Brown of Kayenta to issue a restraining order against the Council action. The Navajo Supreme Court (which had replaced the Supreme Judicial Council) overruled Brown's order. The Court concluded that Brown did not have jurisdiction in the case, and as MacDonald's brother-in-law, was not an impartial observer. On March 10, the Council selected Leonard Haskie as interim chairman. In April, District Court Judge Robert Yazzie ruled that MacDonald and his administrative staff members must vacate their offices. Confrontations continued as emotional supporters of the former chairman protested his eviction. In one of his first official actions, Haskie fired police chief Bill Kellogg, whom most of the three hundred police officers continued to support rather than the new chief, George John. On April 19, Lieutenant Patrick Platero followed the orders of his supervising officer, George Wabenais, who had just been terminated by John, and arrested John for "impersonation of a police officer."[47]

The spring session of the Council opened in mid-May with about one hundred MacDonald supporters picketing and protesting. One day they came into the Council chambers, igniting shouting matches between supporters and critics of MacDonald. Tribal police eventually removed all but the Council members from the building. Later, when Haskie's security guard attempted to leave, the MacDonald forces attempted to stop him. These incidents reveal the high emotions of the era and provide context for understanding what happened next.[48]

MacDonald continued to argue that he was still chairman and to assert to his followers that he had been illegally removed from office. On July 20, he signed an executive order in the form of a memorandum to William Kellogg, whom he listed as Chief of Police. The memo was typed on official Navajo Nation stationery. The memo directed Kellogg to take immediate action. It said:

THE NAVAJO NATION
Window Rock, Arizona 86515

PETER MACDONALD
CHAIRMAN

EXECUTIVE ORDER
JULY 20, 1989

To: William Kellogg, Chief of Police
Division of Public Safety
From: Peter MacDonald, Sr., Chairman
Navajo Tribal Council

By virtue of the powers invested in me, as the Chief Executive Officer of the Navajo Nation, you are hereby directed as follows:

1. Effective immediately, you shall resume the position as Chief of the Navajo Police.
2. You are ordered to immediately take all action necessary to reinstate tribal law enforcement officers under your command who were terminated since February 1989 by order of the interim government.
3. You are further ordered to assist with the orderly restoration and transition of the administration of the Navajo Government which is to take place this 20th day of July, 1989.

Peter MacDonald, Sr., Chairman
Navajo Tribal Council[49]

On that day MacDonald and Johnny Thompson, the former vice chairman, met with supporters at Willie Keeto's house and urged the crowd to help restore them to their positions of leadership. "We will be leaders again," they said. Around five o'clock on the evening of July 20, more than 250 demonstrators assembled in front of an administration building. Navajo police lieutenant Daniel Hawkins came to the site about half an hour later and asked if this would be a peaceful gathering. However, Willie Keeto responded by trying to place Hawkins under citizen's arrest. The protesters had brought a typed, unsigned document on official

Navajo Nation stationery, which said: "I place you under Citizen's Arrest as provided under the Navajo Tribal Law for: 1. For Criminal Conspiracy to illegally overthrow the Navajo Tribal Government." They planned to arrest a tribal official and take that arrest to court in order to argue that MacDonald had been illegally removed from office. As Keeto and the others attempted to carry out this arrest, Hawkins ran back to his police car, with the crowd right behind him. The group shattered the car's window, pulled out Hawkins, and took his service revolver. Employees inside the building called the police. Three police cars arrived and were surrounded. Police officers from two of these cars used mace in order to escape. A riot erupted. When it was over two people had been killed, three others shot, and six more injured.[50]

The two sides gave dramatically different versions of what had happened. Keeto said, "Our security tried to place him [Lt. Hawkins] under arrest, but he resisted. Our security had plain old lumber sticks; it was totally in self-defense." He charged that the officers opened fire without warning. MacDonald held a press conference the next day and compared the event to Tiananmen Square, when "innocent, armless protestors were confronted by armed policemen who opened fire on them." He contended that the demonstrators "were the victims of a harsh, brutal attack." However, a witness to the riot said that the police responded with gunfire only after a demonstrator had fired on Sergeant Daniel Lee with a gun taken from another officer. The witness added that one police officer fired when he saw Lee fall.[51]

MACDONALD GOES TO PRISON

In late July 1991, MacDonald, Thompson, and thirty other Navajos were indicted by a federal grand jury on charges relating to the riot. The indicted included current or former members of the Council, including Donald Benally (Shiprock), Wallace McGilbert (Teec Nos Pos), and Seymour Tso, Sr. (Cameron and Bodaway), as well as Howard Bitsui, Lenora Yazzie Fulton, Paula Ann Martin, Edison Wauneka, and Kee Ike Yazzie. Eleven of these individuals wound up spending time in prison. U.S. District Court Judge Robert Broomfield sentenced MacDonald to fourteen years and seven months for conspiracy to commit kidnapping and burglary of tribal buildings as well as for receiving kickbacks in the Big Boquillas purchase.[52]

Peter MacDonald began serving his sentence in Pennsylvania in 1993. He was incarcerated for more than seven years, spending much of that time at a federal medical center in Fort Worth, Texas, because of diabetes and heart problems. MacDonald underwent quadruple bypass surgery in the late 1990s. Continual appeals for his release eventually succeeded, aided by the Navajo Nation Council pardoning MacDonald in 1995. Just before leaving office, President William Clinton commuted MacDonald's sentence.

Although not a full pardon, the act produced the former chairman's immediate release. He returned to the Tuba City area in late January 2001. Several other people, including Rocky MacDonald, served time in prison for their part in these events. At the time of MacDonald's release, Donald Benally, Ned McKenzie, and Earl Lee remained imprisoned.[53]

The bitterness created by the events of the late 1980s and early 1990s has not entirely dissipated in Navajo country. MacDonald support groups are no longer needed, but the former chairman's return has not healed the deep wounds. When MacDonald was released, Council speaker Edward T. Begay commented, "The Navajo Nation went through tremendous turmoil in 1989 and the Navajo people learned a difficult, but important, lesson as a result regarding the importance of the rule of law. And that lesson is that there are consequences if one breaks the law. Elected Navajo Nation officials hold a sacred trust given to us by the Navajo people and if we violate that trust we will be held responsible."[54]

As a result of the excesses and problems of the MacDonald administration, the Navajo governmental system was altered to reduce the power of the council president. Political scientist David E. Wilkins explains: "One of the central issues that arose in the wake of that scandalous period was a realization on the part of the council that the position of chair must be split into two wholly separate positions—the speaker of the Council (legislative leader) and the president of the Council (executive leader)." The Tribal Council passed on December 15, 1989, what Wilkins terms "a landmark resolution amending Title II of the Tribal Code." The resolution formally separated powers between the executive and legislative branches, created the office of Navajo Nation and President, created a speaker to preside over the Council, limited the powers of these two branches, decreased the number of standing committees, and took the power to appoint membership on legislative committees from the chairman/president and gave it to the speaker of the Council.[55]

Peterson Zah was elected president in 1991, but was defeated in 1995 by Window Rock attorney Albert Hale. Hale benefited from the support of MacDonald backers who remained bitter about his deposition and his imprisonment as well as from being a new face in Navajo politics. Although Zah failed to win reelection, he and members of his administration at least could take some satisfaction from the absence of scandal during the course of his term, for in the final years of the twentieth century turmoil again returned to Navajo politics. Hale was forced out of office in 1998 amidst charges that he had spent tribal money inappropriately, had accepted bribes, and had an affair. His successor, Thomas Atcitty, served only four months before also being forced out for having taken gifts from corporations. Milton Bluehouse became president for a brief amount of time, to be succeeded by current president, Kelsey Begaye. Nelson Gorman, Jr., Kelsey Begaye, and Edward T. Begay have been the most recent speakers.[56]

THE ONGOING CONFLICT WITH THE HOPIS

The partitioning of the former joint-use area dictated the relocation of over 10,000 Navajos and 100 Hopis. Although this relocation was supposed to be accomplished by July 1986, the date came and went without final resolution of this issue. By September 1, 1999, most of the 3,513 Navajo families had been relocated, but 446 remained on the land. Those who moved generally did not fare very well. Anthropologist Orit Tamir concluded that the relocation process was "carried out in ignorance of Navajo economic production and subsistence practices and of Navajo residence patterns and land tenure."

Some of those who relocated moved to the Pinon area. Tamir discovered that relocation "particularly taxed the well-being of traditional Navajos for whom physical and spiritual life, identity, and customary land-use area are one." A seventy-eight-year-old Diné widow spoke about the trauma she had experienced: "It nearly killed me just even to move a short distance. I prefer the old place, although we lived poorly. We had space, privacy, and livestock. We had everything."[57]

Many people who relocated to Pinon lived as close as they could to their former home. One relocatee explained: "This is our birth land. We were born and raised there at home. My sisters and me, we lived there with my mom when we were children, our umbilical cords were buried in the corral." Relocatees hated feeling dependent on the federal government for new housing and for forcing them to sell their livestock. Losing their stock, one suggested, was "like cutting off one of our arms."[58]

Relocation especially adversely affected women. One said, in almost a whisper, "I have not been feeling well in the past few months. I miss my land, my home, my livestock. I am very lonely." She added, "I had sheep, now I don't and it is really hard on me. There is nothing for me to do. It is like being buried alive." Even though relocation provided a new home, it did not replace what had been left behind. One woman said, "The JUA housing may have all the modern facilities and may look good, but I miss my old way of living. The cornfield where I grew corn and squash that I used for food all year. Now I don't have a field to farm. The grazing area for my sheep and horses was larger. Here I have hardly enough range for my livestock." In addition, the new homes looked nice, but many of them did not have running water or receive electric power. The homes also were not well constructed and demonstrated signs of wear very quickly.

Residents in the Pinon area did not always welcome the relocatees. They resented land being taken away and being given to outsiders. New land disputes broke out between old-timers and newcomers. Newcomers reported vandalism to their homes and problems with the adjustment of their children to their changed surroundings. High unemployment in the Pinon area forced many to drive to Chinle for work.

The two nations eventually forged a compromise that allowed Navajo families to remain on the Hopi land by signing a seventy-five-year lease. Not all Diné were willing to agree to such an arrangement, but 570 people did sign this accommodation agreement. A relatively small number of other Navajos continued to hold out against this arrangement. In the summer of 2001, Hopi officials tore down a Sun Dance ceremonial ground in the Big Mountain area. They complained that Navajos were employing the Sun Dance as a political weapon and as these Diné were on Hopi land without a permit, the Hopi Tribe had every right to take this action. Kelsey Begaye countered by saying that it was morally wrong for the Hopis to bulldoze this ground, even if they claimed legal jurisdiction over that land, and pledged that Navajos residing on this land would have access to legal assistance.[59]

In 2000, the Navajos and Hopis finally agreed to a settlement of $29 million for land use and damages to Hopi partition land by Navajo residents. Navajo Nation President Kelsey Begaye and Hopi Tribal Council Chairman Wayne Taylor, Jr., sent out a joint press release about the settlement. Begaye commented, "This resolution is clearly in the best interest of the Navajo Nation. The creative and intelligent approach developed by the leadership of the Navajo Nation Council enabled this agreement to be struck." The Hopis had argued that Navajos had damaged this land through overgrazing.[60] This agreement represented a significant landmark

The continuing conflict between the Hopis
and Navajos. Photograph by Monty Roessel.

in Navajo history. In an effort to expedite Navajo negotiations with the Hopis, Commissioner of Indian Affairs Robert Bennett in 1966 had halted development of any kind on the lands west of the 1882 reservation. This placed an enormous hardship on Diné families who could not even repair their homes in the affected area. The Bennett Freeze continued into the new century, adding to the legacy of this terrible conflict.

ACHIEVEMENTS IN EDUCATION

After Peterson Zah lost in his bid for reelection in 1995, he accepted an invitation from Arizona State University to serve as special advisor for Indian affairs to Lattie Coor, the university's president. Zah had not been pleased by the outreach effort of the admissions office at his alma mater. Nor had he been satisfied with the retention rate at the university. Zah went to every school district in Arizona and talked with all the counselors. He took eleven people from the university, including its president, on one of these excursions. The results have been impressive. Arizona State University's Native American enrollment doubled in five years from about five hundred to about one thousand. With 70 percent of that enrollment Navajo, and with graduation rates on the rise, there are encouraging signs at this university and others in the Southwest of the steady growth of trained Navajo professionals.

These results have not been simply due to chance. Students are coming to college better prepared. High school counselors have made an extra effort to locate additional scholarship assistance for their students. Navajo and other Indian faculty and staff at regional institutions have made a major commitment, not only to recruitment but retention. The existence of Indian student services programs and the development of American Indian studies programs have been important to the students and have contributed to the retention rate. So, too, have many high school teachers and counselors who, contrary to Zah's experience, believe that their students can succeed in college. Each spring at Arizona State University, there is a ceremony to honor Navajo and other Indian students. It is an emotional gathering, filled with testimony, praise, tears, and acknowledgments. It takes longer each year.

At the same time that the major universities of the region have made some progress in the programs they offer Navajo students, the Navajos' own college continued to struggle. Renamed Diné College, the institution's development remained limited. Individuals within the Diné studies program at the college were doing important work, but insufficient funding and disagreement about direction continued to plague the school. Political considerations affected the college's board of regents, and low salaries and heavy teaching loads prompted significant faculty turnover. A number of observers hailed the arrival of the college's first woman president in 2000. Cassandra Manuelito-Kerkvliet expressed her enthusiasm and her eagerness aimed at "re-strengthening the original goals and prayers" of the school.[61]

In the summer of 1991, the *Navajo Nation Today* raised a centrally important question about Navajo education. It asked, "How many schools does it take to educate the 90,000 plus students on the Navajo Nation?" It also gave the correct answer: "Too many." The maze of contract schools, BIA schools, and public schools left parents and students confused and discouraged. A number of people welcomed the addition of charter schools in the 1990s, but their existence also presented yet another layer of schooling. Two words appeared to be vital to the ongoing discussion about how to fashion a unified Navajo school system: control and money. Kayenta School Superintendent Joe Martin said in 1991, "Creating one school system on the reservation is an ideal situation. But the funding is the key question." Things had not changed a decade later.[62]

Nevertheless, there were schools that made pathbreaking efforts to improve the quality of Navajo education. Rough Rock Community School welcomed back Bob and Ruth Roessel in the mid-1990s and with Bob Roessel's retirement in 1999, Monty Roessel succeeded him as executive director. Rough Rock remained the only nonsectarian school permitted to recruit and enroll students from throughout the Navajo Nation. It continued its commitment to Navajo language and culture at a time when the percentage of Navajo language speakers was decreasing dramatically. *Navajo Culture Today*, a monthly newspaper, effectively presented important dimensions of Navajo culture. In a way, Rough Rock demonstrated that education had come full circle. Now parents were sending their children to a boarding school so that they could be exposed more fully to traditional cultural teachings.[63]

The Seba Dalkai Boarding School in Winslow, Arizona, also attempted to encourage a systemic reform of its curriculum and environment. Aided by a grant from the National Endowment for the Humanities, the school expressed its intent to "nurture critical thinking and the intellectual growth of Navajo students by guiding them in the exploration of rich humanities texts and sources, so that they will become knowledgeable of their culture and heritage and be equipped to succeed in the Navajo and other cultures." Seba Dalkai intended to create a humanities learning center in which seventh- through twelfth-grade students would "compare and interpret traditional histories and cultural texts within the context of Navajo history, heritage, and culture." The initiative embraced technology "to access libraries throughout the world to examine significant humanities texts, to interact with primary sources, and to showcase their work." Projected study themes included families and clans; history and ramifications of the Navajo-Hopi land dispute and relocation; people and their land; coming of age; healing and wholeness; a comparison of traditional Navajo, Native American Church, and Christian ceremonial dimensions; sovereignty; language; and sustainable economic development.[64]

As in previous generations, there were wonderful success stories to be noted and accomplishments to be recognized. Three examples illustrate the many intellectual achievements of this era. In the 1980s and 1990s, Tuba City High School students won applause not only on the basketball court but also in the highly competitive world of chess. Employing what their coach, John Nesbit, called "the Tuba City fighting style," the chess team won four Arizona championships, defeating teams from the largest high schools in the state. Harold Yazzie and Ryan Begay also won individual titles. "In the past," said Shaun Stevens, "Indians were just shoved aside and expected to shut up. We showed that doesn't need to happen any more, that if we work hard, we can do anything." Ryan Begay added, "When I come to Phoenix, I'm not try[ing] to prove that I can beat them. I already know I can. What I really want is a good game."[65]

On April 6, 1991, Velma Kee became the first Navajo to win the state spelling bee and competed in Washington, D.C., in the national spelling bee. She made it through six rounds and finished in a tie for fourth place among 277 contestants, spelling correctly words such as "trypanosome" and "osteogenous" before misspelling "bandalore." "People ask me if I was nervous," she later wrote. "I wasn't going to throw up or anything, but I was a little nervous. Once I got the feel of it and knew how it was to get up there in front of everyone, it all went away." She took pride and satisfaction in her achievement, noting, "[A]ll the time and effort I put into this has paid off."[66]

Jennifer Nez Denetdale became the first Navajo to hold a Ph.D. in history. Completing her work at Northern Arizona University, she wrote a dissertation—"Remembering Juanita Through Navajo Oral Tradition: Out of the Shadow of Chief Manuelito"—that honored her great-great-great-grandmother and made a significant contribution to Navajo history. Now an assistant professor of humanities at Northern Arizona University, she began to exert intellectual leadership by organizing the 2001 Navajo Studies conference and by refuting the attempt by Martin Link to deemphasize the amount of pain and suffering experienced by the Diné on the Long Walk and at Fort Sumner. In an eloquent letter to the *Navajo Times*, she articulated the value of oral history and recognized the importance of what the Diné had endured during the 1860s. "I will continue to be appreciative of and awed at the integrity and courage of my ancestors," she wrote. "Because of their love and bravery, their faith in the Navajo way, we survive as a people."[67]

THE STATUS OF WOMEN

There is a moment in the film, *A Weave of Time*, that always generates discussion among Navajo college students. It is when Isabel Myers Descheeny decides to go back to school. She leaves her family to return to finish up her degree at Northern Arizona University. It is in the mid-1980s and there isn't necessarily overwhelming support for her course of action. But it is something that she must do.[68]

Despite the standard generalizations about Navajo society being matriarchal and women having all the power behind the scenes, many Navajo women have long argued that they do not enjoy equal status within the workings of the Diné world. The modern Navajo government, AnCita Benally argues, is patriarchal in practice because it reflects Euro-American ideas about leadership. Moreover, the influence of Christianity and the Native American Church affected perspectives. There remain prevailing attitudes about career choices, political involvement, marriage, and other matters that often restrict individual options and limit possibilities for achievement and fulfillment. Women now form the clear majority of college graduates among the Diné and are gradually moving into leadership roles in fields such as education and health care that have been somewhat more open to their inclusion. But even in these areas, there is resistance. Many women teach first grade; too few serve as principal of the school or superintendent of the school district. Glojean Todacheene demonstrated at Mesa School in Shiprock the kind of warmth, toughness, and dedication that any school would be fortunate to claim in its principal, but she remained a relative rarity. In the same sense, there were many nurses, but few physicians. When Beulah Allen decided to become a doctor, she did so in part because of a kind of backhanded compliment paid to her by a male physician. He said she was too outspoken to be a nurse.[69]

The world of Navajo politics has remained largely a men's club. Although most men serving on the Council held Annie Wauneka in high regard, she had to make her way within a male culture and find a way to fit into that culture. She was, after all, the only woman Council delegate for many years. Even given her considerable ability, had she not been Chee Dodge's daughter, she may well have not been able to get in the door in the first place.[70]

There are a few more women delegates now on the Council and they do not seem inclined to keep quiet when men do not treat them as equals. Thus, for example, when Freddie Howard said on the Council floor in 1995 that the Navajos' Washington, D.C., office was in disarray because women were running it, the remark did not go unchallenged. Delegate Genevieve Jackson of Shiprock immediately attempted to get him called out of order. Interim Council Speaker Alfred Yazzie of Rough Rock paid no attention. Later, when recognized, Jackson observed that the delegates "occupy these chairs through the grace and good will of the public. And women are a majority of the voting public." Jackson asked for an apology, but Howard was not about to give it. After all, the unrepentant representative concluded, Jackson had "never apologized for all the bad things she said about us men in council." Council delegate Julia Mose of Crystal, however, emphasized that Howard had been totally out of line. "What he said was inappropriate," she asserted.[71]

Statistical evidence from the 1994 election supported Jackson's claim about women forming the majority. A total of 47,114 women voted in that election compared to 36,300 men.

During the 1990s, Navajo women were working to gain a more significant voice in politics and other venues of Diné life. Only 6 women served on the Council. Fourteen held the position of chapter president, 21 as chapter vice president, and 81 as chapter secretary treasurer. Ten women served on land boards or as grazing officials. Women accounted for 112 school board members. "The bottom line is that we need more women leaders," said Dorothy Denetclaw. "There are many issues that affect women and children." She contended that only by electing more women to leadership positions would things change.[72]

Conferences centering on empowerment began to be held with increasing frequency. The Navajo Women's Commission, for example, sponsored one such meeting in 1996. "This is a way of life; we're a matriarchal society," commissioner Gloria Means said. "I think it is time for women to support one another and praise one another." Conference attendees could attend sessions on such topics as single parenting, women in politics, childbirth, sexual harassment, and the possibilities of a Navajo woman becoming president of the Navajo Nation.[73]

There were both signs of change and signs of resistance to change as the new century began. Optimists could cite examples of accomplishment that attested to progress, or at least to individual perseverance and determination. The example of Lori Arviso Alvord, the first Diné woman surgeon, is well known, in part because of her co-authored memoir. Claudeen Bates Arthur, the first Navajo attorney general, is another well-publicized case in point. However, Teresa Lynch's story is more recent and has received less publicity, so it will be used here as an alternative illustration. Lynch grew up hearing her father's stories about being a pilot during World War II. Her mother died when she was young and she spent a great deal of time with her father, memorizing his tales about what it was like to take command of what the Diné call a *chidí naat'a'í*—a car that flies or a flying car. Lynch finally decided to become a pilot.

"It's not the flying that is hard," she said. "That's the easy part. It's the belief that I could become a pilot, that was the hard part." She pondered the Navajo stories about the hero twins traveling to meet their father, the sun, traveling on an eagle feather. Today, however, the humans were on the earth and birds were in the sky. Was it culturally appropriate to enter the world of the birds?

During the time she attended Arizona State University, she asked Peterson Zah about this question. He talked to a traditional healer who told him that she would need an introduction to the bird people. Zah gave her a beaded eagle feather. She employs it to mark her flight log and to protect her when she enters the world of the birds. Teresa Lynch graduated from Arizona State University in the spring of 2000. She now has her pilot's license and plans to become a commercial pilot.[74]

GAINING MORE CONTROL OVER HEALTH CARE

The Diné worked successfully to gain greater control over health care during this period, but a greater degree of self-determination did not automatically improve conditions. The IHS in 1991, for example, reported that obesity had become a major problem for the Navajos. Steve Mader, coordinator of the Gallup Indian Medical Center's health promotion and disease prevention program, pointed out that changing times and conditions had had a negative impact on the Diné. He cited a lack of exercise as a key part of the problem.[75]

The ten leading causes of death indicated that certain diseases and problems still had a lot of impact on individual Diné: accidents (motor vehicle, especially), heart disease, malignant neoplasms, influenza and pneumonia, homicide, diabetes, cerebrovascular diseases, suicide, chronic liver disease and cirrhosis, and chronic obstructed pulmonary condition. Significant progress was recorded during this era in combating tuberculosis and reducing the rate of infant mortality. However, diabetes became an even more crucial problem by century's end. Wade Davies observes that the percentage of Navajos diagnosed with diabetes doubled from the 1960s to the 1990s, with one out of every three Diné receiving that diagnosis for the more recent period.[76]

State involvement in providing Navajo health care increased in the 1990s. The advent of the Arizona Health Care Cost Containment System in 1981 eventually prompted more state coverage of Navajos residing away from the Navajo Nation. A few Diné received coverage through the Arizona Long-Term Care Service. At the federal level, the Clinton administration disappointed the Diné by cutting the Public Health Service budget, including a reduction in staff positions.[77]

With the passage in 1990 of the Radiation Exposure Compensation Act, Navajo uranium miners who had radon-related illnesses anticipated receiving a payment of $100,000. But the application process turned out to be both complicated and the wait time extended, so very few benefited from this new legislation. The agony continued for most Navajo uranium miners and their families. Doug Brugge, Timothy Benally, and others maintained their commitment to providing justice to the hundreds of former uranium miners through meetings, publications, and ongoing lobbying efforts.[78]

New IHS hospitals and clinics provided somewhat improved access to better care. However, the IHS "often found it easier to provide good facilities than the employees necessary to operate them." For example, comparatively low salaries made it difficult to obtain orthopedic surgeons, anesthesiologists, and psychiatrists. The service offered people with this

Peyote road man. Photograph by Monty Roessel.

kind of specialized training less than half of what they would expect to receive elsewhere.[79]

The Navajo Nation played a central role in combating HIV and the hanta virus and also mounted a concerted campaign against alcoholism. However, the Diné ultimately hesitated about assuming full control over the delivery of health care. Given the chance to vote to assume that responsibility, Diné voters declined, mainly because of anxieties over funding. Navajos were encouraged about the growth in the number of Diné involved as administrators or serving as physicians.[80]

Within the Navajo Nation one form of ceremonial healing continued to decline while the other continued to increase. Traditional Navajo healing practitioners dwindled in number and most of the healers were elderly. There was more than a little irony to the situation. Just as the IHS began to adopt somewhat more pluralistic attitudes, the employment of traditional healers became more problematic. As the new century got underway, only three hundred or so people were available to lead ceremonies. The average healer now was in his sixties.

Ceremonies did more than offer healing. As Ruth Roessel noted, they were "becoming a way for families on the reservation to get together, since many of the younger children are now living off the reservation attending college or working." A new program inaugurated by the Navajo Nation in 1998 offered some hope that the number of singers would not continue to decrease. The coordinator of this initiative, Ed Tso, announced that forty ceremonial leaders were currently training about fifty apprentices, who received a stipend to support them during the course of their instruction. Whether this program could be sustained, of course, remained to be seen. A related worry concerned the necessary use of the Navajo language in the ceremonies with so many younger people now only speaking English.[81]

The continuing growth of membership in the Native American Church clearly ranked as a very important development during this era. In 1993, a former president of the Native American Church of Navajoland, David Clark, estimated that thirty thousand Diné were members, but by the mid-1990s church membership had doubled from Clark's estimate. Many Diné take advantage of what traditional Navajo ceremonialism, Christianity, and the Native American Church (NAC) each offer, but all one has to do is drive around the Navajo Nation to see the number of sites for NAC ceremonies is obviously on the rise. Davies reports that 1996 marked an important event in the history of the NAC in Diné Bikéyah. The Navajo Nation in that year provided $25,000 for Diné NAC members to construct a church. The 1,300-square-foot building encompassed a meeting room, offices, and a museum. Church members also built a hogan and erected teepees nearby. Not too many years ago such support would have been unimaginable.[82]

NAVAJO ATHLETES RECORD ACHIEVEMENTS IN BASKETBALL AND RODEO

Communities always search for things to unite them. In the 1980s and 1990s the best place to look for a community speaking with one voice was the school gym. Basketball solidified its position as the universal community activity of the era. Navajo fans—loud, emotional, and there in force—heightened their teams' chances for success. After his team had won a championship game, one coach said, "The fans made a big difference for us. There was so much emotion that it just carried our kids like a big wave."

The town of Kirtland adjoins the Navajo Nation in northwestern New Mexico. The Kirtland Central Lady Broncos have won fourteen state championships, most recently in March 2001, and finished second eight times. It is the most successful girls' basketball program in state history. Sparked by Diné stars Nadia Begay, Shantel Begay, and Jamie Tanner, Kirtland defeated its old rival, the Farmington Lady Scorpions, 66 to 55, for the title. In the semifinals, the Lady Broncos overwhelmed the Española Valley Lady Sun Devils, 89 to 30. To win 3A, you must travel highway 64. You must keep an eye on Shiprock, winners in the past, but you always must watch out for Kirtland.

In Arizona, Jimmy Skeet's teams started it all. He coached six Window Rock girls' teams to 3A state championships, beginning in 1986 with a memorable overtime win over Flagstaff Coconino, at 47 to 46. Skeet's successes included a remarkable four consecutive titles from 1992 to 1995. In 1996, Amelia Holtsoi replaced Skeet and her team won, too. Three of Window Rock's triumphs came at the expense of Kayenta's Monument Valley High School, but after a fourth loss in the finals to Snowflake in 1997, the Lady Mustangs finally emerged with a championship in 1999. In 2000 and 2001, the Tuba City Lady Warriors won the title under the direction of new coach Tamrya Rogers. Among the state's smallest schools, the St. Michaels girls team has also carved out an impressive record, winning the 1A title in 1993, 1994, 1997, and 2000. The Lady Cardinals, coached by Joey Rollings, won the 2000 title game handily, defeating Joseph City, 57 to 36. Carla Nez, Nina Chester, and Ariana Watchman were named to the all-tournament team.[83]

After finishing second in 1992, Coach Aaron Anderson's Monument Valley Mustangs team in 1993 became the first Navajo boys' team to take the state championship, defeating Lakeside Blue Ridge in a low-scoring game, at 42 to 36. The fan support for the Mustangs that season bordered on the unbelievable. "It was amazing," Anderson said. "We'd drive five or six hours for a game and have more people there than the home team."

Since that breakthrough victory, witnessed by nearly ten thousand Diné fans at America West Arena, Navajo teams have won five of the past eight titles, with Window Rock (1995), Monument Valley (1996 and 1997), and Tuba City (2000 and 2001) sharing the honors. Always at a height disadvantage, the Navajo teams compensate with speed, defense, and heart.

Many learn to play as T. J. Begay of Monument Valley's first championship team did. He shot his first baskets through a baling wire hoop attached to a plywood backboard nailed to a juniper log on a dirt "court."[84]

Ryneldi Becenti knows about Navajo fan loyalty. After starring at Window Rock High School, Becenti became the first Navajo basketball player to play an important role on a university team. Arizona State University women's teams generally play before pitifully small audiences, but when Becenti competed for the Lady Sun Devils in the early 1990s, the attendance skyrocketed. Hundreds of Navajos drove all the way down to Tempe to watch her. As Arizona State's team huddled before Becenti's first game, one of her teammates peeked at the crowd. "Oh, my, Ryneldi," she gasped. "Look! Look at all those . . . all those . . . Indians!"[85]

More Navajo women than men have followed Becenti's lead into major college basketball. Other than Edison Bahe, who played at the community college level, Navajo men have been disadvantaged by height and by unwillingness of coaches to recruit Native American players. That may be beginning to change. On January 2, 2002, when the Air Force Academy played Northern Arizona University in Flagstaff, a Diné player started for each team. Despite Kodiak Yazzie's seventeen points, the Falcons edged the Lumberjacks, 57 to 56. Lamoni Yazzie made nine of ten free throws and a total of fifteen points for the Academy. Northern Arizona reported a larger attendance than usual for what Kody Yazzie preferred to see as "just another game."[86]

It is not just another rodeo, but it is one of those days when you wouldn't mind a few more clouds. The bleachers at the Eastern Navajo Fair and Rodeo are doing a pretty good job of reflecting the early August sun. The familiar voice of broadcaster Ernie Manuelito advises spectators to get something to eat. "Try the mutton stew," he counsels. "It's the breakfast of champions."

One of the few Anglos present is writing a book on Indian rodeo. Notebook in hand, he heads over toward the food booths. He notices that the Crownpoint Youth Athletic Association is selling fourteen flavors of snow cones and starts copying the list. "Can I help you?" asks a frowning rodeo official, who appears out of nowhere. The visitor knows she means, "What are you doing?" He hurriedly explains. "Oh, that's fine," responds the official. "We thought you were a food inspector from the Indian Health Service."[87]

Like the residents of Aneth, people from the New Mexico checker-board area generally feel slighted and have good reason to be wary of strangers with notebooks. The rodeo at the Eastern Navajo Fair, like most Diné rodeos, is meant to be a gathering of locals. That remains one of the best things about rodeo in Diné Bikéyah. It is a competition, family reunion, and celebration of community all rolled into one. People want to see skilled cowboys and cowgirls. But they also want to see relatives and friends who live elsewhere and who have returned for the occasion.

The first cowboy to enter the arena this afternoon is Bennie Begay. He draws a pretty good horse and has a good ride in the bareback event. Begay receives a reasonably high point total from the judges, who are often reluctant to reward the first competitor. Begay looks like the real deal, though. At the end of the season he qualifies for the Indian National Finals Rodeo. At a Phoenix arena later in the fall he winds up being co-champion. He adds his name to those who have won at the INFR, names that need no introduction to those who know Navajo rodeo. He is now in the company of people like Felix Gilbert, John Boyd, Jr., Wally Dennison, Ed Holyan, James Hunt, Jr., and Carole Jackson, and he knows what kind of company that represents.[88]

In this election year of 1998, a number of Diné politicians show up in Phoenix for the finals. Some look like they haven't been on a horse for a while, but Arizona state senator Jack Jackson appears to be right at home. He should. Jackson still competes in rodeo at the senior level. Senior rodeo gives those over forty a chance to do something more than grow nostalgic over past triumphs. Now they can continue to participate in something that has meant so much to them.

If someone is born into a Navajo rodeo family, he or she is likely to be a part of rodeo, too. Jack Jackson insists there are Navajo children born with their boots on. Emerson Long, Sr., concludes, "Competing in rodeo has really helped my children. They learn more about livestock and responsibility. It's educational and it keeps them busy." As they advance from woolly riding, perhaps, to bull riding, rodeo offers friendships, recognition, a sense of achievement, stories that may or may not be true, and, almost always, the chance to sample a snow cone.[89]

ARTISTS AND STORYTELLERS

The period since 1982 has been an especially productive time for Diné writers, weavers, and other artists. Rather than provide an encyclopedic listing, this brief overview offers a representative sample to allow for discussion of a particular individual's work in somewhat greater detail. This section considers a writer (Luci Tapahonso), a painter (Anthony Chee Emerson), a weaver (Mary Lee Begay), a potter (Alice Cling), another weaver (Grace Nez), and another painter (David Johns).

"There is such a love of stories among the Navajo people," Luci Tapahonso writes, "that it seems each time a group of more than two gather, the dialogue eventually evolves into sharing stories and memories, laughing, and teasing." One of eleven children, she grew up in Shiprock with "lots of relatives around and lots of storytelling." In collections of her work, such as *Sáanii Dahataal: The Women Are Singing* or *Blue Horses Rush In*, she emphasizes the connections between and among generations. "Who I am is my mother, her mother, and my great-grandmother, Kinlichii'ini Bitsi."

Tapahonso's words have earned her an impressive audience both within the Navajo Nation and throughout the United States. She writes about candles and cowboys, horses and Hills Brothers Coffee, rain and raisin eyes. Her writing is often some form of restoration, of the spirit and of the heart. But it is also about the fragility and uncertainty and the unanticipated turns that our lives may take. Her writing suffused with homesickness for Shiprock during the time she lived in Lawrence, Kansas, speaks to all Diné who have had to leave the boundaries of the four sacred mountains. Tapahonso is still beyond that boundary, but living near the Rio Santa Cruz is a lot closer to home than residing near the Kaw.

She often employs a familiar setting, such as the Shiprock Fair, and invests it with special meaning. Tapahonso takes the ordinary and the familiar and makes it yield a portrait that is often poignant and always true. She portrays her family going to Farmington from Shiprock: "My oldest brother always went because he drove, my other brother went because he helped carry laundry, my father went because he was the father, and my mother went because she had the money and knew where to go and what to buy." Diné readers appreciate her sure sense of place and her depiction of characters they recognize: the uncle drinking his coffee, or the woman who has to keep reminding herself that cowboys "are just bad news." Tapahonso's work always seems to circle back to the land, to the place where the Diné prayers begin. "This is How They Were Placed For Us," she declares. "[T]hese mountains and the land keep us strong. From them and because of them we prosper."[90]

Anthony Chee Emerson illustrated Tapahonso's *Songs of Shiprock Fair*. Emerson now lives in Kirtland and owns and operates a gallery in Farmington. His understanding of the four directions has had a fundamental impact on his work. Emerson says the East is a place of beginnings, "where family and life experiences are interpreted into folk art painting with intense colors," producing a "yesteryear as if seen through the eyes of a child." The South "is the developmental stage," bringing forth "whimsical and free falling designs and patterns" that express Navajo spirituality. The West "represents growth and maturity" and presents a more abstract style, influenced by "a higher spirit," mirroring the gift and blessing of imagination. Finally, the North is the source for a more representational style, as seen in landscapes, portraits, and depictions of wildlife. Much of Emerson's work results from a meeting of two directions, making possible new ideas and energy.

Emerson dedicated *Songs of Shiprock Fair* to "my wife, Michele, and my children, Cheyanne and Zack, my inspiration." He credits Cheyanne and Zack for inspiring not only his illustrations for four books for children, but also for influencing him to become a storyteller through his paintings, etchings, and collographs. His sepia etchings of work, home, play, song and dance, and the trading post present familiar scenes that prompt memories and stories. Emerson also paints large canvases of everyday

Anthony Chee Emerson, artist. Photograph by Marc Henning.
Courtesy of Anthony Chee Emerson, Farmington, New Mexico.

life, such as a waiting room at an IHS clinic, that, like his other work, bring a smile of recognition from Diné viewers. Although much of his work may seem timeless and idealized, it often reflects whimsy and the impact of changing times. A recent example, "Where Have All the Sheep Gone?", asks a centrally important question about contemporary Navajo society. Since 1996, Emerson has won thirteen first-place awards at the Santa Fe Indian Market and the Gallup Intertribal Ceremonial and two best-in-division awards at the Heard Museum Indian Market.

His gallery furnishes a venue for folk art by his mother and his brother as well as the creations of Randall Chitto and other nationally known artists. Emerson recognizes the importance of Native artists gaining more control within the workings of the marketplace. A journey to the gallery reveals an ordinary room that has been transformed through imaginative use of available space as well as a meeting ground for American Indian art.[91]

Mary Lee Begay's room is an ordinary one that has not been transformed. For many years she has worked at the Hubbell Trading Post, demonstrating the fine art of Navajo weaving to tourists who somehow manage to make it all the way from Blackwell's Corner to just beyond Burnside's Corner. Navajo weaving authority Ann Hedlund describes her as "proficient and versatile. . . . Although Ganado Red and Hubbell revival styles are her usual choices, she also makes Burntwater, Two Grey Hills, Storm, Wide Ruins, and many other patterns. Because she excels in designing, her work is often copied by other weavers."

Begay does not speak a great deal of English, but she responds to the constant barrage of questions at the Hubbell site in a gracious and patient manner, all the while continuing work on her latest rug. She wears "a multitiered broomstick skirt of satin or calico, a long-sleeved velveteen or satin blouse, and silver and turquoise jewelry." Somehow she manages to focus on her work, all the while fielding questions she has generally heard hundreds of times before. Begay is a kind of Diné ambassador to the world, showing the kind of imagination, creativity, and effort that goes into a finished weaving.

She acknowledges that it is indeed hard work: "Weaving takes a lot of hard thinking," she says. "It takes careful measuring, too." Begay notes that she measures again and again as she moves forward with a weaving. It has to be done right or she will start over. She will not take shortcuts nor tolerate something not done properly. Mary Lee Begay is an artist and interpreter whose beautiful work has enriched the lives of countless guests to the Navajo Nation. She represents herself, her family, her community, Hubbell's, and the Navajo Nation in a productive, appropriate, and considerate way.[92]

Like Mary Lee Begay, Alice Williams Cling was born in the 1940s. However, unlike Begay, she has worked in an art form that until quite recently went unrecognized and unappreciated. Alice Cling is a potter.

She is seen as one of the great Navajo potters of the past quarter-century, and perhaps the best. Her work, signed "Alice Williams" and later, "Alice Cling," after her marriage to Jerry Cling, is unmistakable and in great demand.

Bill Beaver, a trader from the Flagstaff area who has done much to promote Navajo pottery, thinks that she may be the best Diné potter, period. He smiles and shakes his head, when describing the confusion some years ago about her name. "I had a woman come up from Scottsdale and say, 'You should see such and such a show! If you see Alice, you tell her"— referring to Alice Williams—"you tell her she'd better be sharp because this Alice Cling is catching up with her real fast!'"

The daughter of master potter Rose Williams, Cling is from the Cow Springs area, the heart of the Navajo pottery revival. Her pots have extraordinary finishes and graceful contours. They possess a quiet elegance that is especially appealing. Like Emerson, she makes the long journey to various art markets. Knowing that her work will sell quickly takes some of the sting out of the extended drive. At the Santa Fe Indian market in 2001, people were camping out overnight in front of her booth so as to be first in line in the morning.

During this era, Navajo pottery gained a new level of respect and regard. No one has been more important to its ascendancy than Alice Cling.[93]

In 1953, when Grace Nez was sixteen years old, her mother's sudden and unexpected departure for the hospital left Nez in charge of her sister in a home without any food or wood. Grace Nez had observed her mother weave and decided to try to weave a saddle blanket in order to obtain some money. Nez strung up a simple warp and over the next several days and nights wove a two-faced saddle blanket. She took the rug in to the local trading post to sell. Entering the post she felt awkward and uncertain about what she had done, but her efforts were rewarded by the fifteen dollars paid to her—enough for food to keep her sister and herself going until their mother returned.

This modest beginning to her career as a weaver suggested resourcefulness but did not anticipate brilliance. Like many weavers, Nez reached a certain plateau and her work never seemed to progress beyond this point. In 1984, however, a trader gave her a copy of Steve Getzwiller's *The Fine Art of Navajo Weaving*. Nez and her daughters pored over the book and then began to create rugs that represented a new level from prior efforts. They started to work directly with Getzwiller in 1992, after he offered some persuasive ideas about design and color. The financial returns from this collaboration soon allowed members of the Nez family to devote full time to weaving.

During the past decade Grace Nez and her daughters have created truly spectacular rugs, many of them in the Teec Nos Pos tradition. These weavings were featured in 2001 in the Getzwiller exhibit of fine contemporary weavings at the Desert Caballeros Western Museum in Wickenburg,

Arizona. The use of churro wool, the employment of rich new colors, and the stunning presentation of extraordinarily intricate and strikingly beautiful designs mark these rugs as among the very finest being woven today.

If we cannot know the future of Navajo weaving, that very uncertainty offers all the more reason to appreciate the masterpieces of matriarch Grace Nez.

David Johns grew up in Seba Dalkai, north of Winslow. This place

Dome mural by David Johns, Phoenix, Arizona. Photograph by Monty Roessel.

continues to influence his art. "My abstract landscapes are all color and light," he says. "The colors of the sand, the bushes of the red rock country, the summer sky." Johns credits the Holy People for his talent and believes his work combines his training and reading at Northern Arizona University with his "Indian philosophy and traditional Navajo teaching to create a style of my own."

Prominent Scottsdale gallery owner Lovena Ohl befriended Johns at a critical stage of his career. She exhibited his work and introduced him to Alex Wareing, the president of Case Construction Company in Phoenix. His company was constructing an office building with a dome and he wanted an artist to paint a mural in the dome. Wareing asked Ohl for a recommendation. She suggested Johns.[94]

Johns had second, indeed third thoughts, about his acceptance of this assignment. It turned out to be a much bigger project than he could have imagined. The room below the dome was 36 feet in diameter. The dome rose 50 feet. Johns's mural covered 1,600 feet. It is a lasting, inspiring monument to Navajo and other Indian cultures.

The four directions organize the mural. In the course of depicting a life journey, it presents designs and symbols, Canyon de Chelly, the San Francisco Peaks and other sites of special significance, and portraits of great leaders, such as Crazy Horse and Quanah Parker, as well as Native peoples from throughout the Americas. An eastern panel symbolizes spirituality, a southern panel life and growth, a western panel creativity and family, and a northern panel knowledge and survival. Informed by his consultations with Diné elders and the world's beauty, the mural is a monument to an artist's creativity, but also a testimony to the way in which the Diné and other Native American worlds intersect. Johns honors the animal world, sacred places, and the diversity of Native peoples. His mural speaks to the increasing connection made by the Diné to the outside, including the incorporation of the Native American Church.

David Johns thinks of the dome "as a Holy place. I wanted to honor my people with this mural, and to make it so spiritual that walking into the room would be like entering a large cathedral." After his work was completed, in the spring of 1990, he and his uncle, Dudley Yazzie, returned to the room, where Yazzie said a Blessingway prayer. "Before me it is blessed. Behind me it is blessed. Above me it is blessed. Below me it is blessed. All around me it is blessed."

It was finished in beauty.[95]

Conclusion

In the final few years of the twentieth century and the first few years of the twenty-first, the Navajos looked back with pride on the sacrifices and achievements of their ancestors. Many, however, worried about the present and agonized over the future. They articulated major concerns about contemporary Navajo society and believed that the future held even greater challenges.

At the beginning of the new century, the Diné faced both old and new questions. Unemployment constituted a perennial issue. So, too, did discrimination in American society. Many concluded that the conflict with the Hopis would never truly be resolved. However, other issues had emerged more recently. Two of the central components of traditional Navajo culture had been the raising of sheep and the speaking of the Navajo language. And yet the numbers of sheep and the percentage of people who could speak the Navajo language were decreasing rapidly. The Diné also expressed concern about the future of their government. The MacDonald scandal and other embarrassments had raised serious questions about its viability. Could a more effective and appropriate plan of government be devised? If it could, who would want to participate in it?

Even with these ongoing uncertainties, the Diné could also perceive a substantial number of positive developments in the present and recent past, examples that attested to their ability to survive, adapt, expand, and continue.

The Diné had always been conscious of the need to defend their lands, their animals, and their people. They had rebuffed the Spaniards on one occasion after another and yet they still lost people to the slave trade. Their stories told about how the Comanches and Utes were willing to travel hundreds of miles to cause five minutes of trouble or years of strife. Their oral histories still resonated with accounts of the "Fearing Time," that terrible period that encompassed the Long Walk and their incarceration so far from their beloved mountains. They recorded as well the success that more than a few of their people had enjoyed in avoiding capture and confinement. Elders within the society could still recall the shock and sadness of the livestock reduction period. They remembered how people had been thrown in jail, how the sheep had been slaughtered. There were still Code Talkers who personified the ability of the people to defend the land and all of its occupants and to demonstrate great courage in the face of adversity.

In July 2001, the Diné witnessed a belated but still significant recognition of these heroic men. Four of the surviving Code Talkers and family members of the remaining twenty-five made their way to Washington, D.C., to receive the Congressional Gold Medal, the highest civilian award Congress can bestow. "Today," President George W. Bush said, "we honor twenty-nine Native Americans who, in a desperate hour, gave their country a service only they could give. Today we give these exceptional Marines the recognition they earned so long ago."

There had been twenty-nine original Code Talkers and now five still lived: John Brown, Jr., Allen Dale June, Chester Nez, Lloyd Oliver, and Joe Palmer. Richard K. Begay, an executive assistant to Navajo President Kelsey Begaye, and Zonnie Gorman, Carl Gorman's daughter, had done the careful research to find more than four hundred Diné who had been Code Talkers. Begay and Gorman felt so strongly that they had not received sufficient recognition. "Bizaa yee nidaaz'baa," Begay said. "They fought the enemy with their language." Senator Jeff Bingaman of New Mexico had helped push for the medals. His website informed thousands of Americans of the Code Talkers' achievements.[1] Visitors to the site saw some outstanding photographs of the young Marines, including a fine image of Carl Gorman. In paying tribute to the Code Talkers, the Diné honored their courage, their intelligence and creativity, and their defense of place. Through their efforts and those countless others through their history, their survival had been made possible.

The theme of adaptation and incorporation also had continuing validity. Students of the Diné past could point to the sheep, goats, cattle, and horses that the Spaniards had brought and how the Navajos had taken these animals, and with absolutely no acknowledgment of Spain, began to make them a central part of their world. The Pueblo people who came to live among them brought useful knowledge about farming and weaving that could be adapted and employed. The Mexicans had taught them silversmithing and then the Navajos had gone on to forge wonderful creations in silver, such as the squash blossom necklaces whose origins one could trace all the way back to North Africa.

In the years after Fort Sumner, the weavers among the Navajos showed an ability to take new design elements and make them "traditional" within a generation. Any student of the weaving could not help but be impressed by the virtuosity and imagination of weavers from Teec Nos Pos, Two Grey Hills, and Ganado. Over time in the twentieth century, yei, yeibichai, and sandpainting rugs came into being. New regional styles such as Burntwater flourished. Pictorial rugs continued to demonstrate both technical virtuosity and, often, a wry sense of humor. Linda Nez depicted dinosaurs and trading posts; she presented the Anasazi and the Navajo Nation fair. Geanetta John created a spectacular weaving of musicians in an orchestra and Elizabeth Yazzie depicted four different ceremonies. Zonnie Bosley wove a Christmas rug, highlighted by a Santa with a mohair beard.[2]

The Native American Church had gone from persecution to incorporation. Diné traditional scholar Harry Walters suggested that the Native American Church constituted a fifth Blessingway for the people. The Church had come a great distance in its acceptance, even for most Navajos who did not participate in it. Its example showed again the capacity of the Navajos to employ a relatively new institution that had much value for many individuals in a complicated, rapidly changing world.[3]

In the spring of 2001, another example of adaptation and incorporation could be viewed in the confines of America West Arena in downtown Phoenix. The state high school basketball tournament brought thousands of Navajos to the Valley. The Tuba City boys' and girls' teams were defending champions in the 3A division, and now they were attempting to become the first school in Arizona history to win consecutive titles for both the boys' and girls' teams. Both teams had won their semifinal games. The Tuba City girls took on Winslow in the first final. Most of the fans in the nearly full arena cheered loudly for Tuba. The Winslow coach had recorded 572 wins, and had several good Navajo players but on this night his team had to settle for runner-up status, as the Lady Warriors triumphed 62 to 44.

All of western Navajo appeared to be on hand for the boys' final, with Tuba City's nineteen cheerleaders leading tributes to their team. In the boys' final, the Warriors took on Coolidge, a traditional powerhouse in 3A competition and the winners of the two state tournaments prior to Tuba's championship season in 2000. The Bears had only lost one game all year. They were taller, more "athletic," and extremely confident. The undersized but more cohesive Warriors outplayed Coolidge from start to finish to win, 69 to 57. The Tuba City fans created their own wave of emotion in support of their teams. They honored their competitiveness and their achievement. It promised to be a noisy ride back up I-17.[4]

A third theme, expansion and well-being, ran through Navajo history. In the Spanish colonial era and again after their lands were claimed by the Americans, the Diné continued to find ways to locate and occupy more land. The people linked expansion with prosperity. They were not nomadic nor were they without roots. They had developed a deep sense of place, yet recognized the need to keep pushing outward. The process of looking to new horizons, of exploration and discovery, was as old as the people themselves. From the time of the Hero Twins to our own day, the

Diné recognized the importance of finding new resources, developing new approaches, and searching for new answers.

After all, the Navajos had succeeded in quadrupling the size of their reservation after the Treaty of 1868. At a time when most American Indian communities were doing well to maintain their landholdings, the Diné had found allies from outside their ranks and champions within who helped them acquire additional acreage. Thanks to Father Anselm Weber, Chee Dodge, and other stalwart defenders, the Navajos fought back land allotment and succeeded in reclaiming vital pieces of land within their traditional domain. During the 1950s, the infusion of money from federal investment through the Long Range Rehabilitation Act and the Navajos' own funds from oil revenues made possible the expansion of a road network and a public school system that had long been dreamed of but not heretofore realized. The Diné did not always succeed. Senator Dennis Chávez, for example, had blocked the acquisition of much-needed land in New Mexico, and the loss of land to the Hopis continued to be a source of anger and sadness.

In 1982, the Navajos had established a new division of their court system. This much-emulated component over the course of a generation won plaudits for its constructive and effective approach. The peacemaker court offered a distinctly Diné alternative to settling a variety of disagreements and its approach had found overwhelming support from within the Navajo population. No process works in every instance, but the peacemaker approach has been very successful.

"This year," wrote Chief Justice Robert Yazzie in 2000, "the Navajo Nation quit jailing people for dozens of offenses that used to land people behind bars. Now tribal courts are turning to peacemakers." Justice Yazzie explains: "In January 2000 the Navajo Nation Council decided to revamp the Navajo Nation Criminal Code. The Council eliminated jail time and fines for seventy-nine offenses, required the use of peacemaking in criminal cases, and required that the courts see to the rights of victims."

In addition, the traditional concept of *nalyeeh*—"the process of confronting someone who hurts others with a demand that they talk out the action and the hurt it caused so that something positive will come out of it"—also became part of the criminal code.

The Navajos know something that the rest of American society is afraid to admit. In Yazzie's words, "[T]he prison approach to crime does not work. Western adjudication is a search for what happened and who did it; Navajo peacemaking is about the effects of what happened. Who got hurt? What do they feel about it? What can be done to repair the harm?" The Diné system brings the person accused of an offense and the person who suffered from it and his or her relatives. A "peacemaker" moderates the discussion. In this manner the act is identified, discussed, and a plan to deal with it is constructed.

Much of the criminal offenses within Navajo society involve assault and battery, often fueled by alcoholism. The peacemaking process involves *naayéé'*—or "monster" within the person who committed the offense—but also the person who has been hurt must be dealt with; otherwise, the abused will later become the abuser. The offender may be also perceived through this process as a victim, too. Sometimes the restitution is symbolic, such as a piece of jewelry or a horse. Yazzie concludes, "We know that peacemaking works. It has proven successful in problem areas such as driving while intoxicated, delinquency, family violence, and alcohol-related crime. It allows families to be involved in helping their relatives (whether they were the ones doing the hurting or the ones who got hurt), and it helps everyone look at the monster of the action and its effects."

The expansion of this dimension of the judicial system is an important means to foster the well-being of individuals, family members, and the community. It allows the offender's excuses to be heard; it permits the injured party's hurt to be explained. It is an emotional process. Philmer Bluehouse says that the tissue is the most important piece of paper in peacemaking. Its success relies to an important extent on the peacemaker, who is not a neutral party in the discussions that take place. Rather, the peacemaker plays a role akin to the *naat'aani,* a traditional community leader "whose leadership depends upon respect and persuasion." Ideally, through this process, an individual may move from *hochxǫ'ó* (roughly, "a state of conflict in which people are not in right relations with their surroundings or environment") to hózhǫ́ (which includes good health, harmony, peace, balance, and positive events). Peacemaking honors the individual and the family and offers the promise of well-being. In its own way, it offers a going forth, a discovery.[5]

Finally, identity and continuation form another constant within the workings of Navajo history. Navajos have always taken collective pride in their land, history, and culture. From the time of Changing Woman to the twenty-first century, there is an appreciation for heritage and an understanding that present actions affect future generations.

The Treaty of 1868 stands out as a document of fundamental importance. By signing the final treaties negotiated by a Native community and the United States and by building from that foundation, the Diné were able to establish a society able to withstand the confusions and complications of twentieth-century life. Although some of the stipulations in the treaty yielded generic aid or promises to improve administration, its real value stemmed from its symbolic importance.

In 1968, the Diné celebrated the 100th anniversary of the treaty. In the following year, the Navajos declared themselves to be "the Navajo Nation." Both occasions allowed individuals within the Diné community to speak to heritage and to possibility. In 1992, President Peterson Zah signed a sovereignty accord with the governors of Arizona, New Mexico, and Utah. The accord emphasized the importance of "a government-to-government relationship" and that the states and the Navajo Nation

Navajo Nation President Peterson Zah and Arizona Governor Fife Symington sign sovereignty agreement, 1992. Zah Papers, Labriola Center, Hayden Library, Arizona State University, Flagstaff.

would deal with each other "in a spirit of cooperation, coordination, communication, and good will."[6]

In 1999, another major gathering celebrated the presence of a copy of the treaty in the Cline Library at Northern Arizona University. For a year, Navajo men and women made the journey to see the treaty. Low lighting and careful supervision of the document allowed a real copy of the treaty to be displayed and respectfully observed by the people. At the end of that year, on June 1, 1999, the Friends of the Navajo Treaty Project presented the Navajo Treaty Day Commemorative Program to honor the treaty and to honor the ancestors of the Diné.

The gathering on June 30 spoke to the value of the day's events. Evangeline Parsons Yazzie had played a central role in obtaining the treaty for a year's time. She attempted to weigh the treaty's significance. Yazzie said the treaty had significance, for it set aside land within the sacred mountains. She said the treaty was not a perfect document but "it knows who we are." Yazzie suggested that the treaty "had not seen us for 130 years. It probably missed us." She expressed her fears about the language. "The white man's language is contagious," Yazzie said. "We want our children to speak our language once again. Language is the path back to sovereignty, back to our culture, back in kindness, back to our elders."[7]

Sovereignty provided a central theme for other speakers. Kelsey Begaye said that sovereignty "really means a proud and independent people, standing up for their rights." He asserted, "We will no longer accept being invisible. . . . We will no longer accept racism." State senator Jack Jackson argued that the Navajos did not have sovereignty, because the Diné lacked complete jurisdiction: "Do we control all our land? Our education—our health system—our culture—No."

Historical events and places allowed for a common theme to be addressed. Joe Kee, Jr., imagined a Navajo woman "alone in that strange place." He paid a tribute to the strength of Navajo women. "You are our backbone, the hearth fire of our society," Kee said. "Our ancestors never gave up. . . . I thank our ancestors for their determination." Amelia Begay told a story about the kidnapping of children by the Spanish. "These stories," she suggested, "teach me a lesson about life. The pain and cries of our ancestors are etched in these stories and in this way the people live on in our hearts forever." Helena Begay read a story about Hwéeldi. She spoke about the food there not knowing the people. But the clan system, the presence of the children, and the stories all helped the Diné to survive. "We must never forget what people went through at Hwéeldi," Begay concluded.

Poet Laura Tohe read from a poem she had written for this occasion, entitled "Within Dinétah, the People Remain Strong." She movingly and eloquently paid tribute to the Diné past. "Carson tried to wrench us from the land," Tohe said. "What was our crime? We wanted only to live within our sacred mountains. The land holds the memories of our people's whispers, cries, and blood." Tohe added, "Hwéeldi was this place of death, of extreme hardship. We vowed we never again would be separated from the land . . .

"We are Code Talkers. We are Annie Wauneka. We are cowboys, teachers, college professors, sheep herders, weavers, and bus drivers.

"We are Diné."

The program concluded not long after a rendition of "Amazing Grace" in Navajo.[8]

The Diné started to make their way from the stadium and Naałtsoos Sání started to make its way back to the National Archives in Washington, D.C. Nearby the sacred mountain of the west, Dook'o'oosłííd, shimmered in the late afternoon sun. To the north in the distance black clouds were beginning to rise.

Appendix

TREATY OF 1868

ANDREW JOHNSON, President of the United States of America, to all and singular to whom these presents shall come, greetings:

Whereas a Treaty was made and concluded at Fort Sumner, in the Territory of New Mexico, on the first day of June, in the year of our Lord one thousand eight hundred and sixty-eight, by and between Lieutenant General W.T. Sherman and Samuel F. Tappan, Commissioners, on the part of the United States, and Barboncito, Armijo, and other Chiefs and Headmen of the Navajo tribe of Indians, on the part of said Indians, and duly authorized thereto by them, which Treaty is in the words and figures following, to wit:

June 1, 1868
15 Stat. L. 667.
Ratified July 25, 1868.
Proclaimed Aug. 12, 1868
Articles of a treaty and agreement made and entered into at Fort Sumner, New Mexico, on the first day of June, one thousand eight hundred and sixty-eight, by and between the United States, represented by its commissioners, Lieutenant General W.T. Sherman and Colonel Samuel F. Tappan, of the one part, and the Navajo Nation or tribe of Indians, represented by their chiefs and head-men, duly authorized and empowered to act for the whole people of said nation or tribe, (the names of said chiefs and head-men being hereto subscribed), of the other part, witness:

Peace and friendship
ARTICLE 1. From this day forward all war between the parties to this agreement shall forever cease. The Government of the United States desires peace, and its honor is hereby pledged to keep it. The Indians desire peace, and they now pledge their honor to keep it.

Offenders among the whites to be arrested and punished.

If bad men among the whites, or among other people subject to the authority of the United States, shall commit any wrong upon the person or property of the Indians, the United States will, upon proof made to the agent and forwarded to the Commissioner of Indian Affairs at Washington City, proceed at once to cause the offender to be arrested and punished according to the laws of the United States, and also to reimburse the injured persons for the loss sustained.

Offenders among the Indians to be given up to the United States.
Rules for ascertaining damages.
If the bad men among the Indians shall commit a wrong or depredation upon the person or property of any one, white, black, or Indian, subject to the authority of the United States and at peace therewith, the Navajo tribe agree that they will, on proof made to their agent, and on notice by him, deliver up the wrongdoer to the United States, to be tried and punished according to its laws; and in case they willfully refuse so to do, the person injured shall be reimbursed for his loss from the annuities or other moneys due or to become due to them under this treaty, or any others that may be made with the United States. And the President may prescribe such rules and regulations for ascertaining damages under this article as in his judgment may be proper; but no such damage shall be adjusted and paid until examined and passed upon by the Commissioner of Indian Affairs, and no one sustaining loss whilst violating, or because of his violating, the provisions of this treaty or the laws of the United States, shall be reimbursed therefor.

Reservation boundaries.
Who not to reside thereon.
ARTICLE 2. The United States agrees that the following district of country, to wit: bounded on the north by the 37th degree of north latitude, south by an east and werst line passing through the site of old Fort Defiance, in Canon Bonito, east by the parallel of longitude which, if prolonged south, would pass through Old Fort Lyon or the Ojo-de-oso, Bear Spring, and west by a parallel of longitude about 109 degree 30' west of Greenwich, provided it embraces the outlet of the Canon-de-Chilly, which canon is to be all included in this reservation, shall be, and the same is hereby, set apart for the use and occupation of the Navajo tribe of Indians, and for such other friendly tribes or individual Indians as from time to time they may be willing, with te consent of the United States, to admit among them; and the United States agrees that no persons except those herein so authorized to do, and except such officers, soldiers, agents, and employees of the Government, or of the Indians, as may be authorized to enter upon Indian reservations in discharge of duties imposed by law, or the orders of the President, shall ever be permitted to pass over, settle upon, or reside in, the territory described in the article.

Buildings to be erected by the United States.

ARTICLE 3. The United States agrees to cause to be built, at some point within said reservation, where timber and water may be convenient, the following buildings: a warehouse, to cost not exceeding twenty-five hundred dollars; an agency building for the residence of the agent, not to cost exceeding three thousand dollars; a carpenter-shop and blacksmith-shop, not to cost exceeding one thousand dollars each; and a schoolhouse and chapel, so soon as a sufficient number of children can be induced to attend school, which shall not cost to exceed five thousand dollars.

Agent to make his home and reside where.

ARTICLE 4. The United States agrees that the agent for the Navajos shall make his home at the agency building; that he shall reside among them, and shall keep an office open at all times for the purpose of prompt and diligent inquiry into such matters of complaint by or against the Indians as may be presented for investigation, as also for the faithful discharge of other duties enjoined by law. In all cases of depredation on person or property he shall cause the evidence to be taken in writing and forwarded, together with his finding, to the Commissioner of Indian Affairs, whose decision shall be binding on the parties to this treaty.

Heads of family desiring to commence farming may select lands, etc. Effect of such selection.

ARTICLE 5. If any individual belonging to said tribe, or legally incorporated with it, being the head of a family, shall desire to commence farming, he shall have the privilege to select, in the presence and with the assistance of the agent then in charge, a tract of land within said reservation, not exceeding one hundred and sixty acres in extent, which tract, when so selected, certified, and recorded in the "land book" as herein described, shall cease to be held in common, but the same may be occupied and held in the exclusive possession of the person selecting it, and of his family, so long a she or they may continue to cultivate it.

Persons not heads of families.

Any person over eighteen years of age, not being the head of a family, may in like manner select, and cause to be certified to him or her for purposes of cultivation, a quantity of land, not exceeding eight acres in extent, and thereupon be entitled to the exclusive possession of the same as above directed.

Certificates of selection to be delivered, etc., To be recorded.

For each tract of land so selected a certificate containing a description thereof, and the name of the person selecting it, with a certificate endorsed thereon, that the same has been recorded, shall be delived to the party entitled to it by the agent, after the same shall have been recorded by him in a book to be kept in his office, subject to inspect, which said book shall be known as the "Navajo Land Book."

Survey.

The President may at any time order a survey of the reservation, and when so surveyed, Congress shall provide for protecting the rights of said settlers in their improvements, and may fix the character of the title held by each.

Alienation and descent of property.

The United States may pass such laws on the subject of alienation and descent of property between the Indians and their descendants as may be thought proper.

The Navajo People must give up the education of their children, between the ages of 6 and 16, to the white man (by attending school).

Duty of agent.

Schoolhouses and teachers.

ARTICLE 6. In order to insure the civilization of the Indians entering into this treaty, the necessity of education is admitted, especially of such of them as may be settle on said agricultural parts of this reservation, and they therefore pledge themselves to compel their children, male and female, between the ages of six and sixteen years, to attend school; and it is hereby made the duty of the agent for said Indians to see that this stipulation is strictly complied with; and the United States agrees that, for every thirty children between said ages who can be induced or compelled to attend school, a house shall be provided, and a teacher competent to teach the elementary branches of an English education shall be furnished, who will reside among said Indians, and faithfully discharge his or her duties as a teacher. The provisions of this article to continue for not less than ten years.

Seeds and agricultural implements.

ARTICLE 7. When the head of a family shall have selected lands and received his certificate as above directed, and the agent shall be satisfied that he intends in good faith to commence cultivating the soil for a living, he shall be entittle to receive seeds and agricultural implements for the first year, not exceeding in value one hundred dollars, and for each succeeding year he shall continue to farm, for a period of two years, he shall be entitled to receive seeds and implements to the value of twenty-five dollars.

Delivery of articles in lieu of money and annuities.

ARTICLE 8. In lieu of all sums of money or other annuities provided to be paid to the Indians herein named under any treaty or treaties heretofore made, the United States agrees to deliver at the agency house on the reservation herein named, on the first day of September of each year for ten years, the following articles, to wit:

Indians to be furnished with no articles they can make.

Clothing, etc.

Census.

Such articles of clothing, goods, or raw materials in lieu thereof, as the agent may make his estimate for, not exceeding in value five dollars per Indian—each Indian being encouraged to manufacture their own clothing, blankets, etc.; to be furnished with no article which they can manufacture themselves. And, in order that the Commissioner of Indian Affairs may be able to estimate properly for the articles herein named, it shall be the duty of the agent each year to forward to him a full and exact census of the Indians, on which the estimate for year to year can be based.

Annual appropriation in money for ten years.

May be changed.

Army officer to attend delivery of goods.

And in addition to the articles herein named, the sum of ten dollars for each person entitled to the beneficial effects of this treaty shall be annually appropriated for a period of ten years, for each person who engages in farming or mechanical pursuits, to be used by the Commissioner of Indian Affairs, in the purchase of such articles as from time to time the condition and necessities of the Indians may indicate to be proper; and if within the ten years at any time it shall appear that the amount of money needed for clothing, under the article, can be appropriated to better uses for the Indians named herein, the Commissioner of Indian Affairs may change the appropriation to other purposes, but in no event shall the amount of this appropriation be withdrawn or discontinued for the period named, provided they remain at peace. And the President shall annually detail an officer of the army to be present and attest the delivery of all the goods herein named to the Indians, and he shall inspect and report on the quantity and quality of the goods and the manner of their delivery.

Stipulations by the Indians as to outside territory.

ARTICLE 9. In consideration of the advantages and benefits conferred by this treaty, and the many pledges of friendship by the United States, the tribes who are parties to this agreement hereby stipulate that they will relinquish all right to occupy any territory outside their reservation, as herein defined, but retain the right to hunt on any unoccupied lands contiguous to their reservation, so long as the large game may range thereon in such numbers as to justify the chase; and they, the said Indians, further expressly agree:

Railroads.

1st. That they will make no opposition to the construction of railroads now being built or hereafter to be built across the continent.

2d. That they will not interfere with the peaceful construction of any railroad not passing over their reservation as herein defined.

Residents, travelers, wagon trains.

3d. That they will not attack any persons at home or traveling nor molest or disturb any wagon trains, coaches, mules, or cattle belonging to the people of the United States, or to persons friendly therewith.

Women and children.

4th. That they will never capture or carry off from the settlements women or children.

Scalping.

5th. They will never kill or scalp white men, nor attempt to do them harm.

Roads or stations.

6th. They will not in future oppose the construction of railroads, wagon roads, mail stations, or other works of utility or necessity which may be ordered or permitted by the laws of the United States; but should such roads or other works be constructed on the lands of their reservation, the government will pay the tribe whatever amount of damage may be assessed by three disinterested commissioners to be appointed by the President for that purpose, one of said commissioners to be a chief or head man of the tribe.

Military posts and roads.

7th. They will make no opposition to the military posts or roads now established, or that may be established, not in violation of treaties heretofore made or hereafter to be made with any of the Indian tribes.

Cession of reservation not to be valid unless, etc.

ARTICLE 10. No future treaty for the cession of any portion or part of the reservation herein described, which may be held in common, shall be of any validity or force against said Indians unless agreed to and executed by at least three-fourths of all the adult male Indians occupying or interested in the same; and no cession by the tribe shall be understood or construed in such manner as to deprive, without his consent, any individual member of the tribe of his rights to any tract of land selected by him provided in article 5 of this treaty.

Indians to go to reservation when required.

ARTICLE 11. The Navajos also hereby agree that at any time after the signing of these presents they will proceed in such manner as may be required of them by the agent, or by the officer charged with their removal, to the reservation herein provided for, the United States paying for their subsistence en route, and providing a reasonable amount of transportation for the sick and feeble.

Appropriations, how to be disbursed.

ARTICLE 12. It is further agreed by and between the parties to this agreement that the sum of one hundred and fifty thousand dollars appropriated or to be appropriated shall be disbursed as follows, subject to any condition provided in the law, to wit:

Removal.

1st. The actual cost of the removal of the tribe from the Bosque Redondo reservation to the reservation, say fifty thousand dollars.

Sheep and goats.

2d. The purchase of fifteen thousand sheep and goats, at a cost not to exceed thirty thousand dollars.

Cattle and corn.

3d. The purchase of five hundred beef cattle and a million pounds of corn, to be collected and held at the military post nearest the reservation, subject to the orders of the agent, for the relief of the needy furing the coming winter.

Remainder.

4th. The balance, if any, of the appropriation to be invested for the maintenance of the Indians pending their removal, in such manner as the agent who is with them may determine.

Removal, how made.

5th. The removal of this tribe to be made under the supreme control and direction of the miltary commander of the Territory of New Mexico, and when completed, the management of the tribe to revert to the proper agent.

Penalty for leaving reservation.

ARTICLE 13. The tribe herein named, by their representatives, parties to this treaty, agree to make the reservation herein described their permanent home, and they will not as a tribe make any permanent settlement else-where, reserving the right to hunt on the lands adjoining the said reservation formerly called theirs, subject to the modifications named in this treaty and the orders of the commander or the department in which said reservation may be for the time being; and it is further agreed and understood by the parties to this treaty, that if any Navajo Indian or Indians shall leave the reservation herein described to settle elsewhere, he or they shall forfeit all the rights, privileges, and annuities conferred by the terms of this treaty; and it is furhter agreed by the parties to this treaty, that they will do all they can to induced Indians now away from reservation set apart for the exclusive use and occupation of the Indians, leading a nomadic life, or engaged in war against the people of the United States, to abandon such a life and settle permanently in one of the territorial reservations set apart for the exclusive use and occupation of the Indians.

In testimony of all which the said parties have hereunto, on this the first day of June, one thousand eight hundred and sixty-eight, at Fort Sumner, in the Territory of New Mexico, set their hands and seals.

W. T. Sherman,
Lieutenant General, Indian Peace Commissioner.

S. F. Tappan,
Indian Peace Commissioner.

Navajo Chiefs:
(Each signed with an X)

Barboncito, Principal Chief
Chiqueto
Armijo
Muerto de Hombre
Delgado
Hombre
Manuelito
Narbona
Largo
Ganado Mucho
Herrero
Narbono Segundo

Navajo Head Men:
(Each signed with an X)

Riquo
Torivio
Juan Martin

Desdendado
Serginto
Juan
Grande
Guero Inoetenito
Gugadore
Muchachos Mucho
Cabason
Chiqueto Segundo
Barbon Segundo
Cabello Amarillo
Cabares Colorados
Francisco

ATTEST

Geo. W.G. Getty, Colonel Thirty-Seveth Infantry, Brevet Major—General U.S. Army

B. S. Roberts, Brevet Brigadier—General U.S. Army, Lieutenant—Colonel Third Cavalry

J. Cooper McKee, Brevet Lieutenant—Colonel, Surgeon U.S. Army

Theo. H. Dodd, United States Indian Agent for Navajos.

Chas. McClure, Brevet Major and Commissary of Subsistence, U.S. Army

James F. Weeds, Brevet Major and Assistant Surgeon, U.S. Army

J. C. Sutherland, Interpreter

William Vaux, Chaplain U.S. Army

In Executive Session, Senate of the United States

Resolved, (two-thirds of the senators present concurring) That the Senate advise and consent to the ratification of the treaty between the United States and the Navajo Indians, concluded at Fort Sumner, New Mexico, on the first day of June, 1868.

Attest:

Geo. C. Gorham,
Secretary.

By W.J. McDonald,
Chief Clerk.

Now, therefore, be it known that I, ANDREW JOHNSON, President of the United States of America, do, in pursuance of the advice and consent of the Senate, as expressed in its resolution of the twenty-fifth of July, one thousand eight hundred and sixty-eight, accept, ratify, and confirm the said treaty.

In testimony whereof, I have hereto signed my name, and caused the seal of the United States to be affixed.

Done at the City of Washington, this twelfth day of August, in the year of our Lord one thousand eight hundred and sixty-eight, and of the Independence of the United States of America, the ninety-third.

ANDREW JOHNSON

By the President:
W. Hunter
Acting Secretary of State.

Notes

ABBREVIATIONS

ARCIA [year]	*Annual Report of the Commissioner on Indian Affairs [year]*
CCF	Central Classified Files (of NA or NAPR)
Dodge Papers	Thomas Dodge Papers, Arizona State University, Tempe, Ariz.
FFP	Franciscan Fathers' Papers, St. Michaels Mission, Special Collections, University of Arizona Library, Tucson, Ariz.
NA	Record Group 75, Bureau of Indian Affairs, National Archives, Washington, D.C.
NAPR	Record Group 75, Bureau of Indian Affairs, National Archives, Pacific Region, Laguna Niguel, Calif.
NARMR	Record Group 75, Bureau of Indian Affairs, National Archives, Rocky Mountain Region, Denver, Colo.
PIPC	Peter Iverson, private collection, Tempe, Ariz.

CHAPTER 1

1. Luci Tapahonso, "This Is How They Were Placed Here For Us," in Tapahonso, *Blue Horses Rush In* (Tucson: University of Arizona Press, 1997), 39–42.
2. *Treaty between the United States of America and the Navajo Tribe of Indians, With a record of the discussions that led to its signing* (Flagstaff, Ariz.: KC Publications, 1968), 5–6.
3. This summary is based primarily on Ethelou Yazzie, ed., *Navajo History* (Rough Rock, Ariz.: Navajo Curriculum Center, Rough Rock Demonstration School, 1971). See also, however, Paul Zolbrod, trans., *Diné bahane': The Navajo Creation Story* (Albuquerque: University of New Mexico Press, 1984), and Jerrold E. Levy, *In the Beginning: The Navajo Genesis* (Berkeley and Los Angeles: University of California Press, 1998). For an annotated bibliography of the vast Navajo literature, see Howard M. Bahr, *Diné Bibliography to the 1990s* (Lanham, Md.: Scarecrow Press, 1999). Bahr's 739-page work is extremely useful.
4. Yazzie, *Navajo History*; Zolbrod, *Diné bahane'*; Levy, *In the Beginning*.
5. Yazzie, *Navajo History*; Zolbrod, *Diné bahane'*; Levy, *In the Beginning*; Harry Walters, "A New Perspective on Navajo Prehistory" (N.d.), photocopy, Peter Iverson, private collection, Tempe, Ariz. (hereafter cited as PIPC).
6. Yazzie, *Navajo History*; Zolbrod, *Diné bahane'*; Levy, *In the Beginning*; Walters, "New Perspective"; Albert W. Yazzie, *Navajo Oral Tradition* (Rough Rock, Ariz.: Navajo Resource Center, Rough Rock Demonstration School, 1984).
7. Yazzie, *Navajo History*; Zolbrod, *Diné bahane'*; Levy, *In the Beginning*; Walters, "New Perspective"; Yazzie, *Navajo Oral Tradition*.
8. Walters, "New Perspective."
9. In "New Perspective," Walters quotes Charlotte J. Frisbie, *Navajo Medicine Bundles, or*

Jish: Acquisition, Transmission, and Disposition in the Past and Present (Albuquerque: University of New Mexico Press, 1987).

10. Walters, "New Perspective." The Enemy Way is known popularly, if unfortunately, in English as the "Squaw Dance."

11. AnCita Benally, "Hané' Béé'ééhaníťh: With Stories It Is Remembered" (master's thesis, Arizona State University, 1993), 41–46. For an example of recent work on Athabaskan languages, see Eloise Jelinek, et al., eds., *Athabaskan Language Studies: Essays in Honor of Robert W. Young* (Albuquerque: University of New Mexico Press, 1996).

12. Benally, "Hané' Béé'ééhaníťh," 46–50.

13. Ibid., 35–36.

14. Ibid., 54–59.

15. Klara Kelley and Harris Francis, "Anthropological Traditions versus Navajo Traditions About Early Navajo History," in *Diné Bikéyah: Papers in Honor of David M. Brugge*, ed. Meliha S. Duran and David T. Kirkpatrick, Series No. 24 (Albuquerque: Archaeological Society of New Mexico, 1998), 143.

16. See, for example, the opinions expressed by some of the contributors to Ronald H. Towner, ed., *The Archaeology of Navajo Origins* (Salt Lake City: University of Utah Press, 1996). Those willing to confront "mitochondrial haplogroup characterizations," "restriction site polymorphisms," and other terms embraced by physical anthropologists, may wish to tackle Shawn W. Carlyle, et al., "Context of Maternal Lineages in the Greater Southwest," *American Journal of Physical Anthropology* 113, no. 1 (2000): 85–102.

17. Kelley and Francis, "Anthropological Traditions," 149.

18. David M. Brugge, "Thoughts on the Significance of Navajo Traditions in View of Newly Discovered Early Athabaskan Archaeology North of the San Juan River," in *Why Museums Collect: Papers in Honor of Joe Ben Wheat*, ed. Meliha S. Duran and David T. Kirkpatrick, Series no. 19 (Albuquerque: Archaeological Society of New Mexico, 1992), 33, cited in Kelley and Francis, "Anthropological Traditions," 148–49.

19. Kelley and Francis, "Anthropological Traditions," 147; Zarana Sanghani, "Descendants of the Anasazi?," *Gallup Independent*, 29 April 2000.

20. For an early presentation of the incorporation thesis, see Evon Z. Vogt, "Navaho," in *Perspectives in American Indian Culture Change*, ed. Edward H. Spicer (Chicago: University of Chicago Press, 1961), 278–336.

21. Kelley and Francis, "Anthropological Traditions," 149.

22. Harry Walters, oral presentation at "Sheep Is Life" conference, Diné College, Tsaile, Ariz., 26 June 1999, in notes, PIPC; Sanghani, "Descendants."

23. Sanghani, "Descendants."

24. This matter surfaced in 1992 at the second meeting of the Native American Graves Protection and Repatriation Review Committee. Archaeologist Alan Downer participated in this discussion. See Minutes, Native American Graves Protection and Repatriation Review Committee, National Park Service, Lakewood, Colorado, 26–28 August 1992. For a subsequent consideration of this issue, see the minutes for the eighteenth meeting of the Native American Graves Protection and Repatriation Review Committee, National Park Service, Lakewood, Colorado, 18–20 November 1999. Richard Begay and Steven Begay of the Navajo Nation attended the 1999 meeting, as did four representatives from the Hopi Tribe. Contributors in Paul F. Reed, ed., *Foundations of Anasazi Culture: The Basketmaker-Pueblo Transition* (Salt Lake City: University of Utah Press, 2000), examine the beginnings of Anasazi culture. The debate continues over the reasons for the dispersal of the Anasazi communities. See, for example, George Johnson, "Social Strife May Have Exiled Ancient Indians," *New York Times*, 20 August 1996.

25. Kelley and Francis, "Anthropological Traditions," 143–51.

26. David M. Brugge, "Navajo Archaeology: A Promising Past," in *Navajo Origins*, ed. Towner, 270–71; Brugge, letter to Peter Iverson, 22 October 2001.

27. The historical literature has not sufficiently emphasized Navajo relations with peoples such as the Comanches and the Utes. Navajo oral history is filled with references to these two communities.

28. Field trip to Dinétah site, Navajo Studies Conference, San Juan College, Farmington, New Mexico, 30 September 2000; James M. Copeland, "Navajo Hero Twin Ceremonial

Art in Dinetah," in *Diné Bikéyah,* ed. Duran and Kirkpatrick, 60; Brochure for Museum of Indian Arts and Culture, Santa Fe, New Mexico, *Of Stone and Stories: Pueblitos of Dinetah* exhibition, 2000, PIPC. Quotes are found in the brochure. See also a review of the Pueblito literature by Ronald H. Towner, "The Pueblito Phenomenon: A New Perspective on Post-Revolt Navajo Culture," in *Navajo Origins,* ed. Towner, 149–70; and Patrick Hogan, "Navajo-Pueblo Interaction During the Gobernador Phase: A Reassessment of the Evidence," in *Rethinking Navajo Pueblitos* (Farmington, N.Mex.: Bureau of Land Management, Albuquerque District, Farmington Resource Area, 1991).

29. David M. Brugge, "Pueblo Influence on Navajo Architecture," *El Palacio* (summer 1968): 19–20.
30. Aileen O'Bryan, trans., "The Story of the Two Boys and the Coming of the Horse," in *Navaho Indian Myths* (New York: Dover Publications, Inc., 1993), reprint edition of *The Diné: Origin Myths of the Navajo Indians* (Washington, D.C.: U.S. Government Printing Office, 1956), 157–63.
31. Spicer, Edward H., *Cycles of Conquest; The Impact of Spain, Mexico, and the United States on the Indians of the Southwest, 1533–1960* (Tucson: University of Arizona Press, 1962), 324.
32. Ibid., 14–15.
33. Gary Witherspoon, "Sheep in Navajo Culture," *American Anthropologist* 72 (1973): 1442.
34. Percy Deal, presentation to "Sheep Is Life" conference, Diné College, Tsaile, Ariz., 26 June 1999, notes, PIPC.
35. Of course, other Indian communities also had the possibility of acquiring livestock and many did, but no one group achieved as dramatic a transformation.
36. Brochure of the Navajo-Churro Sheep Association (Ojo Caliente, N.Mex.) distributed at the "Sheep Is Life" conference, Diné College, Tsaile, Ariz., 26 June 1999, PIPC.
37. Stefani Salkald, *Southwest Weaving: A Continuum* (San Diego, Calif.: San Diego Museum of Man, 1996), 11.
38. Joe Ben Wheat, "Rio Grande, Pueblo, and Navajo: Cross-Cultural Influence," in *Rio Grande Textiles,* ed. Nora Fisher (Albuquerque: Museum of New Mexico Press, 1994), 22.
39. Spicer, *Cycles of Conquest,* 283–84.
40. Andrew L. Knaut, *The Pueblo Revolt of 1680: Conquest and Resistance in Seventeenth-Century New Mexico* (Norman: University of Oklahoma Press, 1995), 45–46. For a Native commentary on this incident, see Charlene Teters, "Whose History Do We Celebrate?" *Indian Artist* 4, no. 3 (1998): 14–15.
41. David Warren, presentation at D'Arcy McNickle Center for American Indian History, Newberry Library, Chicago, 15 October 1973, notes, PIPC.
42. Frank McNitt, *Navajo Wars: Military Campaigns, Slave Raids, and Reprisals* (Albuquerque: University of New Mexico Press, 1972); J. Lee Correll, *Through White Men's Eyes: A Contribution to Navajo History* (Window Rock, Ariz.: Navajo Heritage Center, 1979), 1:29.
43. Correll, *Through White Men's Eyes,* 1:30–32.
44. Ibid.; David M. Brugge, *Navajos in the Catholic Church Records of New Mexico, 1694–1875* (Tsaile, Ariz.: Navajo Community College Press, 1985).
45. David M. Brugge, "Jemez Pueblos and the Navajos: Part 1, to 1800" (paper presented at Navajo Studies Conference, Farmington, New Mexico, 28 September 2000).
46. Benally, "Hané' Béé'ééhanííh," 67. See also Jack Forbes, *Apache, Navajo, and Spaniard* (Norman: University of Oklahoma Press, 1960).
47. McNitt, *Navajo Wars,* 14.
48. Ibid., 39–40.
49. Correll, *Through White Men's Eyes,* 1:39–40. See also a series of articles by Frank D. Reeve, all published in the *New Mexico Historical Review:* "Seventeenth Century Navaho-Spanish Relations," 32, no. 1 (1957): 36–52; "Navaho-Spanish Wars, 1680–1720," 33, no. 3 (1958): 205–31; "The Navaho-Spanish Peace, 1720s–1790s," 34, no. 1 (1959): 9–40; and "Navaho-Spanish Diplomacy, 1770–1790," 35, no. 3 (1960): 200–235. A final article, edited by Eleanor B. Adams and John L. Kessell after Reeve's death, "Navaho Foreign Affairs, 1790–1845," was published in 1971 (45, nos. 2–3), and later reprinted as Reeve, *Navajo Foreign Affairs, 1795–1846* (Tsaile, Ariz.: Navajo Community College Press, 1983).
50. Rick Hendricks and John P. Wilson, eds., *The Navajos in 1705: Roque Madrid's Campaign Journal* (Albuquerque: University of New Mexico Press, 1996), 100.

51. Thomas D. Hall, *Social Change in the Southwest, 1350–1880* (Lawrence: University Press of Kansas, 1989), 134–64.
52. Of course, the Comanches, among others, furnished other possibilities for disaster. Navajo oral historical accounts speak of Comanches raiding and abducting captives throughout Diné Bikéyah.
53. David M. Brugge, "A Military History of Canyon de Chelly," in *Tse Yaa Kin: Houses Beneath the Rock*, ed. David Grant Noble (Santa Fe, N.Mex.: School of American Research, 1986), 44–45.
54. John Wilson, *Military Campaigns in the Navajo Country, Northwestern New Mexico, 1800–1846* (Santa Fe: Museum of New Mexico Press, 1967), 9; McNitt, *Navajo Wars*, 40–44; Campbell Grant, *Canyon de Chelly: Its People and Rock Art* (Tucson: University of Arizona Press, 1978), 84–86; Brugge, "Military History," 45.
55. William W. Quinn, Jr., "Comparative Ethnohistorical Report on the Canoncito and Navajo Bands" (Branch of Acknowledgment and Research, Bureau of Indian Affairs, 1991), photocopy, PIPC.
56. Ibid.; McNitt, *Navajo Wars*, 26–51.
57. Letters from Spanish colonial administrators in New Mexico, 1793 and 1794, Archivo General de Indias, Seville, Spain, photocopies, PIPC.
58. According to the description included with the letter containing the pursuer's comments, it was sent to a "cordillera," or chain of towns: "It is a letter from Antonio Olgin, received from the town of San Antonio de la Mora by the Deputy Alcalde Mayor Don Antonio Maria Trujillo at Rio Arriba, and sent by him to Don Matias Ortiz, Alcalde Mayor at Cuyamungue. October 6, 1818." Juan Antonio Cabesa de Baca to Governor Facundo Melgares, 8 March 1821, Fray Angélico Chávez History Library, Santa Fe, N.Mex.
59. Nemesio Salcedo, report, 5 July 1806, Fray Angélico Chávez History Library, Santa Fe, N.Mex.
60. Laurance D. Linford, *Navajo Places: History, Legend, Landscape* (Salt Lake City: University of Utah Press, 2000), 193–94, 236–37, 275–76.
61. Virginia Hoffman, "Narbona," in Hoffman and Broderick H. Johnson, *Navajo Biographies* (Rough Rock, Ariz.: Navajo Curriculum Center, 1970), 17–35; Linford, *Navajo Places*, 236–37.
62. Scott Preston, "The Oraibi Massacre," in *Navajo Historical Selections*, ed. Robert W. Young and William Morgan (Phoenix, Ariz.: Bureau of Indian Affairs, 1954), 31–33. The Navajo language text appears on pages 105–7.
63. Arthur Woodward, "Romance of Navajo Silver," *Arizona Highways* 20, no. 3 (1944): 32–37. For an introduction to the art and architecture of Muslim Spain, see Robert Hillenbrand, "The Muslim West," in Hillenbrand, *Islamic Art and Architecture* (London: Thames and Hudson, 1999), 167–95. Richard Fletcher provides a brief introduction to the more general subject in his *Moorish Spain* (New York: Henry Holt and Company, 1992).
64. Kate Peck Kent, *Navajo Weaving: Three Centuries of Change* (Santa Fe, N.Mex.: School of American Research Press), 10–11.
65. Excerpt from Josiah Gregg, *Commerce of the Prairies*, reprinted in Correll, *Through White Men's Eyes*, 1:182.
66. Correll, *Through White Men's Eyes*, 1:182.
67. Ibid., 1:182, 184.
68. Ibid., 1:192–96.

CHAPTER 2

1. Luci Tapahonso, "In 1864," in Tapahonso, *Sáanii Dahataal/The Women Are Singing* (Tucson: University of Arizona Press, 1993), 10.
2. Bernard DeVoto, *The Year of Decision: 1846* (Boston: Little, Brown, and Company, 1943).
3. Alexis de Tocqueville, "The Present and Probable Future Condition of the Indian Tribes That Inhabit the Territory Possessed by the Union," in *Democracy in America* (New York: Random House, 1945), 1:366.

4. Robert F. Berkhofer, Jr., "Expansion with Honor: Problems in Practice," in Berkhofer, *The White Man's Indian: Images of the American Indian from Columbus to the Present* (New York: Alfred A. Knopf, 1978), 145–53.
5. Edward T. Begay, remarks at Treaty Day, Northern Arizona University, Flagstaff, 1 June 1999, PIPC.
6. Correll, *Through White Men's Eyes*, 1:203, 205.
7. Charles Bent to James Buchanan, 15 October 1846; Bent to William Medill, 10 November 1846, both in Correll, *Through White Men's Eyes*, 1:206, 210.
8. Hoffman, "Narbona," 28–29; Correll, *Through White Men's Eyes*, 1:213.
9. Correll, *Through White Men's Eyes*, 1:213.
10. Ibid.
11. Ibid., 1:221–22.
12. John Macrae Washington to Adjutant General Jones, 3 February 1849, in Correll, *Through White Men's Eyes*, 1:234.
13. Robert F. Berkhofer, Jr., presents a very insightful discussion of this development in *The White Man's Indian*.
14. Correll, *Through White Men's Eyes*, 1:238–42; Hoffman, "Narbona," 31–35.
15. Correll, *Through White Men's Eyes*, 1:241–44.
16. Ibid., 1:245–50.
17. bid., 1:311–12. See also Maurice Frink, *Fort Defiance and the Navajos* (Boulder, Colo.: Pruett, 1968).
18. Correll, *Through White Men's Eyes*, 1:349–50.
19. Robert W. Young, *The Role of the Navajo in the Southwestern Drama* (Gallup, N.Mex.: The Gallup Independent, 1968), 36.
20. Governor James S. Calhoun, proclamation, 18 March 1851, and Governor James S. Calhoun to Caciques, Governors, and Principals of Pueblos, 19 March 1851, in Correll, *Through White Men's Eyes*, 1:287–88.
21. John Greiner to "Sir," 31 March 1852, in Correll, *Through White Men's Eyes*, 1:327.
22. Major Electus Backus to Acting Assistant Adjutant General, 5 November 1851, and Major Electus Backus to Henry Schoolcraft, 10 February 1853, in Correll, *Through White Men's Eyes*, 1:315.
23. Articles in Santa Fe *Gazette*, 25 June 1853, 17 June 1854, and 24 June 1853, reprinted in Correll, *Through White Men's Eyes*, 1:359, 361, 382–84.
24. Henry Dodge to Governor David Meriwether, 13 November 1854, in Correll, *Through White Men's Eyes*, 1:392–96.
25. Administrative correspondence and *Gazette* articles reprinted in Correll, *Through White Men's Eyes*, 3:59–65.
26. Notes on the treaty talks, and Governor David Meriwether to George Manypenny, 27 July 1855, in Correll, *Through White Men's Eyes*, 3:404–5; Hoffman, "Zarcillos Largos," in Hoffman and Johnson, *Navajo Biographies*, 30–32.
27. Hoffman, "Zarcillos Largos," in *Navajo Biographies*, 30–32; "Articles of Agreement and Convention," 18 July 1855, in Correll, *Through White Men's Eyes*, 3:406–8.
28. W. W. H. Davis, in Correll, *Through White Men's Eyes*, 3:407.
29. General William Thomas Harbaugh Brooks to Assistant Adjutant General, 11 April 1858, in Correll, *Through White Men's Eyes*, 2:123.
30. General William Thomas Harbaugh Brooks to Asst. Atty. Gen., 15 July 1858, and postscript, 16 July 1858, and articles in the Santa Fe *Gazette*, 24 July, 31 July, 7 August, 14 August, 21 August 1858, in Correll, *Through White Men's Eyes*, 2:133–34; Gerald Thompson, *The Army and the Navajo: The Bosque Redondo Reservation Experiment, 1863–1868* (Tucson: University of Arizona Press, 1976), 7.
31. Agent Samuel Yost Correspondence, 7 December 1858; Treaty, 25 December 1858; and General Orders No. 11, Fort Defiance, 25 December 1858, in Correll, *Through White Men's Eyes*, 2:231.
32. James L. Donaldson to Brantz Mayer, May 1860, Western Americana Collection, Beinecke Library, Yale University, New Haven, Conn.
33. Thompson, *The Army and the Navajo*, 7–9; Donaldson to Mayer.
34. For details of the Canby campaign, see reprints of pertinent documents in Correll, *Through White Men's Eyes*, 2:80–132.
35. This transition is discussed in Robert A. Trennert, *Alternative to Extinction: Federal*

Indian Policy and the Beginnings of the Reservation System, 1846–1851 (Philadelphia: Temple University Press, 1975). For the history of federal Indian policy, see Francis Paul Prucha, *The Great Father: The United States Government and the American Indians,* 2 vols. (Lincoln: University of Nebraska Press, 1984).

36. James Carleton, quoted in Thompson, *The Army and the Navajo,* 28.
37. William P. Dole to Caleb Blood Smith, 27 November 1861, in Correll, *Through White Men's Eyes,* 3:186–88.
38. James S. Collins to William P. Dole, 10 October 1862, in Correll, *Through White Men's Eyes,* 3:234–36.
39. James Carleton to Lorenzo Thomas, 6 March 1864, and 12 March 1864, in Correll, *Through White Men's Eyes,* 3:83–84, 99–101.
40. James Carleton to William Nichols, 28 October 1854, in Correll, *Through White Men's Eyes,* 1:391–92.
41. James M. McNulty, Joseph Updegraff, and Allen L. Anderson to Assistant Adjutant General, 4 December 1862, in Correll, *Through White Men's Eyes,* 3:242–43.
42. James Carleton to Manuel Chavez, 7 August 1863, in Correll, *Through White Men's Eyes,* 3:332.
43. For different portrayals of Carson, see Tom Dunlay, *Kit Carson and the Indians* (Lincoln: University of Nebraska Press, 2000) and the stories told by Navajos in Ruth Roessel and Broderick Johnson, eds., *Navajo Stories of the Long Walk Period* (Tsaile, Ariz.: Navajo Community College Press, 1973).
44. Lawrence Kelly, ed., *Navajo Roundup: Selected Correspondence of Kit Carson's Campaign Against the Navajo, 1863–1868* (Boulder, Colo.: Pruett, 1970), 19–21.
45. Neal W. Ackerley, "A Navajo Diaspora: The Long Walk to Hweeldi" (Silver City, N.Mex.: Dos Rios Consultants, 1998). Available at: Members.tripod.com/ bloodhound/longwalk.htm.
46. See, for example, Dunlay, *Kit Carson and the Indians,* and Martin Link's findings on the Long Walk, reported in the *Gallup Independent,* 30 January 2001. See also the rebuttal to Link by Jennifer Denetdale, published in the *Navajo Times,* 8 March 2001.
47. "Frank Goldtooth," in *Navajo Stories,* ed. Roessel and Johnson, 151; "Howard Gorman," in *Navajo Stories,* ed. Roessel and Johnson, 23–24; "Charley Sandoval," in *Navajo Stories,* ed. Roessel and Johnson, 142; "Helen Begay's Story," in *Oral History Stories of The Long Walk (Hweeldi Baa Hane),* Patty Chee, et al., collectors and recorders, (Crownpoint, N.Mex.: Lake Valley Navajo School, 1991), 13.
48. "Howard Gorman," in *Navajo Stories,* ed. Roessel and Johnson, 25.
49. "Curly Tso," in *Navajo Stories,* Roessel and Johnson, 103.
50. Tiana Bighorse, *Bighorse the Warrior* (Tucson: University of Arizona Press, 1990), 28–35.
51. A. H. Pfeiffer to Lawce G. Murphey, 20 January 1864, in *Navajo Roundup,* ed. Lawrence Kelly, 102–4. Kelly's book furnishes an extensive collection of federal documents from the campaign.
52. Bighorse, *Bighorse the Warrior,* 28–35.
53. Tapahonso, "In 1864," 9.
54. Lieutenant George Pettis to his wife, 26 February 1864, "Long Walk Lesson," Regional Educational Technology Assistance Program, in cooperation with the Museum of New Mexico Office of Statewide Programs and Education, available at http://reta.nmsu.edu:16080/techshare/modules/longwalk/lesson/document/ index.htm.
55. John Thompson to Julius Shaw, 12 August 1864, in Correll, *Through White Men's Eyes,* 4:210–11.
56. Kelly, ed., *Navajo Roundup,* 151–67.
57. "Henry Zahne," in *Navajo Stories,* ed. Roessel and Johnson, 234.
58. "Ernest Nelson," in *Navajo Stories,* ed. Roessel and Johnson, 173.
59. "Frank Goldtooth," in *Navajo Stories,* ed. Roessel and Johnson, 152.
60. Bighorse, *Bighorse the Warrior,* 40–45.
61. David M. Brugge, *The Navajo-Hopi Land Dispute: An American Tragedy* (Albuquerque: University of New Mexico Press, 1994), 21–22.
62. Thompson, *The Army and the Navajo,* 18–19, 118–19.
63. "Rita Wheeler," in *Navajo Stories,* ed. Roessel and Johnson, 84–85.

64. Lieutenant George Pettis to his wife, 26 February 1864.
65. Robert A. Trennert, *White Man's Medicine: Government Doctors Among the Navajo, 1863–1955* (Albuquerque: University of New Mexico Press, 1998), 28–32.
66. "Mose Denejolie," in *Navajo Stories*, ed. Roessel and Johnson, 244–45. See also Trennert, *White Man's Medicine*, 32–34, and Katherine Marie Birmingham Osburn, "The Navajos at Bosque Redondo: Cooperation, Resistance, and Initiative, 1864–1868," *New Mexico Historical Review* 60 (October 1985): 403–5.
67. Prucha, *The Great Father*, 1:485–92.
68. Thompson, *The Army and the Navajo*, 137–39.
69. John L. Kessell, "General Sherman and the Navajo Treaty of 1868: A Basic and Expedient Misunderstanding," *Western Historical Quarterly* 12, no. 3 (1981): 257.
70. Thompson, *The Army and the Navajo*, 139; "Treaty," in DeVoto, *The Year of Decision*, 1–2; Edward Sapir, ed., *Navaho Texts* (Iowa City: Linguistic Society of America, University of Iowa, 1942); David Brugge, e-mail to Peter Iverson, 22 October 2001. Barboncito's statement appears in DeVoto.
71. "Treaty," DeVoto, *The Year of Decision*, 2–6.
72. Ibid., 6–11; AnCita Benally, e-mail to Peter Iverson, 28 November 2001.
73. Thompson, *The Army and the Navajo*, 158–65.
74. Luci Tapahonso mentions the origins of this "traditional" clothing and of fry bread in her poem, "In 1864."

CHAPTER 3

1. William Haas Moore, *Chiefs, Agents, and Soldiers: Conflict on the Navajo Frontier, 1868–1882* (Albuquerque: University of New Mexico Press, 1994), 33.
2. Ellen McCullough-Brabson and Marilyn Help, *We'll Be in Your Mountains, We'll Be in Your Songs: A Navajo Woman Sings* (Albuquerque: University of New Mexico Press, 2001), 63–65; McCullough-Brabson and Help, presentation, Museum of Indian Arts and Culture, Santa Fe, New Mexico, 18 August 2001, notes, PIPC.
3. Moore, *Chiefs, Agents, and Soldiers*, 33.
4. "Francis Toledo," in *Navajo Stories*, ed. Roessel and Johnson, 133.
5. "Akinabh Burbank," in *Navajo Stories*, ed. Roessel and Johnson, 147.
6. Moore, *Chiefs, Agents, and Soldiers*, 27–28.
7. Kessell, "General Sherman," 262–63.
8. Ibid., 263–66; "Francis Toledo," in *Navajo Stories*, ed. Roessel and Johnson, 147.
9. Frederick E. Hoxie, *A Final Promise: The Campaign to Assimilate the Indians, 1880–1920* (Lincoln: University of Nebraska Press, 1984), xii.
10. For a more extensive discussion of the so-called "witch purge" of this era, see Martha Blue, *The Witch Purge of 1878: Oral and Documentary History in the Early Reservation Years* (Tsaile, Ariz.: Navajo Community College Press, 1988), and Moore, *Chiefs, Agents, and Soldiers*, 185–98.
11. Kessell, "General Sherman," 264–65.
12. Peter Iverson, *Barry Goldwater: Native Arizonan* (Norman: University of Oklahoma Press, 1997), 20–21.
13. J. Lee Correll and Alfred Dehiya, *Anatomy of the Navajo Indian Reservation: How It Grew* (Window Rock, Ariz.: Navajo Times Publishing, 1972). Missionary William R. Johnston helped make the Leupp addition a reality.
14. Brugge, *The Navajo-Hopi Land Dispute*, 27; Peter Iverson, "Knowing the Land, Leaving the Land: Navajos, Hopis, and Relocation in the American West," *Montana: The Magazine of Western History* 38, no. 1 (1988): 67–70.
15. Robert S. McPherson, *The Northern Navajo Frontier, 1860–1900: Expansion Through Adversity* (Albuquerque: University of New Mexico Press, 1988), 39–50.
16. Thomas V. Keam to E. H. Plummer, 6 May 1893, Record Group 75, Bureau of Indian Affairs, National Archives, Rocky Mountain Region, Denver, Colorado (hereafter cited as NARMR), Navajo Agency, Letters Received, 1890–1911.
17. Ralph P. Collins to Plummer, 7 May 1893, NARMR, Navajo Agency, Letters Received, 1890–1911.

18. C. M. Goodman to E. H. Plummer, 19 September 1893, and 23 November 1893, NARMR, Navajo Agency, Letters Received, 1890–1911.
19. W. R. Campbell to Plummer, 9 July 1893, NARMR, Navajo Agency, Letters Received, 1890–1911.
20. M. E. DeSelte to Plummer, 17 July 1893, NARMR, Navajo Agency, Letters Received, 1890–1911.
21. Walter Hinnes to E. H. Plummer, 18 August 1893, NARMR, Navajo Agency, Letters Received, 1890–1911.
22. S. V. Berlin, et al., to Plummer, 10 November 1893, NARMR, Navajo Agency, Letters Received, 1890–1911.
23. W. R. Jones to Plummer, 29 November 1893, NARMR, Navajo Agency, Letters Received, 1890–1911.
24. H. Cousins Jennings to Plummer, 16 August 1893, NARMR, Navajo Agency, Letters Received, 1890–1911.
25. C. H. Fancher to E. H. Plummer, 27 December 1893, NARMR, Navajo Agency, Letters Received, 1890–1911.
26. Chas. Babbitt to Navajo Indian Agent, 28 April 1893, NARMR, Navajo Agency, Letters Received, 1890–1911.
27. Plummer to Indian Agent, Fort Apache, 3 August 1893, NARMR, Navajo Agency, Letters Received, 1890–1911.
28. *Coconino Sun* (Flagstaff, Ariz.), 18 November 1899, Museum of Northern Arizona, Flagstaff, Ariz.; Jerry Snow, "Tolchaco," *Plateau* (Winter 2000): 49. William R. Johnston's son, Philip, helped develop the idea for the Navajo Code Talkers.
29. Marsha L. Weisiger, "Sheep Dreams: Environment, Cultural Identity, and Gender in Navajo Country" (New Mexico State University, 2001), 186–87, PIPC. Weisiger's forthcoming study, a revision of her doctoral dissertation in history, will be an extremely important contribution to the literature.
30. See Willow Roberts Powers, *Navajo Trading: The End of an Era* (Albuquerque: University of New Mexico Press, 2001), as well as the pioneering volume by Frank McNitt, *The Indian Traders* (Norman: University of Oklahoma Press, 1962).
31. Keam and Hubbell have been the subjects of new biographies. See Laura Graves, *Thomas Varker Keam: Indian Trader* (Norman: University of Oklahoma Press, 1998), and Martha Blue, *Indian Trader: The Life and Times of J. L. Hubbell* (Walnut, Calif.: Kiva Publishing, 2000).
32. Frank L. Bennett, "The Navajos," in *Annual Report of the Commissioner on Indian Affairs, 1869* (Washington, D.C.: Government Printing Office, 1870), 49. (This series hereafter cited as *ARCIA [year].*)
33. *ARCIA 1870,* 149.
34. *ARCIA 1872.*
35. "Reports of Agents in New Mexico," in *ARCIA 1879,* 115.
36. *ARCIA 1880,* 131.
37. Weisiger, "Sheep Dreams," 92–96.
38. Ibid., 127–28.
39. Alice Kaufman and Christopher Selser, *The Navajo Weaving Tradition, 1650 to the Present* (New York: E. P. Dutton, 1985), 53.
40. See, among others, David M. Brugge, *Hubbell Trading Post: National Historic Site* (Tucson, Ariz.: Southwest Parks and Monuments Association, 1993), and Kathleen L. Howard and Diana F. Pardue, *Inventing the Southwest: The Fred Harvey Company and Native American Art* (Flagstaff, Ariz.: Northland Publishing, 1996).
41. Blue, *Indian Trader,* 236.
42. Thomas Keam to J. D. C. Atkins, 2 January 1886, Frank McNitt Collection, New Mexico State Records Center and Archives, Santa Fe, New Mexico.
43. For a wide-ranging discussion of education provided to American Indians at this time, see David Wallace Adams, *Education for Extinction: American Indians and the Boarding School Experience, 1875–1928* (Lawrence: University Press of Kansas, 1995).
44. Robert W. Young, ed., *The Navajo Yearbook* (Window Rock, Ariz.: Bureau of Indian Affairs, 1961), vol. 8. For an overview of the "peace policy" and the Navajos, see Norman J. Bender, *"New Hope for the Indians": The Grant Peace Policy and the Navajos in the 1870s* (Albuquerque: University of New Mexico Press, 1989).

45. F. T. Bennett to William Clinton, 19 August 1870, in *ARCIA 1870*, 147–53.

46. Charity A. Gaston to William Clinton, 23 August 1870, in *ARCIA 1870*, 153–54.

47. J. V. Lauderdale to the Fort Defiance Indian Agency, 30 November 1874, Special Collections, Beinecke Library, Yale University, New Haven, Conn.

48. W. F. Hall to Nathaniel Pope, 9 September 1872, in *ARCIA 1872*, 302–3.

49. W. F. M. Arny to the Commissioner of Indian Affairs, in *ARCIA 1873*, 272–73.

50. John Bowman, annual report to Commissioner of Indian Affairs, 1885.

51. Frank Mitchell, *Navajo Blessingway Singer: The Autobiography of Frank Mitchell, 1881–1967*, edited by Charlotte J. Frisbie and David A. McAllester (Tucson: University of Arizona Press, 1978), 78, quoted in Adams, *Education for Extinction*, 116–17.

52. Moore, *Chiefs, Agents, and Soldiers*, 258–59.

53. Ibid., 259.

54. The photographs of Torlino are included on the dust jacket of Adams's *Education for Extinction*, for example.

55. For a discussion of the competition among schools, see Scott Riney, *The Rapid City Indian School, 1898–1933* (Norman: University of Oklahoma Press, 1999).

56. C. E. Vandever to Commissioner of Indian Affairs, 22 August 1890, copy, Museum of Northern Arizona, Flagstaff, Ariz.

57. Theo. G. Lemmon to the Commissioner of Indian Affairs, 3 July 1893, Record Group 75, Bureau of Indian Affairs, National Archives, Washington, D.C. (hereafter cited as NA), Jacob C. Morgan file.

58. Brenda Child emphasizes the importance of this factor in her study, *Boarding School Seasons: American Indian Families, 1900–1940* (Lincoln: University of Nebraska Press, 1998).

59. See Riney, *The Rapid City Indian School;* Child, *Boarding School Seasons;* Margaret L. Archuleta, Brenda J. Child, and Tsianina Lomawaima, eds., *Away From Home: American Indian Boarding School Experiences, 1879–2000* (Phoenix: Heard Museum, 2000).

60. Vandever, annual report to Commissioner of Indian Affairs, 1890.

61. David M. Brugge, "Henry Chee Dodge," in *Indian Lives: Essays on Nineteenth-and Twentieth-Century Native American Leaders*, ed. L. G. Moses and Raymond Wilson (Albuquerque: University of New Mexico Press, 1985), 93–97.

62. Robert W. Young and William Morgan, eds., *The Trouble at Round Rock* (Phoenix: Bureau of Indian Affairs, 1952), 9.

63. Ibid.

64. Ibid., 9–10.

65. Ibid., 11.

66. Ibid.

67. Ibid.

68. Ibid., 12.

69. Ibid.

70. Ibid.

71. Edward Plummer to Commissioner of Indian Affairs, 26 December 1893, NA.

72. C. W. Goodman to Edward Plummer, 15 September 1893, NARMR, Navajo Agency, Letters Received.

73. *ARCIA 1894*, 5.

74. Trennert, *White Man's Medicine*, 91.

75. Plummer is quoted in Garrick Bailey and Roberta Glenn Bailey, *A History of the Navajos: The Reservation Years* (Santa Fe, N.Mex.: School of American Research Press; distributed by Seattle: University of Washington Press, 1986), 101. This study includes a large amount of statistical data on Navajo livestock holdings from 1868 to 1975.

76. Henry Dodge to Edward Plummer, 31 May 1893, NARMR, Navajo Agency, Letters Received.

77. This subject has been probed by many western historians, including Gerald D. Nash, *The American West in the Twentieth Century: A Short History of an Urban Oasis* (Albuquerque: University of New Mexico Press, 1977); Michael P. Malone and Richard W. Etulain, *The American West: A Twentieth Century History* (Lincoln: University of Nebraska Press, 1989); and Richard White, *"It's Your Misfortune and*

None of My Own": A New History of the American West (Norman: University of Oklahoma Press, 1991).

78. See Hoxie, *A Final Promise,* and Prucha, *The Great Father.*

79. Kathleen P. Chamberlain, *Under Sacred Ground: A History of Navajo Oil, 1922–1982* (Albuquerque: University of New Mexico Press, 2000), 12. Chamberlin's valuable study offers a thorough review of this subject.

80. Lease between George F. Huff and the Navajo Tribe of Indians, 1901, NARMR, Navajo Agency, Letters Received, 1890–1911.

81. Chamberlain, *Under Sacred Ground,* 15.

CHAPTER 4

1. Yanapah Tsosie and Sam Ahkeah, writings at San Juan School, 18 June 1910 (date received in National Archives, Washington, D.C.), NA, Central Classified Files (hereafter cited as CCF), San Juan Agency. These letters are included in *"For Our Navajo People."*

2. Chee Dodge, speech delivered at "yabichi dance," St. Michaels, Arizona, 16 November 1905, NA, CCF, Navajo Agency. This speech is included in *"For Our Navajo People."*

3. Lawrence C. Kelly, *The Navajo Indians and Federal Indian Policy, 1900–1935* (Tucson: University of Arizona Press, 1968), 27. This pathbreaking study remains an important source for our understanding of this period.

4. Hoxie, *A Final Promise,* 113.

5. Quoted in Brian W. Dippie, *The Vanishing American: White Attitudes and U.S. Indian Policy* (Middletown, Conn.: Wesleyan University Press, 1982), 209.

6. By 1915 at least five Diné owned automobiles. Brugge, "Henry Chee Dodge," 100.

7. The quotations are from a letter circulated by New Mexico livestock growers during this era in Record Group 75, Bureau of Indian Affairs, National Archives, Pacific Region, Laguna Niguel, Calif. (hereafter cited as NAPR), CCF, Eastern Navajo Agency.

8. Kelly, *The Navajo Indians,* 20–21.

9. Dennis Riordan, report, in *ARCIA 1883,* cited in Marsha L. Weisiger, "Sheep Dreams," 210–11.

10. Bailey and Bailey, *A History of the Navajos,* 124–38.

11. Inspector H. S. Traylor, report, 1916, NA, San Juan Agency.

12. Cato Sells to Samuel F. Stacher, 20 September 1918, NAPR, Pueblo Bonito Agency, General Correspondence.

13. Stacher to Sells, 21 October 1918, NAPR, Pueblo Bonito Agency, General Correspondence.

14. Sells to Stacher, 28 February 1920, NAPR, Pueblo Bonito Agency, General Correspondence.

15. See chapter six, "Hoofed Locusts," in Weisiger, "Sheep Dreams," 169–211.

16. Joseph E. Maxwell to Leupp, 28 May 1909, NARMR, Leupp Training School, Letters Sent, 1909.

17. Peter Iverson, *"We Are Still Here": American Indians in the Twentieth Century* (Arlington Heights, Ill.: Harlan Davidson, 1998), 32–36; Hoxie, *A Final Promise,* 154–57, 164–65. See also Blue Clark, *Lone Wolf v. Hitchcock: Treaty Rights and Indian Law at the End of the Nineteenth Century* (Lincoln: University of Nebraska Press, 1994).

18. Chee Dodge to Franklin L. Lane, 2 February 1914, Franciscan Fathers' Papers, St. Michaels Mission, Special Collections, University of Arizona Library, Tucson (hereafter cited as FFP). This letter is included in *"For Our Navajo People."*

19. Robert L. Wilken, *Anselm Weber, O.F.M., Missionary to the Navaho, 1898–1921* (Milwaukee, Wisc.: Bruce Publishing, 1955), does mention Weber's work rather briefly, although he clearly understands its importance. Published by an obscure company, the biography received little attention and had a minimal impact on the overall Navajo literature. It has long been out of print.

20. Anselm Weber to Charles Curtis, 24 November 1909, FFP.

21. Ibid.

22. Father Anselm Weber, "The Navajo Indians: A Statement of Facts," 1917, Fray Angélico Chávez History Library, Santa Fe, New Mexico.

23. Ibid.

24. Kelly, *The Navajo Indians*, 33–34, 36. Garrick Bailey and Roberta Glenn Bailey note that the newspapers in Farmington, New Mexico, were particularly vocal in their opposition to allotments for the Navajos in the public domain and in their support for throwing open the Navajo reservation for non-Indian settlement (Bailey and Bailey, *A History of the Navajos*, 116–17). David Brugge, letter to Peter Iverson, 22 October 2001.

25. Samuel F. Stacher to Cato Sells, 6 May 1918, NAPR, Pueblo Bonito Agency, General Correspondence.

26. Ibid.

27. Hoxie, *A Final Promise*, 187.

28. Wilken, *Anselm Weber*, 173–74, 232.

29. Peter Paquette to Commissioner of Indian Affairs, 13 October 1922, NA, CCF, Navajo Agency.

30. E. B. Meritt to Peter Paquette, 21 October 1922, NA, CCF, Navajo Agency.

31. Wilken, *Anselm Weber*, 174–78; Reuben Perry to the Commissioner of Indian Affairs, 22 November 1905, and 30 November 1905; Telegram, Captain Williard to Commanding General, Department, Colorado, 2 December 1905, NA, Navajo Agency.

32. Acting Commissioner of Indian Affairs to Secretary of the Interior, 5 December 1905, NA, Navajo Agency.

33. Peshlakai, et al., statement, 29 November 1905, NA, Navajo Agency.

34. Francis Leupp to Secretary of the Interior, 13 December 1905, NA, Navajo Agency.

35. C. F. Larrabee, Acting Commissioner, to Superintendent, Navajo Agency, 8 January 1906, 27 January 1906, 15 February 1906, 21 May 1906, 14 August 1906, NA, Navajo Agency.

36. W. T. Shelton to Samuel F. Stacher, 2 December 1913, NAPR, San Juan Agency.

37. Wilken, *Anselm Weber*, 178–81. See also Donald L. Parman, "The 'Big Stick' in Indian Affairs: The Bai-a-lil-le Incident in 1909," *Arizona and the West* 20 (winter 1978): 343–60.

38. Wilken, *Anselm Weber*, 181–82; Franc Johnson Newcomb, *Navaho Neighbors* (Norman: University of Oklahoma Press, 1966), 31–35; McNitt, *The Indian Traders*, 347–49.

39. Transcript of discussion with Be-zho-she (Bizhoozhí), N.p., 1 November 1913, FFP; Wilken, *Anselm Weber*, 182–83; Newcomb, *Navaho Neighbors*, 35; McNitt, *The Indian Traders*, 349. The discussion with Be-zsho-she is included in *"For Our Navajo People."*

40. Wilken, *Anselm Weber*, 183–85; Newcomb, *Navaho Neighbors*, 36–37; McNitt, *The Indian Traders*, 349–55.

41. Wilken, *Anselm Weber*, 185–86; Newcomb, *Navaho Neighbors*, 36–37; McNitt, *The Indian Traders*, 355–56.

42. Wilken, *Anselm Weber*, 186–89; Newcomb, *Navaho Neighbors*, 37–38; McNitt, *The Indian Traders*, 357–58.

43. W. T. Shelton to Samuel Stacher, 2 December 1913, NAPR, San Juan Agency.

44. Chee Dodge, two-page financial record, FFP.

45. See, for example, C. F. Larrabee to Superintendent, Navajo Agency, 11 October 1906, copy, Richard Van Valkenburgh Papers, Arizona Historical Society, Tucson.

46. Nelson Etcitty to S. F. Stacher, 4 April 1922, and 26 April 1922, NAPR, CCF, San Juan Agency. Etcitty's letters are included in *"For Our Navajo People."*

47. Stacher to Etcitty, 26 April 1922, NAPR, CCF, San Juan Agency.

48. Willie George to S. F. Stacher, 9 April 1922, NAPR, CCF, San Juan Agency. This letter is included in *"For Our Navajo People."*

49. John Yazza to S. F. Stacher, 24 June 1916, NAPR, CCF, San Juan Agency. This letter is included in *"For Our Navajo People."*

50. George to Stacher, 9 April 1922.

51. Trennert, *White Man's Medicine*, 95–102.

52. Ibid., 122–27.

53. Rose Mitchell, *Tall Woman: The Life History of Rose Mitchell, a Navajo Woman, ca. 1874–1977*, ed. Charlotte J. Frisbie (Albuquerque: University of New Mexico Press, 2001), 128–35.

54. Evan W. Estep to the Commissioner of Indian Affairs, 20 July 1920, NA, CCF, San Juan Agency.

55. Ibid.

56. H. V. Hailman, Special Assistant to Commissioner of Indian Affairs Charles M. Burke, 9 June 1922, NA, CCF, Western Navajo Agency.

57. Trennert, *White Man's Medicine*, 95–117.

58. Wade Davies, *Healing Ways: Navajo Health Care in the Twentieth Century* (Albuquerque: University of New Mexico Press, 2001); Mitchell, *Navajo Blessingway Singer*, 113.

59. Trennert, *White Man's Medicine*, 95–117.

60. "Indian Mothers, Save Your Babies," n.d., NAPR, Eastern Navajo Agency, General Correspondence, Box 7.

61. Trennert, *White Man's Medicine*, 95–117. See also Davies, *Healing Ways*.

62. H. S. Traylor, 1916 Report, NA, CCF, San Juan Agency.

63. Ibid.

64. Hoxie, *A Final Promise*, 189–97, 209–10.

65. Prucha, *The Great Father*, 2:814.

66. Young, *Navajo Yearbook*, 8:10–11.

67. Henry Greenberg and Georgia Greenberg, *Power of a Navajo: Carl Gorman: The Man and His Life* (Santa Fe, N.Mex.: Clear Light Publishers, 1996), 33–38. For more on runaways, see Riney, *The Rapid City Indian School*, 151–65, and Child, *Boarding School Seasons*, 87–95.

68. Samuel F. Stacher to Commissioner of Indian Affairs, 9 November 1923, NA, CCF, Pueblo Bonito Agency.

69. Charles H. Burke to Samuel F. Stacher, 19 November 1923, NA, CCF, Pueblo Bonito Agency. Burke eventually banned all corporal punishment in the federal schools, although he waited until 1929 to do so, following the indictment of Indian education in the Meriam report of 1928.

70. Kenneth R. Philp, *John Collier's Crusade for Indian Reform, 1920–1954* (Tucson: University of Arizona Press, 1977), 56–62, 99.

71. H. S. Traylor, report on schools, 1916, NA, CCF, San Juan Agency.

72. Jake C. Morgan to Charley Day, 27 August 1902, Day Family Papers, Special Collections, Cline Library, Northern Arizona University, Flagstaff.

73. Jake C. Morgan to Dr. W. H. Harrison, 14 January 1907, NARMR, Navajo Agency, Letters Received, 1890–1911.

74. Jake C. Morgan to Samuel F. Stacher, 4 February 1913, and 10 September 1913, NA, Eastern Navajo Agency, General Correspondence, 1910–1916.

75. Pueblo Bonito School 4th of July Program, 4 July 1913, NA, Eastern Navajo Agency, General Correspondence.

76. Prucha, *The Great Father*, 2:704.

77. Riney, *Rapid City Indian School*, 116.

78. Calendar of the Pueblo Bonito Boarding School, 1921–1922 at Crown Point, New Mexico, A United States Government School for Indian Boys and Girls, NAPR, CCF, Pueblo Bonito Agency. (The idiosyncratic capitalization has been maintained.)

79. Katherine Atencia to Samuel F. Stacher, 11 May 1914, NAPR, Eastern Navajo Agency, General Correspondence.

80. Alice Becenti to Stacher, 24 May 1914, 24 August 1914, 3 November 1916, and May 1916, NAPR, Eastern Navajo Agency, General Correspondence (quote from May 1916).

81. Lilly Julian to Stacher, NAPR, Letters Received.

82. Becenti to Stacher, 24 August 1914, NAPR, Eastern Navajo Agency, General Correspondence.

83. John Charles to Stacher, 30 November 1915, NAPR, Letters Received.

84. Grace Padilla to Stacher, 19 July 1914, NAPR, Eastern Navajo Agency, General Correspondence. The children's letters are included in *"For Our Navajo People."*

85. Samuel F. Stacher to Eske Pahe, 27 November 1915, NAPR, Eastern Navajo Agency, General Correspondence.

86. Samuel F. Stacher to Reuben Perry, 17 August 1916, NAPR, Eastern Navajo Agency, General Correspondence.

87. Young, *Navajo Yearbook*, 8:47–57.

88. Kristie Lee Butler, "Along the Padres' Trail: The History of St. Michael's Mission to the Navajo (1898–1939)" (master's thesis, Arizona State University, 1991), passim.

89. Gertrude Lynch to Anselm Weber, 19 April 1915, FFP; Day Family Papers, Special Collections, Cline Library, Northern Arizona University, Flagstaff. Gertrude Lynch's letter is included in *"For Our Navajo People."*

90. Greenberg and Greenberg, *Carl Gorman*, 34.

91. Patrick Dinealtsihi to Anselm Weber, April 1915, FFC, Special Collections, University of Arizona.

92. End of year program, Day Family Papers, Special Collections, Cline Library, Northern Arizona University.

93. Patrick Dinealtsihi to Anselm Weber, April 1915, FFC, Special Collections, University of Arizona.

94. Day Family Papers, Series 3, Special Collections, Cline Library, Northern Arizona University, Flagstaff.

95. Cato Sells, Circular No. 1079 to Superintendents, 26 January 1916, NAPR, Eastern Navajo Agency, General Correspondence.

96. McNitt, *The Indian Traders*, 345.

97. Ibid., 345–46.

98. Navajo Fair Association Officers and Exhibits, 1916, General Correspondence, Eastern Navajo, Laguna Niguel.

99. Marian E. Rodee, *One Hundred Years of Navajo Rugs* (Albuquerque: University of New Mexico Press, 1995), 117–19.

100. Navajo Fair Association Officers and Exhibits, 1916; Samuel Stacher, announcement of second annual Crownpoint Fair, August 6, 1917, General Correspondence, Eastern Navajo, Laguna Niguel.

101. Premium List, (Eastern) Navajo Fair, NAPR, Eastern Navajo Agency, General Correspondence, 1910–1916.

102. W. T. Shelton to Samuel F. Stacher, 20 August 1914, NAPR, Eastern Navajo Agency, General Correspondence, 1910–1916.

103. Samuel F. Stacher to Cato Sells, 5 October 1916, NA, Pueblo Bonito; Stacher to Sells, 6 October 1917, NAPR, Eastern Navajo Agency.

104. Luci Tapahonso and artist Anthony Chee Emerson have created an appealing book about the contemporary Shiprock fair, *Songs of Shiprock Fair* (Walnut, Calif.: Kiva Publishing, 1999).

105. Rodee, *One Hundred Years of Navajo Rugs*, 74. Two recent, magnificently illustrated books on weaving from the Caucasus are Richard E. Wright and John T. Wertime, *Caucasian Carpets and Coverlets: The Weaving Culture* (London: Laurence King in association with Hali Publishing, 1995), and Ralph Kaffel, *Caucasian Prayer Rugs* (London: Laurence King in association with Hali Publishing, 1998).

106. Rodee, *One Hundred Years of Navajo Rugs*, 117–19, 152; Kent, *Navajo Weaving*, 89–90.

107. Rodee, *One Hundred Years of Navajo Rugs*, 117–19, 152. See also Rebecca M. Valette and Jean-Paul Valette, *Weaving the Dance: Navajo Yeibichai Textiles (1910–1950)* (Albuquerque: Adobe Gallery, 2000), 13–17.

108. Rodee, *One Hundred Years of Navajo Rugs*, 37–38; Steve Getzwiller, notes from interview by Peter Iverson, Santa Fe, 13 August 2001, PIPC. Conversations during the past several years with Getzwiller, Mark Winter, Bill Malone, Bruce Burnham, Hank Blair, and others added to my understanding of traders and the world of Navajo weaving.

109. First Assistant Secretary of the Interior to the Postmaster General, 1910, NA, Navajo Agency. Advertisements are included with the letter.

110. Howard and Pardue, *Inventing the Southwest*, 58–68; see also Blue, *Indian Trader*, 151–55.

111. Powers, *Navajo Trading*.

112. Blue, *Indian Trader*, 147.

113. Evelyn Yazzie Jensen, transcript of interview by Karen Underhill, 10 February 1998, Trading Post Oral History Project, Special Collections, Cline Library, Northern Arizona University, Flagstaff.

114. J. B. Moore, "Foreword," *Collection of Catalogs Published at Crystal Trading Post, 1903, 1911* (Santa Fe, N.Mex.: Avanyu Publishing, 1987), 3. See 1911 catalog.

115. John P. Clum to W. E. Cochran, 23 March 1911, NA, Navajo Agency.

116. Abbott to Sara T. Kinney, 4 February 1911, NA, Navajo Agency.
117. Abbott to Sara T. Kinney, 15 September 1911, NA, Navajo Agency.
118. Chamberlain, *Under Sacred Ground*, 17–18.
119. Ibid., 19–25; Kelly, *The Navajo Indians*, 71.
120. Chamberlain, *Under Sacred Ground*, 26.
121. Kelly, *The Navajo Indians*, 71.
122. Ibid.
123. Chee Dodge to Charles H. Burke, 2 March 1923, FFP.
124. Robert W. Young, *A Political History of the Navajo Tribe* (Tsaile, Ariz.: Navajo Community College Press, 1978), 61–62.
125. Ibid., 62.
126. Ibid., 58–65; David E. Wilkins, *The Navajo Political Experience* (Tsaile, Ariz.: Diné College Press, 1999), 82–84.
127. The quotation by Chee Dodge is included in Kelly, *The Navajo Indians*, 66.
128. Atsidi Nez to "Father Webber," 31 December 1920, NAPR, CCF, Navajo Agency.
129. Young, *Political History*, 62.
130. Ibid., 68.
131. This millennial moment did cause some concern, but the failure of the world to come to an end tended to diminish the influence of this particular healer. An archivist at the Pacific Region branch of the National Archives in Laguna Niguel, California, calmly filed the exchange about the event under the subject heading "World, End of the." Frank E. Andrews, telegram to Samuel F. Stacher, 30 June 1920; Stacher, telegram to Andrews, 1 July 1920, NAPR, Eastern Navajo Agency, Subject Files, "World, End of the."

CHAPTER 5

1. Buck Austin, "We Have Lived on Livestock a Long Time," "The Blind Man's Daughter," and "The Special Grazing Regulations," in *Navajo Historical Selections*, ed. Young and Morgan, 62–64, 74, 135–37, 147.
2. Dan Phillips, "Our Abuse," in *Navajo Historical Selections*, ed. Young and Morgan, 142–44.
3. Jacob C. Morgan, article in *Farmington Hustler*, 18 February 1927. This article is included in *"For Our Navajo People."*
4. Hola Tso and Kenneth Kirk, letter to editor, *Farmington Hustler*, March 1928.
5. J. C. Morgan to H. J. Hagerman, 10 May 1927, NA, Navajo Agency. This letter is included in *"For Our Navajo People."*
6. Felix S. Cohen, memorandum for the Solicitor, 24 September 1943, Felix Cohen Papers, Beinecke Library, Yale University, New Haven, Conn.
7. This summary is based on Kelly, *The Navajo Indians*, 104–14.
8. St. Michaels community petition to the President, 26 February 1924, FFP. This petition is included in *"For Our Navajo People."*
9. Samuel F. Stacher to Herbert J. Hagerman, 14 April 1924, NAPR, Navajo Agency.
10. C. L. Walker to Commissioner of Indian Affairs, 4 November 1926, NA, Western Navajo. See Correll and Dehiya, *Anatomy of the Navajo Indian Reservation*.
11. Statements by Chief Salatouche and Otto Lamavitu in U.S. Senate, Committee on Indian Affairs, *Hearing on a Proposed Bill to Define the Exterior Boundaries of the Navajo Indian Reservation in Arizona, and for Other Purposes*, 7 December 1932.
12. Kelly, *The Navajo Indians*, 103–12.
13. Mitchell, *Tall Woman*, 439; Tara Travis and Scott Travis, notes from interviews by Peter Iverson, September 1999–January 2002, PIPC. Tara Travis is a historian for the National Park Service and is writing a history of Canyon de Chelly. Scott Travis, an archaeologist, is the current superintendent of Canyon de Chelly National Monument.
14. Young, *The Role of the Navajo*, 66–67.
15. Weisiger, "Sheep Dreams," 127–29.
16. Ibid.
17. S. F. Stacher, Order No. 2 to the Navajo Indians, Field Stockmen, Missionaries, and

the Indian Traders of This Jurisdiction, 3 December 1930, NAPR, CCF, Eastern Navajo Agency.

18. William H. Zeh, "General Report Covering the Grazing Situation on the Navajo Indian Reservation," 23 December 1930, in U.S. Senate, Committee on Indian Affairs, *Survey of Conditions of the Indians in the United States*, 71st Cong., 1st sess., 1931, pt. 18:91212–32; E. A. Johnson to Commissioner of Indian Affairs, 26 September 1931, NA, CCF, Northern Navajo Agency.

19. E. A. Johnson to Commissioner of Indian Affairs, NA, CCF, Northern Navajo Agency.

20. Ibid.

21. Ibid.; E. R. McCray to Commissioner, 25 August 1931, NA, CCF, Northern Navajo Agency, 1907–1939.

22. Floyd W. Lee, resolution adopted by the New Mexico Wool Growers Association, in U.S. Senate, Committee on Indian Affairs, *Survey of Conditions;* David Brugge, letter to Peter Iverson, 22 October 2001.

23. Tom Ration for Smith Lake area residents to the President, 21 July 1932, NAPR, CCF, Eastern Navajo Agency. This letter is included in *"For Our Navajo People."*

24. Minutes, Meeting of the Navajo Tribal Council, Fort Wingate, New Mexico, 7–8 July 1933, Thomas Dodge Papers, Arizona State University, Tempe, Ariz. (hereafter cited as Dodge Papers).

25. Ibid. Donald Parman presents a somewhat similar summary in *The Navajos and the New Deal* (New Haven, Conn.: Yale University Press, 1976), 40–42.

26. Minutes, Meeting of the Navajo Tribal Council, For Wingate, New Mexico, 7–8 July 1933, Dodge Papers; Parman, *The Navajos and the New Deal*, 40–42.

27. Minutes, Meeting of the Navajo Tribal Council, Tuba City, Arizona, 30 October–1 November 1933, Dodge Papers. This speech is included in *"For Our Navajo People."*

28. Ibid.; Ben Morris, interview, Doris Duke Oral History Project, tape transcription 415, Zimmerman Library, University of New Mexico.

29. Minutes, Navajo Tribal Council, Crownpoint, New Mexico, 9–11 April 1934, Dodge Papers.

30. Ibid.

31. Ibid.

32. Cohen refers here to the current Japanese occupation of Manchuria and the creation of a puppet state labeled Manchukuo. Felix Cohen, supplementary memorandum for Director of Forestry, Indian Office, concerning proposed grazing regulations, 1 June 1935, Felix Cohen Papers, Beinecke Library, Yale University, New Haven, Conn.

33. Ibid.

34. Ibid.

35. Minutes, Meeting of the Navajo Tribal Council, 6 June 1940, Dodge Papers. Davis's speech is included in *"For Our Navajo People."*

36. Minutes, Meeting of Navajo Tribal Council, Crownpoint, New Mexico, 9–11 April 1934, Dodge Papers. Shirley's remarks are included in *"For Our Navajo People."*

37. E. R. Fryer, presentation to the annual meeting of the Organization of American Historians, 6 April 1971, PIPC.

38. William Y. Adams, "Growing Up in Colonial Navajoland," *Papers From the Third, Fourth, and Sixth Navajo Studies Conferences*, ed. June-el Piper, Alexandra Roberts, and Jenevieve Smith (Window Rock, Ariz.: Navajo Nation Historic Preservation Department, 1993), 305.

39. Ibid.

40. Ibid.; W. G. McGinnies, "Stock Reduction and Range Management," in *Proceedings of the Navajo Service Land Management Conference, March 2–6, 1937* (Window Rock, Ariz.: Bureau of Indian Affairs, 1937), 11.

41. Memorandum to Mr. Fryer, 31 May 1938, and "Tennis Court Rules," NAPR, CCF, Navajo Area Office.

42. Edward T. Hall, *West of the Thirties: Discoveries Among the Navajo and Hopi* (New York: Doubleday, 1994), 131–33.

43. Howard Gorman, oral historical account, in *Navajo Livestock Reduction: A National Disgrace*, ed. Ruth Roessel and Broderick Johnson, (Tsaile, Ariz.: Navajo Community College Press, 1974), 47.

44. Marilyn Help, quoted in McCullough-Brabson and Help, *We'll Be in Your Mountains,* 115–16.

45. Grazing Regulations for the Navajo and Hopi Reservations, 2 June 1937, NA, CCF, Navajo Area Office.

46. Tom Dodge to Harold Ickes, 26 June 1935, Dodge Papers.

47. Young, *Political History,* 87–114.

48. Ibid.

49. Henry Dodge to James Stewart, 20 April 1936, NA, CCF, Navajo Area Office. Chee Dodge's letter is included in *"For Our Navajo People."*

50. Tom Dodge to John Collier, 7 May 1936, Dodge Papers. Tom Dodge's letter is included in *"For Our Navajo People."*

51. Ibid.

52. Tom Dodge to Harold Ickes, 26 June 1935, Dodge Papers.

53. E. R. Fryer, "The Navajo Service," in *Proceedings of the Navajo Service Land Management Conference, March 2–6, 1937* (Window Rock, Ariz.: Bureau of Indian Affairs, 1937).

54. William W. McClellan, Jr., to E. R. Fryer, 30 November 1937, NA, CCF, Navajo Area Office.

55. Harold Ickes to Henry Taliman, 2 August 1937, photocopy, Richard Van Valkenburgh Papers, Arizona Historical Society, Tucson.

56. Department of the Interior Memorandum for the Press, 14 August 1937, Dodge Papers.

57. Paul B. Palmer to E. R. Fryer, 19 February 1938, NAPR, CCF, Navajo Area Office.

58. E. R. Fryer to Woehlke, 5 August 1937, NAPR, CCF, Navajo Area Office.

59. E. R. Fryer, Confidential Memorandum to District Supervisors, 16 September 1937, NAPR, CCF, Navajo Area Office.

60. William W. McClellan, Jr., to H. E. Holman, attention E. R. Fryer, 29 July 1938, NAPR, CCF, Navajo Area Office.

61. A. G. Hutton to Lucy Wilcox Adams, 6 June 1938, NAPR, CCF, Navajo Area Office.

62. Rudolph Zweifel to Lucy Wilcox Adams, 14 June 1938, NAPR, CCF, Navajo Area Office.

63. H. H. Smith to Lucy Wilcox Adams, 10 June 1938, NAPR, CCF, Navajo Area Office.

64. Willard Brimhall to Adams, 9 June 1938, NAPR, CCF, Navajo Area Office.

65. William W. McClellan, Jr., to Adams, 8 June 1938, NAPR, CCF, Navajo Area Office.

66. M. J. Bedwell to Adams, 15 June 1938, NAPR, CCF, Navajo Area Office.

67. E. G. Stocks to Adams, 14 June 1938, NAPR, CCF, Navajo Area Office.

68. William Thomason to Adams, 4 June 1938, NAPR, CCF, Navajo Area Office.

69. Hugh D. Carroll to Adams, 17 June 1938, NAPR, CCF, Navajo Area Office.

70. Tom Dodge to E. R. Fryer, 24 March 1938; Fryer to Tom Dodge, 2 April 1938, both in NAPR, CCF, Navajo Area Office. Dodge's letter is included in *"For Our Navajo People."*

71. Memorandum from Fryer to Lucy Wilcox Adams and John C. McPhee, 1 December 1938, NA, CCF, Navajo Area Office.

72. Minutes, Navajo Tribal Council, 8 November 1938, Dodge Papers. Morgan's speech is included in *"For Our Navajo People."*

73. J. C. Morgan, "The Place of the Tribal Council in the Navajo Program," text for radio broadcast from KTGM, Window Rock, 7 March 1939, FFP. Morgan's address is included in *"For Our Navajo People."*

74. Minutes, Navajo Tribal Council, 15 May 1939, Dodge Papers. The exchange between Morgan and Gorman is included in *"For Our Navajo People."*

75. See, for example, E. R. Fryer's report to John Collier, 10 June 1941, NAPR, CCF, Navajo Area Office; William W. McClellan, Jr., to E. R. Fryer, 17 January 1940, and 24 January 1940, NAPR, CCF, Navajo Area Office. McClellan merely echoed Ickes, who in a memorandum dated 30 April 1934 (NAPR, CCF, Navajo Area Office), informed all employees of the Indian Service that opposition to "the new Indian program" on the part of employees would not be tolerated. Those guilty of "disloyal and pernicious" behavior should anticipate "dismissal from the service."

76. William W. McClellan, Jr., to E. R. Fryer, 26 January 1940, NAPR, CCF, Navajo Area Office.

77. Ibid.

78. Ibid.

79. Scott Preston, Julius Begay, Frank Goldtooth, and Judge Many Children to John Murdoch 14 February 1940, NA, CCF, Navajo Agency. This letter is included in *"For Our Navajo People."*
80. Deshna Clah Cheschillige to Dennis Chávez, 8 December 1940, Dennis Chávez Papers, Center for Southwest Research, Zimmerman Library, University of New Mexico, Albuquerque. This letter is included in *"For Our Navajo People."*
81. Navajo Rights Association By-Laws and Resolutions, Shiprock, Arizona, 15 November 1941, Dennis Chávez Papers, Center for Southwest Research, Zimmerman Library, University of New Mexico, Albuquerque. This material is included in *"For Our Navajo People."*
82. Felix Cohen, memorandum for the Solicitor, 24 September 1943, Felix Cohen Papers, Beinecke Library, Yale University, New Haven, Conn.
83. "Possible Principles of Livestock Reduction," Navajo Planning and Policy Conference, Window Rock, Arizona, 21–30 October 1940, NA, CCF, Navajo Area Office.
84. Wilkins, *Navajo Political Experience*, 81.
85. Kinlichee chapter members to Commissioner of Indian Affairs, 25 December 1937, NAPR, CCF, Navajo Area Office. This petition is included in *"For Our Navajo People."*
86. Toadlena chapter officers Henry Mike, Clyde Beyall, and Mrs. Yanapah Yazzie to W. W. Peter, 30 January 1937; Greasewood chapter officers Billy Pete, Little Judge, and Youataile to Commissioner of Indian Affairs, 14 April 1932; Rock Point residents to Commissioner of Indian Affairs, 18 November 1940, all in CCF, NAPR, Navajo Area Office; Charles Platero, et al., to E. F. Myer, NAPR, CCF, Navajo. These petitions are included in *"For Our Navajo People."*
87. Fred Nelson, Billy Pete, and Paul Williams, resolutions adopted by the local Navajo council of Hopi reservation, 26 June 1933, Dodge Papers.
88. Shonto residents to Commissioner of Indian Affairs, February 1937, NAPR, CCF, Navajo Area Office.
89. Rodee, *One Hundred Years of Navajo Rugs*, 143–50; Kent, *Navajo Weaving*, 97.
90. John Adair, *The Navajo and Pueblo Silversmiths* (Norman: University of Oklahoma Press, 1975), 55–72. A ketoh originally referred to a bow guard (to protect your wrist when you shot an arrow from a bow). Later it became ornamental—the leather covered by hammered or cast silver.
91. Franc Johnson Newcomb, *Hosteen Klah: Navaho Medicine Man and Sand Painter* (Norman: University of Oklahoma Press, 1964), 202–7.
92. Tom Dodge, inaugural speech to Navajo Tribal Council, 15 May 1933, Dodge Papers. This speech is included in *"For Our Navajo People."*
93. B. P. Six to Commissioner of Indian Affairs, 24 September 1930, and 24 October 1930; R. B. Burnham to Commissioners of Indian Affairs, 27 October 1930; C. J. Rhoads to Roy B. Burnham, 8 October 1930 and 18 March 1931; E. R. McCray to Roy Burnham, 9 September 1931, all in NARMR, Northern Navajo Agency, General Correspondence.
94. M. L. Woodard to Burton K. Wheeler, 25 February 1939, NARMR, Northern Navajo Agency, General Correspondence.
95. Ibid.
96. Howard Gorman to E. R. Fryer, 20 December 1939, NAPR, Navajo Area Office, General Correspondence. This letter is included in *"For Our Navajo People."*
97. Minutes, Navajo Tribal Council, 16 May 1939, Dodge Papers. Gorman's report is included in *"For Our Navajo People."*
98. Ann Clark, *Little Herder in Winter (Daago Na'naakkaadi Yazhi)* (Phoenix, Ariz.: U.S. Office of Indian Affairs, 1942), 101.
99. Robert W. Young, notes from interview by Peter Iverson, Albuquerque, N.Mex., 2 June 1990, PIPC; Peter Iverson, "Speaking Their Language: Robert W. Young and the Navajos," in *Between Indian and White Worlds: The Cultural Broker*, ed. Margaret Connell Szasz (Norman: University of Oklahoma Press, 1994), 263.
100. George Boyce, "A Short History of Navajo Service Schools," NAPR, Navajo Area Office, 1940–1943.
101. Ibid.
102. Lucy Harvey, letter, March 1939, NAPR, CCF, Navajo Area Office, Box 166. This letter is included in *"For Our Navajo People."*

103. Crownpoint Boarding School, Thanksgiving program, 25 November 1936, NAPR, CCF, Eastern Navajo Agency.
104. Plan for meals for one week, Crownpoint Boarding School, 1937, NAPR, CCF, Eastern Navajo Agency.
105. In PIPC.
106. Paul N. Schmitt to Lucy W. Adams, 22 August 1939, NAPR, Navajo Area Office.
107. Paul N. Schmitt to George Boyce, 3 October 1942, NAPR, Navajo Area Office.
108. Waldo Emerson to Mr. Rushton, 10 November 1935, CCF, NARMR, Navajo Area Office.
109. Navajo Agency School Bus Route Survey, 1939–1940, NA, Navajo Area Office. This letter is included in *"For Our Navajo People."*
110. Trennert, *White Man's Medicine*, 155–99.
111. Program for the dedication of Sage Memorial Hospital, 14 May 1930, Day Family Papers, Special Collections, Cline Library, Northern Arizona University, Flagstaff.
112. Trennert, *White Man's Medicine*, 180–83.
113. U.S. Senate, Committee on Indian Affairs, *Survey of Conditions*, 91217.
114. See David F. Aberle, with field assistance by Harvey C. Moore, *The Peyote Religion Among the Navajo* (Chicago: Aldine, 1966).
115. Navajo Tribal Council resolution, 4 June 1940, NAPR, Navajo Area Office.
116. Franklin D. Roosevelt to J. C. Morgan, 25 July 1940, NAPR, Navajo Area Office.

CHAPTER 6

1. Marine Corps hymn in Navajo, 5 October 1944, on Harrison Lapahie, Jr.'s website, available at http://www.lapahie.com/NavajoCodeTalker.cfm. Accessed on 25 January 2002. My thanks to Laura Wallace for providing a correct written Navajo version of this rough approximation of the language.
2. Cozy Stanley Brown, oral historical account, in *Navajos and World War II*, ed. Broderick H. Johnson (Tsaile, Ariz.: Navajo Community College Press, 1977), 61. James M. Stewart, "The Navajo Indian at War," *Arizona Highways* (June 1943): 20.
3. Adam Adkins, "Secret War: The Navajo Code Talkers in World War II," *New Mexico Historical Review* (October 1997): 322–23; Iverson, *"We Are Still Here,"* 50–51; Henry Greenberg and Georgia Greenberg, *Carl Gorman's World* (Albuquerque: University of New Mexico Press, 1984), 60.
4. Lapahie website (see n. 1); Adkins, "Secret War."
5. Greenberg and Greenberg, *Carl Gorman's World*, 58–59.
6. *In Search of History: Navajo Code Talkers*, History Channel video (AAE-40428); U.S. Naval Historical Center website on the Code Talkers, at http://www.history.navy.mil/faqs/faq61–2.htm, accessed on 3 March 2002; Adkins, "Secret War." Details of the code are reprinted in *"For Our Navajo People."*
7. Stewart, "The Navajo Indian at War," 40.
8. Adkins, "Secret War." See, for example, the tribute in Kayenta's Burger King restaurant, where Navajo entrepreneur Richard Mike has created a wonderful series of displays in honor of his father, King Mike.
9. Adkins, "Secret War."
10. Alison Bernstein, *American Indians and World War II: Toward a New Era in Indian Affairs* (Norman: University of Oklahoma Press, 1991), 75–78; John S. Westerlund, "'U.S. Project Men Here': Building Navajo Ordnance Depot at Flagstaff," *Journal of Arizona History* (summer 2001): 201–26; Westerlund, "Bombs From Bellemont: Navajo Ordnance in World War II," *Journal of Arizona History* (autumn 2001).
11. Dan Keyonie, speech to the Navajo Tribal Council, 10 July 1943; Many Farms petition, 23 November 1943, Special Collections, University of Arizona Library, Tucson. Keyonie's speech and the full text of the petition are included in *"For Our Navajo People."*
12. Jack D. Jones to J. M. Stewart, 15 April 1945; James Oliver and Sam Capitan to J. M. Stewart, both in NAPR, Navajo Area Office. These letters are included in *"For Our Navajo People."*

13. Ralph W. Anderson to J. M. Stewart and Chairman of the Navaho Tribe, 30 April 1943, NAPR, Navajo Area Office. This letter is included in *"For Our Navajo People."*
14. James M. Stewart to William A. Brophy, 23 March 1945 and 4 April 1945; Stewart telegram to Office of Indian Affairs, 4 January 1945; William Zimmerman, Jr., to John Collier, 5 January 1945; Paul Palmer to Brophy, 12 March 1945, NA, Navajo Area Office; "Capiton Benally," in *Navajo Livestock Reduction,* ed. Roessel and Johnson, 31–38.
15. George A. Boyce, "First Report on Education to the Navajo People," NAPR, Navajo Area Office.
16. Ned Hatathli, speech to the Navajo Tribal Council, 14 October 1955, Dodge Papers.
17. Synopsis of Navajo Tribal Council requests from government, NAPR, Navajo Area Office.
18. Ibid., 2.
19. Ibid., 3.
20. Ibid., 15–16.
21. Young, *Navajo Yearbook,* vol. 8, documents and details the results of this initiative. These statistics are included on page 5 of this invaluable volume.
22. Young, *Navajo Yearbook,* 8:133–34.
23. Paul Jones, inaugural address, 1959, Special Collections, University of Arizona Library, Tucson; Ruth Roessel, ed., *Navajo Studies at Navajo Community College* (Many Farms, Ariz.: Navajo Community College Press, 1971), 39. The address by Jones is included in *"For Our Navajo People."*
24. Navajo Tribal Council resolution, 12 July 1945; William Zimmerman, Jr., to Chee Dodge, 27 August 1945, NAPR, Navajo Area Office.
25. Chee Dodge, testimony, U.S. Senate, Committee on Indian Affairs, 12 May 1946, NA, CCF, Navajo Area Office. This testimony is included in *"For Our Navajo People."*
26. Sam Ahkeah, Scott Preston, Sam Gorman, and Billy Norton, testimony, U.S. Senate, Committee on Indian Affairs, 12 May 1946, NA, CCF, Navajo Area Office.
27. Dan Keyonie and Roger Davis, speeches to the Tribal Council, 18 February 1947; Lilly J. Neil to Willard Beatty, 18 September 1947, NA, Navajo Area Office. These documents are included in *"For Our Navajo People."*
28. George I. Sánchez, *"The People": A Study of the Navajos* (Lawrence, Kans.: Department of the Interior, March 1948); Julius A. Krug, *The Navajo: A Long Range Program for Rehabilitation* (Washington, D.C.: Department of the Interior, 1948).
29. Robert A. Roessel, Jr., *Navajo Education, 1948–1978: Its Progress and Its Problems* (Rough Rock, Ariz.: Navajo Curriculum Center, Rough Rock Demonstration School, 1979), 18–19.
30. "Intermountain Indian School: A New Opportunity for Navajo Children" (Phoenix, Ariz.: Bureau of Indian Affairs, May 1950).
31. Navajo Service Pupils Enrolled in Non-Reservation Indian Service Schools, 1948–49 School Year, NAPR, Navajo Area Office.
32. Young, *Navajo Yearbook,* 8:21–24, 29–33.
33. Alice John Bedoni, letter, in *Adahooniligii* (Navajo-language monthly newsletter, Window Rock, Ariz.), 1 June 1954, Dodge Papers. This letter is included in *"For Our Navajo People."*
34. Young, *Navajo Yearbook,* 8:56–69; Margaret Connell Szasz, *Education and the American Indian: The Road to Self-Determination Since 1928* (Albuquerque: University of New Mexico Press, 1974), 181–82.
35. Hoskie Cronemeyer, speech to the Tribal Council, 11 August 1952, Dodge Papers. This speech is included in *"For Our Navajo People."*
36. David Lee, "Student Council Member Asks Us to Speak English," *Smoke Signals from Intermountain Indian School,* 29 January 1952, NARMR, CCF, Navajo Area Office; Sam Gorman, speech to the Tribal Council, 4 November 1953, Dodge Papers.
37. Roessel, *Navajo Education,* 39.
38. Sam Ahkeah, speech to the Tribal Council, 20 July 1953, Dodge Papers. This speech is included in *"For Our Navajo People."*
39. Dillon Platero, address to a conference on Navajo education, Flagstaff, 25 January 1960, Dodge Papers. This speech is included in *"For Our Navajo People."*
40. Trennert, *White Man's Medicine,* 204–13.

41. Davies, *Healing Ways*, 54–55; George A. Boyce, "Facts About the Navajos" (Window Rock, Ariz.: Bureau of Indian Affairs, 1947, mimeographed), 10; Krug, *The Navajo*, 6–7.

42. John Adair, Kurt Deuschle, and Clifton Barnett, *The People's Health*, rev. ed. (Albuquerque: University of New Mexico Press, 1988), 29–32.

43. Davies, *Healing Ways*, 67–72.

44. See Peter Iverson, "Building Toward Self-Determination: Plains and Southwestern Indians in the 1940s and 1950s," *Western Historical Quarterly* 16, no. 2 (1985): 163–73.

45. Carolyn Niethammer, *I'll Go and Do More: Annie Dodge Wauneka, Navajo Leader and Activist* (Lincoln: University of Nebraska Press, 2001), 31–45, 71–77.

46. Ibid., 75–76, 84.

47. Davies, *Healing Ways*, 73–75; Young, *Navajo Yearbook*, 8:73, 77. For the most detailed discussion of the Cornell project, see Adair, Deuschle, and Barnett, *The People's Health*.

48. Annie Wauneka, speech to the Tribal Council, 12 October 1955, College of Law Library, University of Arizona, Tucson. This speech is included in *"For Our Navajo People."* Annie Wauneka, speech to the Tribal Council, 2 November 1953, College of Law Library, University of Arizona, Tucson. This speech is also included in *"For Our Navajo People."* Wauneka issued the challenge earlier in the 1950s. The quotation is from a 15 January 1959 speech to the Tribal Council in which she recalled this event. Preston's remarks are quoted in several sources, but initially in Adair, Deuschle, and Barnett, *The People's Health*, 33.

49. "Orientation to Health on the Navajo Indian Reservation: A Guide for Hospital and Public Health Workers" (Washington, D.C.: U.S. Public Health Service, June 1959), PIPC.

50. J. M. Stewart to Ralph W. Anderson, 13 May 1943, NAPR, Navajo Area Office.

51. Daniel McCool, "Indian Voting," in *American Indian Policy in the Twentieth Century*, ed. Vine R. Deloria, Jr. (Norman: University of Oklahoma Press, 1984), 107–10.

52. Clyde Hunter to J. M. Stewart, 6 February 1945, NAPR, Navajo Area Office.

53. Ibid.; Affidavits of John Dayish, Harry Denetclaw, Julia Denetclaw, Jimmie K. King, and Howard H. Nez, NARMR, Navajo Area Office.

54. William Ashley, affidavit, 3 May 1946, Apache County, Arizona; William Ashley, Affidavit of Registration, Apache County, 3 May 1946; Complaint in the U.S. District Court for the District of Arizona by William Ashley, Tom Irving, and James Charlie Manuelito, v. R. K. Karigan; R. E. Karigan to J. M. Stewart, 3 May 1946, all in NARMR, Navajo Area Office.

55. Frank Peralta, affidavit, Apache County, May 1946, relating to attempt to register in McKinley County, NARMR, Navajo Area Office.

56. Levi S. Udall to R. E. Karigan, 11 April 1946, NARMR, Navajo Area Office.

57. *Harrison and Austin v. Laveen*, Arizona Supreme Court, 15 July 1948, NARMR, Navajo Area Office; McCool, "Indian Voting," 110–11.

58. Navajo tribal delegation meeting on peyote, 13 May 1946, NAPR, Navajo Area Office.

59. Ibid.

60. *Native American Church v. Navajo Tribal Council*, 272 F. 2d 131, 10th Cir. (1959), reprinted in Wilcomb Washburn, ed., *The American Indian and the United States* (New York: Random House, 1973), 2788–90.

61. See Aberle, *The Peyote Religion Among the Navajo*.

62. Brugge, "Henry Chee Dodge," 91.

63. J. Wesley Huff, "Chee Dodge, Old Mr. Interpreter Is Laid to Rest," *Gallup Independent*, 10 January 1947.

64. Hoffman and Johnson, *Navajo Biographies*, 215–36. See also the depiction of Ahkeah in "A Fair Deal for the Navajos," a chapter in Kenneth R. Philp, *Termination Revisited: American Indians on the Trail to Self-Determination* (Lincoln: University of Nebraska Press, 1999), 50–67.

65. Young, *Political History*, 125–26.

66. *Navajo Times*, 4 November 1965.

67. Robert W. Young, interview by Peter Iverson, Albuquerque, N.Mex., 25 February 1974.

68. Norman Littell, "Reflections of a Tribal Attorney," *Adahooniligii*, 1 April 1957, Dodge Papers.

69. Ibid.
70. Young, *Political History*, 129–30.
71. "Fryer Given Old Post on Reservation," *Arizona Republic,* 22 December 1947; "Ahkeah Protests Return of Fryer to Navajo Agency," *Arizona Republic,* 24 December 1947.
72. *Williams v. Lee,* 358 US 217 (1959), and *Native American Church v. Navajo Tribal Council,* in Washburn, *The American Indian,* 2785–87, and 2788–91, respectively; Fred Ragsdale, letter to Peter Iverson, 31 October 1984.
73. Howard Gorman, speech to the Navajo Tribal Council, 13 January 1959; Annie Wauneka, speech to the Tribal Council, 23 January 1956. Both speeches are included in *"For Our Navajo People."*
74. *Adahooniligii,* August–September 1953, June–July 1956, Dodge Papers.
75. Paul Jones, inaugural address, Window Rock, Arizona, January 1959, Special Collections, University of Arizona Library, Tucson. The address is included in *"For Our Navajo People."*
76. Mary Shepardson, *Navajo Ways in Government: A Study in Political Process,* American Anthropological Association Memoir 96 (Menasha, Wisc.: American Anthropological Association, June 1963), 85–97.
77. Irene Stewart, *A Voice in Her Tribe: A Navajo Woman's Own Story,* ed. Doris Ostrander Dawdy (Socorro, N.Mex.: Ballena Press, 1980), 59. See Navajo Council Resolution CJ-20-55 in Navajo Nation, *Navajo Tribal Code,* 144; Aubrey Williams, *Navajo Political Process,* Smithsonian Contributions to Anthropology, no. 9 (Washington, D.C.: Smithsonian Institution Press, 1970), 41–42.
78. Hoffman and Johnson, *Navajo Biographies,* 256–74.
79. Ibid.
80. Shepardson, *Navajo Ways,* 98–101.
81. Ibid., 101–5.
82. For a more extended discussion of the Navajo court system, see Mary Shepardson, "Problems of the Navajo Tribal Courts in Transition," *Human Organization* 24, no. 3 (1965): 250–53. On the legal services program, see speeches given by Howard Gorman and attorney Lawrence Davis to the Tribal Council on 9 October 1958, Museum of Northern Arizona Library, Flagstaff. Gorman's speech is included in *"For Our Navajo People."* On the Navajo police, see Alfred W. Yazzie, *Navajo Police* (Rough Rock, Ariz.: Navajo Curriculum Center, Rough Rock Demonstration School, 1980).
83. Eugene Gordy and Marcus Kanuho, speeches to the Tribal Council, 8 December 1954; Memo from Adolph Maloney for Sam Ahkeah, in regard to livestock trespass between Navajo and Hopi reservations, 27 September 1954; Horses trespass meeting, Keams Canyon, 3 November 1954, all in NAPR, Navajo Agency.
84. This discussion is based primarily on Brugge, *The Navajo-Hopi Land Dispute,* passim.
85. Ibid., 68.
86. Ibid., 72–89.
87. Ibid., 93–100. See also Jerry Kammer, *The Second Long Walk: The Navajo-Hopi Land Dispute* (Albuquerque: University of New Mexico Press, 1980).
88. William Y. Adams, *Shonto: A Study of the Role of a Trader in a Modern Navaho Community,* Smithsonian Institution, Bureau of American Ethnology, Bulletin no. 188 (Washington, D.C.: Government Printing Office, 1963), 290.
89. Dewey Etsitty and Roger Davis, speeches before the Tribal Council, 26 June 1948, NAPR, Navajo Area Office. These speeches are included in *"For Our Navajo People."*
90. See the minutes of the Navajo Tribal Council for this period, College of Law Library, University of Arizona, Tucson, and Willow Roberts, *Stokes Carson: Twentieth Century Trading on the Navajo Reservation* (Albuquerque: University of New Mexico Press, 1987), 127–36; Max Drefkoff, "An Industrial Program for the Navajo Indian Reservation" (Report presented to the Council, 1948). Drefkoff is nowhere to be seen in Powers, *Navajo Trading.*
91. Sallie Wagner, *Wide Ruins: Memories from a Navajo Trading Post* (Albuquerque: University of New Mexico Press, 1997), 143–46.
92. Morris H. Burge, "Report to the Commissioner of Indian Affairs on Navajo Trading," April 1949, Dodge Papers; J. M. Stewart, remarks to the Tribal Council, 1 April 1948, Dodge Papers; Young, *Political History,* 138–39.
93. Wagner, *Wide Ruins,* 143–46.

94. Adams, *Shonto*, 129–33; Colleen O'Neill, "The Making of a Navajo Wage-Worker: The Navajo Household and Wage-Work, 1948–1972" (paper presented at Western History Association conference, 18 October 1977).

95. For a more general discussion, see Donald L. Fixico, *The Urban Indian Experience in America* (Albuquerque: University of New Mexico Press, 2000).

96. See, for example, the commentary by Rachel L. Spieldoch, "Uranium Is in My Body," *American Indian Culture and Research Journal* 20, no. 2 (1996): 173–85.

97. Frank Bradley, speech to the Council, 3 November 1953, Zimmerman Library, University of New Mexico, Albuquerque. This speech is included in *"For Our Navajo People."*

98. Timothy Benally, interview, Navajo uranium workers oral history project, Doug Brugge, coordinator, PIPC.

99. Iverson, *"We Are Still Here,"* 168.

100. Young, *Navajo Yearbook*, 8:268.

101. Ibid., 269.

102. Ned Hatathli, speech to Tribal Council, 19 September 1957, Dodge Papers. This speech is included in *"For Our Navajo People."*

103. Dewey Etsitty to Douglas McKay, 18 April 1953; Grazing District 14 letter to Glenn Emmons, 18 September 1953, NA, Navajo Area Office. The first letter is included in *"For Our Navajo People."*

104. Young, *Navajo Yearbook*, 8:155–66; Gilbert Fite, *American Farmers: A New Minority* (Bloomington: Indiana University Press, 1981).

105. Young, *Navajo Yearbook*, 8:155–66.

106. Ibid.

107. Ibid., 178–84.

108. Drefkoff, "Industrial Program."

109. Young, *Navajo Yearbook*, 8:192.

110. Ibid., 197–208.

111. Samuel Moon, *Tall Sheep: Harry Goulding, Monument Valley Trader* (Norman: University of Oklahoma Press, 1992), 144–51.

112. This quotation is from Riitta Laitinen, a graduate student from Finland, who said her father had told her to greet John Wayne when she arrived in Monument Valley. Laitinen, conversation with Peter Iverson, Monument Valley, Ariz., 8 April 1998. See also Moon, *Tall Sheep*, 1999, 223–29.

113. Gilbert S. Maxwell, *Navajo Rugs: Past, Present, and Future* (Palm Desert, Calif.: Best-West Productions, 1963), 52.

CHAPTER 7

1. Raymond Nakai, inaugural address, 13 April 1963, PIPC.

2. Ibid.

3. Broderick H. Johnson, "Raymond Nakai," in Hoffman and Johnson, *Navajo Biographies*, 332–37.

4. Deenise Becenti, "We Are One," in *Star Torch II: An Anthology of Student Writings* (Gallup, N.Mex.: McKinley County Schools, 1977).

5. Raymond Nakai, "Will We Meet the Challenge?," an address delivered to the Governor's Interstate Indian Council, Denver, Colo., 24 September 1964, reprinted in *Journal of American Indian Education* 4, no. 1 (1964): 10–12.

6. Ibid.

7. Littell to Thomas M. Storke, 3 April 1964, 15 May 1964, 17 August 1964, 21 October 1966, 25 November 1966, 30 November 1966, 4 February 1967, 3 March 1967, 27 November 1967, Thomas M. Storke Papers, Bancroft Library, University of California, Berkeley.

8. *Littell v. Nakai* 344 F2d 486, 488 (9th Cir., 1965), reprinted in Washburn, *The American Indian*, 2854–58; *Navajo Times*, 23 February 1967.

9. *Navajo Times*, 23 February 1967. Shiprock councilman Carl Todacheene believed that "Littell was too much of a chief, but firing him was a mistake. The Tribe went down

hill after he departed." Todacheene, interview by Peter Iverson, Kirtland, N.Mex., 8 June 2000.

10. Peter Iverson witnessed such scenes when he taught at Navajo Community College. The report about Intermountain is covered in the 13 February 1969 issue of the *Navajo Times*.

11. Fannie Chee to David Cargo, 7 October 1969, David Cargo Papers, Box 62, New Mexico State Archives and Records Center, Santa Fe, N.Mex. Other children at Crownpoint also wrote to Cargo using the same words, so Chee's letter must be seen as part of a campaign or class exercise or both. Nevertheless, the letter gives voice to common sentiments of the time.

12. *Navajo Times*, 6 May 1965; Roessel, *Navajo Education*, 49–58, 200–211; Bob Roessel, various conversations with Peter Iverson, 1997–2001.

13. Donald A. Erickson and Henrietta Schwartz, "Community School at Rough Rock" (Rough Rock Demonstration School, Rough Rock, Ariz., 1969, mimeograph); Broderick H. Johnson, *Navaho Education at Rough Rock* (Rough Rock, Ariz.: Rough Rock Demonstration School, 1968).

14. For an example of national publicity given to Rough Rock, see Estelle Fuchs, "Time to Redeem an Old Promise: American Indian Education," *Saturday Review*, 24 January 1970, 54–57; and Larry A. Van Dyne, "Navajos, Stressing Heritage, Claim Nation's Only Indian College," *The Chronicle of Higher Education* 8 May 1972, 4. A long article by Daniel Rosenfelt in a law journal also highlighted Rough Rock. See Rosenfelt, "Indian Schools and Community Control," *Stanford Law Review* (April 1973): 489–550.

15. Monty Roessel, "Building a Nation with Leadership," *Navajo Culture Today* (Rough Rock, Ariz.), January 1999. Peter Iverson taught at the college from 1969 to 1972; the other information presented here is archived in PIPC.

16. PIPC; Iverson, "The Early Years of Navajo Community College," *Journal of American Indian Education* 38, no. 3 (1999): 34–43.

17. Evan Roberts, "Early History of ONEO" (paper prepared for the Office of Navajo Economic Opportunity Supervisory Training Workshop, Farmington, N.Mex., 11 March 1974); *Navajo Times*, 8 October 1964, 2 December 1965.

18. These statistics do not include people served by DNA Legal Services, which initially was part of ONEO. Office of Navajo Economic Opportunity, "A History and a Report," June–November 1967, 31, 33, 39, 41, PIPC.

19. *ONEO Newsletter* (Window Rock, Ariz.), July 1970, PIPC.

20. *Navajo Times*, 5 January 1967.

21. Ibid.

22. Farmington Vehicles is a fictional place of business, but this kind of transaction occurred all too frequently at bordertown dealers. For information about Gallup at this time, see the *Gallup Independent*, in particular the issues of 5 February 1967, 6 February 1967, 21 February 1967, and 23 March 1967. The period from the late 1960s through the mid-1970s was marked by tension and conflict in Gallup and Farmington. The death of Larry Casuse in Gallup in 1973 and the murder of three Navajo youths in Farmington in 1974 brought national attention to the problems existing in both towns.

23. Brad Blair to Louis Bruce, 15 September 1969, copy, Barry Goldwater Papers, Arizona Historical Foundation, Hayden Library, Arizona State University, Tempe, Ariz.

24. *Gallup Independent*, 9 August 1968; Niethammer, *I'll Go and Do More*, 170–74.

25. *Gallup Independent*, 9 August 1968; Niethammer, *I'll Go and Do More*, 170–74. As of 2001, Mitchell was still working in Micronesia.

26. *Navajo Times*, 10 September 1970; David Ralph Graham, *The Role of Business in the Economic Redevelopment of a Rural Community* (Austin: Bureau of Business Research, University of Texas, 1973), 43–59; Lorraine Turner Ruffing, "Economic Development and Navajo Social Structure" (paper prepared for the Economic Development Administration, U.S. Department of Commerce, Washington, D.C., April 1973).

27. Bailey and Bailey, *A History of the Navajos*, 238; Philip Reno, *Mother Earth, Father Sky, and Economic Development: Navajo Resources and Their Use* (Albuquerque: University of New Mexico Press, 1981), 127–31.

28. Peter Iverson showed a film about coal mining in Appalachia to Navajo Community College students during the 1969–1970 academic year and was impressed by their absolute astonishment at the damage caused by coal mining.

29. Eugene Gade, "Environmental and Economic Issue: The Strip Mining of Black Mesa and the Coal Burning Power Plants of the Southwest" (Many Farms High School, Many Farms, Ariz., 1971, mimeograph).

30. *Diné Baa-Hani* (Crownpoint, N.Mex., Eastern Navajo Agency), October 1970, PIPC.

31. Gade, "Environmental and Economic Issue."

32. Boyden died in 1980, long before his role as a double agent was revealed. Charles Wilkinson, *Fire on the Plateau: Conflict and Endurance in the American Southwest* (Washington, D.C.: Island Books, 1999), 298–304.

33. *Navajo Times*, 26 February 1970.

34. Raymond Nakai, speech delivered at the opening of the centennial year, Window Rock, Ariz. (p. 108), and preface to Martin A. Link, ed., *Navajo: A Century of Progress, 1868–1968* (Window Rock, Ariz.: Navajo Tribe, 1968).

35. Navajo Nation, *Navajo Tribal Code* (Orford, N.H.: Equity, 1969), 1:7–8.

36. Charlotte Raub, "A Time to Celebrate and Remember: November is National Native American Month," *Inscom Journal* 21, no. 4 (1998).

37. *Navajo Times*, 26 February 1970.

38. These biographical details are drawn from various issues of the *Navajo Times* as well as materials provided by Chairman MacDonald's office during the 1970s.

39. *Navajo Times*, 28 July 1966.

40. *Navajo Times*, 23 June 1966.

41. *Gallup Independent*, 25 August 1970; *Navajo Times*, 27 August 1970; *Gallup Independent* and *Navajo Times*, September–November 1970.

42. *Navajo Times*, 7 January 1971.

43. Anonymous scholar's comment to Peter Iverson during the late 1970s.

44. Peter MacDonald, "Preconditions for Growth" (address given at "The Rise of the Southwest: Promises and Problems" conference, Phoenix, Arizona, 21 April 1977), PIPC.

45. Lawrence Ruzow, tape-recorded commentary prepared at Peter Iverson's request, November 1974; Jeff Gillenkirk and Mark Dowie, "The Great Indian Power Grab," *Mother Jones* (January 1982): 24–26.

46. *DNA Newsletter* (Window Rock, Ariz.), 30 August 1973; James Wechsler, interview by Peter Iverson, Window Rock, Ariz., May 1973.

47. *Navajo Times*, 23 December 1976, 30 December 1976, 6 January 1977, 20 January 1977, 4 January 1979. Other significant victories included *Goodluck v. Apache County* 417 F. Supp. 13 (D. Ariz. 1975) (gaining the right to vote in county elections and being eligible to run for positions in county government) and *Natonabah v. Board of Education of Gallup-McKinley School District* 355 F. Supp. 716 (D.N.M. 1973) and *Bigman v. Utah Navajo Development Council Inc.* C77-0031 (Utah) (forcing states and counties to build public school facilities on Navajo Nation land so that Diné children did not have to make round-trip journeys of up to 150 miles to attend off-reservation public schools).

48. *Navajo Times*, 26 January 1978; 2 February 1978; 9 February 1978; 16 February 1978; 23 February 1978; 23 March 1978; 20 April 1978; 4 May 1978; 1 June 1978; 8 June 1978; Mark N. Trahant, "MacDonald Has Long History of Legal Woes," *Navajo Nation Today* (Window Rock, Ariz.), 31 July–6 August 1991; Gillenkirk and Dowie, "Power Grab," 46.

49. Gillenkirk and Dowie, "Power Grab," 47.

50. Navajo Nation, *Navajo Tribal Code*, 24.1–24.2.

51. Navajo Division of Education, "Strengthening Navajo Education" (Window Rock, Ariz., 1973); Peter MacDonald, "Education for Survival" (address given at the state convention of Delta Kappa Gamma International, Clarksville, Ind., 23 April 1977), PIPC; Roessel, *Navajo Education*, 291.

52. Roessel, *Navajo Education*, 292–308.

53. Office of Research, Navajo Community College, "High Schools' Views of NCC and Its Recruitment Program: Report of a Survey" (Tsaile, Ariz.: Navajo Community College, October 1972).

54. Yazzie, *Navajo History*; Roessel and Johnson, *Navajo Stories of the Long Walk Period*; Roessel and Johnson, *Navajo Livestock Reduction*; Broderick H. Johnson, ed., *Stories of Traditional Navajo Life and Culture* (Tsaile, Ariz.: Navajo Community College Press, 1977).

55. *Navajo Times,* 9 November 1973.
56. Irene Nakai, "Bridge Perspective," in *The South Corner of Time: Hopi, Navajo, Papago, Yaqui Tribal Literature,* ed. Larry Evers (Tucson: Sun Tracks and University of Arizona Press, 1980), 91.
57. *Navajo Times,* 5 December 1974; Davies, *Healing Ways,* 131–32.
58. Davies, *Healing Ways,* 132–34.
59. *Diné Baa-Hani,* June–July 1970.
60. Davies, *Healing Ways,* 140–49.
61. Ibid., 174.
62. Program, dedication of the Chinle Comprehensive Health Care Facility, 28 August 1982, PIPC.
63. Powers, *Navajo Trading;* Jim Babbitt, interview by Bradley Cole, United Indian Traders Association Oral History Project, 21 July 1999, Cline Library, Northern Arizona University, Flagstaff.
64. Kent Gilbreath, *Red Capitalism* (Norman: University of Oklahoma Press, 1973), 12.
65. Babbitt, interview.
66. Ibid.; Powers, *Navajo Trading,* 149–93.
67. Bruce Burnham, conversations with Peter Iverson, 1997–2000; Powers, *Navajo Trading,* 221.
68. Richard Mike and several representatives of the Crownpoint Rug Auction, conversations with Peter Iverson, 1997–2000.
69. Office of Navajo Economic Opportunity, "How to Organize and Operate a Cooperative: A Handbook for Chapter Members" (Window Rock, Ariz.: Office of Navajo Economic Opportunity, 1973); *Diné Baa-Hani,* 7 July 1972; *Navajo Times,* 6 April 1978, 7 December 1978.
70. *Navajo Times,* 19 August 1976, 22–23 December 1976, 30 December 1976, 6 January 1977, 20 January 1977, 4 January 1979.
71. "An Interview with Peter MacDonald," *American Indian Journal* (June 1979): 11–12.
72. Bruce A. Johansen, "The High Cost of Uranium in Navajoland," *Akwesasne Notes,* n.s., April–June 1997: 10–12. See also Harrison Lapahie website (n. 1, chapter 6).
73. Robert M. McPherson, "Poverty, Politics, and Petroleum: The Utah Navajos and the Aneth Oil Field," in McPherson, *Navajo Land, Navajo Culture: The Utah Experience in the Twentieth Century* (Norman: University of Oklahoma Press, 2001), 179–98. For a useful overview of Navajo and other Indian efforts to gain greater control over their mineral resources, see Marjane Ambler, *Breaking the Iron Bonds: Indian Control of Energy Development* (Lawrence: University Press of Kansas, 1990).
74. Navajo Forest Products Industries, annual report, 1978 (Navajo, N.Mex.); *Navajo Times,* 29 June 1978, 6 July 1978; Carl Todacheene, interview.
75. Gordon Denipah, Navajo Housing Authority, interview by Iverson, Window Rock, Ariz., May 1973.
76. LeNora Begay Trahant, *The Success of the Navajo Arts and Crafts Enterprise: A Retail Success Story* (New York: Walker and Company, 1996), 13–22.
77. Kammer, *The Second Long Walk,* 202.
78. *Navajo Times,* 19 September 1976, 17 February 1977, 7 April 1977, 25 May 1978, 31 August 1978, 5 October 1978, 19 October 1978, 9 November 1978.
79. Iverson, *Barry Goldwater,* 179–81.
80. Brugge, *The Navajo-Hopi Land Dispute,* 236–38.
81. Ibid.
82. Kaufman and Selser, *The Navajo Weaving Tradition,* 106; Ann Lane Hedlund, *Reflections of the Weaver's World: The Gloria F. Ross Collection of Contemporary Navajo Weaving* (Denver, Colo.: Denver Art Museum; distributed by Seattle: University of Washington Press, 1992), 21–22.
83. Conversations with Bruce Burnham; Rodee, *One Hundred Years of Navajo Rugs,* 170.
84. Hedlund, *Reflections of the Weaver's World,* 9; "Navajo Pictorial Weaving—The Rug That's a Picture," *New Mexico Magazine,* February 1976, 20–25.
85. This discussion is based the authors' observations; Hedlund, *Reflections of the Weaver's World,* 9; Tony Hillerman, "The Crownpoint Rug Weavers Auction: Going . . . Going . . . ," *New Mexico Magazine,* February 1976, 28–29, 36–37; Fred Hirschmann, "Crownpoint Rug Auction," *Native Peoples* (winter 1989): 2–9.

86. This discussion is based on my observations and Peter Iverson, *Riders of the West: Portraits from Indian Rodeo* (Seattle: University of Washington Press, 1999). The quotations derive from pages 17 and 32. The story about Michael Bia is based on an article by Marley Shebala published in the 20 January 2000 issue of the *Navajo Times*.

87. Iverson, *Riders of the West*, 64; *Diné Baa-Hani*, June–July 1970.

88. *Navajo Times*, 23 March 1972. See also, for example, the *Navajo Times* of 13 February 1969, for a photograph of the Fort Wingate Bearettes. Pictured are Edith James, Elouise Johnson, Irene Harrison, Leta Garcia, Betty Nez, Cora James, Nancy Watchman, Irma Harrison, Rachel Shack, and Sara Begay.

89. Peterson Zah press release, "Peterson Zah: A Profile of a Navajo Leader," 15 March 1988, PIPC.

90. George M. Lubick, "Peterson Zah: A Progressive Outlook and a Traditional Style," in Moses and Wilson, *Indian Lives*, 190–206.

91. *Arizona Republic*, 4 November 1982; Peter MacDonald, "Navajo Nationhood: The Time of Emergence (The MacDonald Years)," statement to the Navajo Tribal Council, 22 December 1982, PIPC.

92. MacDonald, "Navajo Nationhood."

CHAPTER 8

1. Betty Reid, "Returning to the Flock," *Arizona Republic*, 9 May 1999.

2. "Unincorporated Communities, Population Growth, 1990–2000," available at: http://www.azcentral.com/news/census_poprural, accessed on 3 March 2002; Associated Press wire story on Indian communities and the 2000 census, 31 March 2001, *Tucson Citizen*.

3. "Unincorporated Communities;" Associated Press wire story, 31 March 2001, *Tucson Citizen*; Betty Reid, "Look at Lukachukai," *Arizona Republic*, 10 March 2001.

4. Deenise Becenti, "Gang Violence Leaves Two Dead," *Navajo Nation Today*, 21–27 August 1991.

5. Navajoland Tourism Department, "Discover Navajoland," Navajoland Visitor's Guide (Window Rock, Ariz., n.d.), PIPC. For a thoughtful overview of the Navajo forests, see Patrick Gordon Pynes, "Erosion Extraction, Reciprocation: An Ethno/Environmental History of the Navajo Nation's Ponderosa Pine Forests" (Ph.D. diss., University of New Mexico, 2000).

6. Navajoland Tourism Department, "Discover Navajoland"; Pynes, "Erosion Extraction"; Many Farms Inn brochure (Many Farms High School, Many Farms, Ariz.), PIPC.

7. See Coyote Pass Hospitality website, available at http://ourworld.compuserve.com/cppage.htm (accessed on 3 March 2002).

8. Monty Roessel, "Where Are the Trading Posts?" *Navajo Nation Today*, 24–30 September 1991.

9. Alice Kaufman, "'New' Grey Hills: A Weaving Revolution," *New Mexico Magazine*, August 2000, 76–81; Nancy Watson, "Mark Winters—An Indian Trader with a Vision," *The Indian Trader*, July 2000, 5–7; Mark Winter, conversations with Peter Iverson, Toadlena, N.Mex., Santa Fe, N.Mex., Mesa, Ariz., 1996–2000; observations by Iverson during visits to Toadlena Trading Post.

10. Bruce Burnham, conversations with Peter Iverson, Tucson, Ariz., Snowflake, Ariz., Prescott, Ariz., 1998–2000; Bill Malone, conversations with Peter Iverson, Ganado, Ariz., 1998–2000; Iverson, visits to Hubbell Trading Post, Arizona, 1996–2001; Steve Getzwiller, conversations with Peter Iverson, 1999–2002; Iverson, visits to Getzwiller home in Benson, Ariz., 1999–2002; Iverson, visits to Crownpoint rug auctions, 1998–2001.

11. Larry Di Giovanni, "Navajo Gambling Before U.S. Indian Gaming Commission," *Gallup Independent*, 7 December 2001; Brenda Norrell, "To'hajiilee Seeks Aid at Gaming Convention," *Navajo Times*, 27 December 2001.

12. George Joe, "The Beginning: The Story of an Effort to Achieve Self-Governance," in Kayenta Township Commission, *The Township Project, Fourteen Years Later: 1985–1999* (Kayenta, Ariz.: Kayenta Township Commission, 1999). Years ago Lakota scholar

Vine Deloria, Jr., expressed his annoyance at "red tape." He insisted "white tape" was a far more appropriate term.

13. Jerry Kammer, "Regulatory Dead Hand Stifles Commerce," *Arizona Republic,* 17 September 1993.
14. "Chronology of Key Events," in Kayenta Township Commission, *The Township Project.*
15. Ibid.; Gerald P. Knowles, *Kayenta Township Pilot Project: Five-Year Report* (Kayenta, Ariz.: Kayenta Planning Board, January 1991); Electa Draper, "For Navajos, Kayenta an Experiment in Civics," *Denver Post,* 5 August 2001.
16. Bill Donovan, "Navajo Ranchers Told of Drought: Tribal Officials Issue Alert on Need to Reduce Herds," *Arizona Republic,* 24 May 1999.
17. Reid, "Returning to the Flock."
18. Bruce Cory, "A New Generation of Navajos," *New York Times Magazine,* 18 November 1984.
19. Ibid.; Talli Nauman, "Peterson Zah Changes Style of Leadership," *Albuquerque Journal,* 8 January 1984; Susan Landon, "A Tough Race Gets Tougher," *Albuquerque Journal,* 26 October 1986; Peterson Zah, presentation to a class taught by Iverson, Arizona State University, Tempe, 12 April 1996. Sidney and Zah both recalled the old school song, "Onward Phoenix" (modeled after "On Wisconsin"). Sidney even sang its opening lines at a conference in Tempe some years ago.
20. Landon, "A Tough Race."
21. Patrice Locke, "MacDonald Scores Landslide Victory Over Zah in Primary," *Albuquerque Journal,* 14 August 1986.
22. Susan Landon, "Zah, MacDonald Exchange Barbs," *Albuquerque Journal,* 23 October 1986.
23. Sandy Tolan, "Showdown at Window Rock," *New York Times Magazine,* 26 November 1989.
24. Duane Beyal, "Peterson Zah: A Profile of a Navajo Leader" (Zah campaign release), 1986, PIPC.
25. Susan Landon, "Navajo Chairman Sworn In," *Albuquerque Journal,* 14 January 1987.
26. United States Commission on Civil Rights, *Enforcement of Indian Civil Liberties Act: Hearing Held in Flagstaff, Arizona, August 13–14 1987* (Washington, D.C.: Government Printing Office, 1988), 194.
27. Ibid., 186–87.
28. Ibid., 176, 185.
29. Ibid., 180, 183; Patrice Locke, "MacDonald's Office Shuts Down Navajo Times," *Albuquerque Journal,* 20 February 1987; Patrice Locke, "Navajo Paper's Closing Called Political Move," *Albuquerque Journal,* 21 February 1987.
30. United States Commission on Civil Rights, *Enforcement of Indian Civil Liberties Act,* 176–82. See also Tim Giago, "Free Press Isn't When Tribal Government Bought, Paid For It," *Albuquerque Journal,* 7 March 1987.
31. Susan Landon, "Big Boquillas: How a Whirlwind Land Deal Turned into a Tribal Storm," *Albuquerque Journal,* 5 March 1989.
32. Tolan, "Showdown."
33. Landon, "Big Boquillas."
34. Susan Landon, "Arizona Ranch Purchase Stirs Navajo Controversy," *Albuquerque Journal,* 23 August 1987.
35. Tolan, "Showdown." Bill Donovan wrote at the beginning of his review of the top news stories for 1987: "Regardless of how one feels about the leadership of Peter MacDonald, his years as chairman will never be viewed by future historians as dull" (*Navajo Times,* 31 December 1987).
36. Susan Landon, "Tribe Picks Hospital Designer: MacDonald Names Cousin's Firm To Plan Shiprock Facility," *Albuquerque Journal,* 21 January 1988; Susan Landon, "Tribe's Hospital Choice Ranked Third, Source Says," *Albuquerque Journal,* 22 January 1988.
37. Mark N. Trahant and Mark Shaffer, "Extravagance, Hint of Scandal Mark MacDonald's Leadership: Navajo Leader Beset by Critics, Federal Probe," *Arizona Republic,* 15 January 1989.
38. Ibid.
39. Landon, "Big Boquillas."

40. Mark N. Trahant, Charles Kelly, and Carol Sowers, "Navajo Leader's Son 'Entangled': Fresh Law Career on Line in Probe of Dad's Dealings," *Arizona Republic,* 22 February 1989.
41. Ibid.
42. Anne Q. Hoy, "Tribal Head Got Ranch Payoff, Panel Told; Secret Tapes of Realty Agent Reveal Dealings," *Arizona Republic,* 8 February 1989; Susan Landon, "Broker Discloses Secret Ranch Deal: Brown Says MacDonald Was to Share Profits," *Albuquerque Journal,* 8 February 1989.
43. Bill Donovan, "Navajo Leader Admits Taking Contractor Gifts: 'No Different' From Lawmaker Fees For Talks," *Arizona Republic,* 9 February 1989.
44. Peter MacDonald, "Navajo Leader Disputes Charges of Greed, Corruption," *Albuquerque Tribune,* 14 February 1989; Peterson Zah, "MacDonald Has Only Himself to Blame," *Albuquerque Journal,* 14 February 1989.
45. Susan Landon, "Chairman Sought Gifts, Witness Says: Contractor Tells of Loans to MacDonald," *Albuquerque Journal,* 3 February 1989.
46. Gina Binole, "Navajo Bribe Alleged: Businessman Says He Paid Tribal Chairman," *Albuquerque Tribune,* 2 February 1989.
47. Susan Landon, "Embattled MacDonald Steps Down," *Albuquerque Journal,* 17 February 1989; Susan Landon, "Council Puts MacDonald on Leave," *Albuquerque Journal,* 18 February 1989; Susan Landon, "Tribal Court Kills Order Reinstating MacDonald: Navajo Chairman Put Out of Office Again," *Albuquerque Tribune,* 25 February 1989; Susan Landon, "MacDonald Supporters Obey Order to Leave," *Albuquerque Tribune,* 20 April 1989; Mark N. Trahant, "Police and Politics: The Trial of Patrick Platero," *Navajo Nation Today,* 6–12 November 1991.
48. Mark N. Trahant, "July 20: Navajo Riots Remembered," *Navajo Nation Today,* 24–30 July 1991.
49. Ibid.
50. Ibid.
51. Ibid.
52. LeNora Begay, "Feds Indict 32 for 1989 Riots," *Navajo Nation Today,* 31 July–6 August 1991.
53. Wilkins, *Navajo Political Experience,* 214–16; Jim Maniaci, "Navajo Leaders Urge Forgiveness: MacDonald Case Spurs Plea For Healing," *Gallup Independent,* 23 January 2001.
54. Maniaci, "Navajo Leaders."
55. Wilkins, *Navajo Political Experience,* 129–35. See also Office of Navajo Government Development, *Navajo Nation Government* (Window Rock: Navajo Nation, 1998).
56. Various issues of the *Navajo Times,* 1998–2001.
57. Orit Tamir, "Assessing the Success and Failure of Navajo Relocation, *Human Organization* 59, no. 2 (2000): 267–71; Tamir, "What Happened to Navajo Relocatees from Hopi Partition Lands in Pinon?" *American Indian Culture and Research Journal* 23, no. 4 (1999): 81–82.
58. Tamir, "What Happened to Navajo Relocatees," 82–83.
59. Ibid., 84–88; Jim Maniaci, "Navajos on Hopi Land to Get Aid," *Gallup Independent,* 10 September 2001.
60. Marley Shebala, "Nation to Pay Hopis $29 Million Settlement for Land Use, Damages," *Gallup Independent,* 13 January 2000; David Brugge, "The Navajo and Hopi Land Dispute from Historic Through Contemporary Times," in *Native Peoples of the Southwest: Negotiating Land, Water, and Ethnicities,* ed. Laurie Weinstein (Westport, Conn.: Bergin & Garvey, 2001), 179–202.
61. "First Woman Selected as President of Dine College," *Gallup Independent,* 20 July 2000.
62. *Navajo Nation Today,* 10–16 July 1991.
63. Bob Roessel, Ruth Roessel, and Monty Roessel, conversations with Peter Iverson, Rough Rock and Chinle, Ariz., 1999–2002.
64. School materials developed at Seba Dalkai School, Winslow, Arizona, 1998–2001, PIPC.
65. Jerry Kammer, "The Spirits of the Chess Board," *Arizona Republic,* 19 September 1993.
66. *Navajo Nation Today,* 14–20 April 1991.

67. Jennifer Nez Denetdale, "The Long Walk: A Response to an Amateur Historian," *Navajo Times*, 8 March 2001.

68. *A Weave of Time* (1987) documents continuity and change in Navajo life and features members of the Burnsides/Myers family of Pine Springs. It includes some wonderful early film shots by anthropologist John Adair in the late 1930s and early 1940s.

69. Glojean Todacheene, conversations with Peter Iverson, Toadlena and Farmington, N.Mex., 1997–2001; "A (Local) Doctor In The House," special edition of the *Navajo Times*, Window Rock, Ariz., 1996.

70. Carolyn Niethammer supports this generalization in *I'll Go and Do More*, her recent biography of Annie Wauneka.

71. Marley Shebala, "Charge of Sexism Rings Through Chamber," *Navajo Times*, 27 July 1995.

72. "Who Has Voting Power? Navajo Women!" *Navajo Times*, 4 September 1997; Deenise Becenti, "Women Tout Leadership Abilities," *Navajo Times*, 20 February 1997; "One Day Session to Focus on Women in Politics," *Navajo Times*, 13 February 1997; Marley Shebala, "Navajo Women Prepare to Enter Political Arena," *Navajo Times*, 8 January 1998.

73. Marley Shebala, "Navajo Women to Share, Explore Ideas and Concerns at Gathering," *Navajo Times*, 11 April 1996.

74. Betty Reid, "Navajo Woman Takes to the Skies," *Arizona Republic*, 14 May 2000.

75. Deenise Becenti, "No Walk, No Run, No Good," *Navajo Nation Today*, 24–30 September 1991.

76. Wade Davies, *Healing Ways*, 154–57.

77. Ibid., 161–69.

78. Doug Brugge, a research scientist, worked for years with Navajos from the affected communities on an oral history project relating the experiences of the uranium miners.

79. Davies, *Healing Ways*, 169–73.

80. Ibid., 193–200.

81. Bill Donovan, "Not Enough Medicine Men," *Arizona Republic*, 21 December 1999.

82. Jerry Kammer, "Peyote Opens 'Access to God,'" *Arizona Republic*, 19 September 1993; Davies, *Healing Ways*, 183.

83. Oree Foster, "Lady Broncos Make History," *Navajo Times*, 8 March 2001. The information on past tournaments is based on a program for the Arizona 3A boys and girls championships. Oree Foster, "How Sweet It Is! St. Michael Lady Cardinals End Banner Season with State Crown," *Navajo Times*, 24 February 2000.

84. Jerry Kammer, "New, Unifying Ritual: 'Rezball,'" *Arizona Republic*, 19 September 1993.

85. Ibid.; Carolyn Calvin, "ASU Basketball Star Picked Up Sport at 4 Years Old," *Navajo Nation Today*, 18–31 December 1991.

86. Gary Fox, "Air Force Slips Past NAU," *Arizona Republic*, 3 January 2002.

87. Peter Iverson is the Anglo visitor; this description is drawn from Iverson, *Riders of the West*.

88. Iverson, *Riders of the West;* Indian National Finals Rodeo programs, 1986, 1997–1999, PIPC.

89. Iverson, *Riders of the West;* Carole Nez, "Bucking the Odds: Rodeo Traditions Keep Children Riding Straight," *New Mexico Magazine*, August 1992, 40.

90. Tapahonso, *Sáanii Dahataal*, x, 15, 92; Tapahonso, *Blue Horses Rush In*, 39–42; Jo Ann Baldinger, "Navajo Poet: Tapahonso Holds Home in Her Heart," *New Mexico Magazine*, August 1992, 34; Tapahonso and Emerson, *Songs of Shiprock Fair;* Luci Tapahonso, conversations with Peter Iverson, 1995–2001.

91. Emerson Gallery website at http://www.emersongallery.com, accessed on 3 March 2002; Tapahonso and Emerson, *Songs of Shiprock Fair;* Anthony Chee Emerson, conversations with Peter Iverson, 1999–2002.

92. Hedlund, *Reflections of the Weaver's World*, 30.

93. Bill Beaver, interview by Bradley Cole, 25 January 2000, United Indian Traders Association Oral History Project, Special Collections, Cline Library, Northern Arizona University, Flagstaff; Alice Cling, conversations with Peter Iverson, 1997–2001.

94. Lois Essary Jacka, *David Johns: On The Trail of Beauty* (Flagstaff, Ariz.: Northland,

1991), 2, 22, 29–38. This discussion of Johns's work is based on Jacka's excellent description and analysis.

95. Ibid., 46–49, 57, 59, 62. Jacka uses a similar ending for her chapter on the mural.

CONCLUSION

1. Betty Reid, "Navajo Code Talkers to Be Honored for WWII Role," *Arizona Republic,* 25 July 2001; Associated Press, "A Tribute To Twenty-Nine Marines," *Arizona Republic,* 27 July 2001; Senator Jeff Bingaman website at http://bingaman.senate.gov/code_talkers/.
2. Susan Brown McGreevy and D. Y. Begay, *The Image Weavers: Contemporary Navajo Pictorial Textiles* (Santa Fe, N.Mex.: Wheelwright Museum, 1994).
3. Harry Walters, conversation with Peter Iverson, Tsaile, Ariz., 26 June 1999.
4. This discussion is based on Iverson's attendance at the 3A state championship games in Phoenix, Ariz., 21 February 2001. The Tuba City girls' team won its third consecutive state championship on 23 February 2002, defeating Chandler's Seton Catholic, 42–32. Coolidge took the boys' title, capping an undefeated season by edging Globe 50–47.
5. Robert Yazzie, "Navajo Justice," *Yes! A Journal of Positive Futures,* fall 2000, available at http://www.futurenet.org/15prisons/yazzie.htm, accessed on 3 March 2002; James W. Zion, "The Dynamics of Navajo Peacemaking," *Journal of Contemporary Criminal Justice* 14, no. 1 (1998): 58–74; Howard Brown, presentation to Iverson seminar on twentieth-century American Indian history, Arizona State University, Tempe, 7 November 2001.
6. Wilkins, *The Navajo Political Experience,* xxv.
7. Evangeline Parsons Yazzie, presentation, Navajo Treaty Day Commemorative Program, 1 June 1999, Flagstaff (notes of presentation recorded by Iverson).
8. Laura Tohe, presentation, Navajo Treaty Day Commemorative Program, 1 June 1999, Flagstaff (notes of presentation recorded by Iverson).

Selected Readings

This book is based mostly on original research in primary sources, but it has been informed by an enormous secondary literature. A portion of that literature is presented here. Many of these selections could be placed in more than one category, but are only listed once below. Because of space limitations, only books are included.

ANTHROPOLOGICAL, ARCHAEOLOGICAL, AND HISTORICAL OVERVIEWS

Acrey, Bill. *Navajo History: The Land and the People*. Shiprock, N.Mex.: Central Consolidated School District Number 22, 1979.

Bailey, Garrick, and Roberta Glenn Bailey. *A History of the Navajos:The Reservation Years*. Santa Fe, N.Mex.: School of American Research Press, 1986.

Basso, Keith, and Morris E. Opler, eds. *Apachean Culture History and Ethnology*. Tucson: University of Arizona Press, 1971.

Benally, Clyde. *Dinéjí Nákéé' Nááahane'—A Utah Navajo History*. Monticello, Utah: San Juan School District, 1982.

Bender, Norman J. *"New Hope for the Indians": The Grant Peace Policy and the Navajos in the 1870s*. Albuquerque: University of New Mexico Press, 1989.

Boyce, George A. *When the Navajos Had Too Many Sheep:The 1940s*. San Francisco: Indian Historian Press, 1974.

Coolidge, Mary Roberts, and Dane Coolidge. *The Navajo Indians*. Boston: Houghton Mifflin, 1930.

Correll, J. Lee, ed. *Through White Men's Eyes: A Contribution to Navajo History: A Chronological Record of the Navajo People from Earliest Times to the Treaty of June 1, 1868*. 6 vols. Window Rock, Ariz.: Navajo Heritage Center, 1979.

Downs, James F. *The Navajo*. New York: Holt, Rinehart, and Winston, 1972.

Duran, Meliha, and David T. Kirkpatrick, eds. *Diné Bikéyah: Papers in Honor of David M. Brugge*. Vol. 24. Albuquerque: Archaeological Society of New Mexico, 1998.

Eck, Norman K. *Contemporary Navajo Affairs*. Rough Rock, Ariz.: Navajo Curriculum Center, Rough Rock Demonstration School, 1982.

Forbes, Jack D. *Apache, Navaho, and Spaniard*. Norman: University of Oklahoma Press, 1960.

Hall, Thomas D. *Social Change in the Southwest, 1350–1880*. Lawrence: University Press of Kansas, 1988.

Hendricks, Rick, and John P. Wilson, eds. *The Navajos in 1705: Roque Madrid's Campaign Journal*. Albuquerque: University of New Mexico Press, 1996.

Iverson, Peter. *The Navajo Nation*. Albuquerque: University of New Mexico Press, 1983.

———. *The Navajos*. New York: Chelsea House, 1990.

Kelly, Lawrence C. *The Navajo Indians and Federal Policy, 1900–1935*. Tucson: University of Arizona Press, 1968.

Kluckhohn, Clyde, W. W. Hill, and Lucy Wales Kluckhohn. *Navaho Material Culture.* Cambridge, Mass.: Belknap Press of Harvard University Press, 1971.
Kluckhohn, Clyde, and Dorothea Leighton. *The Navaho.* Cambridge, Mass.: Harvard University Press, 1946.
Link, Martin, ed. *Navajo: A Century of Progress.* Window Rock: Navajo Tribe, 1968.
McPherson, Robert S. *The Northern Navajo Frontier: Expansion Through Adversity, 1860–1900.* Albuquerque: University of New Mexico Press, 1988.
———. *Navajo Land, Navajo Culture: The Utah Experience in the Twentieth Century.* Norman: University of Oklahoma Press, 2001.
Moore, William Haas. *Chiefs, Agents, and Soldiers: Conflict on the Navajo Frontier, 1868–1882.* Albuquerque: University of New Mexico Press, 1994.
Ortiz, Alfonso, ed. *Southwest.* Vol. 9, *Handbook of North American Indians.* Washington, D.C.: Smithsonian Institution, 1979.
Parman, Donald L. *The Navajos and the New Deal.* New Haven, Conn.: Yale University Press, 1976.
Roessel, Robert A., Jr. *Dinetah: Navajo History.* Vol. 2. Rough Rock, Ariz.: Navajo Curriculum Center, Rough Rock Demonstration School, 1983.
Sánchez, George I. *"The People": A Study of the Navajos.* Lawrence, Kans.: U.S. Indian Service, 1948.
Schaafsma, Curtis. *Apaches de Navajo: Seventeenth-Century Navajos in the Chama Valley of New Mexico.* Salt Lake City: University of Utah Press, 2002.
Towner, Ronald H., ed. *The Archaeology of Navajo Origins.* Salt Lake City: University of Utah Press, 1996.
Underhill, Ruth. *Here Come the Navaho!* Lawrence, Kans.: U.S. Indian Service, 1953.
———. *The Navajos.* Norman: University of Oklahoma Press, 1956.
Van Valkenburgh, Richard F. *A Short History of the Navajo People.* Window Rock, Ariz.: Navajo Service, 1938.
Young, Robert W. *The Role of the Navajo in the Southwestern Drama.* Gallup, N.Mex.: Gallup Independent, 1968.

AGRICULTURE AND RANCHING

Bailey, Lynn R. *If You Take My Sheep: The Evolution and Conflicts of Navajo Pastoralism, 1630–1868.* Pasadena, Calif.: Westernlore Publications, 1980.
Bingham, Sam, and Janet Bingham. *Navajo Farming.* Rock Point, Ariz.: Rock Point Community School, 1987.
Downs, James F. *Animal Husbandry in Navajo Society and Culture.* Berkeley: University of California Press, 1964.
Hill, W. W. *The Agricultural and Hunting Methods of the Navaho Indians.* New Haven, Conn.: Yale University Press, 1938.
Kelley, Klara Bonsack. *Navajo Land Use: An Ethnoarchaeological Study.* New York: Academic Press, 1986.
Kelley, Klara, and Peter M. Whiteley. *Navajoland: Family and Settlement and Land Use.* Tsaile, Ariz.: Navajo Community College Press, 1989.
Ward, Elizabeth. *No Dudes, Few Women: Life with a Navajo Range Rider.* Albuquerque: University of New Mexico Press, 1951.
Weisiger, Marsha. *"Sheep Dreams: Environment, Cultural Identity, and Gender in Navajo Country."* Ph.D. diss., University of Wisconsin-Madison, 1998.
White, Richard. *The Roots of Dependency: Subsistence, Environment, and Social Change Among the Choctaws, Pawnees, and Navajos.* Lincoln: University of Nebraska Press, 1983.
Wood, John J., Walter M. Vannette, and Michael J. Andrews. *"Sheep Is Life": An Assessment of Livestock Reduction in the Former Navajo-Hopi Joint Use Area.* Anthropological Paper No. 1. Flagstaff: Northern Arizona University, 1982.

ARCHITECTURE

Carlson, Roy. *Eighteenth-Century Navajo Fortresses of the Governador District.* Studies in Anthropology. Boulder: University of Colorado, 1965.

Jett, Stephen C. and Virginia E. Spencer. *Navajo Architecture: Forms, History, Distribution.* Tucson: University of Arizona Press, 1981.

McAllester, David P. *Hogans: Navajo Houses and House Songs.* Middletown, Conn.: Wesleyan University Press, 1980.

Powers, Margaret A., and Byron P. Johnson. *Defensive Sites of Dinetah.* Albuquerque, N.Mex.: Bureau of Land Management, 1987.

BIBLIOGRAPHY

Bahr, Howard. *Diné Bibliography to the 1990s: A Companion to the Navajo Tribal Bibliography of 1969.* Lanham, Md.: Scarecrow Press, 1999.

Correll, J. Lee, David M. Brugge, and Editha L. Watson. *Navajo Bibliography With Subject Index.* Rev. ed. Window Rock, Ariz.: Navajo Tribal Research Section, 1974.

Iverson, Peter. *The Navajos: A Critical Bibliography.* Bloomington: Indiana University Press, 1976.

BIOGRAPHY, AUTOBIOGRAPHY, AND LIFE HISTORY

Alvord, Lori Arviso, with Elizabeth Cohen Van Pelt. *The Scalpel and the Silver Bear: The First Navajo Woman Surgeon Combines Western Medicine with Traditional Healing.* New York: Bantam, 1999.

Bennett, Kay. *Kaibah: Recollections of a Navajo Girlhood.* Los Angeles: Westernlore Press, 1964.

Bighorse, Tiana. *Bighorse the Warrior.* Edited by Noel Bennett. Tucson: University of Arizona Press, 1990.

Dyk, Walter. *Son of Old Man Hat.* Lincoln: University of Nebraska Press, 1938.

Dyk, Walter and Ruth Dyk. *Left Handed: A Navajo Autobiography.* New York: Columbia University Press, 1980.

Hoffman, Virginia, and Broderick H. Johnson. *Navajo Biographies.* Rough Rock, Ariz.: Rough Rock Demonstration School, 1970.

MacDonald, Peter, with Ted Schwarz. *The Last Warrior: Peter MacDonald and the Navajo Nation.* New York: Orion Books, 1993.

McPherson, Robert S., ed. *The Journey of Navajo Oshley: An Autobiography and Life History.* Logan: Utah State University Press, 2000.

Mitchell, Emerson Barney Blackhorse. *Miracle Hill: The Story of a Navajo Childhood.* Norman: University of Oklahoma Press, 1967.

Mitchell, Frank. *Navajo Blessingway Singer: The Autobiography of Frank Mitchell, 1881–1967.* Edited by Charlotte J. Frisbie and David McAllister. Tucson: University of Arizona Press, 1978.

Mitchell, Rose. *Tall Woman: The Life Story of Rose Mitchell, A Navajo Woman, c. 1874–1977.* Edited by Charlotte J. Frisbie. Albuquerque: University of New Mexico Press, 2001.

Moses, L. G., and Raymond Wilson, eds. *Indian Lives: Essays on Nineteenth- and Twentieth-Century Native American Leaders.* Albuquerque: University of New Mexico Press, 1993.

Newcomb, Franc J. *Hosteen Klah: Navajo Medicine Man and Sand Painter.* Norman: University of Oklahoma Press, 1964.

Niethammer, Carolyn. *I'll Go and Do More: Annie Dodge Wauneka, Navajo Leader and Activist.* Lincoln: University of Nebraska Press, 2001.

Stewart, Irene. *A Voice in Her Tribe: A Navajo Woman's Own Story.* Edited by Doris Ostrander Dowdy. Socorro, N.Mex.: Ballena Press, 1980.

DEMOGRAPHY

Goodman, James M. *The Navajo Atlas: Environments, Resources, People, and History of the Diné Bikéyah.* Norman: University of Oklahoma Press, 1982.

Hodge, William H. *The Albuquerque Navajos.* Tucson: University of Arizona Press, 1969.

Howard, Cheryl. *Navajo Tribal Demography, 1983–1986: A Comparative and Historical Perspective.* New York: Garland, 1993.

Johnston, Denis Foster. *An Analysis of Sources of Information on the Population of the Navaho.* Washington, D.C.: Bureau of American Ethnology, 1966.

ECONOMY

Ambler, Marjane. *Breaking the Iron Bonds: Indian Control of Energy Development.* Lawrence: University Press of Kansas, 1990.

Chamberlain, Kathleen P. *Under Sacred Ground: A History of Navajo Oil.* Albuquerque: University of New Mexico Press, 2000.

Eachstaedt, Peter. *If You Poison Us: Uranium and Native Americans.* Santa Fe, N.Mex.: Red Crane Books, 1994.

Gilbreath, Kent. *Red Capitalism: An Analysis of the Navajo Economy.* Norman: University of Oklahoma Press, 1973.

Howard, Kathleen L., and Diana F. Pardue. *Inventing the Southwest: The Fred Harvey Company and Native American Art.* Flagstaff, Ariz.: Northland, 1996.

Ortiz, Roxanne Dunbar, ed. *American Indian Energy Resources and Development.* Native American Studies. Albuquerque: University of New Mexico, 1980.

Reno, Philip. *Mother Earth, Father Sky: Navajo Resources and Economic Development.* Albuquerque: University of New Mexico Press, 1981.

Trahant, LeNora Begay. *The Success of the Navajo Arts and Crafts Enterprises: A Retail Success Story.* Photographs by Monty Roessel. New York: Walker and Company, 1996.

EDUCATION

Connell-Szasz, Margaret. *Education and the American Indian: The Road to Self-Determination Since 1928.* 3d ed. Albuquerque: University of New Mexico Press, 2000.

Coombs, L. Madison. *Doorway Toward the Light: The Story of the Special Navajo Education Program.* Brigham City, Utah: Bureau of Indian Affairs, 1962.

Johnson, Broderick. *Navaho Education at Rough Rock.* Rough Rock, Ariz.: Rough Rock Demonstration School, 1968.

Leighton, Dorothea, and Clyde Kluckhohn. *Children of the People: The Navaho Individual and His Development.* Cambridge, Mass.: Harvard University Press, 1947.

Reyhner, Jon, Joseph Martin, Louise Lockard, and W. Sakiestewa Gilbert, eds. *Learn in Beauty: Indigenous Education for a New Century.* Flagstaff: Northern Arizona University Center for Excellence in Education, 2000.

Roessel, Robert A., Jr. *Indian Communities in Action.* Tempe: Arizona State University, 1967.
———. *Navajo Education, 1948–1978.* Rough Rock, Ariz.: Navajo Curriculum Center, Rough Rock Demonstration School, 1979.

Thompson, Hildegard. *The Navajos' Long Walk for Education: A History of Navajo Education.* Tsaile, Ariz.: Navajo Community College Press, 1975.

Young, Robert W., ed. *The Navajo Yearbook: A Decade of Progress, 1951–1961.* Vol. 8. Window Rock: Bureau of Indian Affairs, 1961.

GENDER

Benedek, Emily. *Beyond the Four Corners of the World: A Navajo Woman's Journey.* New York: Alfred A. Knopf, 1995.

Denetdale, Jennifer Nez. "Remembering Juanita Through Navajo Oral Tradition: Out of the Shadow of Chief Manuelito." Ph.D. diss., Northern Arizona University, 1999.

McCullough-Brabson, Ellen, and Marilyn Help. *We'll Be In Your Mountains, We'll Be In Your Songs: A Navajo Woman Sings.* Albuquerque: University of New Mexico Press, 2001.

Reichard, Gladys A. *Dezba: Woman of the Desert.* New York: J. J. Augustin, 1939.

Roessel, Ruth. *Women in Navajo Society.* Rough Rock, Ariz.: Navajo Resource Center, Rough Rock Demonstration School, 1981.

Schweitzer, Marjorie M., ed. *American Indian Grandmothers: Traditions and Transitions.* Albuquerque: University of New Mexico Press, 1999.

Witherspoon, Gary. *Navajo Kinship and Marriage.* Chicago: University of Chicago Press, 197

GEOLOGY

Baars, Donald L. *Navajo Country: A Geological and Natural History of the Four Corners Region.* Albuquerque: University of New Mexico Press, 1995.

GOVERNMENT

Bingham, Sam, and Janet Bingham. *Navajo Chapters.* Rev. ed. Tsaile, Ariz.: Navajo Community College Press, 1987.

Philp, Kenneth R. *John Collier's Crusade for Indian Reform, 1920–1954.* Tucson: University of Arizona Press, 1977.

Shepardson, Mary. *Navajo Ways in Government: A Study in Political Process.* Menasha, Wisc.: American Anthropological Association, 1963.

Wilkins, David E. *The Navajo Political Experience.* Tsaile, Ariz.: Diné College Press, 1999.

Williams, Aubrey W. *Navajo Political Process.* Washington, D.C.: Smithsonian Institution Press, 1970.

Young, Robert W. *A Political History of the Navajo Tribe.* Tsaile, Ariz.: Navajo Community College Press, 1978.

HEALTH CARE

Adair, John, Kurt W. Deuschle, and Clifford R. Barnett. *The People's Health: Anthropology and Medicine in a Navajo Community.* Rev. ed. Albuquerque: University of New Mexico Press, 1988.

Davies, Wade. *Healing Ways: Navajo Health Care in the Twentieth Century.* Albuquerque: University of New Mexico Press, 2001.

Kane, Robert L., and Rosalie A. Kane. *Federal Health Care (With Reservations!).* New York: Spring, 1972.

Trennert, Robert. *White Man's Medicine: Government Doctors and the Navajo, 1863–1955.* Albuquerque: University of New Mexico Press, 1998.

LANGUAGE

Franciscans, St. Michaels, Ariz. *An Ethnologic Dictionary of the Navaho Language.* Saint Michaels, Ariz.: Franciscan Fathers, 1910.

Goossen, Irvy W. *Diné Bizaad: Speak, Read, Write Navajo.* Flagstaff, Ariz.: Salina Bookshelf, 1995.

House, Deborah. *Language Shift Among the Navajos: Identity Politics and Cultural Continuity.* Tucson: University of Arizona Press, 2002.

Jelinek, Eloulse, Sally Midgette, Keren Rice, and Leslie Saxon, eds. *Athabaskan Language Studies: Essays in Honor of Robert W. Young.* Albuquerque: University of New Mexico Press, 1996.

McLaughlin, Daniel. *When Literacy Empowers: Navajo Language in Print.* Albuquerque: University of New Mexico Press, 1992.

Neuendorf, Alice. *Atchini Binaaltsoostsoh: A Navajo/English Bilingual Dictionary.* Albuquerque: Native American Materials Development Center, 1983.

Parnwell, E. C. *The New Oxford Picture Dictionary: English/Navajo.* Translated by Marvin Yellowhair. New York: Oxford University Press, 1989.

Platero, Paul, et al. *Diné Bizaad Bee Na'adzo: A Navajo Language Literacy and Grammar Text.* Farmington, N.Mex.: Navajo Academy, 1986.

Witherspoon, Gary. *Language and Art in the Navajo Universe.* Ann Arbor: University of Michigan Press, 1977.

Young, Robert W., and William Morgan, Sr. *Analytical Lexicon of Navajo.* Albuquerque: University of New Mexico Press, 1982.

———. *The Navajo Language: A Grammar and Colloquial Dictionary.* 2d ed. Albuquerque: University of New Mexico Press, 1987.

MIGRATION

Hester, James J. *Early Navajo Migrations and Acculturation in the Southwest.* Santa Fe: Museum of New Mexico, 1962.

NAVAJO STUDIES PROCEEDINGS

Piper, June-el, ed. *Diné Baa Hane Bi Naaltsoos: Collected Papers from the Seventh Through Tenth Navajo Studies Conferences.* Window Rock, Ariz.: Navajo Nation Historic Preservation Department, 1999.

Piper, June-el, Alexandra Roberts, and Jenevieve Smith, eds. *Papers from the Third, Fourth, and Sixth Navajo Studies Conferences.* Window Rock, Ariz.: Navajo National Historic Preservation Department, 1993.

ORAL HISTORY

Blue, Martha. *The Witch Purge of 1878: Oral and Documentary History in the Early Reservation Years.* Tsaile, Ariz.: Navajo Community College Press, 1988.

Brugge, Doug, ed. *Memories Come to Us in the Rain and the Wind: Oral Histories and Photographs of Navajo Uranium Miners and Their Families.* Jamaica Plain, Mass.: Red Sun Press, 1997.

Johnson, Broderick H., ed. *Navajos and World War II.* Tsaile, Ariz.: Navajo Community College Press, 1977.

———, ed. *Stories of Traditional Navajo Life and Culture.* Tsaile, Ariz.: Navajo Community College Press, 1977.

Roessel, Ruth, ed. *Navajo Stories of the Long Walk Period.* Tsaile, Ariz.: Navajo Community College Press, 1973.

Roessel, Ruth, and Broderick H. Johnson, eds. *Navajo Livestock Reduction: A National Disgrace.* Tsaile, Ariz.: Navajo Community College Press, 1974.

Young, Robert W., and William Morgan, eds. *Navajo Historical Selections.* Phoenix, Ariz.: Bureau of Indian Affairs, 1954.

———, eds. *The Trouble at Round Rock.* Phoenix, Ariz.: Bureau of Indian Affairs, 1952.

ORIGIN STORIES AND OTHER TRADITIONAL STORIES

Haile, Berard. *Navajo Coyote Tales: The Curly Tó Aheedlíinii Version.* Edited by Karl W. Luckert. Lincoln: University of Nebraska Press, 1990.

Klah, Hosteen. *Navajo Creation Myth: The Story of the Emergence.* Santa Fe, N.Mex.: Museum of Navajo Ceremonial Art, 1942.

Matthews, Washington. *Navajo Legends.* New York: American Folklore Society, 1897.

O'Bryan, Aileen, and Sandoval. *The Diné: Origin Myths of the Navaho Indians.* Washington, D.C.: Bureau of American Ethnology, 1956.

Roessel, Robert A., Jr. and Dillon Platero, eds. *Coyote Stories of the Navaho People.* Rough Rock, Ariz.: Navajo Curriculum Center, Rough Rock Demonstration School, 1968.

Sapir, Edward. *Navaho Texts.* Iowa City, Iowa: Linguistic Society of America, 1942.

Yazzie, Alfred. *Navajo Oral Tradition.* 3 vols. Rough Rock, Ariz.: Rough Rock Demonstration School, 1984.

Yazzie, Ethelou, ed. *Navajo History.* Rough Rock, Ariz.: Rough Rock Demonstration School, 1974.

PHILOSOPHY

Farella, John. *The Main Stalk: A Synthesis of Navajo Philosophy.* Tucson: University of Arizona Press, 1984.

———. *The Wind in a Jar.* Albuquerque: University of New Mexico Press, 1993.

McNeley, James Hale. *Holy Wind in Navajo Philosophy.* Tucson: University of Arizona Press, 1981.

PHOTOGRAPHY

Adair, John, and Sol Worth. *Through Navajo Eyes*. Bloomington: Indiana University Press, 1976.

Doty, C. Stewart, Dale Mudge, and Herbert John Benally. *Photographing Navajos: John Collier, Jr. on the Reservation, 1948–1953*. Albuquerque: University of New Mexico Press, 2002.

Faris, James C. *Navajo and Photography: A Critical History of the Representation of an American People*. Albuquerque: University of New Mexico Press, 1997.

Forrest, Earle R. *With a Camera in Old Navajoland*. Norman: University of Oklahoma Press, 1970.

Gilpin, Laura. *The Enduring Navaho*. Austin: University of Texas Press, 1968.

Grimes, Joel. *Navajo: Portrait of a Nation*. Englewood, Colo.: Westcliffe Publishers, 1992.

Heisey, Adriel, and Kenji Kawano. *In the Fifth World: Portrait of the Navajo Nation*. Tucson, Ariz.: Rio Nuevo, 2001.

Kawano, Kenji, and Carl Gorman. *Warriors: Navajo Code Talkers*. Flagstaff, Ariz.: Northland, 1990.

Long, Paul V. *Big Eyes: The Southwestern Photographs of Simeon Schwemberger, 1902–1908*. Albuquerque: University of New Mexico Press, 1992.

MacCannell, Linda. *Riders of the West: Portraits from Indian Rodeo*. Text by Peter Iverson. Seattle: University of Washington Press, 1999.

Roessel, Robert A., Jr. *Pictorial History of the Navajo From 1860 to 1910*. Rough Rock, Ariz.: Navajo Curriculum Center, Rough Rock Demonstration School, 1980.

POETRY, SHORT STORIES, FICTION, CHILDREN'S LITERATURE

Begay, Shonto. *Navajo: Visions and Voices Across the Mesa*. New York: Scholastic, 1995.

Clark, Ann Nolan. *Little Herder in Autumn*. Illustrated by Hoke Denetsosie. 1940. Reprint, Santa Fe: Ancient City Press, 1988.

Jim, Rex Lee. *Duchas Taa Koo Dine: A Trilingual Poetry Collection in Navajo, Irish, and English*. Beal Feirste, Ireland: An Clochan, 1998.

Morris, Irvin. *From the Glittering World: A Navajo Story*. Norman: University of Oklahoma Press, 1997.

Roessel, Monty. *Kinaaldá: A Navajo Girl Grows Up*. Minneapolis: Lerner Publications, 1993.

———. *Songs from the Loom: A Navajo Girl Learns to Weave*. Minneapolis: Lerner Publications, 1995.

Tapahonso, Luci. *Sáanii Dahataal/The Women Are Singing*. Tucson: University of Arizona Press, 1993.

———. *Blue Horses Rush In*. Tucson: University of Arizona Press, 1997.

———. *Songs of Shiprock Fair*. Illustrated by Anthony Chee Emerson. Walnut, Calif.: Kiva Publishing, 1999.

Tapahonso, Luci, and Eleanor Schick. *Navajo ABC: A Diné Alphabet Book*. New York: Macmillan, 1995.

Tohe, Laura. *No Parole Today*. Albuquerque: West End Press, 1999.

PLACE AND COMMUNITY

Bingham, Sam, and Janet Bingham, eds. *Between Sacred Mountains: Navajo Stories and Lessons from the Land*. Tucson: Sun Tracks and University of Arizona Press, 1984.

Brugge, David M. *A History of the Chaco Navajos*. Washington, D.C.: National Park Service, 1980.

Brugge, David M., and Raymond Wilson. *Administrative History, Canyon de Chelly National Monument*. Washington, D.C.: National Park Service, 1976.

Frink, Maurice. *Fort Defiance and the Navajos*. Boulder, Colo.: Pruett, 1968.

Grant, Campbell. *Canyon de Chelly: Its People and Rock Art*. Tucson: University of Arizona Press, 1978.

Jett, Stephen C. *House of Three Turkeys: Anasazi Redoubt*. Photography by Dave Bohn. Santa Barbara, Calif.: Capra Press, 1977.

————. *Navajo Place Names and Trails of the Canyon de Chelly System*. With the assistance of Chauncey M. Neboyia, William Morgan, Sr., and Robert W. Young. New York: Peter Lang, 2000.

Kelley, Klara Bonsack, and Harris Francis. *Navajo Sacred Places*. Bloomington: Indiana University Press, 1994.

Lamphere, Louise. *To Run After Them: Cultural and Social Bases of Cooperation in a Navajo Community*. Tucson: University of Arizona Press, 1977.

Linford, Laurence D. *Navajo Places: History, Legend, Landscape*. Salt Lake City: University of Utah Press, 2000.

McPherson, Robert S. *Sacred Land, Sacred View: Navajo Perceptions of the Four Corners Region*. Provo, Utah: Brigham Young University Press, 1992.

Sasaki, Tom. *Fruitland, New Mexico: A Navaho Community in Transition*. Ithaca: Cornell University Press, 1960.

Shepardson, Mary, and Blodwen Hammond. *The Navajo Mountain Community*. Berkeley: University of California Press, 1970.

Van Valkenburgh, Richard. *Diné Bikéyah*. Window Rock: U.S. Indian Service, 1941.

Watson, Editha. *Navajo Sacred Places*. Window Rock, Ariz.: Navajo Tribal Museum, 1964.

RELIGION

Aberle, David F. *The Peyote Religion Among the Navaho*. 2d ed. Chicago: University of Chicago Press, 1982.

Begay, Shirley M. *Kinaaldá: A Navajo Puberty Ceremony*. Rev. ed. Rough Rock, Ariz.: Rough Rock Demonstration School, 1983.

Blanchard, Kendall. *The Economics of Sainthood: Religious Change Among the Rimrock Navajos*. Cranbury, N.J.: Associated University Presses, 1977.

Bodo, Murray, ed. *Tales of an Endishodi: Father Berard Haile and the Navajos, 1900–1961*. Albuquerque: University of New Mexico Press, 1999.

Brugge, David M. *Navajos in the Catholic Church Records of New Mexico, 1694–1875*. 2d ed. Tsaile, Ariz.: Navajo Community College Press, 1986.

Brugge, David M., and Charlotte Frisbie, eds. *Navajo Religion and Culture: Selected Views. Papers in Honor of Leland C. Wyman*. Papers in Anthropology. Santa Fe: Museum of New Mexico, 1982.

Faris, James. *The Nightway: A History and a History of Documentation of a Navajo Ceremonial*. Albuquerque: University of New Mexico Press, 1990.

Frisbie, Charlotte J. *Kinaaldá: A Study of the Navaho Girl's Puberty Ceremony*. Reprint with new preface. Salt Lake City: University of Utah Press, 1993.

————. *Navajo Medicine Bundles or Jish: Acquisition, Transmission, and Disposition in the Past and Present*. Albuquerque: University of New Mexico Press, 1987.

Gill, Sam. *Sacred Words: A Study of Navajo Religion and Prayer*. Westport, Conn.: Greenwood Press, 1981.

Griffin-Pierce, Trudy. *Earth Is My Mother, Sky Is My Father: Space, Time, and Astronomy in Navajo Sandpainting*. Albuquerque: University of New Mexico Press, 1992.

Haile, Berard. *Origin Legend of the Navaho Enemy Way*. New Haven, Conn.: Yale University Press, 1938.

————. *Origin Legend of the Navaho Flintway*. Chicago: University of Chicago Press, 1943.

————, Maud Oakes, and Leland C. Wyman. *Beautyway: A Navaho Ceremonial*. New York: Pantheon Books, 1957.

————. *Women versus Men: A Conflict of Navajo Emergence*. Lincoln: University of Nebraska Press, 1981.

————. *Head and Face Masks in Navaho Ceremonialism*. 1947. Reprint, Salt Lake City: University of Utah Press, 1996.

Halpern, Katherine Spencer, and Susan Brown McGreevy, eds. *Washington Matthews: Studies of Navajo Culture, 1880–1894*. Albuquerque: University of New Mexico Press, 1997.

Klah, Hosteen. *Navajo Creation Myth*. Recorded by Mary C. Wheelwright. Santa Fe, N.Mex.: Museum of Navajo Ceremonial Art, 1942.

———. *Myth of Mountain Chant and Myth of Beauty Chant.* Edited by Mary Cabot Wheelwright. Santa Fe, N.Mex.: Museum of Navajo Ceremonial Art, 1951.

Kluckhohn, Clyde. *Navaho Witchcraft.* 1944. Reprint, Boston: Beacon Press, 1967.

Levy, Jerrold E. *In the Beginning: The Navajo Genesis.* Berkeley: University of California Press, 1998.

Luckert, Karl W. *Navajo Mountain and Rainbow Bridge Religion.* Flagstaff: Museum of Northern Arizona Press, 1977.

———. *Coyoteway: A Navajo Holyway Healing Ceremony.* Tucson and Flagstaff: University of Arizona Press and Museum of New Mexico Press, 1979.

Matthews, Washington. *The Mountain Chant: A Navajo Ceremony.* Washington, D.C.: Smithsonian Institution, 1887.

———. *The Night Chant: A Navaho Ceremony.* 1902. Reprint, Salt Lake City: University of Utah Press, 1995.

Newcomb, Franc Johnson. *Navajo Omens and Taboos.* Santa Fe, N.Mex.: Rydal Press, 1940.

Reichard, Gladys. *Navaho Religion.* Princeton, N.J.: Princeton University Press, 1950.

Spencer, Katherine. *Mythology and Values: An Analysis of Navaho Chantway Myths.* Philadelphia: American Folklore Society, 1957.

Wheelwright, Mary Cabot. *Hail Chant and Water Chant.* Santa Fe, N.Mex.: Museum of Navajo Ceremonial Art, 1946.

———. *Wind Chant and Feather Chant.* Santa Fe, N.Mex.: Museum of Navajo Ceremonial Art, 1946.

———, ed. *Emergence Myth According to the Hanelthnayhe or Upward-Reaching Rite.* Recorded by Berard Haile. Santa Fe, N.Mex.: Museum of Navajo Ceremonial Art, 1949.

———. *The Myth and Prayers of the Great Star Chant and the Myth of the Coyote Chant.* Santa Fe, N.Mex.: Museum of Navajo Ceremonial Art, 1956.

———. *Red Ant Myth and Shooting Chant.* Santa Fe, N.Mex.: Museum of Navajo Ceremonial Art, 1958.

Wilken, Robert L. *Father Anselm Weber, O.F.M.: Missionary to the Navaho.* Milwaukee, Wisc.: Bruce Publishing, 1955.

Wyman, Leland C. *Beautyway: A Navaho Ceremonial.* Princeton, N.J.: Princeton University Press, 1957.

———. *Blessingway.* Tucson: University of Arizona Press, 1970.

———. *The Windways of the Navaho.* Colorado Springs: Taylor Museum, 1962.

———. *The Red Antway of the Navaho.* Santa Fe, N.Mex.: Museum of Navajo Ceremonial Art, 1965.

———. *Blessingway.* Tucson: University of Arizona Press, 1970.

———. *The Mountainway of the Navaho.* Tucson: University of Arizona Press, 1975.

———. *Southwest Indian Drypainting.* Santa Fe, N.Mex.; Albuquerque: University of New Mexico Press, 1983.

Zolbrod, Paul G. *Diné Bahane': The Navajo Creation Story.* Albuquerque: University of New Mexico Press, 1984.

TRADING POSTS

Adams, William Y. *Shonto: A Study of the Role of the Trader in a Modern Navajo Community.* Smithsonian Institution, Bureau of American Ethnology, Bulletin no. 188. Washington, D.C.: Government Printing Office, 1963.

Blue, Martha. *Indian Trader: The Life and Times of J. L. Hubbell.* Walnut, Calif.: Kiva Publishing, 2000.

Brugge, David M. *Hubbell Trading Post National Historic Site.* Tucson, Ariz.: Southwest Parks and Monuments Association, 1993.

Cousins, Jean, and Bill Cousins. *Tales From Wide Ruins.* Edited by Mary Tate Engels. Lubbock: Texas Tech University Press, 1996.

Gillmor, Frances, and Louisa Wade Wetherill. *Traders to the Navajo.* Albuquerque: University of New Mexico Press, 1934.

Graves, Laura. *Thomas Varker Keam, Indian Trader.* Norman: University of Oklahoma Press, 1998.

Hall, Edward T. *West of the Thirties: Discoveries Among the Navajo and Hopi*. New York: Doubleday, 1994.

Hegemann, Elizabeth C. *Navaho Trading Days*. Albuquerque: University of New Mexico Press, 1963.

James, H. L. *Rugs and Posts: The Story of Navajo Weaving and Indian Trading*. West Chester, Penn.: Schiffer Publishing, 1988.

Kennedy, Mary Jeanette. *Tales of a Trader's Wife*. Albuquerque, N.Mex.: Valliant Company, 1965.

Manchester, Albert, and Ann Manchester. *Hubbell Trading Post National Historic Site: An Administrative History*. Santa Fe, N.Mex.: National Park Service, Southwest Cultural Resources Center, 1993.

McNitt, Frank. *The Indian Traders*. Norman: University of Oklahoma Press, 1962.

Moon, Samuel. *Tall Sheep: Harry Goulding, Monument Valley Trader*. Norman: University of Oklahoma Press, 1992.

Newcomb, Franc J. *Navaho Neighbors*. Norman: University of Oklahoma Press, 1966.

Powers, Willow Roberts. *Navajo Trading: The End of an Era*. Albuquerque: University of New Mexico Press, 2001.

Richardson, Gladwell. *Navajo Trader*. Tucson: University of Arizona Press, 1986.

Roberts, Willow. *Stokes Carson: Twentieth-Century Trading on the Navajo Reservation*. Albuquerque: University of New Mexico Press, 1987.

Wagner, Sallie Lippincott. *Wide Ruins: Memories from a Navajo Trading Post*. Albuquerque: University of New Mexico Press, 1997.

TREATIES AND AGREEMENTS

Correll, J. Lee, and David M. Brugge. *The Story of the Navajo Treaties*. Window Rock, Ariz.: Navajo Tribal Research Section, 1971.

Correll, J. Lee, and Alfred Dehiya. *Anatomy of the Navajo Indian Reservation: How It Grew*. Window Rock, Ariz.: Navajo Times Publishing, 1978.

WAR/CONFLICT

Bailey, Lynn R. *The Long Walk, A History of the Navajo Wars, 1846–68*. Los Angeles: Westernlore Press, 1964.

———. *Bosque Redondo: An American Concentration Camp*. Pasadena, Calif.: Socio-Technical Books, 1970.

Benedek, Emily. *The Wind Won't Know Me: A History of the Navajo-Hopi Land Dispute*. New York: Alfred A. Knopf, 1992.

Brugge, David M. *The Navajo-Hopi Land Dispute: An American Tragedy*. Albuquerque: University of New Mexico Press, 1994.

Hill, W. W. *Navaho Warfare*. New Haven, Conn.: Yale University Press, 1936.

Kammer, Jerry. *The Second Long Walk: The Navajo-Hopi Land Dispute*. Albuquerque: University of New Mexico Press, 1980.

Kelly, Lawrence C., ed. *Navajo Roundup: Selected Correspondence of Kit Carson's Campaign Against the Navajos, 1863–1865*. Boulder, Colo.: Pruett, 1970.

McNitt, Frank. *Navajo Wars, Military Campaigns, Slave Raids and Reprisals*. Albuquerque: University of New Mexico Press, 1972.

Paul, Doris. *The Navajo Code Talkers*. Philadelphia: Dorrance, 1973.

Scudder, Thayer. *No Place to Go: Effects of Compulsory Relocation on Navajos*. Philadelphia: Institute for the Study of Human Issues, 1982.

Thompson, Gerald. *The Army and the Navajo: The Bosque Redondo Reservation Experiment, 1863–68*. Tucson: University of Arizona Press, 1976.

Trafzer, Clifford. *The Kit Carson Campaign*. Norman: University of Oklahoma Press, 1972.

Wilson, John P. *Military Campaigns in the Navajo Country, Northwestern New Mexico, 1800–1846*. Santa Fe: Museum of New Mexico Press, 1967.

WEAVING, ART, POTTERY, SANDPAINTING, SILVERSMITHING

Adair, John. *The Navajo and Pueblo Silversmiths*. Norman: University of Oklahoma Press, 1944.

Amsden, Charles. *Navaho Weaving, Its Technic and History*. Santa Ana, Calif.: Fine Arts Press, 1934.

Bedinger, Margery. *Indian Silver: Navajo and Pueblo Jewelers*. Albuquerque: University of New Mexico Press, 1973.

Bennett, Noel. *The Weaver's Pathway: A Clarification of the "Spirit Trail" in Navajo Weaving*. Flagstaff, Ariz.: Northland Press, 1974.

Bennett, Noel, and Tiana Bighorse. *Working With the Wool: How to Weave a Navajo Rug*. Flagstaff, Ariz.: Northland Press, 1971.

Bonar, Eulalie H., ed. *Woven by the Grandmothers: Nineteenth-Century Navajo Textiles from the National Museum of the American Indian*. Washington, D.C.: Smithsonian Institution Press in association with the National Museum of the American Indian, Smithsonian Institution, 1996.

Bryan, Nonabah G., and Stella Young. *Navajo Native Dyes: Their Preparation and Use*. Washington, D.C.: Bureau of Indian Affairs, 1940.

Campbell, Tyrone, Joel Kopp, and Kate Kopp. *Navajo Pictorial Weaving, 1880–1950*. New York: Dutton Studio Books, 1991.

Edison, Carol, ed. *Willow Stories: Utah Navajo Baskets*. Salt Lake City: Utah Arts Council, 1996.

Getzwiller, Steve. *Ray Manley's The Fine Art of Navajo Weaving*. Tucson: Ray Manley Publications, 1984.

Greenberg, Henry, and Georgia Greenberg. *Carl Gorman's World*. Albuquerque: University of New Mexico Press, 1984.

Hartman, Russell, and Jan Musial. *Navajo Pottery: Tradition and Innovation*. Flagstaff, Ariz.: Northland, 1987.

Hedlund, Ann Lane. *Reflections of the Weaver's World*. Denver, Colo.: Denver Art Museum, 1992.

Hollister, U.S. *The Navajo and His Blanket*. 1903. Reprint, Glorieta, N.Mex.: Rio Grande Press, 1972.

Hucko, Bruce. *A Rainbow at Night: The World in Words and Pictures by Navajo Children*. San Francisco: Chronicle Books, 1995.

Jacka, Lois Essary. *David Johns: On the Trail of Beauty*. Photographs by Jerry Jacka. Flagstaff, Ariz.: Northland, 1991.

———. *Enduring Traditions: Art of the Navajo*. Photographs by Jerry Jacka. Flagstaff, Ariz.: Northland, 1994.

———. *Navajo Jewelry: A Legacy of Silver and Stone*. Photographs by Jerry Jacka. Flagstaff, Ariz.: Northland, 1995.

Kaufman, Alice, and Christopher Selzer, eds. *The Navajo Weaving Tradition, 1650 to the present*. New York: E. P. Hutton, 1985.

Kent, Kate Peck. *Navajo Weaving: Three Centuries of Change*. Santa Fe, N.Mex.: School of American Research Press; Distributed by Seattle: University of Washington Press, 1985.

Kline, Cindra. *Navajo Spoons: Indian Artistry and the Souvenir Trade, 1880–1940*. Santa Fe: Museum of New Mexico Press, 2001.

M'Closkey, Kathy. *Swept Under the Rug: A Hidden History of Navajo Weaving*. Albuquerque: University of New Mexico Press, 2002.

McGreevy, Susan Brown, and D. Y. Begay, curators. *The Image Weavers: Contemporary Navajo Pictorial Textiles*. An Exhibition at the Wheelwright Museum of the American Indian, Santa Fe, New Mexico, May 15–October 26, 1994. Santa Fe, N.Mex.: Wheelwright Museum of the American Indian, 1994.

Moore, J. B. *The Catalogues of Fine Navajo Blankets, Rugs, Ceremonial Baskets, Silverware, Jewelry & Curios, Originally Published Between 1903 and 1911*. Albuquerque, N.Mex.: Avanyu, 1987.

Parezo, Nancy. *Navajo Sandpainting: From Religious Art to Commercial Art*. Albuquerque: University of New Mexico Press, 1983.

Reichard, Gladys A. *Navajo: Shepherd and Weaver*. New York: J. J. Augustin, 1936.

————. *Spider Woman: A Story of Navajo Weavers and Chanters.* 1934. Reprint, Albuquerque: University of New Mexico Press, 1992.

Rodee, Marian E. *One Hundred Years of Navajo Rugs.* Albuquerque: University of New Mexico Press, 1995.

Roessel, Robert A., Jr. *Navajo Arts and Crafts.* Rough Rock, Ariz.: Navajo Curriculum Center, Rough Rock Demonstration School, 1983.

Rosenek, Chuck, and Jan Rosenek. *Navajo Folk Art: The People Speak.* Flagstaff, Ariz.: Northland, 1994.

Salkald, Stefani. *Southwest Weaving: A Continuum.* San Diego, Calif.: San Diego Museum of Man, 1996.

Valette, Rebecca M., and Jean-Paul Valette. *Weaving the Dance: Navajo Yeibichai Textiles (1910–1950).* Albuquerque, N.Mex.: Adobe Gallery, 2000.

Wheat, Joe Ben. *Blanket Weavers of the Southwest.* Edited by Ann Hedlund. Tucson: University of Arizona Press, 2002.

Whitaker, Kathleen. *Common Threads: Pueblo and Navajo Textiles in the Southwest Museum.* Los Angeles: Southwest Museum, 1998.

Witherspoon, Gary, and Glen Peterson. *Dynamic Symmetry and Holistic Asymmetry in Navajo and Western Art and Cosmology.* New York: Peter Lang, 1995.

Woodward, Arthur. *Navajo Silver: A Brief History of Navajo Silversmithing.* Flagstaff, Ariz.: Northland, 1971.

Zolbrod, Paul and Roseann S. Willink. *Weaving a World: Textiles and the Navajo Way of Seeing.* Santa Fe: Museum of New Mexico Press, 1996.

Index

Weisiger, Marsha, 76, 78
*We'll Be In Your Mountains,
    We'll Be In Your Songs*
    (McCullough-Brabson
    and Help), 67
West of the Thirties (Hall),
    153
Wetherill, Louisa, 172
Wheat, Joe Ben, 24
Wheeler, Burton K., 171
Wheeler, Charles L., 222
Wheeler, Rita, 59
Wheelwright, Mary Cabot,
    170
White House Ruins, 17
Wigglesworth, Albert,
    116–17
Wilkins, David E., 297
Wilkinson, Charles, 244
Williams, Alice, 310, 313–14
Williams, Paul, 168
Williams, Rose, 314
Williams v. Lee, 209–10, 231,
    252
Willie, Jacob, 271
Willie, John W., 183
Wilson, Alvin, 202
Wilson, John P., 28
Wilson, William Dean, 252
Window Rock, Ariz., 5, 151

Winny, Reed, 161
Winter, Mark, 267, 279
witchcraft, 70–71
Witherspoon, Gary, 23
Woehlke, Walter V., 160
Women, status of, 302–5
Woodard, M. L., 171
Woods, Hoska, 128
Woodward, Arthur, 32
Wooton, E. O., 105
Work, Hubert, 134
World War II, 2, 4, 166, 180,
    182–88

Yabeney, Chee, 187
Yabeney, Ned, 187
Yabeney, Slim, 161
Yabeney, Walter, 187
Yázhí, Histalí, 110–11
Yazza, John, 114
Yazzie, Agatha, 236
Yazzie, Alfred, 303
Yazzie, Allen, 233, 235
Yazzie, Elizabeth, 319
Yazzie, Ethelou, 256
Yazzie, Evangeline Parsons,
    323
Yazzie, George, 202
Yazzie, Harold, 302
Yazzie, Kee Ike, 296

Yazzie, Kodiak, 309
Yazzie, Lamoni, 309
Yazzie, Leonard, 271
Yazzie, Maxwell, *150*
Yazzie, Norman, 202
Yazzie, Robert, 294, 320–21
Yazzie, William, 183
Yazzie, Woody, 202
Yellowhair, Atah Chee, 236
Yellowhair, Chester, 235,
    252
Yonnie, Oscar, 215
Young, Charles, 283
Young, Robert W., 25, 119,
    135, 156, 173, 207, 221,
    222
Youngblood, Bonney, 217

Zagenitzo, 134
Zah, Peterson, 5, 228, *241*,
    242, 252, 256, 271–73,
    282–83, 285–89, 291, 293,
    297, 300, 304, 321, 322
Zahne, Herbert, 57
Zeh, William, 143
Zhin, Tol, 108–9
Zimmerman, William J.,
    217
Zunis, 14, 51
Zweifel, Rudolph, 161, 187